MAGIC IN CHRISTIANITY: FROM JESUS TO THE GNOSTICS

For Morton Smith
1915 — 1991

ολιγους οσους των κοφινων εκφορησας...

MAGIC IN CHRISTIANITY: FROM JESUS TO THE GNOSTICS

ROBERT CONNER

Published by
Mandrake of Oxford
PO Box 250
OXFORD
OX1 1AP (UK)

Cover art by Christopher Cochran

Other books by Robert Conner:
Jesus The Sorcerer: Exorcist, Prophet of The Apocalypse
Magic in The New Testament: A survey and appraisal of the evidence

CONTENTS

INTRODUCTION

In 1906, Albert Schweitzer, a German theologian, wrote a book, *Geschichte der Leben Jesu-Forschung: Von Reimarus zu Wrede*, translated into English in 1910 as *The Quest of the Historical Jesus: From Reimarus to Wrede.*[1] *The Quest*, which initiated the modern search for the Jesus of history, would prove to be one of the most important works on Christianity written in the 20th century. As one effect of the change in focus achieved by the historical approach, scholars steadily accumulated evidence for magical practices in the New Testament—in the 1920's occasional articles on the subject began to appear in specialty journals and by the 1970's books setting out the evidence were published. In the final decades of the past century academic interest in magic in the Greco-Roman world increased dramatically with the result that further connections between Christian and pagan magic were documented.[2] It is that continuously expanding body of knowledge and commentary that has made this survey of the evidence possible.

However, the double barrier of theological commitment on one hand and a materialist approach to religious praxis on the other

[1] A new and superior translation, *The Quest of the Historical Jesus: First*

[2] Notably with C. Bonner (1927) and P. Samain (1932). Samain's article stands as one of the most completely documented and tightly reasoned summaries in the literature. Among the early book length treatments are Hull's *Hellenistic Magic and the Synoptic Tradition* (1974) and Smith's *Jesus the Magician* (1978). More recent works include Arnold's *Ephesians: Power and Magic* (1989), Klauck's *Magic and Paganism in Early Christianity*, first published in German in 1996, Janowitz' *Magic in the Roman World: Pagans, Jews and Christians* (2001), Strelan's *Strange Acts* (2004), and Thomas' *Magical Motifs in the Book of Revelation* (2010), to name but a few of many examples.

continues to impede evidence-based assessment of the documents of early Christianity. As Strelan points out, "angels, dreams, visions and supernatural experiences"—to say nothing of magic—have been placed off limits to New Testament scholars in particular "by a scientific method that ruled out the supernatural *a priori*" and to publish on any aspect of the subject "put their credibility and academic acceptability on the line."[3] Until quite recently most dismissed the history of magic as beneath the dignity of academic discourse, if not, in fact, beneath contempt. The majority of scholars considered "the study of exorcism, the most highly rated activity of the early Christian church, a historiographical 'no-go' area."[4] Horsley has characterized "modern Western interpreters" as "skittish about demon possession and exorcism"[5] because these phenomena, which were central to primitive Christian experience, cannot be a accommodated by modern scientific rationalism.

However, it is not rationalism but advocacy scholarship that has been and still remains the single greatest obstacle to understanding the founding documents of Christianity. To take but one of many possible examples, the author Richard Bell finds it "highly problematic that some have understood Jesus' 'career' as that of a magician." Bell concedes, "there may be some similarities" between Jesus and pagan magicians but claims "there really is no basic similarity when one views the context of these miracles."[6] To the contrary, it is precisely the context of Jesus' miracles that marks them as examples of ancient magical practice and the number of scholars who have published on the topic of magic in Christianity is a fair few larger than "some."

---

[3] Strelan, *Strange Acts*, 9.

[4] Brown, *The Cult of the Saints*, 108.

[5] Horsley, *Experientia*, I, 41.

[6] Bell, *Deliver Us from Evil: Interpreting the Redemption from the Power of Satan in New Testament Theology*, 185-186.

In point of fact, the details of the exorcism stories of the synoptic gospels conform very closely to spells from the surviving magical papyri as well as agreeing point by point with accounts of such ancient miracle workers as Apollonius of Tyana. Lucian of Samosata, an astute and skeptical observer of Christians and similar miracle workers, did not distinguish Christian from pagan magic, nor did the pagan critic Celsus, who regarded Christians as magicians on par with street performers who exorcized demons and cured diseases. His attack on Christianity, *True Doctrine*, preserved in part in Origen's *Contra Celsum*, provides extensive evidence that Christian sects were known for magical practice.

Regarding the editor and contributors to the *Theologisches Wörterbuch zum Neuen Testament*, the German corpus translated into English as the *Theological Dictionary of the New Testament*, a work much admired by some evangelical scholars, Aune remarks, "[they] write as if they were involved in a conspiracy to ignore or minimize the role of magic in the New Testament and early Christian literature."[7] In fact, the editor was involved in somewhat more than that. Kittel and a number of his contributors were Nazi collaborators who were attempting to systematically write the Jewish background out of the life of Jesus, to make Jesus of Nazareth *judenfrei* in order to to adapt German Christianity to a virulently racist ideology.[8]

Samson Eitrem, a very thorough scholar, pointed to numerous parallels between the miracles of Jesus and the spells of the magical papyri only to conclude, "It is, indeed, very difficult to detect any *magical method* in the cures of Jesus...He was no thaumaturge trained in magical technique: this, at least, we know from our sources."[9] Quite to the contrary, what we know

---

[7] Aune, *Aufstieg und Niedergang der Römischen Welt*, II.23.2: 1508.

[8] Ericksen, *Theologians Under Hitler: Gerhard Kittel, Paul Althaus, and Emanuel Hirsch*.

[9] Eitrem, *Some Notes on the Demonology in the New Testament*, 40.

from ancient sources is that magic flourished in Palestine from the beginning of recorded history, that magic was ubiquitous in Palestine and the Mediterranean world generally in the time of Jesus, that Jesus and early Christians were accused of practicing magic by their pagan opponents and by their Jewish contemporaries, and that Christians were accused of practicing magic *by other Christians.* As will be pointed out repeatedly in the pages that follow, it is embarrassingly easy to demonstrate "magical method" in the cures and exorcisms of Jesus. The notion that Jesus somehow transcended his own era, place and culture, while simultaneously using its language, behavior and frame of reference, is based on theology, not evidence, and it is worth reminding ourselves that pagans invented theology long before the arrival of Christianity and were well aware of its uses and abuses.

Apologetic study of ancient texts is hardly limited to Christianity, however. Following the discovery of the trove of manuscripts in the Cairo *genizah*, the two Jewish scholars who examined the material "had to sift through the thousands of magical texts strewn there," eventually producing thorough coverage of the material "with the glaring exception of its numerous fragments which deal with magic, divination, and the occult sciences, fragments which both scholars treated as if they did not exist."[10] Mordecai Margalioth, the scholar who reconstructed the *Sepher Ha-Razim*, a book of magical spells, "was convinced that the book was the product of Jewish heretics" operating on the fringes of normative Judaism. Schäfer concludes, "This statement does not come as a surprise, but it is no doubt wrong."[11]

The neglect of magical material extended even to classicists who convinced themselves the Greeks of yore were the epitome of rationalism. "More than 70 years went by after the discovery of

---

[10] Bohak, *Ancient Jewish Magic: A History*, 8.

[11] Schäfer, *Envisioning Magic: A Princeton Seminar and Symposium*, 38.

magical papyri before they became known to a large number of scholars: Wilamowitz and the majority of Hellenists preferred to ignore them as a degenerate by-product of the Greek spirit."[12] "Classicists, whose attention was riveted solely on things Attic, denigrated and decried [the magical papyri] as the barbaric products of a bastard culture unworthy of their study."[13]

These are merely a few examples of distortion that could be cited in the long history of scholarly conformity. If the gospels were to be allowed as evidence, it would appear that the origins of Christianity itself began to be falsified soon after Jesus' death. This work explores how Jesus' apocalyptic message, which was central to his preaching, came to be explained away and then quietly abandoned, how magical details of Jesus' charismatic performance were excised from the gospels and how spirit possession, once central to what became orthodox Christianity, was allowed to wither and disappear. It is a pivotal argument of this book that apologetic scholarship is inevitably dishonest scholarship that does violence to the evidence and that the field of 'Jesus Studies' is so riddled with special pleading and question begging that it barely qualifies as an academic discipline. Fortunately, we have several ancient sources, Lucian, Celsus, Philostratus, Irenaeus and Origen, which allow us to reconstruct the magico-religious milieu of Jesus' era.

The facticity of Jesus' miracles is not the concern of this book. I am in agreement with Hull on the subject: "The crucial point of inquiry into the miracles of Jesus, as of those of the early church, was not whether they had in fact happened but the nature and origin of the power used to perform them. By means of such as these 'the apostles gave witness with great power,' i.e., not simply with great impact but the aid of a mighty force (Acts 4.33)."[14] There is no Jesus apart from miracles; they are by far

---

[12] Mastrocinque, *From Jewish Magic to Gnosicism*, 221.
[13] Brashear, *Aufstieg und Niedergang der römischen Welt* II, 18.5: 3399.
[14] Hull, *Hellenistic Magic and the Synoptic Tradition*, 108.

the best-attested feature of his life and the basis of his fame. None of his opponents tried to deny their reality. Jürgen Becker says of Jesus, "To no miracle worker of Antiquity were as many miracles attributed as there were to Jesus. All four gospels, including their sources (the synoptic sayings source and Johannine signs source), without exception bear witness to Jesus as a powerful miracle worker…"[15] Had Jesus and his earliest followers no fame for performing miracles, it is doubtful there would be any such religion as Christianity or that the world would recall Jesus' existence.[16] I leave it to readers to make of Jesus' miracles what they will.

This is as good a place as any to briefly address the proposed differences between *religion* and *magic*, a distinction designed to raise the petticoats of faith above the gutter of superstition. I will spare the reader a lengthy rehearsal of the tortured logic that has dominated much of that exercise. Suffice to say that in past decades scores of scholars have written many hundreds of pages in an attempt to establish some difference and yet no consensus of opinion has emerged, an observation that suggests ipso facto that there is no clear distinction to be made. To the contrary, every set of criteria proposed to establish some difference has met with solid criticism and the effort has been gradually abandoned as useless for the study of religion in the ancient Near East. "…there can be no doubt that magic is regarded as part of, and not opposed to religion…The notion of magic as distinct from religion seems to be alien to the Hebrew Bible."[17] Attempts to distinguish religion from magic in the New Testament and primitive Christianity will not repay the effort, a claim this work intends to verify *in extenso*. "The death blow for absolute definitions for miracle and magic is simply the ambigu-

---

[15] Becker, *Jesus of Nazareth*, 170.

[16] A point emphasized by MacMullen, *Christianizing he Roman Empire*, 22.

[17] Schäfer, *Envisioning Magic: A Princeton Seminar and Symposium*, 33.

ous nature of the ancient evidence itself."[18] In his discussion of the magical symbolism of Revelation, Thomas concludes, "there were no clear-cut parameters between magic and religion."[19] "Such private dealings with supernatural beings make up most of what we call 'magic' as well as what we call 'private religion.' There is no clear line between the two."[20]

Distinguishing magic from religion or from medicine in antiquity fails in part because all three shared the same assumption: *human fate is under the control of spirit forces.* Modern scholars who accept the efficacy of magic on some level tend to explain its effects in terms of psychology, but that was not the paradigm in force in the era we are about to examine.[21] That magic, religion, and medicine shared the same basic premise at the time Christianity emerged and that all ancient religions and many philosophies also shared the same premise makes it impossible to distinguish between magic and religion. For a clear majority of people living in the 1st century who bothered to give it any thought, *magic* basically meant *bad religion*—"activities or beliefs that the speaker regards with disapproval...religious practices...considered immoral, fraudulent, or otherwise unacceptable."[22] However, as the magical papyri, amulets, and other sources prove, magic was nearly universal and taken with all seriousness at every level of society. For all practical purposes there

---

[18] Reimer, *Miracle and Magic: A Study in the Acts of the Apostles and the Life of Apollonius of Tyana*, 7.

[19] Thomas, *Magical Motifs in the Book of Revelation*, 35.

[20] Smith, *Jesus the Magician*, 69.

[21] Stratton makes a convincing case that a small number of intellecttual elites considered the effects of magic to be psychological—"because they believe in them" (30)—but that was certainly not the opinion of the hoi polloi or Christian apologists, who believed magic worked by demonic force as the Judeo-Christian spells, curses and amulets amply attest. See particularly her comments on *impia religio* (*Naming the Witch: Magic, Ideology and Stereotype in the Ancient World*, 32).

[22] Rives, *The Religious History of the Roman Empire*, 73, 74.

is no difference between magic and medicine or healing and exorcism in our sources. That magic and medicine interpenetrated then and for centuries to follow can be confirmed by the survival of such ideas as *cosmobiology* or *iatromathematics*, the attempt to correlate physical and mental illness with astrology, until well into the 17th century.

In a particularly incisive discussion of the supposed distinction between religion and magic, Mastrocinque stresses that the difference was particularly acute for the early Christians owing to "the need to reject the accusations that Christ and his followers were practitioners of magic." That urgency continued due to early Christianity's conflict both with pagan wonder workers and to internal conflicts between competing Christian sects that used accusations of practicing magic as a standard polemic device. Under the pagan emperors "the [magical] sphere of evil was very limited" but after Christianity became the state religion and the pagan religions became magic by definition that "sphere of evil" was vastly enlarged.[23] Most subsequent efforts to distinguish magic from religion flow more or less directly from those early Christian attitudes. Morton Smith: "Christianity gave to magic Satan—a supreme ruler of the powers of evil…an empire opposed to that of God…The triumph of Christianity, however, brought also the triumph of Satan, though this consequence was only slowly recognized."[24]

For the purposes of this book, *religion* will be defined as *magic for the masses* and *magic* as *religion for the individual.* Religion typically deals with the future after death, and magic with more immediate concerns, but when the immediate concern *is* death, religion displays its magical face in various rituals of last rites. To observe the fluid boundary between magic and religion in our sources, we need look no further than the story in the Old Testament about the magical serpent staff fashioned to relieve

---

23 Mastrocinque, *From Jewish Magic to Gnosticism*, 214, 217.

24 Smith, *Studies in the Cult of Yahweh*, II, 215.

victims of snakebite,[25] that later becomes a named object of religious veneration and is for that reason destroyed,[26] yet raising the snake is subsequently applied allegorically to Jesus[27] and becomes a feature of the Christian Ophite—from Greek *οφις*, *snake*—theology. The Ophites and other groups such as the Marcionites "identified the serpent in the Garden of Eden with the bronze serpent made by Moses and the serpent into which the rod of Moses had been transformed..."[28]

Moses raising the brazen serpent (Doré).

[25] Numbers 21:6-9.

[26] 2 Kings 18:4.

[27] John 3:14.

[28] Mastrocinque, *From Jewish Magic to Gnosticism*, 46.

Animal talismans or *telesmata* such as the brazen serpent of Numbers 21:4-9 were a widely employed form of magic around the ancient Mediterranean: "brazen replicas of obnoxious insects and vermin were often erected to avert the pests they represented...after Moses' intercession Yahweh instructs that a brazen serpent be fashioned and set up on a staff, and promises that whoever looks at the serpent will be instantly cured."[29] The power of the copper serpent is greater than that of the real snakes and "works automatically and without restriction. This is magic, pure and simple..."[30] The story of the copper serpent is a perfect example of the validity Bohak's observation that "the contents of what we might label 'magic' could change from one period to the next, and even from one Jewish group or community to another at one and the same time."[31]

This work assumes that Jesus was a real person and that the gospels contain a core of historical material. Although "mythicists" argue that Jesus of Nazareth never existed and that the gospels are a complete fabrication, a recent summary of the evidence for such claims concludes, "The theory of Jesus' nonexistence is now effectively dead as a scholarly question."[32] "No ancient opponent of Christianity ever denied Jesus' existence."[33] Jesus was scarcely mentioned outside the New Testament for a century or more after his death because he was insignificant in the greater scheme of things, not because he was fictional. In any case, *the Jesus of the gospels is already a mythic figure* and the charge of magical praxis still applies to him, historical, mythical, or some mixture of both. Be that as it may, this book entirely dispenses with the pleasant pretext that the life of Jesus was truly relevant then or now. Christianity began as an obscure apocalyptic sect of Palestinian Judaism. Its "founder" thought the

---

[29] Faraone, *Talismans and Trojan Horses*, 40-41.

[30] Schäfer, *Envisioning Magic*, 30.

[31] Bohak, *Ancient Jewish Magic: A Hisory*, 66.

[32] Van Voorst, *Jesus Outside the New Testament*, 14.

[33] Stanton, *Jesus of Nazareth Lord and Christ*, 165, footnote 7.

world would end in his lifetime. It is certainly fair to say that Jesus was personally unknown to the majority of Christians—"a tiny, peculiar, anti-social, irreligious sect"[34] from a Roman perspective—who could have been his contemporaries. In fact, it appears that he was personally unknown even to Saul of Tarsus who, writing as the apostle Paul, became orthodox Christianity's chief spokesman. The Lord Jesus Christ of Paul's cult of spirit possession is clearly a construct of myth, not history, and if his epistles are any indication, it appears that Paul knew little and cared less about the historical Jesus.

Strictly speaking, the New Testament consists of 27 documents *written in Greek*. No informed person disputes that translation from a source language into a target language is an interpretive, even creative, act that involves decisions not only about vocabulary and tone, but also inevitably reflects what the translator thinks the source document as a whole means. While enabling a measure of comprehension, translation inevitably loses most of the deep field of association that every word has in its own language, era and culture.

New Testament writers sometimes coin words,[35] or use established vocabulary in idiosyncratic ways—a number of famous passages exist for which no satisfactory explanation has ever emerged. But even if the language is clear and the translator can tell the reader word for word what the author *said*, that still does not necessarily clarify what the author *meant*. Although the failings of translators are widely known, it is less often acknowledged that translators more often overachieve. Translators paper over grammatical inconcinnities and non sequiturs, assign familiar definitions to unknown words, and make sense of statements that are incomprehensible in the original. A rigorously

---

[34] Wilken, *The Christians as the Romans Saw Them*, xv.

[35] An easy example is the term δευτεροπρωτος (deuteroprōtos), "second-first," of Luke 6:1. No one actually seems to know what it means and a number of translations simply omit the word.

honest translation of ancient texts would bracket some words and expressions as untranslatable, but this rarely occurs, particularly in bibles. In actual practice, most translations are also *emendations*. In this manner also, translation can misrepresent by creating the false impression of a seamless, uncomplicated text the meaning of which is readily apparent. Which word (if any) in English appropriately translates a word in Hebrew, Greek, or Coptic is often a matter of conjecture, particularly it seems, at those points where the text is of greatest interest to us.

Unfortunately, there are much more fundamental problems with translation. It is very convenient, to say nothing of naïve, to assume that English words simply translate Greek words and that the multiple associations an English word calls to mind are the same associations a Greek word called to mind 2000 years ago. It has been one of the subtexts of my work that the mental world of the 1st century simply does not translate into the mental world of the 21st century. In my view claiming to be a literalist believer in any religion of antiquity confirms either deep intellectual dishonesty or abysmal ignorance. It suggests that one is willing and able to suspend common knowledge about the extent of space and time, ignore basic categories of modern thought such as cause and effect and the principle of least action, and perform an intellectual leap backward into an era with which we have only the most superficial familiarity.

To cite a pertinent example, consider the Greek word *σεληνιαζομαι* (selēniazomai),[36] which means "to be moonstruck" but is typically translated "to be epileptic," a translation Botha characterizes as "an unfortunate instance of ethnocentrism," while pointing out the mistaken assumption that "events and words

---

[36] Formed off *σεληνη* (selēnē), *moon*, the verb occurs at Matthew 4:24 and 17:15.

The majority of English translations render the term as *epilepsy* or as *lunatics*. Neither translation accords with a modern understanding of seizures or mental illness.

can be freed from historical and cultural contingency."[37] The ancients, who knew nothing of neurons, synapses or electrochemical impulse transmission, and hardly suspected the function of the central nervous system, would have regarded our understanding of epilepsy as every bit as bizarre as we do their notion that the moon caused seizures. Not only does the English *epilepsy* not actually translate *σεληνιαζομαι*, it obscures what the word meant to ancient Greeks.

The late Morton Smith, to whose memory this book is dedicated, contributed much to the study of ancient magic in general, and to the role of magic in early Christianity in particular. Smith looked behind the theologized Jesus, situated him in the culture of his time, contextualized his actions and his reported vocabulary, and revealed that the clothes had no Emperor, that the Jesus of the gospels had embarrassingly little of substance to say to those who struggled against the surge of the crowd to touch the hem of his garment. In short, if Smith's evaluation of Jesus were true, it meant the academy would have to come to grips with the evidence for magic and stop faking Jesus' actions.

Shawn Eyer put his finger directly into the wound that Smith opened up in the side of Jesus studies, noting that he "took the Gospels as more firmly rooted in history than in the imagination of the early church," that he "refused to operate with an artificially thick barrier between pagan and Christian," and that he published his theories "in plain, understandable and all-too-clear language,"[38] offenses the present writer hopes to emulate. It is my expectation that those for whom this book has been written will easily rise above disputes about personalities and credentialism, and judge the arguments made herein on their factual merits.

---

[37] Botha, *Health Sa Gesondheid*, 1, No. 2, 3.

[38] Eyer, *Alexandria: The Journal for the Western Cosmological Tradition* 3:103-129.

To a large extent this book is a survey of the evidence rather than an original investigation. As such, critical points in primary references are quoted verbatim, usually in Greek since the New Testament documents and other primary sources closest to the gospels are in Greek, and secondary sources are quoted or closely paraphrased, allowing their authors to speak in their own voices. The use of footnotes instead of endnotes allows the reader the convenience of staying on the same page as the main text when looking for references, and full citations are supplied in place of abbreviations.

A penultimate observation should be made regarding citations from the magical papyri. The two collections most often referenced, the *Papyri Graecae Magicae* and the *Supplementum Magicum*, are cited differently. In the case of the *Papyri Graecae Magicae*, the individual papyri are referenced by number and by line of text: PGM IV, 286, for example, refers to document number 4, line 286. The papyri included in *Supplementum Magicum*, issued in two volumes, are numbered by document, but are accompanied by additional pages of commentary. Individual documents in the *Supplementum Magicum* are referenced by number; the commentary is referenced by volume and page. *Supplementum Magicum* 24 refers to document 24, whereas *Supplementum Magicum* II, 67, refers to commentary in volume II, page 67.

Unless otherwise noted, all translations from Greek are my own. Unaccented Greek text is still considered "regrettable, if not even scandalous"[39] by many scholars, but following the eminently sensible lead of Wenham, I consider the inclusion of accents a pointless affectation and have dispensed with them.

[39] Duff, *The Elements of New Testament Greek*, xi.

CHAPTER 1: THE SOURCES

For all practical purposes the reconstruction of Jesus' life and teaching is based entirely on the documents of the New Testament. By some estimates over thirty gospels were produced in the first two centuries following Jesus' death, but most of those gospels have disappeared and those outside the New Testament that survive are fragmentary, distorted by time and fabulist tendencies, and contain little to nothing of biographical interest. Some 21 gospels in various states of preservation are known, as well as the names of 13 others that have not survived.

Preservation of the oral tradition.

In daily conversation Jesus and his disciples spoke a dialect of Palestinian Aramaic, a Semitic language closely related to Hebrew. In a few places the writer of the gospel of Mark records Aramaic words or phrases and provides a Greek translation, particularly when the words in question are "words of power" that accompany the performance of healings and exorcisms—in the technical literature, a "word of power" is often called a *vox magica* (plural, *voces magicae*).

> Foreign words are a very familiar feature of magic spells and the papyri are full of examples...In the Coptic magical papyri Greek appears as the strange and forbiddingly authentic sound, while in the Greek magical world Jewish names and words had special prestige...The foreign expressions are sometimes translated into Greek for the professional use of healers and exorcists...The continued use of Ephphatha in the baptismal ritual of the church (which was also exorcism) can hardly be accounted for except by the supposition that the

word was believed in itself to possess remarkable power."[40]

Two clear examples are ταλιθα κουμ (talitha koum), "get up, little girl,"[41] and εφφαθα (ephphatha), "be opened."[42] Commenting on the words of power used in Mark 5:41, Smith noted of the formula used by Peter to raise a dead woman—Ταβιθα αναστηθι: "Tabitha, rise!"[43]—"*Tabitha* is a mispronunciation of *talitha*, which the storyteller mistook for a proper name."[44] As we will have occasion to note, such invocations tend to gain in length and complexity with the passage of time. In some manuscripts, Peter's "Tabitha rise!" expands to include "in the name of our Lord Jesus Christ."Aune addresses the motive for retaining Aramaic words:

> Why then are these Aramaic healing formulas preserved in the tradition used by Mark? In view of the importance attributed to preserving adjurations and incantations in their original languages, these formulas were probably preserved for the purpose of guiding Christian thaumaturges in exorcistic and healing activities. In early Christianity, therefore, these Aramaic phrases may have functioned as magic formulas.[45]

There will be much to say in the following chapters about the magical power ascribed to the "Hebrew" language and divine names. It must suffice for now to mention that the importance was such that a Coptic spell written long after Jesus died says, "The angels that call all *the names* (N̄ONOMⲀCIⲀ) that are written *in Hebrew* (M̄MN̄TϨEBPⲀIOC), in the language of heaven..." The

---

[40] Hull, *Hellenistic Magic and the Synoptic Tradition*, 85-86.
[41] Mark 5:41.
[42] Mark 7:34.
[43] Acts 9:40.
[44] Smith, *Jesus the Magician*, 95.
[45] Aune, *Aufstieg und Niedergang der Römischen Welt*, II.23.2:1535.

Hebrew names ensure that the angels will "listen to every man who will perform this spell"[46] because the magician is speaking the language of the angels. The reader familiar with the New Testament will be instantly reminded of Paul's "tongues of men and angels."[47] In any case, it was apparently widely believed in antiquity that translation would "empty the name" of magical power and that the sound of sacred names had to be preserved exactly, transmitted *literatim.*[48]

Of course the official language of Rome and the Italian peninsula was Latin, but in most of the eastern Roman territories of Jesus' time the language most commonly used from day to day was not Latin, but Greek. Much elevated discourse, writing on philosophy and theology in particular, was carried forward in Greek. The New Testament is also written in Greek, but not in the polished language of the rhetoricians of classical literature:

> As we study the New Testament…the first great impression we receive is that the language to which we are accustomed in the New Testament is on the whole just the kind of Greek that simple, unlearned folk of the Roman Imperial period were in the habit of using.[49]

Whether Jesus spoke any language other than Aramaic or was even able to read has been the subject of some debate. Modern societies expend enormous resources to educate their populations, but pre-industrial societies had neither the resources nor the motivation to teach many people to read and write. Reading

---

[46] Worrell, *The American Journal of Semitic Languages and Literature* 46: 243, 256.

[47] 1 Corinthians 13:1.

[48] DeConick, *Mystery and Secrecy in the Nag Hammadi Collection and Other Ancient Literature*, 14.

Compare *Contra Celsum* V, 45, where Origen claims that spells translated into another language lose their effect due to the change in pronunciation.

[49] Deissmann, *Light from the Ancient East*, 62.

was simply not necessary for the types of work that the majority of people performed. It has been estimated that about 90% of the population in the 1st century was completely illiterate[50] and the New Testament specifically states of Peter and John that they were *αγραμματος* (agrammatos), "without letters," unable to read or write[51]—Peter betrays himself in the gospels by his rustic Galilean accent.[52] Since Jesus' closest disciples were predominantly men who worked with their hands, an inability to read or write would have been completely in keeping with their time and station in life, a point conceded by Origen who says "*they had not received even the rudiments of learning* (*μηδε τα πρωτα γραμματα μεμαθηκοτας*) even as the gospel records about them."[53] Origen reports the charge that Christians were known for their utter lack of education (*απαιδευτοτατους*) and ignorance (*αμαθεστατους*) and that they were "sorcerers" (*γοητας*) who gained converts by misdirection: "they set traps for complete yokels" (*παλευομεν δε τους αγροικοτερους*).[54]

Early Christian converts were most frequently women, slaves and laborers, i.e., members of groups with very low rates of literacy. Making a virtue of necessity, Paul openly acknowledged Christianity's appeal to the humble and disenfranchised: "not many wise by human standards, not many powerful, nor many well-born…"[55] "Not many" in this case evidently meant "precious few." Paul's first letter to the Corinthians begins by making the case for more or less pure fideism, dumbing down the gospel historically, and early pagan critics such as Celsus clearly considered gullibility and ignorance to be notable Christian attributes, "to believe without reason."[56] In his biography of the

---

[50] The position of William.V. Harris, *Ancient Literacy*, pages 147-175.
[51] Acts 4:13.
[52] Watt, *Diglossia and Other Topics in New Testament Linguistics*, 107-120. Compare Matthew 27:73.
[53] Origen, *Contra Celsum* I, 62.
[54] Ibid, VI, 14.
[55] 1 Corinthians 1:26.
[56] Origen, *Contra Celsum*, I, 9.

colorful religious huckster Peregrinus, the satirist Lucian describes the Christians as ιδιωταις ανθρωποις, "ill-informed men,"[57] gullible rubes eager to believe and easily misled—"He does not scruple...to call the Christians *idiōtai*, a word which was then applied by the philosophers to those whom they regarded as incapable of elevated thought."[58]

The low social status of the early Christians and of Jesus himself reflects a bitter reality of the ancient world generally. Lane Fox: "The social pyramid tapered much more steeply than we might now imagine when first surveying the monuments and extent of the major surviving cities. By itself, a specialized ability in a craft was not a source of upward mobility. Its adepts were often slaves themselves, and even if they were not, they were competing with slave labour, which kept the price of their own labour low. The most upwardly mobile figures were the veteran soldier, the athlete, the retired gladiator and perhaps (if we knew more) the traders in slaves themselves."[59]

All the gospels agree that Jesus taught in synagogues. On one such occasion the gospel of Luke has Jesus being handed a scroll from which he reads a passage from Isaiah,[60] but the accuracy of this account, like the rest of Luke's history, is questionable. Regarding the reaction to Jesus' teaching, John says, "Consequently the Jews were amazed, saying, 'How does this man know letters when he has not been taught?'"[61] The clear implication is that Jesus himself was "without letters," or at the very least exhibited some evident deficiency. Joseph Hoffman: "...even the members of the synagogue in Nazareth, not the most cultivated of towns (see John 1:46), were offended at the sight of someone

---

[57] Lucian, *On the Death of Perigrinus*, 13.

[58] Edwards, *Christians, Gnostics and Philosophers in Late Antiquity*, 95.

[59] Lane Fox, *Pagans and Christians*, 59.

[60] Luke 4:16-20.

[61] John 7:15. "Letters," γραμματα (grammata), i.e., *reading and writing*. The villagers of Nazareth raise the same question according to Matthew 13:34-38.

with this background teaching in public."[62] Contemporaries of Jesus such as Philo reveal "the association of magic with the poor and uneducated."[63] The Greek of the magical papyri, like the Greek of the gospels, "is the unpretentious common language of the people, not the cultivated, and atticistic language of the educated."[64] In short, Jesus and his early followers belonged to the stratum of society most closely identified by ancient critics as susceptible to the conjuring tricks of sorcerers and the blandishments of magicians.

As strange as it may seem, it is not certain that the synagogue Jesus supposedly taught in was even a building dedicated to Jewish worship. Regarding the "enigmatic archaeological remains" that have been identified as synagogues, McKay observes that "synagogue" refers primarily to closed religious communities, perhaps exclusively male, and not to physical structures that in contemporary sources tend to be identified as *προσευχαι* (proseuchai) or *places of prayer*,[65] like the one utilized by Paul,[66] that "may have been an informal meeting place, per[haps] in the open air."[67]

Jesus is sometimes referred to as "rabbi," which means *teacher* or *master*. However, just what the speakers meant by this title is unclear. In Mark 9:5, for instance, Jesus is so addressed after Peter, James, and John witness the transfiguration. In John 3:2, Nicodemus also calls Jesus "rabbi," but appears to do so in recognition of his miraculous signs. In other words, it is not Jesus' remarkable erudition that calls forth this title of respect, but rather the visions and miracles associated with him. In a subse-

---

[62] Hoffman, *Jesus Outside the Gospels*, 29.

[63] Seland, *The New Testament and Early Christian Literature in Greco-Roman Context*, 338.

[64] Aune, *Aufstieg und Niedergang der Römischen Welt*, II, 23.2, 1521.

[65] McKay, *Currents in Research: Biblical Studies* 6:103, 121.

[66] Acts 16:13,16.

[67] Bauer, Arndt & Gingrich, *Greek-English Lexicon of the New Testament and Other Early Christian Literature*, 855.

quent chapter, I will briefly make the case that "teaching" had little to nothing to do with reading and everything to do with the performance of miracles. Whether something like the office of rabbi as currently understood even existed in the 1st century is doubtful, but in any case several recent assessments of Jesus conclude that he did not conform to "the rabbinic model," but instead "fits well with the general image of a traveling exorcist and miracle-worker."[68]

The villagers of Nazareth ask concerning Jesus, "Isn't this the laborer, the son of Mary and the brother of James and Joses and Judas and Simon, and aren't his sisters here among us?"[69] In this passage, the word *τεκτων* (tektōn), "laborer," refers to a *carpenter* or *mason*, a person who in Jesus' times would hardly have been expected to be literate. Matthew, on the other hand, rephrases the question to avoid making Jesus out to be a mere laborer: *ουκ ουτος εστιν ο του τεκτονος υιος*, "Isn't this the son of the laborer…?"[70] The Christian apologist Origen, writing in the early 3rd century, castigated the pagan Celsus for calling Jesus a carpenter, claiming Celsus was "unaware that in none of the gospels proclaimed in the churches has 'carpenter' (*τεκτων*) been used to describe Jesus himself,"[71] thereby revealing either Origen's incomplete knowledge of the gospels or his willingness to misrepresent the record. Luke and John simply omit any reference to Jesus' day job. Modern historians tend to place 1st century artisans such as carpenters below agricultural workers in the social hierarchy.[72]

Might Jesus have spoken Greek or at least understood it to some degree? The idea derives some support from the fact that a Hellenistic enclave, Sepphoris, lay a mere four miles from Jesus'

---

68 Grabbe, *Judaism from Cyrus to Hadrian*, II, 521.

69 Mark 6:3.

70 Matthew 13:55.

71 Origen, *Contra Celsum* 6.36.

72 Crossan, *The Historical Jesus*, 46.

boyhood home of Nazareth. It has been claimed by some that Jesus might have spent part of his youth working in Sepphoris as a carpenter and may have thus acquired some familiarity with Greek language and culture.. However, there is no evidence in the gospels that Jesus spent any time in any pro-Roman city of his day. In fact, Sepphoris is not even mentioned in the New Testament and it appears doubtful that a very large Greek-speaking population existed in the Galilee of Jesus' day. Much of the reconstruction of Galilee in Jesus' time is based on remains dating from centuries after his death.[73] Stanley Porter has recently addressed the complex question of who spoke what in 1st century Palestine.[74]

Contrary to seeking out non-Jews, Jesus appears to have actively avoided any contact with major towns and cities, and his disciples were specifically instructed not to enter Gentile or Samaritan cities.[75] "When Jesus engages in his ministry, according to our Gospels, he *avoids* all major cities but spends his time in small villages and remote rural areas, until his final trek to Jerusalem to celebrate Passover."[76] Of an apparently long-standing antipathy Crossan notes: "Peasant hatred for administrative centers such as Sepphoris and Tiberias...points toward social revolution or...at least toward social insurrection. The Galilean peasants might not have been able to imagine a new social order, but they could well imagine a world with certain administrative centers razed to the ground."[77]

> The ancient world operated very much in terms of élites who, despite the more democratic outlook created by the diffusion of the Greek πολις, still lived for each other

---

[73] Chancey, *Biblical Archaeology Review* 33/4: 43-50.
[74] Porter, *Diglossia and Other Topics in New Testament Linguistics*, 53-75.
[75] Matthew 10:5.
[76] Ehrman, *The New Testament: A Historical Introduction to the Early Christian Writings*, 254.
[77] Crossan, *The Historical Jesus*, 193.

> to the exclusion of the vast majority of the population ...If in fact Jesus avoided all the Herodian cities, Sepphoris and Tiberias, which for all their Jewishness were alien centres as far as peasant Jews were concerned—as well as the cities, but not the villages of the surrounding territories, as Mark suggests—the assumption that his message was inspired by the universalist outlook of the Greek world would seem to be a priori less likely.[78]

Despite occasional encounters with Gentiles, Jesus' general attitude toward them appears to have been openly antagonistic. Jesus refers to Gentiles as "dogs" as at Mark 7:27 where he tells the Gentile woman whose daughter he eventually heals, "It is not right to take the children's bread and throw it to the curs." Some commentators have interpreted Jesus' use of *κυναριον* (kunarion), the diminutive of *κυων* (kuōn), *dog*, as ironic or even affectionate,[79] but as corrected by Grant, "the diminutive form rather expresses contempt and distaste."[80] Jesus intends to draw the strongest possible distinction between the Jews, to whom alone he has been sent[81] and the Gentile mongrels—"Do not give what is holy to dogs"[82]—which he generally avoids.[83] To be called a dog is never a good thing: "Beware of the dogs!"[84] The "dogs" are included with murderers, idolaters and sorcerers.[85]

The gospels are not histories in any modern sense of the word, *nor do they contain direct eyewitness accounts of Jesus' career*—Eusebius says of Mark, the putative author of the earliest gospel,

---

[78] Freyne, *Galilee, Jesus and the Gospels*, 173.
[79] Connolly, *New Documents Illustrating Early Christianity: A Review of the Greek Inscriptions and Papyri published in 1979*, 158.
[80] Grant, *Jesus*, 122.
[81] Matthew 15:24.
[82] Matthew 7:6.
[83] Matthew 10:5.
[84] Philippians 3:2.
[85] Revelation 22:15.

"he had not heard the Lord, nor had he followed him"[86]—and reconstructions of Jesus' life must necessarily work within the severe limitations imposed by those conditions. Those who accept that Jesus was a real person and not merely an invention must do as best they can with the preponderance of the evidence and this work will argue that the evidence indicates that Jesus of Nazareth fits a well-known type: *the apocalyptic preacher who authenticated his message by charismatic performances*, performances that were understood as miracles by his followers but as magic by other Jews and pagans.

Of the many gospels rejected by the early church, Eusebius remarked, "they obviously turn out to be inventions of heretical men."[87] In short, the victors of the various early doctrinal wars declared their gospels to be "orthodox," and labeled the numerous gospels and acts used by the losers "heretical." In the past, scholars assumed that only the heretical sects sought to change the text of the New Testament. However, recent attention to the evidence has demolished that comfortable position. There are abundant indications that the suppression of the many early forms of Christianity that diverged from the orthodox position also entailed making "refinements" of the New Testament text.[88] The 4th century church historian Eusebius made this revealing complaint about the copying and alteration of gospels up to his time, alterations that may have involved a primitive form of textual criticism:

> For this reason [i.e., confidence in "the techniques of unbelievers"] they fearlessly put their hands on the di-

[86] Eusebius, *Ecclesiastical History* III, 39.

[87] Ibid, III, 25.

[88] Ehrman's *The Orthodox Corruption of Scripture*, which concentrates on the effects of the emerging christological controversies on the New Testament text, is a comprehensive examination of the evidence for doctrinally motivated textual tampering. The corrupted form of the text is essentially that of the *King James Version*, the so-called "majority text."

> vine scriptures, purporting to have corrected them, and that I utter no false allegation against them anyone who wishes can learn, for if any man so desire, collect the copies to closely compare each with the other. He would find many discrepancies and variances between those of Asklepiades and Theodotus, and it is possible to acquire an abundance of them since their disciples have copied them diligently, "set aright" as they call it, but in fact corrupted.
>
> Again, the copies of Hermophilus do not agree with these, nor do those of Apollonides even agree with one another, for the copies they produced first can be compared to those which later on they even further corrupted, and they will be discovered to differ greatly.[89]

As Hector Avalos has pointed out, the search for an autograph—even if it were to ultimately succeed—which stands behind the surviving texts would still not return us to the authentic sayings of Jesus:

> So even if we were to find the original Greek texts behind all the Greek manuscripts we now have, we would end up only finding a translation of Jesus' words. And Greek translations, by definition, cannot be the "originnal" text of anything Jesus said in Aramaic.[90]

That the quest for the "authentic" Greek text of the New Testament is a fool's errand is now more commonly acknowledged by central figures in biblical studies. "Moreover, there can be no question that the Gospels, from the very beginning, were not archive materials but used texts. This is the worst thing that could happen to any textual tradition. A text, not protected by canonical status, but used in liturgy, apologetics, polemics, homiletics, and instruction of catechumens is most likely to be

[89] Eusebius, *Ecclesiastical History*, V, 28.
[90] Avalos, *The End of Biblical Studies*, 71.

copied frequently and is thus subject to frequent modifications and alterations."[91] According to Christian apologists, Jesus' life was the most important life ever lived, "the greatest story ever told," and yet amazingly none of our surviving documents appear to contain the direct personal account of anyone who actually saw it.

Magical texts.

The number of scholarly references to which a work such as this might appeal is quite large. Potentially relevant books and articles on religious movements, magic, history, sociology, law, papyrology and archaeology exist by the hundreds in the major European languages and Hebrew and additional books and articles on magic in antiquity as well as closely related subjects appear with great regularity. I make no pretense of having surveyed the totality of this material, a procedure that would have resulted in a book at least several times the size of the present work. In fact, it is doubtful that any work that did complete justice to the evidence for magical praxis, vocabulary, and thought in the career of Jesus and the first centuries of the church could be fit into less than a thousand pages.

The mere possession of magical books in antiquity was a crime and sanctions against owning them were severe. Magical works were gathered up by the authorities and burned, and the first recorded incident of Christian book burning (Acts 19:19) involved magical books. The oldest of our Hebrew magical works, ספר הרזים, the *Sepher Ha-Razim*, was reconstructed from scattered fragments of text by the scholar Mordecai Margalioth during the 1960's and published in Hebrew in 1966. Margalioth's work, while admirable, is widely regarded to have missed

[91] Koester, *Gospel Traditions in the Second Century*, 20.

the complete reconstruction of the text, hardly surprising given the nature of the surviving evidence. The *Sepher Ha-Razim* describes seven ascending heavens populated by a bureaucracy of angels, reflecting the same sort of cosmology as the Enoch and Hekhalot texts.[92]

The Greek magical papyri, which are quoted extensively in the chapters that follow, are often fragmentary and were inexpertly copied. That they have survived at all is due to the dry conditions of Egypt where they were discovered plus an amazing stroke of luck. The majority of these documents, which came to the attention of Europeans in the 1800's as part of the antiqueties trade, may have originated in a single library. Some were published as early as 1843, but the most widely used collection, *Papyri Graecae Magicae*, published in Greek with a German translation, was issued in two volumes in 1928 and 1931 by Karl Preisendanz. Bombing during World War II destroyed the proofs of a third projected volume. The most comprehensive introduction by far to the magical papyri is the exhaustively referenced article, "The Greek Magical Papyri: An Introduction and Survey; Annotated Bibliography (1928-1994)" by the late William Brashear.[93]

A lesser-known collection of magical texts, the *Supplementum Magicum*, was published in two volumes in 1990 and 1992. *Supplementum Magicum*, which is, unfortunately, of quite limited availability, records a broad collection of Greek spells with English translations and commentary by Robert Daniels and Franco Maltomini. Christian spells in Coptic have been gather-

---

92 Morgan, *Sepher Ha-Razim: The Book of the Mysteries*, 6.

93 Brashear, *Aufstieg und Niedergang der Römischen Welt* II, 18.5: 3380-3684.

ed from various sources, translated, and published by Marvin Meyer and Richard Smith.[94] Other magical works of antiquity continue to be published and described in specialty journals.

Outside of Egypt the textual material that has survived consists of curse spells inscribed on folded lead sheets (*defixionum tablellae*), amulets inscribed on metals (*lamellae*) and inscribed gems, and incantation bowls with Aramaic and Hebrew text that have been excavated in numbers in present-day Iraq. The incantation bowls, like the papyri that preceded them over a century ago, are typically dug up by treasure hunters and appear on the antiquities market before coming to the attention of experts. Besides these primary materials there are other important witnesses to ancient magical practice who were well-informed witnesses to primitive Christianity. Three pagan sources are of particular interest.

Lucian of Samosata

Lucian of Samosata (c. 120-180)—a self-confessed "hater of frauds" (*μισογοης*) and "hater of liars" (*μισοψευδης*)[95]—relates sharply observed accounts of magic and miracle mongering. "Lucian's knowledge of magical beliefs and practices is very exact."[96] Lucian's *Lover of Lies* is a virtual compendium of magical belief and practice; *On the Death of Peregrinus* offers a critical outsider's view that situates Christian magic in a broader culture

[94] Meyer & Smith, *Ancient Christian Magic: Coptic Texts of Ritual Power.*

[95] Lucian, *The Dead Come to Life* (Αναβιουντες η αλιευς), 20.

[96] Jones, *Culture and Society in Lucian*, 48.

For Lucian's obvious familiarity with Christian miracle, see Edwards, "Satire and Versimilitude: Christianity in Lucian's Peregrinus," *Christians, Gnostics and Philosophers in Late Antiquity*, 89-98.

of religious hoax and flimflammery. Of all the writers of antiquity, Lucian comes closest to the thinking of a modern skeptic.

Besides surviving images of the cult of the oracular man-snake Glycon, a bizarre religious movement that survived for over a century, Lucian's *Alexander the False Prophet*[97] is the most important witness to the career of Alexander of Abonoteichus and the source of nearly all that is known about his cult. Lucians' exposé of Alexander is directed to "my dear Celsus," who wrote "against magicians" (*κατα μαγων*),[98] possibly the same Celsus who wrote *The True Doctrine*,[99] an early refutation of Christian belief and the subject of Origen's belated reply.

It is probable that Lucian was familiar with the gospel of Matthew as well as the content of early Christian preaching. Lucian tells of an exorcism performed by a "Syrian from Palestine," i.e., a Jew, who cast out demons (*τους δαιμονωντας*), demanding to know from whence they came,[100] and by threatening them,[101] heals a man "fallen due to the moon" (*καταπιπτοντας προς την σεληνην*),[102] and brings rotting corpses to life.[103] When a story touches on the subject of ghosts of those who die violently, it may be significant that "someone who hanged himself," (*τις απηγξατο*)[104] or was beheaded,[105] or crucified[106] are singled out

---

[97] *Αλεξανδρος η ψευδομαντις*, *Alexander the False Prophet*, is available in Harman's *Lucian*, IV, in the Loeb classical series.

[98] Origen, *Contra Celsum* I, 68.

[99] See Chadwick, *Origen: Contra Celsum*, xxiv-xxvi and Clay, *Aufstieg und Niedergang der römischen Welt* II.36.5, 3406-3450.

[100] Matthew 12:43.

[101] Matthew 8:29.

[102] Lucian, *Lover of Lies* (*Φιλοψευδης η απιστων*), 16.
Compare Matthew 4:24, "possessed by demons and moonstruck" (*δαιμονιζομενους και σεληνιαζομενους*).

[103] John 11:39.

[104] *και απελθων απηγξατο*, "and he went off and hanged himself..." (Matthew 27:5).

[105] Matthew 14:10.

as exemplary. Lucian recounts a miraculous pick-up-your-cot-and-walk story[107] and it is easy to suspect that his mention of a son sent to Egypt as a youth by his father[108] is a joking reference to the gospel account of Jesus' legendary sojourn in Egypt.[109] Lucian mocks "half-baked philosophers drawn from cobblers and carpenters" (*αυτοσχεδιοι φιλοσοφοι εκ σκυτοτομων η τεκτονων*),[110] a possible gibe aimed at Jesus in particular[111] and Christians in general, who were derided by Celsus as "ignorant and utterly unlettered" (*ιδιωται και αγροικοτεροι*),[112] "ignorant (*αμαθης*)...witless (*ανοητος*)...uneducated (*απαιδευτος*)...infantile (*νηπιος*)."[113] Gathered in "private houses," the Christian mob is composed of "wool carders and *shoe makers* (*σκυτοτομους*) and fullers and *the most uneducated and biggest bunch of yokels*" (*τους απαιδευτοτατους τε και αγροικοτατους*).[114] That Christian converts were generally recruited from the lowest strata of society is clear from New Testament references.[115]

Celsus

It is not true, as claimed by David Brakke in an otherwise impeccable book, that "Irenaeus is the only author of the second century who provides any detailed account of the Christian di-

---

[106] Matthew 27:35.
[107] Lucian, *Lover of Lies*, 11. Compare John 5:8.
[108] Ibid, 33.
[109] Matthew 2:13.
[110] Lucian, *The Double Indictment* (*Δις κατηγορυμενος*), 6.
[111] *ουχ ουτος εστιν ο του τεκτονος υιος*: "isn't this the son of the carpenter?" (Matthew 13:55).
[112] Origen, *Contra Celsum* I, 27.
[113] Ibid, III, 44.
[114] Ibid, III, 55.

In the Roman era, *fulling*, the preparation of wool for cloth production, was done by slaves who worked the fibers with their feet while the material soaked in tubs of urine.

[115] Acts 4:13, 1 Corinthians 1:26-27, 7:21, for example.

versity of his day."[116] The pagan philosopher Celsus wrote a pamphlet, Αληθης λογος, *True Doctrine* or *True Discourse*, an attack on the profusion of Christian sects, about the year 178 C.E., late in the reign of Marcus Aurelius. In a belated reply, Origen wrote a lengthy defense, *Contra Celsum*, around 248 C.E. Celsus' knowledge of Egyptian religion and Christian groups currently considered gnostic suggests that he composed his work in Alexandria. Origen's logorrheic rebuttal, written some 70 years later, implies not only that *True Doctrine* was still in circulation in his time but also that Celsus' criticisms hit painfully close to the bone.

Celsus clearly knew a fair bit about the various Christian factions: their members formed "secret compacts with each other" (*συνθηκας κρυβδην προς αλληλους*) that were in violation of legal norms,[117] some sects rejected the Hebrew God and the Hebrew scriptures,[118] some offered different interpretations of the gospels—Origen concedes the existence of Marcion, Valentinus, Lucian, the Ophites, Simonians, Marcellians, Harpocratians, Sibyllists, Ebionites, and Encratites[119]—rejected "the doctrine of the resurrection according to scripture" (*το περι αναστασεως κατα τας γραφας δογμα*),[120] denied that Jesus suffered and died in reality (Docetism),[121] and worshipped "a god above heaven, who transcends the heaven of the Jews" (*τον υπερουρανιον θεον υπεραναβαινοντας τον Ιουδαιων ουρανον*).[122] Celsus also knew of a Christian diagram illustrating ten heavens represented as circles

---

[116] Brakke, *The Gnostics: Myth, Ritual, and Diversity in Early Christianity*, 30.

Chadwick characterizes Celsus as a "a remarkable well-informed opponent" and notes that "Celsus is excellently informed about the Gnostic sects." (Chadwick, *Origen: Contra Celsum*, ix, xxiii).

[117] Origen, *Contra Celsum* I, 1.

[118] Ibid, II, 3, IV, 2, V, 54.

[119] Ibid, II, 27, III, 10, 13, V, 61-62, 64-65, VI, 19.

[120] Ibid, V, 22.

[121] Ibid II, 16.

[122] Ibid, VI, 19 (compare V, 61, VI, 21, VIII, 15).

guarded by theriocephalic angels—a form of the diagram still existed in Origen's day.[123] The "god above heaven" had deep magical significance. Kotansky has published an example of a spell that begins, Ορκιζω σε τον επανω του ουρανου, "I invoke you, the One above heaven..."[124]

Celsus compared the internecine squabbles of Christians and Jews to "frogs debating with one another around a pond"[125] or the proverbial "fight about the shadow of an ass."[126] The Christian sects "slander one another with dreadful and unspeakable words of abuse ...they would not make even the least concession to reach agreement...they utterly detest each other."[127]

In fact, Celsus anticipated the findings of mainstream New Testament studies by many centuries. He knew that the original text of the gospel had been changed, in some cases several times, a charge Origen could not deny[128]—an unstable early gospel text is now recognized as a given among textual critics and that multiple gospels existed in the 2nd century is universally conceded. Celsus knew of "certain sects" (τινες αιρεσεις) that denied Christ was the person prophesied in the Hebrew Bible[129]—the popular Christian teacher Marcion denied that Jesus was the messiah of the Old Testament. In short, Celsus knew in the 2nd century that "there was never a single Christianity," that by the end of the 1st century "numerous independent Christian communities come into view," and that Christian teaching was a mixture of "disparate cultural elements," a doctrinal smorgasbord that current scholarship labels "hybridity."[130]

---

[123] Ibid, VI, 21, 24-32.

[124] Kotansky, *Greek Magical Amulets: The Inscribed Gold, Silver, Copper, and Bronze Lamellae*, I, 276, 280).

[125] Origen, *Contra Celsum* IV, 23.

[126] Ibid III, 1.

[127] Ibid V, 63 (translation of Henry Chadwick).

[128] Ibid, II, 27.

[129] Ibid, IV, 2.

[130] Brakke, *The Gnostics*, 7, 12.

Apollonius of Tyana.

Philostratus' *Life of Apollonius of Tyana* recreates the career of an itinerant miracle-working holy man with many similarities to Jesus who was probably his near contemporary. It is instructive to compare pagan descriptions of magical technique contained in the *Life* with early Christian praxis.

Jesus, the family, sexual metaphor, and magic.

As Crossan observes, "It is impossible to avoid the suspicion that historical Jesus research is a very safe place to do theology and call it history, to do autobiography and call it biography."[131]

> The earliest Christians did not write a narrative of Jesus' life, but rather made use of, and thus preserved, individual units—short passages about his words and deeds. These units were later moved and arranged by editors and authors. This means that we can never be sure of the immediate context of Jesus' sayings and actions.[132]

To the modern mind, the gospels contain a host of glaring omissions. There is no physical description whatever of Jesus or of any of his disciples. "Nobody remembered what Jesus looked like…by c. 200, he was being shown on early Christian sarcophagi in a stereotyped pagan image, as a philosopher teaching among his pupils or as a shepherd bearing sheep from his flock."[133] The very earliest representation of Jesus appears to be

---

[131] Crossan, *The Historical Jesus: The Life of a Mediterranean Jewish Peasant*, xxviii.

[132] Sanders, *The Historical Figure of Jesus*, 57.

[133] Lane Fox, *Pagans and Christians*, 392.

the Roman *Alexamenos grafitto*, which depicts Jesus as a crucified man with a donkey's head.

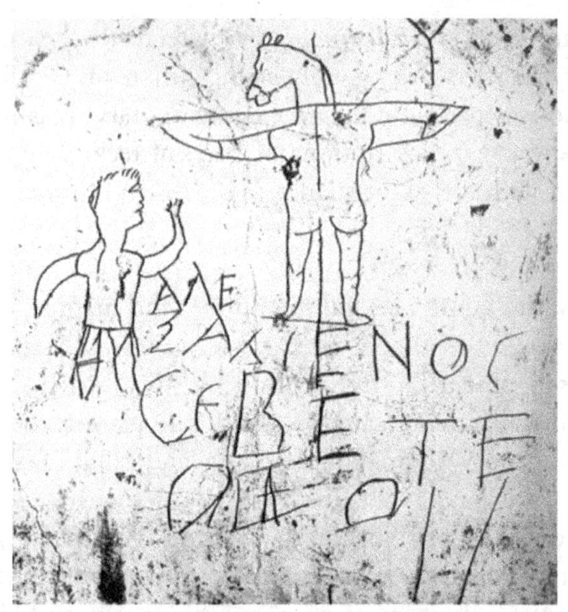

The *Alexamenos graffito*, discovered in Rome in 1857, the earliest known depiction of the crucifixion. The crude inscription reads: *Αλεξαμενοc cεβετε* (sic) *θεον*, "Alexamenos worships god."

Only Jesus' mother, brothers, and sisters are mentioned in Mark,[134]—Joseph never appears in Mark—and none of the gospels has anything to say about his father once Jesus' career begins. Of Jesus' own marital status nothing is said and it is difficult to know just what to make of the gospels' silence on this subject. A strand of the early tradition claimed that Jesus had a twin brother, Judas Thomas—*Thomas* is derived from the

---

[134] Mark 3:31.

Jesus' brothers are also mentioned at John 7:3, 1 Corinthians 9:5, and Galatians 1:19. According to Paul, Jesus' brothers and the other apostles were married.

Aramaic word for *twin*—also known as *Didymus* from the Greek word for *twin.* He may be the same as the famous "Doubting Thomas" of the gospel of John,[135] and is the probable subject of the apocryphal *Acts of Thomas.* In general, however, the New Testament obscures the "factual origins of Jesus" and a case has even been made on the basis of ancient sources that Jesus was conceived as a result of Mary having been raped by a Roman soldier named Pantera.[136] Despite all attempts by historians to determine them, the exact dates of Jesus' birth and death remain a matter of conjecture. The length of Jesus' life and career are also uncertain; the chronology of the gospel of John suggests a career of about three years, but the earlier account of Mark is consistent with a much shorter period, perhaps less than a year in length.

The later synoptic gospels, Matthew and Luke, both polish Mark's prose and ease into Jesus' story by including infancy narratives that are clearly fictitious. Matthew and Luke also omit many of the more radical details and sayings found in Mark, features with which they were apparently uncomfortable. The progressive editing of magical details from the gospel accounts suggests that at some point in the first century evidence of magical praxis became an embarrassment—the Aramaic words of power found in Mark are omitted by Matthew and Luke and exorcism, which features prominently in the synoptics (Mark, Matthew, Luke), is altogether missing from John.

The gospel of Mark contains this revealing snatch of dialogue:

> Peter began to say to him, "Look, we have given up everything and followed you."
>
> Jesus replied, "Truly I say to you, there is no one who has left house or brothers or sisters or mother or father

---

[135] John 20:27-28.

[136] Hanson, *Palestine in the Time of Jesus: Social Structures and Social Conflicts*, 57-58.

> or children or fields on my account and on account of the good news who will not receive a hundred times as much now in this present time, houses and brothers and sisters and mothers and children and fields—with persecutions—and in the age to come, eternal life."[137]

It appears that Jesus' closest disciples abandoned their homes, families, and livelihood to follow him. This naturally raises the question of what happened to those families his disciples left behind—*wives and children are never mentioned as a part of Jesus' entourage*. "Jesus appears to have challenged some to a lifestyle which left local family responsibilities behind. He, himself, appears to have lived such a lifestyle."[138] Jesus' admonition that his followers make eunuchs of themselves (Matthew 19:12) is "yet another extravagant gesture of renunciation" that included abandonment of family, wealth and concern for daily cares.[139] How Jesus and his band of followers managed to support themselves is also unclear, but the accounts imply that while on the road they lived from the charity of those receptive to Jesus' message. Women are mentioned who provided for Jesus[140] and the gospel of John mentions that the disciples kept a purse.[141] Lucian charged that Alexander lived off the public and took financial advantage of a woman *d'un certain âge*,[142] implying that it was a custom of magicians everywhere.

The saying at Luke 18:29 specifically includes *wives* along with brothers, parents and *children* among those to be renounced. Various writers have speculated that Jesus married, but none to my knowledge have read Jesus' words as evidence that he abandoned his own family. Could Jesus have led by example, leaving

---

137 Mark 10: 28-30.
138 Loader, *Sexuality and the Jesus Tradition*, 134.
139 Kueffler, *The Manly Eunuch: Gender Ambiguity, and Christian Ideology in Late Antiquity*, 259.
140 Luke 8:1-4.
141 John 12:6, 13:29.
142 Lucian, *Alexander the False Prophet*, 6.

behind a wife and children and insisting his followers do the same? Thirty years old when he appeared for baptism,[143] he was old enough to have married and fathered children. Did Jesus hate his own wife and children? Did he leave them behind?

Several passages imply that Jesus was alienated from his own family:

> And his mother and brothers came, and standing outside, they sent for him, calling him. A crowd sat around him, and they said to him, "Look, your mother and brothers and sisters are outside asking for you."
>
> He answered, "Who are my mother and brothers?" And looking at those who were sitting around him, he said, "Behold my mother and my brothers! For whoever does the will of God, this is my brother and sister and mother."[144]

Matthew and Luke also report this episode.[145] Morton Smith suggested that Jesus' saying that his disciples must hate their families as well as their own lives (Luke 14:26) may have reflected his own psychology.[146] Myers is certainly correct when he states, "kinship is the backbone of the very social order Jesus is struggling to overturn," and notes that "community of discipleship"[147] is the basis for the new apocalyptic society.

Based on the gospel material, it is difficult to know quite what to make of Jesus' relationship to his family. The brief exchange between Jesus and his mother at the wedding in Cana contains this startling comment:

---

[143] Luke 3:23.

[144] Mark 3:31-35.

[145] Matthew 12:46-50, Luke 8:19-21.

[146] Smith, *Jesus the Magician: Charlatan or Son of God?*, 24-28.

[147] Myers, *Binding the Strong Man: A Political Reading of Mark's Story of Jesus*, 168.

> And when they ran out of wine, Jesus' mother said to him, "They don't have any wine."
> Jesus said to her, "What have I to do with you, woman? My time is not yet here."
> His mother said to the servants, "Do whatever he tells you."[148]

I have translated the Greek idiom *τι εμοι και σοι*—literally "what [is it] to me and to you"—as "What have I to do with you?" It is a carryover of a Semitic expression into Greek that means something like "What do you have against me?" or "What have I done to you that you should attack me?" It is, in fact, the identical idiom used by the demons when addressing Jesus (Mark 1:24) : "What have we to do with you, Jesus the Nazarene (*τι ημιν και σοι* Ιησου Ναζαρενε)? Have you come to destroy us?" The expression, fairly common in the Greek translation of the Hebrew Old Testament, is often linked by the context to violent intentions.[149] The hostility implicit in this idiom has been papered over by any number of Mary-Mother-of-God apologists, whose diligent misreading of the passage has successfully generated an enduring fog of misimpression. "Any hero who speaks to his mother only twice, and on both occasions addresses her a 'Woman,' is a difficult figure for sentimental biographers."[150]

Jesus' disciples must *hate* their parents, siblings, wives and children according to the form of the saying in Luke 14:26—"If anyone comes to men and *does not hate* (*ου μισει*) his father and mother and wife and children..." The remarkable similarity of this saying to magical spells of attraction is discussed below. Jesus' prickly family relationship appears repeatedly in the gos-

---

[148] John 2:3-5.

[149] As at Judges 11:12, 1 Kings 17:18, 2 Chronicles 35:21, for example, where in each case one party contemplates the death of the other.

[150] Smith, *Jesus the Magician*, 25.

pels in connection with his mission. Barton notes that Capernaum and the inner circle of the twelve "replaces Nazareth and the community of Jesus' own family," and concludes that the ominous "those outside" for whom everything is obfuscation includes Jesus' own relatives[151]—Jesus' own brothers did not believe in him.[152] Those looking for support for conventional "family values" may take cold comfort from the words of Jesus of Nazareth. As Andrew Jacobs notes, the language of the gospels is the language of "domestic demolition."[153]

> ...Jesus hated families...By "family values" conservative politicians mean "hierarchical values," imposed not only on children but on lots of adults, often punitively. "Family values" forcibly infantilize most of the population. Jesus rejects families in part because he insists upon a different hierarchy: God is the father, which means that all humans are children...that slaves were attracted to Christianity is not surprising.[154]

As Edwards remarks, the apocalyptic fixation of Jesus' first disciples, "when it was thought that the transition would be sudden and universal," soon shifted to a fixation on martyrdom "and celibacy was not only a desirable condition for the zealot, but a proof of zeal in those who would not be given the opportunity to die...it was the duty of an Apostle to break up marriages and of virgins to avoid them."[155]

Few scholars competent in the field of New Testament studies appear to question the conclusion that Jesus was a confirmed bachelor. As to Jesus' sex life, the relevant facts are these: at

---

[151] Barton, *Discipleship and Family Ties in Mark and Matthew*, 68, 72.
[152] John 7:5.
[153] Jacobs, *Journal of Early Christian Studies* 7:107.
[154] Taylor, *Castration: An Abbreviated History of Western Manhood*, 199-200.
[155] Edwards, "Some early Christian immoralities," *Christians, Gnostics and Philosophers in Late Antiquity*, 78-79.

thirty years of age Jesus was presumably a single man, a feature of his life that would have been remarked upon in his time and culture: "Singleness—an unmarried lifestyle—was exceptional, even suspicious among the Jews, because it was seen as an offense to the divine obligation to procreate (Gen. 1:28). Jesus, however, was apparently single."[156] If a childless woman was considered a scandal worthy of intervention from On High, we can barely imagine the amount of malicious whispering a childless man must have produced. "Celibacy is prohibited in Jewish law. The rabbis consider procreation the first command recorded in the Bible...Marriage and study of Torah are put ahead of all other religious obligations."[157]

It is not that celibacy was unknown in 1st century Judaism. The Essenes practiced celibacy as a part of their severely legalistic and isolationist religious movement, or possibly because of "the embattled character of the Community as a whole,"[158] but there is no evidence that Jesus was legalistic or isolationist to the same extent, so one might fairly ask why he remained unmarried. Martin, who discusses various forms of asceticism practiced in Jesus' day, notes that sexual abstinence usually accompanied other forms of abstinence or avoidance (wine, food, social relations, contact with the dead) and concludes, "... though we can now admit that sexual abstinence was indeed practiced by Jews of Jesus' day, what we know about Jesus does not fit any of the forms of ascetic Judaism we know about. If Jesus was a sexual ascetic, he was a queer one."[159]

Of course, various motives for celibacy may have overlapped: Jesus' intensely apocalyptic fixation (discussed in the next chap-

---

[156] Nissinen, *Homoeroticism in the Biblical World: A Historical Perspective*, 119.

[157] Epstein, *Sex Laws and Customs in Judaism*, 141.

[158] Brown, *The Body and Society: Men, Women and Sexual Renunciation in Early Christianity*, 38.

[159] Martin, *Sex and the Single Savior: Gender and Sexuality in Biblical Interpretation*, 97.

ter) may have been expressed as avoidance of sex, as well as a concern for purity, defined both in Jesus' cultural milieu and in the magical papyri as "abstention from sexual activity," which in certain extreme cases extended to not speaking to women and avoiding food served by them.[160] The Hebrew book of magical spells, the *Sepher Ha-Razim,* repeatedly admonishes the magician, "Purify yourself from all impurity and cleanse your flesh from all carnality and then you will succeed...Perform the entire rite in purity, and you will succeed."[161] Morton Smith pointed to Paul's "recommendation of celibacy on the ground that it would free the Christian from distractions and make him *euparedron* for the Lord...the lack of normal sexual satisfaction is likely to lead to compensatory connections with spirits, hence the requirement of celibacy by many shamanistic and priestly groups has probably some functional justification."[162] Temporary sexual abstinence was a condition of purity for Egyptian priests[163]—who practiced magic as part of their duties—and sexual abstinence played a significant role in Greco-Egyptian magic which in the 1st century included the characteristically Jewish element of exorcism: "virginity...gave efficacy to the exorcist's words."[164] The *Leyden Papyrus*, an Egyptian magical text, provides another witness to the importance of purity defined by the formula: "a boy, pure, before he goes with a woman."[165]

It is remarkable how closely Jesus' words to his disciples match those of an *αγωγη* (agōgē), a sexual attraction spell:

---

[160] Rebecca Lesses, *Harvard Theological Review* 89: 57.
[161] Morgan, *Sepher Ha-Razim: The Book of the Mysteries*, 24, 31, 42, etc.
[162] Smith, *Harvard Theological Review* 73: 244.
Paul's term *ευπαρεδρος* (euparedros) receives further comment in a subsequent chapter.
[163] Brier, *Ancient Egyptian Magic: Spells, Incantations, Potions, Stories, and Rituals*, 38.
[164] Brenk, *Aufstieg und Niedergang der Römischen Welt*, II, 16.3, 2112.
[165] Griffith & Thompson, *The Leyden Papyrus: An Egyptian Magical Book*, III, 11; XXV, 20; XXVII, 15.

> If anyone comes to me and does not hate his father and mother and wife and children and brothers and sisters and his own soul as well, he cannot be my disciple.[166]

> Make her leave father, mother, brothers, sisters, until she comes to me...with an endless divine passion and frenzied devotion.[167]

> Frenzied (*μαινομενη*), let [Name] throw herself at my doors, forgetting children, and life with her parents, detesting the race of men and women, let her hold me and me alone...[168]

> ...may you forget your parents, children, friends![169]

Faraone points out that erōs-type spells, which urge the victim to abandon family relationships, are typically employed by "men, courtesans, or whores"[170] and in another work comments on the "attendant shift in loyalties" attraction spells effected in addition to drawing attention to the fact that Jesus' command at Luke 14:26 "seems to echo the language of contemporary love spells."[171]

It may be simple coincidence that the language of religious devotion tends to mimic the language of sexual infatuation, but Jesus is quoted as using metaphors of virgins[172] and brides[173] in connection with his followers, and the trope is carried over into

---

[166] Luke 14:26.

[167] Martinez, *Ancient Magic and Ritual Power*, 358, quoting *Supplementum Magicum* I, 45.

[168] Preisendanz, *Papyri Graecae Magicae* IV, 2756-2761.

[169] Ibid, XV, 4.

[170] Faraone, *The World of Ancient Magic*, 279.

[171] Faraone, *Ancient Greek Love Magic*, 88, 89.

[172] Matthew 25:1-13.

[173] Mark 2:19-20, John 3:29.

the letters of Paul.[174] It is well known from modern examples that a certain erotic glamour is sometimes associated with the most unlikely religious figures, at least in the minds of their followers, and such appears to have been the case with Paul. In the *Acts of Paul and Thecla*, a leering novella about virginity retained, Thecla, a maiden betrothed, sits "like a spider at the window ...bound by [Paul's] words" in a "a fearful passion."[175]

The effect of Paul's enchantment is sexual renunciation, leading the people of the city to shout, "Away with the sorcerer!"[176] Brown notes of *Paul and Thecla*, "The ancient scenario of supernatural violence exercised through love-spells was a device exploited with gusto by all writers in the second century."[177] However, the acrobatics in Thecla's case are revealed to be more religious than sexual, as perfect an example as could be hoped for that abstinence is merely one of the many uses to which the sexual impulse may be put. The pure Christian 'nottie-as-hottie' has an ancient pedigree; early Christian sources describe in some detail the effects of spell-induced erotic frenzy on virginal Christian maidens as well as the detection and reversal of such spells.[178]

Jesus relationship to his body of disciples is frequently likened to marriage, particularly in the apocalyptic passages of the New Testament.[179] The 144,000 who are the collective "bride of the Lamb" are virgin males: "these are the ones who were not defiled with women, for they are virgins. These are the ones who follow the Lamb wherever he goes..."[180] It may be difficult for

---

[174] 2 Corinthians 11:2.
[175] Henneke, *Acts of Paul*, 9.
[176] Ibid, 15.
[177] Brown, *The Body and Society: Men, Women and Sexual Renunciation in Early Christianity*, 157.
[178] Faraone, *Ancient Greek Love Magic*, 88, ff.
[179] As at Matthew 9:15, 25:1-10, Mark 2:19-20, Revelation 18:23, 21:2, for instance.
[180] Revelation 14:4.

the post-modern reader to avoid seeing a camp *bouleversement* in this image, a twee Sunday school Jesus accompanied by an army of virginal men, and it would come as little surprise if some early Christian sects interpreted the union as more than merely spiritual.

Indeed, the language of the gospels frequently contains sexual overtones, a fact obscured by the usual selection of English equivalents for Greek words. Jesus is the *οικοδεσποτης* (oikodespotēs), the *master of the house*, or if a more literal but still accurate rendering is preferred, the *house despot*, a term "redolent with hegemonic assumptions about masculine destiny."[181] The lord and master of the house 'can do as he pleases with what belongs to him.'[182] In a further evocation of a patriarchal household, the master of the house commands slaves as at Matthew 13:27, for instance—*οι δουλοι του οικοδεσποτου*: "the housemaster's slaves" which often rendered by innocuous translation, "the householder's servants."

"The kingdom of the heavens may be compared to a man who sowed good seed in his field."[183] The good seed—*καλον σπερμα* (kalon sperma)—is a thinly veiled sexual metaphor and the sowing is promiscuous: on the path, the rocks, among the thorns, and on good soil.[184] The metaphor is carried over into the epistle of John: "Every man who has been begotten from God cannot commit a sin because his seed remains in him,[185] and he is not able to sin because he has been begotten."[186]

---

[181] Anderson, *New Testament Masculinities*, 79, 102. The term occurs in Matthew 13:52, 20:1, 21:33, Mark 14:14, Luke 12:39, 13:25, 14:21, 22:11, for example.

[182] Matthew 20:15.

[183] Matthew 13:24.

[184] Mark 4:1-9.

[185] *οτι σπερμα αυτου εν αυτω μενει*: "because his seed remains in him ..." 1 John 3:9.

[186] 1 John 3:9.

It is in connection with the sort of devotion, "the likes of which not even a slave would do," that David Martinez notes "the close parallel between magical ερως θειος and the exclusive devotion demanded by Jesus in Lk 14:26" where the oft-repeated demand to hate one's family members is stipulated as a requirement for discipleship.[187] The phenomenon of ερως θειος (erōs theios), *the love due a god*, or φιλια μανικη (philia manikē), *maniacal devotion*, is a feature of the erotomagical spells in the papyri as previously noted. The connection between nocturnal mystery rites and sexual acts, a point explored in a subsequent chapters, is also well attested: "The modern use of the word 'orgies,' from *orgia*, reflects the puritan's worst suspicions about secret nocturnal rites. There is no doubt that sexuality was prominent in mysteries."[188] The term οργια (orgia) referred to worship generally, rites and sacrifices, but when applied to the mystery cults, it meant the *secret rite* practiced by an initiate.

Samuel Angus:

> Another conception of communion with the deity in the Mysteries was a religious marriage—a conception the roots of which can be traced back to the Egyptian and Asiatic belief and practice of copulation with deity...Such *synousia* had a double underlying idea: first, an erotic-anthropomorphic, in which *synousia* has the character of an offering or sacrifice (of purity); secondly, the magical, whereby the worshippers participated in the god's *Mana* and secured life and salvation."[189]

---

[187] Martinez, *Ancient Magic and Ritual Power*, 357, 358.

Compare Matthew 10:37, 19:29, Mark 10:29-30, Luke 14:26, 18:29.

[188] Burkert, *Ancient Mystery Cults*, 104.

[189] Angus, *The Mystery Religions: A Study in the Background of Early Christianity*, 222-223.

Συνουσια (sunousia), *communion, social intercourse*, or even *unio mystica, mystical union.*

A few commentators, most famously Morton Smith, suggested that in some sects primitive Christian ritual included an overtly homosexual element, a claim that is not particularly controversial if read against the background of possession cults generally: "ecstatic possession seizures are sometimes explicitly interpreted as acts of mystical sexual intercourse between the subject and his or her possessing spirit...all over the world we find this conception of a spiritual union, paralleling human marriage, used to image the relationship between a spirit and its regular devotee."[190] Their early opponents claimed that magic and sexual rites played a central role in certain gnostic sects. The Basilidians were alleged to "employ magic and images, incantations, invocations and all the rest of the arsenal of magic" and their rites were claimed to include the use of sexual secretions:

> Man and woman take the male sperm in their hands, step forward, look up to the sky, and with the defilement still on their hands, evidently pray..."We present unto you this gift, the Body of Christ." So they eat it while participating in their infamies...They behave in a similar way with what comes from the woman when she menstruates: the monthly blood of impurity from her is collected by them; they take it, eat it in common and say: "This is the blood of Christ"...they prohibit the generation of children during intercourse...they smear their hands with the ignominy of their seminal ejaculations, and rise and pray with polluted hands, completely naked...The power which is contained in the blood of menstruation and the reproductive organs, however, is Psyche, which we collect and eat.[191]

---

[190] Lewis, *Ecstatic Religion: An Anthropological Study of Spirit Possession and Shamanism*, 58-59.

[191] Haardt, *Gnosis: Character and Testimony*, 43, 71-73.

The *Gospel of Judas*, discovered in 1978 and first published in English translation in 2006, reflects internecine doctrinal conflict between competing Christian sects so its accusations presumably apply to Christians. Among the "lawless acts" alleged are "those who sleep with men." The Coptic text in question reads ϩN̄ΚΟΟΥЄ ЄΥN̄ΚΟΤΚЄ ΜN̄ N̄ϩΟΟΥΤ[192] in which the verb, ΝΚΟΤΚ (*to sleep*) plus the preposition ΜN̄ (*with*) is a euphemism for sexual intercourse.[193] It is the same expression used in the Coptic version of Genesis 39:10 and Leviticus 18:22 where the meaning is clearly "to lie down with" in order to engage in sexual relations. The text literally breaks down as follows: ϩN̄ (some) ΚΟΟΥЄ (others) ЄΥN̄ΚΟΤΚЄ (they sleep) ΜN̄ (with) N̄ (the) ϩΟΟΥΤ (males).

The text is a clear, if euphemistic, accusation of same-sex activeity made by Christians against other Christians but does it reflect reality, and if so, how would we know? Several early Christian sects generally considered to be "Gnostic," including the Nicolaitans, Phibionites, and Naassenes, were accused by proto-orthodox writers of a range of outré sexual practices that included ritual ingestion of semen. Mastrocinque cautions, "the documentation as a whole is a compound of polemical arguments, not a historical picture, although the specific descriptions of sexual abuses supported by theological doctrines could not be entirely without a historical basis."[194]

Epiphanius characterized the multitude of sects in competition with the orthodox as "like a swarm of insects, infecting us with diseases."[195] He claims the "so-called Gnostics"[196] "avoid inter-

---

[192] Kasser, et al, *The Gospel of Judas: Critical Edition*, 195.
[193] Crum, *A Coptic Dictionary*, 224.
[194] Mastrocinque, *From Jewish Magic to Gnosticism*, 136-138.
[195] Williams, *The Panarion of Epiphanius of Salamis, Book I (Sects 1-46)*, 2nd edition, 90 (*Panarion*, Book I, XXVI, 1.1).

I have followed Williams' numbering system for the sections, but have produced a more explicit translation of the text.

course with women" (*γυναιξι μη πλησιαζοντες*) and ejaculate onto their own hands, and "even the rest who have promiscuous intercourse with women do not achieve satiety, *becoming inflamed* [with passion] *for one another* (*εις αλληλους εκκαιονται*), *men with men* (*ανδρες εν ανδρασι*)."[197]

Regarding those the Gnostics call "Levites," Epiphanius bluntly states, "Those they call 'Levites' *do not have intercourse with women, but have intercourse with each other* (*ου μισγονται γυναιξι αλλα αλληλοις μισγονται*), and those persons they regard as *the elect, indeed, the exalted ones* (*οι προκριτεοι παρ' αυτοις δηθεν και επαινετοι*)."[198] Concerning the Carpocratians, he says, "The [disciples] of this wicked sect put their hand to every kind of hideous and destructive practice. They have contrived various magical *devices* (*μηχανην*) and *charms* (*επωδας*), concocted *philtres* (*φιλτρα*) and *attraction spells* (*αγωγιμα*), and not only that, they conjure *familiar spirits* (*παρεδρους δαιμονας*) for their use to exert great power over many *by magical arts* (*δια...μαγγανειας*)...and besides that, every lewdness and wicked act—which it is not even decent to utter with one's mouth—these people perform every kind of pederasty[199] and the most salacious sexual intercourse with women in every part of the body, and carry out magic (*μαγαιας*) and witchery (*φαρμακειας*)[200] and idolatry."[201] Whatever one may make of the accusations of sexual license, it is certain that both orthodox and heterodox Christian groups

---

[196] *Κατα των λεγομενων γνοστικων*, "Against the so-called Gnostics", *Panarion* Book I, XXVI.

[197] Epiphanius, *Panarion*, Book I, XXVI, 11.1, 11.7.

[198] Ibid, Book I, XXVI, 13.1.

[199] Epiphanius employs a late and uncommon word, *ανδροβασια*, a synonym of *παιδεραστια*, *boy love* (See Sophocles, *Greek-English Lexicon of the Roman and Byzantine Periods*, 158). His choice of words may reflect the fact that the latter still carried positive connotations among pagans and that the sexual relations he describes were between adults of equal age and status.

[200] *Potions* or *poisons*, likely including abortifacients.

[201] Epiphanius, *Panarion*, Book I, XXVII, 3, 1; 4, 6-7.

practiced magic, the orthodox in the form of exorcism and healing, cursing, and prophecy by spirit possession,[202] and the heterodox by more typically pagan means.[203] According to the best evidence, the charge that the Christian gnostics practiced magic is sustained.

One accusation in particular in Celsus' *True Doctrine* sent Origen off on an extended tangent: that Jesus was merely "a worthless sorcerer, hated by God" (*θεομισους ην τινος και μοχθηρου γοητος*)[204] and that he had learned magic in Egypt, the ancient home of magic and the ultimate source of Jesus' miraculous powers. Attempting to disprove the accusation that Christ and his followers practiced magic, Origen poured out page after page on the subject, providing us with antiquity's most complete, not to mention most voluble, explanation of the theory of magical names.[205]

Although Origen could hardly say enough about Christian magic and magical diagrams, he proved considerably more reticent about Celsus' charge that the worship of Jesus was similar to the adoration of Antinous, universally regarded (as far as we know) as the Emperor Hadrian's deified "catamite."[206] Only in

---

[202] Conner, *Magic in the New Testament: A Survey and Appraisal of the Evidence*, 149-312.

[203] The writer Porphyry preserves the pagan Plotinus' attack on the magic of the gnostics (*Προς τους γνωστικους*) in the *Enneads* (II, 9, 15). Preisendanz' collection of magical spells (*Papyri Grae-cae Magicae*) preserves at least one recognized to have a gnostic orientation (XIII, 139-213, 442-563).

[204] Origen, *Contra Celsum* I, 71.

[205] Ibid, I, 6,22,24-27,38,46,60,68,71, II, 9,32,34,48-55, III, 1,5,24,46, 50,68, IV, 33-35,86,88,92-95, V, 6,9,38,42,45-46,51, VI, 38-41, VII, 4, 47,59-60.

[206] That was clearly Origen's opinion; he describes Antinous as Hadrian's *παιδικα*, *favorite* or *darling boy*, mentions Hadrian's "unnatural lust" and attributes the healing and prophecy that allegedly

his late teens or perhaps slightly older, Antinous drowned in the murky waters of the Nile under equally murky circumstances and "was automatically identified with that other young god of myth," Osiris, likewise drowned in the sacred Nile. Dead before his time, deified, reputed to grant healing miracles and foretell the future, pagans noted similarities "between Antinous, the young, sacrificial and resurrected god from Bithynion, and Christ, the young, sacrificial and resurrected go from Nazareth." From the Roman point of view the cults of Jesus and Antinous were simply more imports of "eastern gods of mystery, salvation, and ecstasy." But the story of Antinous has one other point in common with the story of Jesus: "We do not have a single word about [Antinous] or a single image of him which can be indubitably dated to his own lifetime."[207]

Origen quotes Celsus as claiming that "other [Christians], *invented another guardian* (ευραντο προστατην) for themselves by wickedly conceiving of *a master and tutelary spirit* (διδασκαλον τε και δαιμονα), and wallow about in utter darkness more lawless and more depraved than *[the rites] of those devoted*[208] *to the Egyptian Antinous...*" (των Αντινου του κατ' Αιγυπτον θιασωτων)[209] It seems clear that the rites of Antinous, particularly his "sacred nights," scandalized Christians and were, by implication at least, "flagrant and uninhibited homosexual orgies."[210] That Celsus' charge of same-sex debauchery even more

---

occurred at Antinous' shrines to the work of demons and sorcerers. (*Contra Celsum* III, 36).

[207] Lambert, *Beloved and God: The Story of Hadrian and Antinous*, 2, 6, 17, 47.

Lambert's book, finished by a co-author after his death by suicide, is an exhaustively researched, well-written and accessible account of the life and cultic afterlife of Antinous.

[208] "of those devoted," from θιασωτης, a *member* of a θιασος, a *cult* or *religious brotherhood*, particularly of the ecstatic god Bacchus to whom Antinous was assimilated.

[209] Origen, *Contra Celsum* V, 63.

[210] Lambert, 186-187. Compare *Contra Celsum* III, 36.

depraved than the sacred nights of Antinous applied to some *Christian* sect(s) known to him is secure. The context makes clear that *Christian factions* are the subject of discussion; the Simonians, Marcellians and Harpocratians are specifically mentioned and Origen's reply, which avoids specifically addressing charges of lawless and depraved behavior, quotes 1 Timothy 4:1-3 which "foretold" that "in the last times *some will apostatize* (αποστησονται τινες) from the faith" by following "the teachings of demons" (διδασκαλιας δαιμονιων) and "forbidding marriage."[211] It is possible that 1 Timothy addresses a late first century Christian gnosticism with tutelary spirits—daemons—similar in character to the deified Antinous.

The reality of "gnosticism" as a category is currently a subject of debate,[212] but in any case it seems clear that gnostic speculation functioned as "a bedrock to build cities of theosophical inquiry without much legalistic zoning"[213] and it is important to note that in the gnostic antinomian tendency there is nothing in principle that would preclude sexual ritual—"For the gnostics bisexuality is an expression of perfection."[214] On the contrary, the very antinomian character of some gnostic sects would appear to encourage it: "...the pneumatic morality is determined by hostility toward the world and contempt for all mundane ties...As the pneumatic is free from the *heimarmene*,[215] so he is free from the yoke of the moral law. To him all things are permitted, since the pneuma is 'saved in its nature' and can be

---

[211] Origen, *Contra Celsum* V, 62-64.

On Gnostic attitudes toward women and marriage see, Kurt Rudolph's *Gnosis: The Nature and History of Gnosticism*, 270-272.

[212] Brakke (*The Gnostics*), King (*What Is Gnosticism*?), Williams (*Rethinking "Gnosticism"*), for example.

Giversen expressed skepticism (in 1963) about labeling "the heterogeneous line of sects and movements which have been classified under Gnosticism." (Giversen, *Apocryphon Johannis*, 13).

[213] Conner, *Voices of Gnosticism*, 3.

[214] Rudolph, *Gnosis*, 80.

[215] *Fate* (ειμαρμενε) as predetermined by the stars.

neither sullied by actions nor frightened by the threat of archontic retribution."[216]

The divine *σπινθηρ* (spinthēr), "spark," synonymous with the *πνευμα* (pneuma), "spirit," is the incorruptible mark and property of the gnostic elect, the "pneumatics." In their most literal sense the words of Paul would describe this spiritual elite: "Now we have been set free from the law, dead to that which restrained us...consequently there is now no judgment on those in Christ Jesus for *the law of the spirit* (*ο...νομος του πνευματος*) of life in Christ Jesus set you free from the law of sin and of death."[217]

This and similar passages were liable to a libertine interprettation: "both the hidden God and the hidden pneuma are nihilistic conceptions: no *nomos* [*law*, my note] emanates from them, that is, no law either for nature or for human conduct as part of the natural order." Repudiation of the lower world and its Creator results in "a positive metaphysical interest in repudiating allegiance to all objective norms and thus a motive for their outright violation."[218] The gnostic elite are "a new kind of man ...*free* from the law."[219]

Whatever the truth of the claims made about Christian splinter groups, there is no doubt that sex magic figured in the wider culture:

> Over [seminal] emission, a good [spell]. After intercourse say: "I have poured out the blood of Abrathiaou into the vagina of woman [Name]. Give your pleasure to [Name]. I have given you part of my pleasure, O

---

[216] Jonas, *The Gnostic Religion*, 46.
[217] Romans 7:6, 8:1-2. Compare Galatians 5:18.
[218] Jonas, 271, 273.
[219] Rudolph, *Gnosis*, 253.

> [Name], I poured the blood of Babraōth in your womb."[220]

The expression is *εις την φυσιν*, literally "into the nature..." In keeping with the broad definition of *φυσις*, *nature*, the principle "which causes growth and preservation in plants and animals"[221] and, by extension, the sexual organs.

Semen is often referred to in the magical papyri as water or as the blood of various gods. "The general notion can be explained in the light of the fact that blood and semen (also saliva, milk, urine, wine, water, honey, etc) were thought to emanate from or to share something with an eternal flow of divine light, which was also viewed as a liquid."[222]

> Φυσικλειδιον[223]
>
> The spell to say:
> I say to you, uterus of [Name], open and receive the seed of [Name], the incontinent sperm of Iarphe Arphe (write it!). Make her, [Name], love me for all her time as Isis loved Osiris...[224]

Some spells list frankly sinister ingredients: "...the fat of a spotted goat and blood and *pollution* (μυσαγμα)[225], the fetus of a dog, *menstruation from a maiden untimely dead* (ιχωρα παρθενου

---

[220] Daniel & Maltomini, *Supplementum Magicum*, 79.
[221] Liddell & Scott, *A Greek-English Lexicon*, 1965.
[222] Ibid, II, 158.
Compare "O lord, almighty, first-begotten, self-begotten, begotten without semen..." (Meyer & Smith, *Ancient Christian Magic: Coptic Texts of Ritual Power*, 47).
[223] Φυσικλειδιον, derived from the words for *vagina* and *key*, hence a "key-to-the-vagina spell."
[224] Preisendanz, *Papyri Graecae Magicae* XXXVI, 286-288.
[225] *Defilement* or *uncleanness*, a variant of *μυσος*, a probable reference to *semen*.

αωρου) and the heart of a young boy..."[226] It should be noted the text is part of a *διαβολη* (diabolē), *a slander spell*—"the projection of a ritual violation onto the party to be affected by the spell"[227]—that accuses the intended victim of violating the sanctity of a ritual, thereby arousing the wrath of the offended deity. In short, the text is an accusation, not a true description of a ritual. "None of this stuff is required for the ritual itself; rather, the performer *imputes* these impurities to the person he is trying to bind—to get Selene angry with her."[228]

There existed a powerful taboo against the revelation of mysteries as this excerpt from a slander spell shows: "For I come proclaiming the slander of the defiled and unholy woman [Name], for she slandered your holy mysteries by revealing them to men..."[229]

Is it possible that sexual elements appeared among some early Christian groups as charged by their opponents? Such accusations have typically been dismissed as over-heated rhetoric by modern scholars who consider them similar to accusation spells (*διαβολαι*), but given the admittedly limited evidence they cannot be discounted absolutely. In any case, the New Testament contains language that could be interpreted sexually: "a man will leave his father and mother behind a stick closely to his wife and the two will be one flesh. This is a great mystery—I am speaking of Christ and the church."[230]

Stars and magic: Matthew's infancy story.

Of the city of Bethlehem the prophet Micah wrote,

---

[226] Preisendanz, *Papyri Graecae Magicae* IV, 2644-2648.
[227] Betz, *The Greek Magical Papyri in Translation*, 83, footnote 314.
[228] Frankfurter, *Greek, Roman, and Byzantine Studies* 46: 53.
[229] Preisendanz, *Papyri Græcæ Magicæ* IV, 2476-2478.
[230] Ephesians 5:31-32.

> But you, O Bethlehem Ephrathah, who are little to be among the clans of Judah, from you shall come forth for me one who is to be ruler in Israel, whose origin is from of old, from ancient days.[231]

The first Christians were eager to apply this prediction to Jesus, but to do so they had to get Jesus born in Bethlehem. There was, unfortunately, a problem: Jesus and his family were from Nazareth, a village so insignificant that it is never even mentioned in the Old Testament. "There seems no good reason why anyone should have invented a connection with a place otherwise so little known."[232] Mark, the writer of the earliest gospel, simply ignored the issue, but Matthew, who had an excellent motive for making a connection between Jesus and Bethlehem, elected to take it up. John knows of the controversy, but did not invent an infancy fable.[233]

It is well known that people of Jesus' time often concocted fabulous stories about the birth and childhood of famous figures. In the centuries after Jesus' death, apocryphal tales about him and his mother were collected in the form of books, two of which, the *Infancy Gospel of Thomas* (not to be confused with the Coptic *Gospel of Thomas*) and the *Gospel of James*, still survive. Matthew needed to get Jesus born in Bethlehem, in David's city,[234] so that David, the past king of Israel, could function as a prophetic prototype of Jesus, the future King of Kings. Matthew places Jesus in the family line of Abraham and David, two pivotal characters in Jewish salvation history, and even enumerates a span of 42 generations between Abraham, David, and Jesus. Strangely enough, Matthew includes several

---

[231] Micah 5:2 (RSV)

[232] Wilcox, *Aufstieg und Niedergang der Römischen Welt*, II.25.1: 143.

[233] John 7:41-42.

[234] David's father, Jesse, was a native of Bethlehem (1 Samuel 16:1).

women of questionable repute in Jesus' family tree: Tamar,[235] who, posing as a prostitute has sex with her father-in-law,[236] Rahab,[237] a prostitute by profession,[238] and Bathsheba, the wife of Uriah,[239] an adulteress.[240] Assuming that Matthew could just have easily omitted these women, "ladies in the holy family who were not wholly holy,"[241] one can only wonder why he chose to include them. It is not impossible that Matthew meant them to be read as a subtext to the story of Jesus' own parentage.

Matthew wishes to complete Jesus' connection to David by having him born in Bethlehem,[242] after which time magi from the east appear at the court of the Judean king, Herod the Great:

> In the days of Herod the king, after Jesus was born in Bethlehem of Judea, magi came from the east to Jerusalem, saying, "Where is he who has been born King of the Jews? For we saw his star ascend, and we came to render homage to him." But after hearing this, King Herod became troubled and all Jerusalem with him, and he assembled all the chief priests and scribes of the people and inquired of them where the Christ was to be born.[243]

If the star was a comet or some other spectacular celestial event, why had Herod and his court not seen it? Matthew probably had Isaiah 60:3 (*RSV*) in mind: "And nations shall come to your light and kings to the brightness of your rising." In any case,

---

[235] Matthew 1:3
[236] Genesis 38:13-26.
[237] Matthew 1:5.
[238] Joshual 2:1.
[239] Matthew 1:6.
[240] 2 Samuel 11:2-5.
[241] Smith, *Jesus the Magician*, 28.
[242] Matthew 1:1, 17, 2:1.
[243] Matthew 2:1-4.

Herod then sends the magi on to Bethlehem with orders to report back.

A *μαγος* (magos) is usually understood to have been a Persian court official, an expert in astrology, dream interpretation, and the occult arts generally.[244] However, in the Greek-speaking world the practice of magic was often attributed to foreigners, particularly Persians and Egyptians, simply as a matter of custom. An intriguing parallel in the Greek translation of the Old Testament recounts how Nebuchadnezzar, disturbed by a prophetic dream, summons the "enchanters," *επαοιδος* (epaoidos), the "magi," *μαγος* (magos), and the "sorcerers," *φαρμακος* (pharmakos), to interpret his dream.[245] Georg Luck: "The history of the terms *magos*, *mageia*, suggests and old misunderstanding. What, for the Persians, was their national religion, was, in the eyes of the Greeks, ritual magic."[246] Morton Smith believed that the story was meant to mark Jesus out as "the supreme magus and master of the art," worthy of the submission of other magi;[247] Jesse Rainbow has made the case that the gold, frankincense and myrrh brought to Jesus by the magi were gifts fit for an accomplished magus.[248] Ancient Christians clearly connected the star of Bethlehem with magic: "a star shone forth in heaven, above all the stars...*therefore all magic was destroyed and every bond* (*ελυετο πασα μαγεια και πας δεσμος*)..."[249] The "star" of Bethlehem was interpreted by some Christians as an "astrological omen," proof that "Christ had set people free from the

---

[244] See especially Becker, *A Kind of Magic: understanding magic in the New Testament and its religious environment*, 87-106.
[245] Daniel 2:2.
[246] Luck, *Witchcraft and Magic in Europe: Ancient Greece and Rome*, 95.
[247] Smith, *Jesus the Magician*, 96.
[248] Rainbow, *Harvard Theological Review* 100: 263.
Compare Jesus' saying in Matthew 12:42 with the Song of Solomon 4:12-15.
[249] Ignatius, *Ephesians* 19:2-3.

bonds which held them fast, including magic and astrological fate."[250]

Origen concocted an elaborate interpretation of the infancy story that explained the defeat of magic: "Magi consort with demons and by invoking them achieve the results they desire and prevail so long as nothing more divine or *stronger* (ισχυροτερον) than the demons and *the spell that summons them* (της καλουσης αυτους επωδης) appears or is spoken..." But when the angels appeared to announce the birth of Jesus, singing "Glory to God on high...because of that the demons became weak and completely lost their strength, *their sorceries were overturned* (ελεγχεισης αυτων της γοητειας) and *their operations destroyed* (καταλυθεισης της ενεργειας)." Feeling their powers waning, the Magi come seeking the reason.[251] Origen's explanation recalls Jesus' parable of the strong man, Satan: "No one is able to enter the house of the strong man...*unless first he binds the strong man* (εαν μη πρωτον τον ισχυρον δηση)."[252]

> This became evident already at Jesus' birth when the power which accompanied him caused a sort of "blackout" in the transfers of common magical powers. All earthly magicians suddenly discovered that their magic formulas no longer worked, and, after seeing the star that defied all of the established astrological categories, they realized that it is not a locally occurring defect...[253]

According to Matthew, the star goes ahead of the magi and stops over the house—*not*, it should be noted, a manger—where the infant Jesus lives with his parents—εως ελθων εσταθη επανω

---

[250] Hegedus, *Laval théologique et philosophique* 59/1 (février 2003), 83, 91.

[251] Origen, *Contra Celsum* I, 60.

[252] Mark 3:27.

[253] Šedina, *Listy filologické* 136, 1-2, 9.

ου εν το παιδιον, "until [the star] stopped over the place where the child was." The sign of the star given to the magi finds a nearly exact parallel in the magical papyri where a "sign"[254] given to a magician is a star that "after descending will stop over the middle of the house"—*κατ' ελθων στησεται εις μεσον του δωματος*.[255] So similar is the language of the gospel that it is tempting to think Matthew might have copied his story straight from some magical text. The appearance of new stars to announce the appearance of new divinities is known from the case of Hadrian's deified lover Antinous: "Finally, he said that he saw a star that he took to be that of Antinous, and listened eagerly to the false stories spun by his associates to the effect that the star had really come into being from the soul of Antinous and had appeared then for the first time."[256]

As things turned out, the star of Bethlehem posed a religious question that festered for several centuries: "since the Magi learned by means of astrology where Jesus had been born, did this mean astrology was in itself a valid type of foreknowledge, apart from prophecy?" Or as Denzey puts it, paraphrasing the critic Celsus, "the star proved not only that Christ's birth was fated but that even Christ was powerless under the inexorable unfolding of a cosmic plan greater than his own."[257] Derived from Babylonian astral magic, astrology implied a "fatalistic consciousness of subjection to a rigid necessity as such, and the passivity to which it seemed to condemn man..."[258]

The magi are warned in a dream not to return to Herod, and an angel appears to Joseph in a dream and warns him to flee with

---

[254] A *sign* , *σημειον* (sēmeion), the usual term for wonder working in the gospel of John.

[255] Preisendanz, *Papyri Graecae Magicae* I, 75.

[256] Dio Cassius, *Roman History* LXIX, 11.

[257] Denzey, *Prayer, Magic, and the Stars in the Ancient and Late Antique World*, 211.

Celsus' objection is found at *Contra Celsum* I, 59.

[258] Jonas, *The Gnostic Religion*, 257.

his family to Egypt. Herod, seeing that the magi have not returned as promised, kills all the children in Bethlehem who are under two years of age. After Herod dies, an angel again appears in a dream to Joseph and orders him to return from Egypt to Judea, but on returning, Joseph discovers that Archelaus, Herod's son, is ruler of Judea (and Bethlehem) and, warned yet again in a dream, resettles his family in Nazareth of Galilee. "The most important of all the modes of divination which link the Hebrews with other nations is that by dreams."[259]

Concerning dreams, the papyri recommend the magician call "the heavenly gods and chthonic demons[260] ...and whenever [Apollo] comes in, ask him what you wish for, about prophecies, about divination by means of Homeric verses, about sending dreams, sending diseases, about everything included in the craft of magic..."[261] "Divination by means of Homeric verses" is a reference to *bibliomancy* or *stichomancy*, a form of divination using first the Homeric epics (*sortes Homerica*), and later the gospels (*sortes sanctorum*), in which a passage taken at random was interpreted prophetically. Homeric verses are used in magical spells in the Greco-Egyptian papyri; New Testament passages were used similarly in later Christian magic. Randomly heard voices were also thought to carry indications of the divine will as in the famous case of "tolle, lege," which resulted in the conversion of Augustine.[262] Dreams were considered of enormous importance and Greek has an impressive number of terms for dreamwork, only a fraction of which occur here: **ονειροπομπεια** (oneiropompeia), *dream sending*, **ονειραιτησια** (oneiraitēsia), *dream revelation*, and **ονειροκρισια** (oneirokrisia), *dream interpretation*.

---

[259] Davies, *Magic, Divination and Demonology among the Hebrews and their Neighbors*, 77.

[260] **καλων τους ουρανιους θεους και χθονιους δαιμονας**, "call the heavenly gods and chthonic demons..."

[261] Preisendanz, *Papyri Graecae Magicae* I, 266, 327-3311.

[262] Augustine, *Confessions* XIII, 28-29.

The spell quoted above mentions technique: "...in the craft of magic," εν τη μαγικη εμπειρια—εμπειρια (empeiria), *craft*, and the related term εμπειρος, from whence our word *empiric*, suggesting that magical spells, like recipes, were based on observation and experiment and were transmitted generation to generation. Ancient magic was therefore much like ancient medicine; the practitioner added personal experience to received opinion.

According to Matthew, all of these events—the flight to Egypt, the slaughter of the children, and the move to Nazareth—supposedly fulfill Old Testament prophecies.[263] As noted by Becker, the Old Testament prophets, not astrologers, are the only true guides to the identity of the Messiah,[264] but that still fails to solve the motive of Matthew's illogical narrative.

There are many problems with Matthew's story, beginning with the magi, who, if represented to be Persian officials, could be presumed to have some slight knowledge of royal courts and how they worked. They appeared before Herod the Great—who no doubt regarded *himself* as King of the Jews—inquiring about "he who has been born King of the Jews." Although his repute-tion for rapacious cruelty was not out of keeping with the standards of his times, this is the same Herod widely known to have murdered two of his ten wives, three sons, a brother-in-law, and a wife's grandfather.[265] How, one cannot help but wonder, did the magi think that Herod would react to the news of the birth of a rival king?

Herod dispatches the magi to Bethlehem on the promise that they will return and report the child's location to him, but according to the story, the magi evade Herod, returning to their

---

[263] Matthew 2:8-23.

[264] Becker, *A Kind of Magic: understanding magic in the New Testament and its religious environment*, 104

[265] Metzger, *The New Testament: Its Background, Growth and Content*, 24.

country by a different route. But if Herod was so disturbed by the news of the kingly birth, "and all Jerusalem with him," why didn't he simply have the magi followed? Why, for that matter, didn't Herod just kill all the children in Bethlehem at once and call it done, having learned about Bethlehem from the prophecy of Micah, not the magi?

When the magi set out from Herod's palace on their mission to find Jesus, the star again appears and stops over the house where Jesus and his parents live. But if the star led them to Jesus, why didn't it just take them there in the first place? Why did it lead them first to Herod and why would they need to inquire of Herod's scribes and priests where the Christ would be born if the star stopped over the very house where Jesus lived? Obviously the story as we have it traces a ridiculously convoluted path to Bethlehem. However, a possible motive for concocting the story of the slaughter of the children by Herod was to create a parallel between Jesus and Moses by recalling Pharaoh's murder of the Israelite boys.[266]

Joseph Hoffman has suggested a strong secondary motive for Matthew's elaborations:

> ...the story of the flight to Egypt (Matt. 2:13-15), which the author of the first Gospel strains to relate to an Old Testament prophecy...is perhaps a response to the Talmudic charge that Jesus had learned magic and sorcery in Egypt. The Talmud knows Egypt as the center of the magical arts: "Ten measures of sorcery descended in the world: Egypt received nine, the rest of the world one. (Talmud b. Qidd. 49). Thus to say that Jesus learned magic in Egypt is to say that he is more powerful as a worker of signs than the local variety of wonder-worker (see Matt. 9.33).[267]

---

[266] Exodus 2:15-16.

[267] Hoffman, *Jesus Outside the Gospels*, 40.

To suggest a connection between Jesus and the magicians of Egypt and their techniques might seem at first to be the pursuit of an exegetical phantom, but it is the New Testament itself that connects Jesus both with magicians and with Egypt.[268] Of particular interest is Koester's observation that the concept of virgin birth, which is foreign to Judaism, "is Hellenistic and, ultimately, Egyptian. No other religious or political tradition of antiquity can be identified as its generator."[269]

According to this reading, Matthew's infancy story reflects past or current accusations of magical practice leveled against Jesus and seeks to disarm them by explaining Jesus' association with Egypt—and its powerful magic—as strictly circumstantial and not as the true source of his amazing powers. Nevertheless, Christian apologists found themselves defending Jesus against charges of practicing sorcery for years after his death, including allegations that he had returned from Egypt with spells tattooed on his body:[270] "But did not Ben Stada [Jesus, *my note*] bring forth witchcraft from Egypt by means of scratches/tattoos upon his flesh?"[271] The Jews, like many ancients, regarded Egypt as the cradle of magic. Clement of Alexandria famously referred to Egypt as "the mother of magicians." Even Pythagoras was said to have traveled to Egypt to receive training in their wisdom, "stored up in secret writings" (*scriptis arcanis*).[272]

The pagan polemicist Celsus, writing about 180 CE, knew of such charges, likely from Jewish informants: "After being brought up in obscurity, he hired himself out in Egypt and having become experienced *in certain magical arts* (δυναμεων τινων), he made his way back and on account of those powers

[268] Matthew 2:1-2, 13, 19.
[269] Koester, *Ancient Christian Gospels*, 306.
[270] Pinch, *Magic in Ancient Egypt*, 47.
[271] Schäfer, *Jesus in the Talmud*, 16.
[272] *Ammianus Marcellinus* XXII, 16.

proclaimed himself a god."[273] Fritz Graf: "...those who accused Jesus of being a magician (they were not few among the pagans) argued that he, after all, had spent part of his youth in the homeland of magic, after the escape from Palestine..."[274]

Seized by a spirit: Luke's infancy story.

If Matthew's story is to be judged improbable, Luke's is even worse. The birth narrative of Luke starts, not with Jesus, but with his predecessor, John the Baptist. According to this version of events, a priest named Zechariah was married to a barren woman named Elizabeth. While Zechariah fulfilled his priestly duties in the temple, the angel Gabriel appeared to him and announced that Elizabeth would bear a son who would be called John. When Zechariah objected that both he and his wife were too old to have children, Gabriel struck him mute.[275] The impregnation of barren women was practically a cottage industry in the Old Testament—Sarah, the wife of Abraham and mother of Isaac, was barren[276] as was Hannah, the mother of Samuel.[277]

In the sixth month of Elizabeth's pregnancy, Gabriel appeared to Mary, a virgin girl living in Nazareth of Galilee.

> In the sixth month, the angel Gabriel was sent forth from God to a city of Galilee called Nazareth to a virgin, the fiancée of a man named Joseph of David's house. The virgin's name was Mary.

---

273 Origen, *Contra Celsum*, I, 38.

Celsus charged that Moses had performed powerful works by means of magic (*Contra Celsum* III, 46).

274 Graf, *Envisioning Magic: A Princeton Seminar and Symposium*, 94-95.

275 Luke 1:5-20.

276 Genesis 17:17-19.

277 1 Samuel 1:6-7.

> When [Gabriel] came in, he said, "Greetings, favored one, the Lord is with you." But she became very troubled by this announcement and began to wonder what kind of salutation this might be.
>
> And the angel said to her, "Do not fear, Mary, for you found favor before God, and behold, you will conceive in your womb and give birth to a son and you will call his name Jesus. This one will be great and will be called Son of the Most High, and the Lord God will give him the throne of David his father, and he will rule over the house of Jacob for all ages and of his kingdom there will be no end."
>
> Mary said to the angel, "How will this happen, since I have no husband?"[278] And the angel said to her in answer, "The holy spirit will come upon you, and power of the Most High will overshadow you,[279] and therefore what is begotten will be called God's son."[280]

"The holy spirit will come upon you..."—*πνευμα αγιον επελευσεται επι σε*—hints at violence in Greek. The verb *επερχομαι*, "to come upon" or "befall," has well-known connotations of robbery or assault.[281] A similar expression occurs in Acts 1:8: *λημψεσθε δυναμιν επελθοντος του αγιου πνευματος εφ' υμας*: "you will receive power when the holy spirit comes upon you..." Being "overshadowed" by the power of the Most High also conveys the sense of force; Moses cannot enter the tabernacle because the cloud representing Yahweh's presence "overshadows" it.[282] Another verb of "overcoming," *επιπιπτω* (epipiptō), is used

---

[278] *επει ανδρα ου γινωσκω*: (literally) "since I know not a man..."

[279] Moses cannot enter the tabernacle because the cloud representing Yahweh's presence "overshadows" it, Exodus 40:34-35. Compare the "cloud" at Matthew 17:5.

[280] Luke 1:26-35.

[281] Moulton & Milligan, *The Vocabulary of the Greek Testament: Illustrated from the Papyri and Other Non-Literary Sources*, 231.

[282] Exodus 40:34-45.

of the crush of a crowd,[283] of being possessed by terror,[284] or by the holy spirit—"praying that [the Samaritans] might receive holy spirit, for as yet *it had not fallen upon them*" (επ' ουδενι αυτων επιπεπτωκος).[285] The "headless demon" that "begets and destroys," a likely reference to the dismembered Osiris, is "the one whose perspiration is the heavy rain *falling upon Earth* (επιπιπτων επι την γην) that it may be inseminated."[286]

A "binding love spell" (φιλτροκαταδεσμος λογος) of the magician Astrapsoukos reads, "Come to me, Lord Hermes, *like the fetuses to the wombs of women* (ως τα βρεφη εις τας κοιλιας των γυναικων)! Come to me, Lord Hermes, who sustains the life of gods and men! Come to me, [Name], Lord Hermes and *give me grace* (δος μοι χαριν), sustenance..."[287] Like the beneficiary of Astrapsoukos' spell, Mary has found "favor before God" (χαριν παρα τω θεω).[288] In fact, χαρις (charis), *grace* or *favor*, can even mean *love spell*; Lucian uses it in that sense in reference to the "magician/lover" (εραστης γοης) of the young and comely Alexander of Abonoteichos. Alexander's mentor produces "magical enchantments (μαγειας) and incantations (επωδας)...and charms for love affairs (χαριτας επι τοις ερωτικοις)..."[289]

It was a well-known Christian slander that "the spirit of Apollo passed into [the Pythia] by means of her genitals."[290] We have no less an authority than Origen on the subject: προφητιδι πνευμα δια των γυναικειων υπεισερχεται το μαντικον, "the prophetic

---

283 Mark 3:10.

284 Luke 1:12; Acts 19:17; Revelation 11:11.

285 Acts 8:15-16.

When holy spirit "falls upon" the Gentiles, they speak in "tongues." (Acts 10:44-46; 11:15).

286 Preisendanz, *Papyri Graecae Magicae* V, 145-155.

287 Ibid, VIII, 1-4.

288 Luke 1:30.

289 Lucian, *Alexander, the False Prophet* (Αλεξανδρος η Ψευδομαντις), 5.

290 Smith, *Greek, Roman, and Byzantine Studies* 44: 199.

spirit secretly enters the oracle through her genitals."[291] Interestingly enough, Origen, like Luke, uses another verb compounded off *ερχομαι*, *υπεισερχομαι*, *to enter upon secretly* or *come upon unawares*.[292] In the same tract Origen claims *η του Απολλωνος προφητις δεχεται το πνευμα δια των γυναικειων κολπων*, "the prophetess of Apollo receives the spirit through her vagina."[293] The expression *δια των γυναικειων κολπων* means something approximating "through the folds in her pudenda," but the reader ancient or modern gets the drift. Given the claim the early churchmen made about the oracle of Apollo, a pagan could easily wonder how they failed to explain the miraculous conception of Jesus by invoking some similar process.

---

[291] Origen, *Contra Celsum* III, 25.
[292] Liddell & Scott, *A Greek-English Lexicon*, 1606.
[293] Origen, *Contra Celsum* VII, 3.

CHAPTER 2: APOCALYPTIC MAGIC

All four gospels agree that Jesus came from Nazareth to John the Baptist and was baptized by him in the Jordan River. The descent of the spirit following his baptism constitutes Jesus' anointing and it is from this point onward that we first hear of his teachings and miracles.

"...into the wilderness."

That wonder-working Judean prophets or a receptive public were rarely in short supply is confirmed by the Jewish historian Flavius Josephus who wrote in the 1st century. Among them were Theudas, who Josephus calls both a *γοης* (goēs), which means *sorcerer* or *impostor*, and a *προφητης* (profētēs), *prophet*. Just what sort of prophet Theudas was is answered by the report that at his command the river Jordan was expected to part so the mob that followed him into the desert could cross over it on dry land.[294] In short, Theudas promised to perform a miracle. Kolenkow: "In the Jewish world, the major motif is proof of prophecy by miracle-sign."[295] "Many sources, especially the NT and Josephus, recount Jewish and Samaritan miracle workers at the time of Jesus. It is not even difficult to name more than ten of them."[296] The New Testament confirms that prophecy was intimately connected with miracle and second sight. When Jesus raises the son of the widow of Nain, the crowd, "seized with fear," proclaims, "A *great prophet* (*προφητης μεγας*) has

---

[294] Josephus, *Jewish Antiquites*, XX, 97.
Theudas and his fate are noted at Acts 5:36.

[295] Kolenkow, *Aufstieg und Niedergang der Römischen Welt* II.23.2: 1471.

[296] Koskenniemi, *Journal of Biblical Literature* 117: 465.

arisen in our midst!"[297] and when Jesus allows his feet to be anointed by a sinful woman, the Pharisee thinks, "If this man were a prophet (ουτος ει ην προφητης), he would know this woman is a sinner."[298]

Theudas' actions constituted insurrection; he was killed and his head brought back to Jerusalem, obviously to be put on display as a warning to other would-be magician/prophets. The Roman authorities clearly meant to set a precedent *pour encourager les autres*. Notwithstanding Theudas' sticky end, Josephus soon tells us of "those deceived by a certain man, a magician, who proclaimed salvation and an end to their troubles" if they chose to follow him "into the wilderness.[299] This man and his followers were also promptly killed. Josephus also tells us about the Egyptian false prophet: "A man came into the countryside, a magician, who established a reputation as a prophet…"[300] This man led 30,000 into the desert, up to the Mount of Olives, and attacked Jerusalem, but was repulsed and escaped.

Bohak has pointed out that the γοητες (goētes), *sorcerers* or *charlatans* of Josephus' accounts are never accused of witchcraft per se or φαρμακα (pharmaka), essentially *black magic* or *poisoning*, "in spite of the obvious opportunity to do so," nor does Josephus say they should have been put to death "in line with the biblical legislation on *keshaphim*," or sorcerers.[301] While true, Josephus also calls them "prophets" and as we will see, prophets proved their bona fides by miracles, i.e., magic, and the Romans

---

[297] Luke 7:16.

[298] Luke 7:39.

[299] τους απατηθεντας υπο τινος ανθρωπου γοητος σωτηριαν επαγγελλουμενου: "those deceived by a certain man, a magician, who proclaimed salvation…" Josephus, *Jewish Antiquites*, XX, 188.

[300] παραγενομενος γαρ εις την χωραν ανθρωπος γοης και προφητου πιστιν επιθεις: "A man came into the countryside, a magician, who established a reputation as a prophet…" Josephus, *Jewish War*, II, 259.
According to Acts 21:38, Paul was mistaken for this man.

[301] Bohak, *Ancient Jewish Magic: A History*, 84.

executed such prophetic figures precisely because their preaching and charismatic performances whipped up excited crowds. Origen acknowledged the existence of prophetic figures who Celsus had compared to Jesus, Theudas, and "a certain Judas of Galilee" who was executed, as well as Dositheus, a Samaritan, supposedly "the Christ foretold by Moses"" (*ο προφητευμενος υπο Μωυσεως*), and (naturally) "Simon the Samaritan magician (*Σιμων ο Σαμαρευς μαγος*) [who] beguiled some *by magic*" (*μαγεια*). According to Celsus, these and many other deceivers "*of Jesus' type*" (*οποιος ην ο Ιησους*) had appeared.[302] It is clear that Celsus recognized Jesus *as belonging to a familiar category* and that Origen regarded "signs and wonders" as the mark of a prophet, even though it might be a false prophet: "If there arise among you *a prophet* (*προφητης*) or *one who receives revelations in dreams* (*ενυπνιαζομενος ενυπνιον*) and he gives you signs and wonders (*σημειον η τερας*)..."[303] Stanton noted in an essay on the terms *πλανος* (deceiver), *μαγος* (magician) and *ψευδοπροφητης* (false prophet) that "the most widely attested ancient criticism of Jesus: he was a magician and a false prophet who deceived God's people…accusations of magic and false prophecy are very closely related to one another."[304]

The attraction of the Jordan River and the adjoining wilderness for prophets and miracle workers was no doubt based on the legendary exploits of Elijah and Elisha. Elijah parted the waters of the river by striking them with his cloak, a wonder that Elisha duplicated, and Elijah ascended heavenward in a chariot of fire from the bank of the river.[305] The waters of the Jordan cured Naaman's leprosy, and Elisha performed magic in its stream by causing an iron ax head to float.[306] Jesus' baptism in the Jordan caused some early Christians to regard the river itself as magi-

---

[302] Origen, *Contra Celsum* I, 57, II, 8.

[303] Ibid, II, 53. The reference is to Deuteronomy 13:1.

[304] Stanton, *Jesus of Nazareth Lord and Christ*, 166-167.

[305] 2 Kings 2:6-14.

[306] 2 Kings 5:14, 6:5-6.

cal—a spell against weakness and witchcraft preserves the words, *ορκιζω σε κατα του Ιορδανου ποταμου και του βαπτισματος αυτου*: "I adjure you by the river Jordan and by his baptism ..."[307] and other examples of spell casting by naming the river Jordan are known as well.

Grant suggests that John the Baptist chose a particular area of the Jordan in which to baptize because it was reputed to be the place where Elijah had ascended and where his successor, Elisha, had commanded the leper Naaman to wash and be cured.[308] After tracing the way in which John's message was adapted to meet Christian needs, Crossan notes "that John's message was an announcement of imminent apocalyptic intervention by God and not at all about Jesus" and of John's execution observes, "No matter what John's intentions may have been, Antipas had more than enough materials on which to act. Desert and Jordan, prophet and crowds, were always a volatile mix calling for immediate preventive strikes."[309] In other words, apocalyptic prophets were *political* figures as pointed out by Horsley: "these prophets and their followers thought they were about to participate in the divine transformation of a world gone awry into a society of justice, willed and ruled by God..."[310]

The suppression of ecstatic religious movements was not isolateed to Palestine. The celebration of the Bacchanalia was savagely crushed when the Roman senate became suspicious that a play for political power lay behind it: "vast numbers of adherents of the cult—men and women, noble and plebian—were executed

---

[307] Giannobile & Jordan, "A Lead Phylactery from Colle san Basilio (Sicily)," *Greek, Roman, and Byzantine Studies* 46: 74-79.

[308] Grant, Jesus, 79.

Compare Matthew 3:13, Mark 1:9, Luke 3:21, John 1:32.

[309] Crossan, *The Historical Jesus*, 235.

[310] Horsley, *Bandits, Prophets and Messiahs: Popular Movements in the Time of Jesus*, 161.

or imprisoned."[311] By the time John the Baptist and Jesus appeared, the Roman state had an established policy dictating that it would brook no interference from apocalyptic or charismatic religious cults.

Regarding the Jewish rebel Bar Kokhba who led the third and final Jewish revolt against Roman occupation—Bar Kokhba means "son of a star" a reference to Numbers 24:17, "A star will come out of Jacob; a scepter will rise out of Israel"—Eusebius says he "claimed to be a luminary who had come down to them from heaven and was magically enlightening those who were in misery."[312] Perhaps the main reason Bar Kokhba is not today regarded as the martyred founder of a world religion is that he lacked a Saul of Tarsus to litigate his case.

Lewis points out in her discussion of the "star of Bethlehem" in Matthew's infancy story, the account of the star was likely inserted to bolster Matthew's case that Jesus was the long-awaited Messiah since the Greek text of Numbers 24:17 in the Septuagint, a version of the Old Testament widely used among Jews in the Hellenistic age, foretold that "*a man* will rise up out of Israel."[313] In Jesus' time the text appears to have been widely regarded as a messianic prophecy. Following three years of war (132-136 C.E.), that were marked by particularly heavy Roman casualties, the Romans retaliated, expelled most of the Jewish population, renamed Judea *Syria Palaestina,* and built a new capital, Aelia Capitolina, on the ruins of Jerusalem. The catastrophic Bar Kokhba war relegated messianism to the fringes of Jewish religious thought.

---

[311] Cohn, *Europe's Inner Demons: An Inquiry Inspired by the Great Witch Hunt*, 12.

[312] Eusebius, *Ecclesiastical History* IV, 7.

[313] Denzey, *Prayer, Magic, and the Stars in the Ancient and Late Antique World*, 216.

ανατελει αστρον εξ Ιακωβ, *αναστησεται ανθρωπος εξ* Ισραηλ, "a star will rise out of Jacob, a man will be raised up out of Israel."

Two additional points must be noted: Jewish and early Christian magic are tightly gender bound. There are no women who resurrect people or perform exorcisms within the Jewish tradetion. Second, magical power, both in the Old and New Testament, becomes a potent source of social control, a point not missed by the Jewish or Roman authorities.

About John himself the gospels have little to report. Herod Antipas, one of the sons of Herod the Great, had John executed after he rashly criticized Antipas' marriage to Herodias, the wife of his brother Philip.[314] Aside from John's critique of Herod's irregular family life, the gospels have this to say about his message:

> So he said to the crowds that were coming out to be baptized by him, "Nest of vipers! Who showed you how to flee from the coming wrath?"
>
> "Therefore produce fruits worthy of repentance and do not start to say among yourselves, 'We have Abraham for a father,' for I tell you that God can raise up children for Abraham from the stones. The ax is already laid at the root of the tree! Every tree not producing good fruit will be cut down and thrown into the fire!"
>
> "The winnowing fork is in his hand, ready to clean out the threshing floor and gather the wheat into his barn, but the husks he will burn with fire that cannot be put out!"[315]

John proclaims a message of rapidly impending judgment that no Jew can escape by pleading special status as a son of Abraham. The separation of righteous from the unrighteous is imminent: the ax is already laid at the root of the tree. We are never informed about what circumstances prompted John's denuncia-

---

[314] Mark 6:17-18.
[315] Luke 3:7-9, 17.

tions, but the fact that Jesus came to him and was baptized indicates that he agreed with John's message and became his disciple.

Whether John performed powerful works as part of his prophetic repertoire, we do not know. In Luke it is promised that John "will go before him in the spirit and power of Elijah,"[316] an apparently clear prediction that John would perform miracles. The gospel of John denies that he did,[317] likely out of deference to the wonders of Jesus, but we are told that John's opponents said, "He has a demon," the very charge Jesus' opponents level against him for performing exorcisms.[318] Jesus himself observes that John "is more than a prophet,"[319] but just how much more we are not told. Given the river's extensive association with the miraculous,[320] it is probable that John chose the site to improve his own bona fides as a prophet. In any case, prophets were expected to perform miracles and John enjoyed quite a reputation as a prophet.

After Jesus feeds the multitude, John tells us, "When the men saw the sign he performed, they said, 'Surely this is the prophet, the one coming into the world!"[321] But being identified as a prophet did not necessarily mean that momentous events had to be predicted, or great wonders performed: when Jesus tells the woman at the well that she has had four husbands and that the man she currently lives with is not her legal husband, she also replies, "I see that you are a prophet"[322] which in her case may mean no more than "mind reader." Nathaniel identifies Jesus as

---

[316] Luke 1:17.
[317] John 10:41.
[318] *δαιμονιον εχει*: "He has a demon." (Matthew 11:18; Luke 7:33).
The meaning of this charge made against Jesus (Mark 3:22; John 7:20) is discussed at length in a subsequent chapter.
[319] Luke 7:26.
[320] 2 Kings 2:8, 14; 5:14; 6:6.
[321] John 6:14.
[322] John 4:19.

the Son of God "because Jesus told him what he had been doing before they met."[323] Likewise, the Samaritan woman exclaims, "Come see a man who told me everything I've ever done! He can't be the Messiah, can he?"[324] Unsurprisingly, mind reading is a magical desideratum: "[Spell for] *foreknowledge* (προγνωσις): *Make me foreknow what is in the mind of each* (ποιησον με προγνωναι τα κατα ψυχην εκαστου) [person] today because I am...Iaō Sabaōth Iaō Thēaēēth...to know each of the men and *to know what he has in mind* (προγνωναι κατα ψυχην εχει)..."[325] "...I [Name], may determine what is in the mind of every person, Egyptians, Syrians, Greek, Ethiopians, every race and nation, *people who put questions to me* (επερωτων με) or come within my sight, whether they speak or remain silent, so that I make known to them (εξαγγειλω)[326] what has happened, is happening, or is going to happen, and I know their trades and lives and habits and their works and names..."[327]

"...by no means will this generation disappear"

According to Mark, Jesus' career begins even as John's is about to end, and Jesus adopted John's apocalyptic message:

> It happened in those days that Jesus came from Nazareth of Galilee and was baptized in the Jordan by John. And at once, while he was coming up out of the water, he saw the heavens being ripped open and the spirit descending on him like a dove. And a voice came out of the heavens, "You are my son, the beloved. In you was I pleased."

[323] Smith, *Jesus the Magician*, 13. The reference is to John 1:48-49.
[324] John 4:29.
[325] Preisendanz, *Papyri Graecae Magicae* III, 263-266, 330.
[326] From εξαγγελλω, *to reveal a secret.*
[327] Preisendanz, V, 289-300.

> At once the spirit drove him out into the wilderness, and he was in the wilderness for forty days being tempted by Satan and he was with the wild animals and the angels served him.
>
> But after John had been arrested, Jesus came into Galilee proclaiming the good news of God, and saying, "The time allotted has run out and the kingdom of God has almost arrived! Repent and believe in the good news!"[328]

The language used to describe Jesus' baptism—*το πνευμα ως περιστεραν καταβαινον εις αυτον*, "the spirit descending *into* him like a dove"—could result in a gnostic interpretation. Regarding the preposition Ehrman observes, "The prepositon *εις* commonly means 'into,' so that the text as Mark originally wrote it is especially vulnerable to the Gnostic claim that at Jesus' baptism a divine being entered into him. Whether Mark himself understood the event in this way is not the question I'm concerned to address here. It is worth noting, however, that both Matthew and Luke changed the preposition to *επι* ("upon").[329]

Like John the Baptist, Jesus proclaimed a message of impending judgment and called for repentance. The kingdom of God was coming quickly. But just how quickly? What sort of judgment did Jesus visualize? And what sort of kingdom? Despite later editing, the gospels provide clear answers to these questions.

That Jesus imagined the kingdom to be coming soon—*very soon*—is made abundantly clear by Mark:

> He said to them, "Truly I say to you, there are some standing here who will by no means taste death until

---

[328] Mark 1:9-15.

[329] Ehrman, *The Orthodox Corruption of Scripture*, 141.

[329] Mark 1:9-15.

> they see the kingdom of God already arrived in power."[330]
>
> "Truly I tell you, by no means will this generation disappear until all these things happen."[331]
>
> The High Priest was standing in their midst, and he asked Jesus, "Have you nothing to say in response? What are these men testifying against you?"
>
> But he kept silent and did not reply to anything. Again the High Priest asked him, "Are you the Christ, the son of the Blessed One?"
>
> Jesus said, "I am.[332] And you will see the Son of Man seated at the right hand of power and coming with the clouds of heaven!"[333]

The High Priest himself will witness the coming of the heavenly Son of Man and Jesus own generation—"*this* generation"—will not disappear before "*all* these things" happen, nor will most of his followers die before personally seeing the kingdom of God arrive "in power."

According to Matthew's version, the disciples will not die before seeing the Son of Man "coming in his kingdom" (Matthew 16:28). The note of immediacy is also present in Luke (4:22). The "some of those standing here" likely included a reference to Jesus' opponents who are being warned of impending judgment. When Jesus sends his disciples out on a round of healing and kingdom preaching, he tells them,

---

[330] Mark 9:1.

[331] Mark 13:30.

[332] Greek does not use inverted word order to indicate a question, so Jesus' reply, εγω ειμι (*I am*), could also be translated, "Am I?" As pointed out by Borg and Crossan, the ambiguous answers recalled by the gospels of Matthew (26:64) and Luke (22:70) seem to favor rendering Jesus' response as neither confirming or denying the charges. Borg, *The Last Week*, 24.

[333] Mark 14:60-62.

> "But whenever they run you out of one town, flee to another, for truly I tell you, by no means will you finish going through all the towns of Israel before the Son of Man arrives."[334]

Given the gospel context, it seems clear that Jesus understood the Aramaic בר-נשא (bar-enosh)[335] to refer to an apocalyptic figure of divine judgment and it is certain that other Jews of Jesus' era had a similar understanding.

The immediate arrival of the kingdom of God is also assumed in Jesus' saying, "...by no means will I drink the fruit of the vine until that day when I drink it anew in the kingdom of God."[336] Such vows of abstention are examples of **אסר** (issar), a binding oath to abstain (usually from eating or drinking) until a goal is accomplished. The root meaning of **אסר** denotes *binding* or *bond* and is similar in meaning to the Greek *καταδεσμος* (katadesmos), *magical bond*, or *αναθεμα* (anathema), *bound with a curse*. The concept of magical binding and releasing is discussed at length in a subsequent chapter.

A similar New Testament usage of *anathema* occurs in Acts 23:12: "The Jews bound themselves with a curse"—*ανεθεματισαν εαυτους*—bound themselves with a curse, or made themselves *αναθεμα, accursed,* until their goal was achieved—"saying they would neither eat nor drink until they killed Paul." Similar binding vows of abstinence are well known elements of the erotic spells of the Greek magical papyri, formulae that, as previously noted, find very close parallels in Jesus' repeated demands for exclusive devotion.[337] Uttering a vow not to eat or drink until an oath is fulfilled clearly does not presume that the consummation is centuries away. It is possible that Jesus thought his confron-

---

334 Matthew 10:23.

335 Daniel 7:13-14.

336 Mark 14:25. Compare Luke 22:16, 18.

337 As, for example, at Matthew 10:37 and Luke 14:26.

tation with the Jewish leaders would somehow trigger the entry of the New Age, an interpretation nearly demanded by the phraseology of the so-called "eucharistic words":

> "Truly I tell you that I will never by any means drink of the fruit of the vine until that day when I drink it anew in the kingdom of God."[338]

> "Truly I tell you that I will by no means eat [the Passover] until it is consummated in the kingdom of God… I tell you that from now on I will by no means drink from the fruit of the vine until the kingdom of God arrives."[339]

As noted by David Martinez, such a self-binding vow of abstinence is employed "to activate the realm in which divine power operates." By vowing abstinence from the Passover meal, the supreme cultic celebration of Judaism,

> Jesus consecrates himself to the necessary action, making himself the instrument through which God will establish the new order…He seals his absolute commitment to the apocalyptic age with the vow that he will not partake of the sacred bread and wine until that age is ushered in.[340]

Regarding the connection between prophecy and magic, Crossan notes, "…among colonized people there appear not only thaumaturgical or magical but also millennial or revolutionary prophets, or, more simply, magicians and prophets."[341]

---

338 Mark 14:25.

339 Luke 22:16, 18.

340 David Martinez, *Ancient Magic and Ritual Power*, 346, 350-351.

341 Crossan, *The Historical Jesus*, 137.

> ...the comparative study of millennial movements has shown that magic functions in such a way that the leaders of such movements are supernaturally legitimated, so the thaumaturgical activities of Jesus appear to have functioned as a form of supernatural legitimation supporting his role as messianic prophet.[342]

Jesus is quite explicit about what the coming of the Son of Man will mean for both the righteous and the wicked:

> "But in those days, after that affliction, the sun will be darkened and the moon will not give its light and the stars will fall out of the sky and the powers in the heavens will be shaken. And they will see the Son of Man coming in the clouds with great power and glory. Next he will send forth his angels and gather his chosen ones from the four winds, from the ends of the earth to the ends of the sky."
>
> "Learn this comparison from the fig tree: whenever you see its branch sprout and put forth leaves, you know that summer is almost here. In the same way, whenever you see these things happening, you know that he is at your door. Truly I tell you, under no circumstances will this generation disappear until all these things happen."[343]
>
> "Just the way it happened in the days of Noah, that is the way it will be in the days of the Son of Man. They were eating and drinking, marrying and giving brides away right up to the day Noah went into the ark, and the Deluge came and destroyed everyone."
>
> "It happened the very same way in the days of Lot. They were eating, drinking, buying and selling, planting and building, but the day Lot left Sodom, fire and

---

[342] Aune, *Aufstieg und Niedergang der Römischen Welt*, II.23.2: 1527.
[343] Mark 13:24-30.

> sulfur rained from heaven and destroyed everyone. It will be like that the day the Son of Man is revealed."[344]

The verb translated "to reveal" in Luke 17:30 is αποκαλυπτω (apokaluptô), and the corresponding noun, αποκαλυψις (apokalupsis), is the source of our word *apocalypse*. *Apocalypticism* is the ideological substrate of the most primitive Christian theology, the sudden revelation of God's judgment with all that that implies. In this particular passage Jesus describes how in the remote past the mundane façade of everyday life was suddenly ripped away by revelations of divine judgment. In the case of Sodom[345] and the near extinction of the human race during the Deluge,[346] the overthrow of the wicked was sudden, violent, and complete. The reversal of fortune for people then living was also total: the complacent wicked were utterly annihilated, the watchful righteous exalted.

The notion of apocalyptic confrontation seized the imagination of Jesus just as it apparently seized the imagination of some of his contemporaries. Of the monastic community at Qumran, Grant notes, "...they were glad to pronounce the revelation of a blood-thirsty holocaust at the end of the world when the Kingdom of God would come...the Qumran devotees expected this final event in the extremely near future. Indeed, they believed that the great battles destined to herald it would be fought in their own lifetimes and that they themselves, as recipients of a New Covenant replacing the Covenant bestowed upon Moses, had been chosen to play a vital part in the world-shattering events of those days."[347]

Did Jesus mean to identify himself with the apocalyptic Son of Man whose coming he foretold? The evidence is ambiguous,

---

344 Luke 17:26-30.
345 Genesis 19:24-27.
346 Genesis 7:1-5.
347 Grant, *Jesus*, 18.

and like many other issues dealing with the correct interprettation of Jesus' words, the controversy has raged back and forth only to end in stalemate. In the passages concerning world judgment such as the ones quoted above, Jesus speaks of the Son of Man in the third person. A reader unacquainted with Christian belief might easily assume that Jesus was speaking of someone else and not himself.

What is clear is that Jesus' earliest followers came to identify him as the Son of Man, probably due to the influence of an apocalyptic passage from Daniel.[348] Mark has Jesus refer to himself as the Son of Man in connection with his betrayal, death, and resurrection,[349] and Matthew relates the term to Jesus' authority to forgive sins, heal on the Sabbath, and with his identification as the Messiah.[350] It has been argued that in these passages the church was simply reading its subsequent understanding of Jesus' mission back into the institutional memory of his life. Neither Hebrew nor 1st century Greek employed lower case letters, so the mere convention of capitalizing "Son of Man" in English makes it into a title, implying that the ancients so regarded it. That, of course, is not necessarily the case.

> As far as we can determine, this was not a message about himself, but a message about the coming day of judgment on which the Son of Man...would be licensed by God to take direct control of a new kingdom (c.f. Mark 14:62). *The failure of these signs to materialize led to the curious result that Jesus was retroactively declared 'Son of Man'... by his followers after his death...*"[351]

---

[348] Daniel 7:13-14.

[349] Mark 8:31, 9:31, 10:33-34.

[350] Matthew 9:5-6, 12:8, 16:13-17.

[351] Hoffman, *Jesus Outside the Gospels*, 11-12.

It is notable that apart from the gospels, the disciple Stephen is the only other person to identify Jesus as the Son of Man,[352] and oddly enough, Paul, for whom the resurrection *cum* glorification of Jesus is the theological event of all time, never speaks of Jesus as the Son of Man, nor do the early church fathers seem at all interested in the term.

Desperate times, it has been said, call for desperate measures. If Jesus really believed in the impending end of the political and religious order, we would logically expect to hear it reflected in his ethical advice, and we do. The disciples are not to imagine that Jesus came to bring peace on earth. Indeed, family members will turn on one another, becoming bitter enemies[353] and those who expect to follow Jesus into the coming kingdom should do so now, not even stopping to say goodbye to those left behind.[354] A man on his roof must not linger to gather his possessions, and a man in the field must not stop even to pick up his cloak.[355] The urgency of the times abrogates even the most basic filial responsibilities:

> Another of his disciples said to him, "Lord, first allow me to go and bury my father." But Jesus said to him, "Follow me and let the dead bury their dead."[356]

For those who expect to inherit the coming kingdom, the costs will be steep. No one can become a disciple without hating his own father, mother, brothers and sisters, or even his wife and children, as well as relinquishing all possessions. The would-be disciple must therefore count the cost. Little wonder that the rich heard Jesus' words with regret.[357] Pitre's remarks on the origin of Jesus' anti-family stance merits an extended quote:

---

[352] Acts 7:56.

[353] Matthew 10:34-37, Luke 12:49-53.

[354] Luke 9:61-62.

[355] Matthew 24:17-18.

[356] Matthew 8:21-22.

[357] Luke 14:26-28, 33, 18:23-25.

> However, one set of familiar texts has repeatedly failed to draw the detailed attention of the Jesus questers: the beatitudes for childless and barren women (Lk 23:29; *Gos. Thom.* 79b) and the warnings to pregnant women and mothers (Mk 13:17-19; Lk 23:28, 30-31)...when the beatitudes and woes to women are understood in the context of Jewish apocalyptic eschatology, they function together as an injunction against procreation ...[Jesus'] message of renouncing reproduction in light of imminent tribulation stands firmly in the tradition of an ancient prophetic predecessor (Jer. 16:1-9)... Jesus' words of renunciation are congruent with his negative response to an unnamed woman who blesses 'the womb that bore' him and 'the breasts that nursed' him (Lk 11:27-28; *Gos. Thom.* 79a)...His retort, 'Blessed rather are those who hear the word of God and obey it!' makes a good deal of sense if, as we have seen, part of his message was to warn women against bearing children.[358]

In short, nothing should distract one from the nearness of the end: neither self-regard,[359] nor standing within the community —"I swear to you that the tax men and the whores are going ahead of you into the kingdom of God!"[360] The flight to safety should not be delayed for any reason. The nearness of the end has rendered the distinctions of daily life irrelevant: "the abandonment of worldly hostilities was not motivated by gentleness, or compassion, or pacifism, but by his concentration on the Kingdom and the all-important task of securing admission to it..."[361]Even Jesus' exorcisms are evidence of the coming kingdom:

---

[358] Pitre, *Journal for the Study of the New Testament* 81: 60, 78.
[359] Matthew 18:3,4.
[360] Matthew 21:31.
[361] Grant, *Jesus*, 30.

"For if I cast out the demons by means of Beezeboul, by whom do your sons cast them out? That is why they will become your judges. But if I cast them out the demons by the finger of God, then the kingdom of God has already overtaken you."[362]

The "finger of God" had long-established magical connotetions—the magical papyri pre-serve a spell for exorcism: *και εξορκιζω κατα του δακτυλου του θεου*, "and I cast [you] out by the finger of God..."[363] Given the connections to pagan magic —"to heathen exorcists the 'Finger of God' was in fact the more expressive phrase"[364]—Matthew changed it to "spirit of God," giving the expression a Christian gloss. John Hull: "Matthew's reticence about technique is seen in 12:28 (= Luke 11:20) where the change from 'finger' to 'spirit' is to be explained in terms of the association with magical technique which the finger of God had. The only place in the gospel where Jesus seems to be on the point of disclosing his method is thus spiritualized."[365] Certainly Jesus' Jewish audience would be familiar with the Exodus story: "The magicians said to Pharaoh, 'This is the finger of God!'"[366]

> This is a perfect example of 'your magic is my miracle' ...Hence, it is not a question of (biblical) religion versus (Egyptian) magic, but of (biblical) magic versus (Egyptian) magic. That the biblical magic is incorporated into the religious system of the Bible does not say that it is not magic.[367]

Twelftree on the significance of the expression "finger of God":

---

362 Luke 11:19-20.

363 Preisendanz, *Papyri Graecae Magicae* II, 209.

364 Eitram, *Some Notes on the Demonology in the New Testament*, 42.

365 Hull, *Hellenistic Magic and the Synoptic Tradition*, 129.

366 Exodus 8:19 (NIV).

367 Schäfer, *Envisioning Magic: A Princeton Seminar and Symposium*, 29.

> This is evidence that [Jesus] understood that he was not operating unaided but was using a power-authority—the Spirit or finger of God. Also, in the previous verse ('If I cast out daimons by Beelzebul, by whom do your sons cast them out?'), Jesus places himself on a level with other healers and takes up the assumption that he is using a power-authority for his exorcisms...it is plain that he shared the same view of exorcism as some of those involved in ancient magic: using a power-authority to perform an exorcism.[368]

The *arm-hand-finger* metaphor as a rhetorical figure for the projection of power carried magical connotations and scores of examples could be adduced. An early Christian prayer—"Stretch out your hand to heal and perform signs and wonders through the name of your holy servant Jesus,"[369] εν τω την χειρα εκτεινειν σε εις ιασιν και σημεια και τερατα γινεσθαι δια του ονοματος του αγιου παιδος σου Ιησου—closely follows the language of a spell from the magical papyri: και λεγε χαιρε θεα μεγαλοδοξε ΙΛΑΡΑ ΟΥΧ και ει μοι χρηματιζεις εκτεινον σου την χειρα επαν εκτεινη αξιου προς τα επερωτηματα, "And say, hail, Goddess, most glorious, ILARA OUCH [magical words, *my note*]. And if you grant me a revelation, extend your hand…"[370]

Works of wonder have a meaning that extends beyond them. Jesus' exorcisms are harbingers of the coming kingdom. The raising of the dead foreshadows the raising of all the dead at the final judgment, the healing of the sick foretells the elimination of all disease, and casting out demons anticipates the final expulsion of the Prince of Demons. So sure is Jesus of this that he describes it proleptically, as if already done:

---

368 Twelftree, *A Kind of Magic*, 81-82.

369 Acts 4:30 (NIV).

370 Preisendanz, *Papyri Graecae Magicae* IV, 3225-3226.

> And the seventy-two returned with rejoicing, saying, "Lord, even the demons are subject to us in your name!" And he said to them, "I saw Satan thrown down from heaven like lightening!"[371]

"This passage, in which Jesus remarks that he saw Satan 'fall like lightening from the sky,' depicts an unabashedly apocalyptic scene in the midst of a document not usually considered to be 'apocalyptic.'"[372] The arrest of Jesus therefore became a temporary triumph of "the power of darkness" (Luke 22:53). The meaning is clear: the Jewish leaders are the minions of Satan, doing his bidding.

If Satan is overthrown, then his followers must also fall. The metaphor of opposing kingdoms of light and darkness is a powerful element in the apocalyptic view. The figure of Satan becomes, among other things, a way of characterizing one's actual enemies as the embodiment of transcendent forces. For many readers of the gospels ever since the first century, the thematic opposition between God's spirit and Satan has vindicated Jesus' followers and demonized their enemies."[373]

It is, in fact, possible to see most of the events of Jesus' career as parables-in-action. The confrontation with the temple authorities is a preview of God's impending judgment of the temple and his rejection of its leadership. Jesus understands Jeremiah as a prototype or forerunner and takes up both the Old Testament prophet's mantle of office and his words. All the judgments of the past, the Deluge, the end of Sodom, and the destruction of Solomon's temple, foretell the judgment Jesus speaks against his own generation, "this generation" that will not pass away until all Jesus' words are fulfilled upon it. In addition to Jesus' openly apocalyptic statements, there are other indications of his intense

---

[371] Luke 10:17-18.

[372] Garrett, *The Demise of the Devil*, 46.

[373] Pagels, *The Origin of Satan*, 13.

animosity toward the temple and its leaders: the cursing of the fig tree, which withers "to the roots," is a sign given to the disciples,[374] a sign rapidly followed by the parable of the vineyard: "What will the master of the vineyard do? He will come and he will destroy the cultivators and give the vineyard to others."[375]

Jesus' disciples envisioned a physical kingdom that would replace the kingdoms soon to be swept away. And how could they have thought otherwise? Jesus had promised them that he would drink wine with them in the kingdom, where they would enjoy families, houses, and fields, and sit on thrones, judging the twelve tribes of Israel. Even the mother of two of the disciples asks Jesus to seat her sons at his right and left hand in his coming kingdom.[376] Paul himself preached that the Christian saints would sit in judgment of the world and the angels.[377] According to Luke, as Jesus approached Jerusalem for his final Passover celebration, the disciples supposed that the kingdom was about to appear, and after Jesus' resurrection they again asked if he was about to restore the kingdom to Israel.[378] In the earliest phase of Christianity, expectations of Jesus' triumphant return ran so high that those with property sold off what they had and Jesus' followers lived communally.[379]

Writing to the newly converted, Paul advised slaves to remain slaves, and virgins and the unmarried to remain in their present state. Married men were to behave as if they had no wife, which probably meant that married couples acted as if celibate, for "the time allotted has become short."[380] It is possible that pagan

---

[374] Mark 11:12-25.

[375] Mark 12:9.

[376] Mark 10:30, 14:25, Matthew 19:28, 20:20-21.

[377] 1 Corinthians 6:2-3. Paul almost certainly had in mind the fallen angels he believed were the real rulers of the world (2 Corinthians 4:3-4).

[378] Luke 19:11, Acts 1:6.

[379] Acts 4:34-35.

[380] 1 Corinthians 7:21-31.

contempt for Christianity arose in part from believers divorcing their mates or denying them conjugal relations. The ascetic tendencies provoked by the looming parousia result in "a household of brothers and sisters rather than husbands and wives, fathers and mothers."[381] "Christians, who expected to live on in a better world, could set less store by having progeny in this... As the New Jerusalem receded, it continued to unlock its gates to martyrs; and celibacy was not only a desirable condition for the zealot, but a proof of zeal in those who would not be given the opportunity to die."[382]

So pervasive was the sense of impending doom that the early Christians resorted to the most extreme behavior: Origen, a church father of the 2nd century went so far as to castrate himself, using Matthew 19:12 as justification, and Justin Martyr, another early church father, praised a young Alexandrian convert who petitioned the Roman governor to give a surgeon permission to castrate him. Like many apocalyptic movements since, early Christianity was characterized by sexual psychopathology and extremism.

Convinced that Jesus had risen and would soon return, the believers waited expectantly. But nothing happened. Schweitzer, in what is perhaps the most important New Testament study of the 20th century, invoked the electrifying image of Jesus crushed by the ever-turning wheel of history and concluded, "The wheel roles onward, and the mangled body of the one immeasurably great Man, who was strong enough to think of Himself as the spiritual ruler of mankind and to bend history of His purpose, is hanging upon it still. That is His victory and His reign.[383]

It is hardly surprising that Christian believers are unhappy with this evaluation of the evidence of the gospels and that they have

---

[381] Martin, *Sex and the Single Savior*, 108.
[382] Edwards, *Christians, Gnostics and Philosophers in Late Antiquity*, 78.
[383] Schweitzer, *The Quest of the Historical Jesus*, 370-371.

concocted a theology that ignores the spectacular failure of Jesus' predictions. In a recent survey of the New Testament evidence regarding the end-of-the-world beliefs of Jesus and the primitive church and the modern theological response, Allison concludes, "I myself do not know what to make of the eschatological Jesus. I am, for theological reasons, unedified by the thought that, in a matter so seemingly crucial, a lie has been walking around for two thousand years while the truth has only recently put on its shoes. But there it is."[384]

The first Christians were convinced the world "was about to go under in a sea of fire" and therefore interested "only in the speedy end of the world, they took no part in the daily life of the city and refused to make even token gestures of loyalty to the emperor, or of reverence to the gods of Rome."[385] This was hardly an attitude that would allow Christianity to become the religion of the Roman state and by the end of the 2nd century the orthodox had abandoned fascination with the apocalypse, never to take it up again. "...Dionysus [the bishop of Alexandria, Egypt, *my note*] explained away the plain words of Revelation as an allegory, and when Iraneus' tract against heresy was translated into Latin in the early fifth century, the translator omitted the millennium from its text. To many thinking Christians it had become an embarrassment.[386]

As reported by Eusebius, by at least the 3rd century the doctors of the church had begun to characterize *chiliasm*, the belief in a 1000-year entertained by many early churches, as "trivial and befitting mortals and too like the present."[387]

---

[384] Allison, *Journal of Biblical Literature* 113: 668.

[385] Cohn, *Europe's Inner Demons: An Inquiry Inspired by the Great Witch Hunt*, 13-14.

[386] Lane Fox, *Pagans and Christians*, 266.

[387] Eusebius, *Ecclesiastical History* VII, 24.

CHAPTER 3: THE TRIAL

Confrontation at the temple.

Six days before the feast of Passover, Jesus and his disciples arrive at Bethany, a small town within walking distance of Jerusalem.[388] Jesus sends two of the disciples into the village where they find a donkey. The disciples throw their cloaks over the animal, Jesus mounts it, and rides into Jerusalem much as described in the prophecy of Zechariah:

> Rejoice greatly, O daughter of Zion! Shout aloud, O daughter of Jerusalem! Lo, your king comes to you; triumphant and victorious is he, humble and riding on an ass, on a colt, the foal of an ass.[389]

The gospel of Matthew reconstructs this prophetic scene as follows:

> This happened to fulfill what was spoken through the prophet, saying, "Tell the daughter of Zion, Behold, your king is coming to you, humble, and mounted on a donkey and on a colt, the foal of a donkey."
>
> And the disciples went and did just as Jesus directed them. They brought the donkey and the colt, and laid their outer garments over them, and he sat upon them. And a very large crowd spread their outer garments in the road, and others cut branches from the trees and were spreading them in the road. And the crowds that preceded him and those following him shouted, saying, "Hosanna to the son of David. Blessed is the one com-

[388] Mark 11:1, John 12.1.

[389] Zechariah 9:9 (RSV).

> ing in the name of the Lord! Hosanna in the highest heavens!"
>
> And coming into Jerusalem, the whole city was in commotion, saying, "Who is this?" And the crowd said, "This is the prophet Jesus from Nazareth in Galilee."[390]

The writer of the gospel was obviously not an eyewitness of the events he describes. He misunderstands the parallelism of the Old Testament passage, misreading the text of Zechariah to refer to *two* animals—Mark, Luke, and John all have one donkey[391] and in John's retelling Jesus finds the donkey on his own —and presents the reader with the absurd image of Jesus astraddle two animals, and adult *and* its colt. The gospel of John nearly concedes that the connection between Jesus' trip into Jerusalem on a donkey and the prophecy of Zechariah is a later invention: "His disciples did not realize these things about him at first, but after he had been glorified, then they recalled that these things had been written about him and they had done these things to him."[392]

On the day of his arrival, possibly the first day of the six days mentioned in John,[393] Jesus went to Jerusalem, entered the temple for a look around, and then left, "as it was already late," and went back to Bethany to spend the night.[394] On the following day—day two according to Mark—he returned from Bethany with a group of disciples and created a disturbance in the temple, overturning the tables of the moneychangers and generally obstructing business, but was not arrested by the temple police at that point. This so-called "cleansing of the temple"[395] was, as

---

390 Matthew 12:4-11.

391 Mark 11:2, Luke 19:30, John 12:14.

392 John 12:16.

393 John 12:1.

394 John 12:1, Mark 11:11.

395 Mark 11:12.

noted by Crossan, "not at all a purification of the Temple but rather a symbolic destruction."[396]

Jesus and his followers left the city that evening and returned on the following day, the third day of Jesus' temple activities according to Mark's account. At this juncture the temple authorities confronted him, but were unable to arrest him publicly because they feared the crowds that Jesus attracted—the gospels are unanimous on this point:[397] the temple authorities *feared* Jesus. Regarding the aggressive and violent imagery of the gospels, Stroumsa notes that the "deep-seated ambiguity is directly related to the radical nature of earliest Christianity, a movement born within the chiliastic content of Jewish apocalypticism."[398]

Freyne says regarding Jesus' hold on the crowds,

> ...as perceived from the centre, these mighty deeds were not just dangerous, they were subversive, and their purveyor needed to be 'destroyed'. We would have to assume that such a reaction on the part of the Jerusalem scribes is a fairly clear intimation that not merely were the miracle stories propagandist within early Christianity, but that also, during the actual ministry of Jesus, reports of his mighty deeds brought the crowds flocking to him, something that all the gospels assume, but that Mark in particular underlines by his use of the term 'hearsay' (*ακοη*, Mk 1:28, 45; 5:20; 7:36; Lk 7:17).[399]

The confrontations the gospels describe between Jesus and the temple authorities were an ugly business. Jesus denounced them in offensive terms, quoting from the prophet Jeremiah:

---

396 Crossan, *The Historical Jesus*, 357.

397 Matthew 21:26, Mark 11:32, Luke 20:19, John 12.19.

398 Stroumsa, *Barbarian Philosophy: The Religious Revelation of Early Christianity*, 10.

399 Freyne, *Galilee, Jesus and the Gospels*, 228

And he was teaching them, saying, "Has it not been written, my house will be called a house of prayer for all the nations? But you have made it a hideout of robbers!" And the chief priests and the scribes heard about this and they began to seek how they might kill him, for they feared him because his teaching overwhelmed the whole crowd.[400]

"Woe to you, scribes and Pharisees! Hypocrites! You build the tombs of the prophets and you adorn the graves of the righteous, and you say, 'If we lived in the days of our forefathers, we would not have been their partners in shedding the blood of the prophets.' So you testify against yourselves that you are sons of those who killed the prophets!"

"Fill up the measure of your fathers, you! Snakes! Offspring of vipers! How are you to flee from the judgment of Gehenna?"

"Why for this reason I am sending forth prophets and wise men and scribes to you. You will kill and crucify some of them and some of them you will whip in your synagogues and pursue from city to city, so that there may come upon you all the righteous blood spilled on earth from the blood of innocent Abel down to the blood of Zechariah the son of Barachiah who you murdered between the sanctuary and the altar."

"Yes, indeed, I say to you, all this will come upon this generation!"

"Jerusalem, Jerusalem, she who kills the prophets and stones those sent forth to her! How many times I wanted to gather your children to me the way a hen gathers her chicks under her wings, but you did not want it. Now look! Your house is left desolate! For I say to you,

---

[400] Mark 11:17-18.

> from now on you will by no means see me until you say, 'Blessed is he who comes in the name of the Lord!'"[401]

As extreme as these words are, the modern reader can scarcely appreciate the offense they must have caused to the temple leaders. The Gehenna to which Jesus refers is the valley of Hinnom, a steep narrow ravine outside the southern wall of the city. In Jesus' day the valley was the receptacle into which the city's sewage drained and rubbish was thrown to be burned. Gehenna was a combination of cesspool and garbage dump. As Grant observes, Jesus' denunciation "is the language not only of invective but of white-hot anger...What Jesus felt and displayed was violent rage."[402]

In this scathing denunciation, Matthew even has Jesus include converts to Judaism, calling them "sons of Gehenna."[403] In short, the context of this bitter denunciation repeatedly associates the temple officials not only with filth, but also with apostasy. Do these exchanges reflect the words of the historical Jesus?[404]

It is nearly certain that they do. The woes pronounced against the temple leadership culminate in the prediction that the temple itself will be destroyed.

> As he left the temple, one of his disciples said to him, "Teacher, look what large stones and amazing buildings!" And Jesus said to him, "Do you see these great

---

[401] Matthew 23:29-39.

[402] Grant, *Jesus*, 77.

[403] Matthew 23:15.

[404] Some of the details of these diatribes are certainly anachronistic: none of Jesus' followers were being pursued or flogged in synagogues at this stage, and the Pharisees were never in charge of the temple cult. As the only religious sect to survive the Roman invasion following the Jewish revolt in 68 CE, they became the source of modern rabbinic Judaism.

> buildings? By no means will a stone be left upon a stone here and not be demolished!"[405]

Jesus' curse upon the temple is reported by all four gospels, repeated by his accusers at his hearing before the temple authorities, and is thrown back in his face as a taunt during his crucifixion. It appears in the Coptic *Gospel of Thomas*, and in Acts the witnesses against Stephen accuse him of repeating Jesus' prediction that the temple will be destroyed.[406] A probable trace of the charge appears to survive in the *Gospel of Peter*: "But I and my companions were grieving and went into hiding, wounded in heart. For we were being sought out by them *as if we were evildoers* (*ως κακουργοι*) who wanted to burn the Temple."[407] Jesus' curse on the temple finds an eerie echo in the magical spells of the *Sepher Ha-Razim*: "Smite it to dust and let it be overturned like the ruins of Sodom and Gemorah, and let no man place stone upon stone on the place…"[408]

There is certainly no reason to doubt Jesus' animosity toward the temple authorities and their fear of him is well documented. They believed the crowd would riot if they arrested him publicly.[409] Freyne describes how the tension between Jesus and the religious authorities builds to a crescendo in the gospel of John:

> John's Pharisees...send emissaries to investigate the identity of John (1:19,24) and they are obviously concerned about the success of new religious movements (4:1); they send servants to arrest Jesus (7:32,ff.); they cross-examine the parents of the man born blind and it is they

---

[405] Mark 13:1-2.

[406] Matthew 24:1-2, Luke 21:5-6, John 2:19-21, Mark 14:58, 15:29-30, *Gospel of Thomas*, 71 ("I shall destroy this house and no one will be able to build it."), Acts 6:13-14.

[407] Ehrman & Pleše, *The Apocryphal Gospels: Texts and Translations*, 383.

[408] Morgan, *Sepher Ha-Razim*, 28.

[409] Mark 14.2.

> who will be responsible for expulsion from the synagogue (9:13,ff.); they are deeply involved in the decision to have Jesus removed, actually summoning a meeting of the council (11:46f.).[410]

Needing a pretext to cover Jesus' arrest that would get the attention of the Roman prefect, the Jewish authorities approached him with a trick question: should Jews pay Roman taxes, taxes that helped support the Roman occupation?[411] A flat refusal would imply that Jesus advocated insurrection; agreement would alienate those in the crowd who were unenthusiastic about paying for their own subjugation. Two types of coinage were used in Jerusalem. Jewish coins had no human or animal images in keeping with the prohibition against such imagery. Roman coins, on the other hand, typically had images of Caesar. By calling attention to the fact that the Jewish authorities used such Roman coins,[412] Jesus pointed to their collaboration. Jesus responded, in effect, "It's Caesar's coin—give it back to him."[413]

The apocalyptic content of Jesus' preaching has been previously touched upon. Jesus came proclaiming the imminent arrival of the kingdom of God and the overthrow of the old order, including, as we have seen, the destruction of Herod's temple. It is impossible to imagine that any prophet foretelling the overthrow of kings and kingdoms in the midst of the vast Passover throngs—caught up during the festival on the high tide of nationalistic religious fervor—would be tolerated. It is also impossible that Jesus did not realize this.

Preventing disturbances during Passover was the job of the Jewish temple police operating under the authority of the High

---

[410] Freyne, *Galilee, Jesus and the Gospels*, 125-126.
[411] Mark 12:14.
[412] Mark 12:13-17.
[413] Borg, *The Last Week*, 64.

Priest, Joseph Caiaphas. For the sake of all involved, it was acknowledged that the administration of Jewish affairs was best left in the hands of the Jewish authorities whenever possible. The provocation of pagan soldiers entering the sacred temple grounds during this most holy of festivals would be a recipe for disaster, so Roman intervention within the temple precinct would have been used only as a last resort. An inscription putting Gentiles on notice not to enter the sacred precinct read, "Let no foreigner enter within the screen and enclosure surrounding the sanctuary. Whosoever is taken so doing will be the cause that death overtaketh him."[414]

Given the potential for rioting among the Passover crowds, the Roman prefect, a symbol of law and order—Pontius Pilate at the time of Jesus' arrest—traveled to Jerusalem from his usual residence in the seacoast city of Caesarea accompanied by a contingent of 3000 troops. A permanent Roman garrison in the fortress of Antonia, adjacent to the temple precinct, warily surveyed the Jewish pilgrims from the ramparts of the heavily fortified walls and towers, alert for any signs of disturbance. In the event of problems during Passover, the entire political leadership, Jewish and Roman, would present a united front, quickly and efficiently dealing with troublemakers. As remarked by Fuhrmann, "When the governor arrived in town, death came with him."[415]

Pontius Pilate, *praefectus* of Judea from CE 26-36, possessed *imperium*, supreme administrative power, which entitled him to deal with virtually any situation as he saw fit, the customary practice when the indigenous people of a province presented special problems of governance. Palestine was part of the imperial province of Syria that, unlike senatorial provinces, was

---

[414] Deissman, *Light from the Ancient East*, 80.

[415] Fuhrmann, *Policing the Roman Empire: Soldiers, Administration and Public Order*, 186.

ruled by a military governor. Prefects or procurators controlled the districts of the province. Pilate was such a prefect.

The festivals were perfect opportunities for cutthroats. Josephus mentions how the *sicarii*, or *daggermen*, assassins who targeted Jewish collaborators, mingled with the crowds the better to conceal themselves after committing murders. One of their victims in the years following Jesus' death was Jonathan, the high priest, an assassination that was one of the causes of the First Jewish War.[416]

Joseph Caiaphas' responsibilities to his people during the festival were particularly extreme: if a mob should slip from the control of the Jewish temple police, the Roman prefect would be forced to intervene, a provocation that would incite the restive population to open rebellion. Should that occur, Pilate would next petition for legions of troops from the neighboring Syrian legate. All of Judea could erupt into war with incalculable loss of life, a disaster for Caiaphas and an even greater tragedy for the Jewish nation.

> Therefore the chief priests and the Pharisees assembled the High Council and they said, "What will we do? This man is performing many signs! If we tolerate him like this, everyone will believe in him and the Romans will come and take over both our place and people!"
>
> But one of them, Caiaphas, being the High Priest that year, said to them, "You don't understand anything! You don't even take into account that it is more advantageous for you that one man die for the people than to have the whole nation destroyed." He did not say that of

[416] Josephus, *Jewish War*, II, 256. The First Jewish War, 66-73 CE, during which the temple built by Herod was destroyed (70), was followed by a second war, the Kitos War, 115-117 CE, and a third, the Bar Kokhba Revolt, 132-135.

Elsewhere Josephus documents other disturbances that occurred during Passover. *Jewish Antiquities*, XX, 106, ff.

> his own accord, but being High Priest that year he prophesied that Jesus was about to die for the nation, and not only for the nation, but to gather together God's dispersed children into one.
>
> So from that day forward they planned how they might kill him.[417]

The betrayal, arrest, and trial of Jesus are deeply overlaid with Christian iconography and the facts of the matter buried under layers of improbable apologetic nonsense. Luke reports that the temple police used spies to follow Jesus[418] in preparation for his delivery to the authorities, so it makes little sense to suppose that they would pay Judas to betray Jesus' location. It has been suggested that Judas betrayed the content of Jesus' secret teaching, an idea supported by the charge that Jesus considered himself the future "King of the Jews."[419] But there is a division of opinion on the matter: "That Jesus never asserted directly or spontaneously that he was the Messiah is admitted by every serious expert…The firmness of early Christian emphasis on Jesus' Messianic status is matched by the reluctance of Synoptic tradetion to ascribe to him any unambiguous public, or even private, declaration in this domain."[420]

Carmichael points out that the gospel accounts of Jesus' arrest and trial are related "in contradictory and ambiguous ways; both the procedure and the content of the trial are deeply confused."[421] "The spectacle of the Roman governor coming out of his court to ask the people assembled outside why they would not try his prisoner, and acquiescing in the finality of their reply that, notwithstanding his invitation, they had no power to, is

---

[417] John 11:47-53.

[418] Luke 20:20.

[419] Ehrman, *Jesus, Apocalyptic Prophet*, 216-219.

[420] Vermes, *Jesus the Jew*, 140, 152.

[421] Carmichael, *The Unriddling of Christian Origins: A Secular Account*, 83.

just too grotesque for credence."[422] In short, the gospels portray Pilate, a Roman governor, as the reluctant puppet of the Jewish leadership when in fact the situation was likely the complete reverse.

Mark has Judas indicate which man is Jesus by approaching him and kissing him. In John's gospel, on the other hand, Jesus steps forward, asks the temple police who they are seeking, and identifies himself not once but three times while Judas simply stands by. At the time of his arrest, the disciples initially offer armed resistance, and then flee.[423] Significantly, Jesus asks if the temple police have come to arrest him as if he were a *ληστης* (lēstēs). The word is multivalent: it can mean *highwayman*, *robber*, or *insurrectionist*, *guerrilla*, i.e., a person who incited rebellion against Roman authority.[424] It is, of course, quite probable that insurrection in Jesus' day was funded by theft in much the same way that unconventional warfare of today is funded by illegal activity, so the two categories no doubt overlapped. If the gospel was written during the last years of the Jewish revolt, certainly after the destruction of Herod's temple, it raises the possibility that Jesus advocated subversion. The term is also used of the two men crucified along with Jesus.[425] "Social banditry and millennial prophecy may, indeed, go hand in hand…Messianic claimants invoke human violence but with divine violence undergirding it.[426] Based on evidence from the gospels, Carmichael makes a case that Jesus attempted an insurrection, concluding: "Since the Romans could scarcely have bothered giving actual trials to the multitude of Kingdom of God activists they crucified, it is clear that 'trying' Jesus—if they did—and identifying him as 'King of the Jews' was a natural way of explaining

---

[422] Cohn, *The Trial and Death of Jesus*, 155.
[423] Mark 14:43-45, John 18:3-10, Matthew 26:56, Mark 14:50.
[424] Mark 14:48.
[425] Luke 23:40.
[426] Crossan, *The Historical Jesus*, 163, 168.

the point of Jesus' execution; it represented the crushing of a national rebellion."[427]

If the disciples abandoned Jesus in disarray and followed the subsequent progression of events from a safe distance,[428] then it was, of course, impossible for them to overhear Jesus' exchanges with his accusers. It is already established by the gospels themselves that the Temple authorities arrested Jesus by night, hastily interviewed him, pronounced his guilt, and hustled him away to Pilate for speedy execution because they were in fear of the reaction of the crowd of Jesus' supporters. It is therefore absurd to have Pilate stand Jesus before the crowd and argue repeatedly for his acquittal. "The gospels, especially Matthew and John, want Jesus to have been condemned by the Jewish mob, against Pilate's better judgment...The stories of Pilate's reluctance and weakness of will are best explained as Christian propaganda; they are a kind of excuse for Pilate's action which reduces the conflict between the Christian movement and Roman authority."[429]

In summary, the chain of events seems to have run roughly like this: Jesus and his disciples left the temple area and crossed the Kidron valley to a garden where the temple police arrested Jesus.[430] He was taken before Annas, the father-in-law of Caiaphas, and other members of the High Council, where he was questioned by some number of Jewish rulers, including the High Priest.[431] The Jewish authorities, satisfied that Jesus was recalcitrant, then sent Jesus posthaste to Pilate with the recommendation that he be executed. Pilate briefly interrogated him and sent him away to die.[432]

---

[427] Carmichael, *The Unriddling of Christian Origins: A Secular Account*, 136.
[428] Matthew 26:56, Mark 14:50.
[429] Crossan, *The Historical Figure of Jesus*, 273-274.
[430] John 18:1-3.
[431] John 18:12-14, 19-24.
[432] John 18:28, 19:1-16.

Luke exonerates the Romans by shifting the blame for Jesus' death to the chief priests and the scribes,[433] omits the presence of Romans at the moment of Jesus' arrest[434]—in contrast with John[435]—and deletes the reference to Gentile "sinners" found in Matthew and Mark.[436] Luke has Herod Antipas' officers abuse Jesus,[437] not the Romans who perform this task in Matthew and Mark.[438] Nevertheless, Luke concedes, perhaps inadvertently, that Pilate murdered Jews.[439] Even the interrogation of Jesus is problematic. If Pilate spoke Latin and Greek, and Jesus spoke Aramaic, then the philosophical discussions reported in the gospels, particularly the gospel of John, could only have transpired through an interpreter and it is doubtful that Jesus received that much of a hearing from Pilate, a man who apparently despised the Jews and their religion.

The accusation of sorcery.

Unless the gospels—canonical as well as apocryphal—are simply lying, Rome in the person of Pontius Pilate found Jesus guilty *of something* and executed him by crucifixion. However, *the specific charges against Jesus are never stated in the New Testament*, which leads us to suppose that the charge that led to Jesus' hasty execution was even more embarrassing to the early church than the fact that Jesus died an ignominious death reserved for felons. In fact, the procedure described in the gospels contains so many incongruities that it has been largely dismissed by all but the most fervent Christian apologists.

---

433 Luke 22:2.
434 Luke 22:52.
435 John 18:12.
436 Matthew 26:45, Mark 14:41.
437 Luke 23:11.
438 Matthew 27:27-31, Mark 15:16-20.
439 Luke 13:1.

> Pilate "went out unto them, and said, What accusation bring ye against this man?" (John 18:29), indicating that, so far, none had been brought. This is—to say the least—most surprising: how could Jesus have been admitted into the *praetorium* unless a charge was pending against him? If he was, as yet, under no indictment, he would not be let in any more than any other member of the public...a Roman cohort under the command of a tribune would never have been detached for the arrest of Jesus unless a charge had already been preferred against him...This is no less surprising: if the Jews were as interested as all that in having Jesus tried on a capital offense, why did they not take the opportunity offered and formulate a charge accordingly?"[440]

An excellent question, but one to which the gospels offer no clear answer.

I will argue that the Jewish leaders accused Jesus of sorcery, and that despite the vigorous editing to which the gospel accounts have been subjected with a view to removing any basis for such charges, the evidence is nonetheless compelling. Clearly the Jewish authorities regarded Jesus as a problem and wanted to be rid of him, but to achieve that end they needed an accusation that would impress the Roman governor. To haul him up before Pilate and accuse him of involvement in a purely religious squabble would not do; the Romans didn't bother to understand, much less enforce, Jewish religious laws. The surviving evidence portrays Pilate "as lacking in concern for Jewish religious sensibilities and as capable of rather brutal methods of crowd control."[441]

---

[440] Cohn, *The Trial and Death of Jesus*, 151-152.

"While mention is made in Luke (23:24) of a 'sentence' pronounced by Pilate, it is significant that none of the Gospels actually quotes or describes the judgment or sentence..." (188).

[441] Crossan, *Who Killed Jesus? Exposing the Roots of Anti-Semitism in the Gospel Story of the Death of Jesus*, 148.

Thanks to Josephus, we understand the tight connections between magic, prophecy, and social disturbance. Kingdom-of-God apocalyptic preachers who established their prophetic bona fides by the performance of miracles were considered *magicians* and the accusation of sorcery was not trivial: "There was thus no period in the history of the empire in which the magician was not considered an enemy of society, subject at the least to exile, more often to death in its least pleasant forms."[442] The charge of practicing magic, which charge could expand to include "prophets who disturb the peace,"[443] could kill more than one's reputation. "The empire had long shown an exceptional interest in the policing of ritual systems—diviners, spell-mongers, *magoi*, 'foreign' cults," and by the time of Jesus magic had become "a criminal form of ritual subversion in the Roman Empire."[444] Roman authorities moved against religious figures "deemed potentially subversive" and various types of "holy men," including astrologers, who "were expelled from Rome at least ten times from 33 BC to AD 93."[445]

The imputation of practicing sorcery is based on two passages, one of which is found in John. Asked by Pilate what charges they are bringing against Jesus, the Jewish leaders reply: "If this man were not an evildoer, we would not have handed him over to you."[446] It is apparent from the context that whatever evil Jesus was accused of doing, it was a capital offense, but the charges are vague. Plumer notes, "In the Johannine trial of Jesus the material evidence for the prosecution has conveniently gone missing!" and concludes that the "material evidence" in question was the Beelzeboul controversy,[447] i.e., the accusation that Jesus

---

[442] MacMullen, *Enemies of the Roman Order*, 125-126.

[443] Rives, *The Religious History of the Roman Empire*, 98.

[444] Frankfurter, *Greek, Roman, and Byzantine Studies* 46: 59.

[445] Fuhrmann, *Policing the Roman Empire: Soldiers, Administration, and Public Order*, 49.

[446] John 18:30.

[447] Plumer, *Biblica* 78: 359-361.

practiced sorcery, hence the charge *ει μη ην ουτος κακον ποιων ουκ αν σοι παρεδοκαμεν αυτον*, "If this man were not an evildoer, we would not have handed him over to you."

It is clear from the gospels that the Jewish authorities considered Jesus to be in control of evil spirits. In addition to *evildoer*, the term *κακοποιος* (kakopoios) could also mean *sorcerer*—the most authoritative lexicon of New Testament Greek offers "sorcerer" as one of several definitions of *κακοποιος*.[448] Calling sorcerers "evildoers" was apparently very old even in Jesus' day. François Lenormant: "As a rule the sorcerer was called 'the evildoer, and the malevolent man' in the old Accadian conjurations…his rites and formulae for enchantment subjected the demons to his orders…He could even take away life with his spells and imprecations…"[449] Among a collection of Babylonian prayers, King translated one, "By the command of thy mouth may there never approach anything evil, the magic of the sorcerer and of the sorceress!...May the evil curse, that is unfavorable, never draw nigh, may it never be oppressive!"[450] (The subject of magical cursing in the New Testament is explored in a later chapter.)

On the use of *κακοποιος*, *evil doing*, Kotansky notes, "the adjective *κακοποιος* is used in the magical papyri specifically of malevolent planetary influences…"[451] In any event, Kotansky documents an amulet with the following text: *πονηρον πνευμα και κακαποιον και φθοροποιον απελασον απο της* [name] *Πτα νεβρ αν θαβιασα*, "Depart from her [name], harmful (*κακοποιον*) and destructive evil spirit! O Ptah, entirely beautiful, thabiasa!" Although short, the spell perfectly captures a syncretistic smorgasbord of magical terms: *πονηρον πνευμα*, *evil spirit*, is a term from

---

[448] Bauer, Arndt & Gingrich, *A Greek-English Lexicon of the New Testament and Other Early Christian Literature*, 482.
[449] Lenormant, *Chaldean Magic*, 60-61.
[450] King, *Babylonian Magic and Sorcery: "The Prayers of the Lifting of the Hand,"* 62.
[451] Kotansky, *Greek Magical Amulets: The Inscribed Gold, Silver, Copper, and Bronze Lamellae*, 102.

the Septuagint carried over into the New Testament, and *φθοροποιος*, *causing destruction*, is used of demons only by Christian writers. But just in case, the spell includes an invocation of the god Ptah and ends with a word, *thabiasa*, likely compounded from Aramaic טב (tāb), *good*, and אסא (asā), *remedy*.[452]

The magical papyri offer this contrast: "for doing good"—*επι μεν των αγαθοποιων*—"offer storax, myrrh, sage, frankincense, fruit pit. But for doing harm,"—*επι δε των κακοποιων*—"offer magical material of a dog and a dappled goat (or in a similar way, of a virgin untimely dead).[453]

Charges of evildoing through magic were leveled at Jesus' closest associates. The *Apocriticus* of Macarius Magnes, an attempted refutation of Porphyry's *Against the Christians*, preserves this charge made against the apostle Peter: "This man Peter is proved unrighteous (*αδικων ελεγχεται*) in other matters also. A certain man called Ananias and his wife called Sapphira...he killed though they had done nothing wrong (*εθανατωσε μηδεν αδικησαντας*)..."[454] From a pagan standpoint, Peter had murdered Ananias and Sapphira by magical cursing, a premeditated criminal action captured by the term *αδικημα* (adikēma), *deliberate wrong*. By the standards of Roman law, Christianity's founding documents exalted criminality. The notion of *evil doing* (*κακον ποιειν*) by magic is common: "...if I have given a *pharmakon* [*φαρμακον*, *potion* or *poison*, my note] to Asklepiadas or contrived in my soul *to do him harm* (*κακον τι αυτω ποισαι*) in any way..."[455] The tradition of magical cursing thrived in early Christianity: "The body and the blood of Jesus Christ, strike Maria daughter of Tsibel..." or "You must bring [Martha] away

---

452 Ibid, 102-103.

453 Preisendanz, *Papyri Graecae Magicae* IV, 2870-2876. I have used the translation in Betz' *The Greek Magical Papyri in Translation*, 92.

454 Blondel, *Μακαριου Μαγνητος Αποκριτικος η Μονογενες*, XXI.

455 Quoted from Versnel, *The world of ancient magic*, 134.

by the method of an ulcerous tumor…she pouring forth worms …My lord Jesus Christ, you must bring her down to an end."[456]

In short, Porphyry charged that Peter's curse on Ananias and Sapphira was subject to legal punishment. Peter is *αδικος*, a *criminal.* Commenting on the phrase *και ει τις με αδικησι επεικινα αποστρεψον*, "And if anyone shall injure me henceforth, turn (him) away!" Kotansky points out that the verb *αδικειν* "generally means 'to damage, injure,' but when it occurs in the formula *ει τις αδικειν* is used specifically of committing *legal* injury or wrong" and cites several instances of such use from decrees and letters.[457] The verb used to describe Peter's magical curse means "*do wrong, act wickedly* or *criminally.*"[458] Roman law considered magic "above all as a murderous activity, which explains the severity of the punishments inflicted to prevent it: banishment, being thrown to the beasts, being burned alive."[459] The New Testament itself connects magic with murder: "Outside are the dogs and the *sorcerers* (*φαρμακοι*)…and the *murderers* (*φονεις*)…"[460] Magic and murder were closely connected in the 1st century; a charge of murder was brought against the famous seer and miracle worker, Apollonius, accused of sacrificing a boy in order to foretell the future by inspecting his entrails.[461] "Religious deviance could indeed play a central part" in accusations of magical practice which, as noted by Rives, included such figures as "magicians, *magi*, and evildoers, *malefici*" as well as "prophets who disturb the peace" and the punish-

---

[456] Meyer & Smith, *Ancient Christian Magic: Coptic Texts of Ritual Power*, 193, 207.

[457] Kotansky, *Greek Magical Amulets*, 183, 184, 189, 190.

[458] Abbott-Smith, *A Manual Greek Lexicon of the New Testament*, 9.

[459] Heintz, *Simon "Le Magicien: Actes 8,5-25 et L'accusation de Magie Contre les Profètes Thaumaturges Dans L'Antiquité*, 34.

"Le fait que la législation romaine considère la magie avant tout comme une activité homicide permet de comprendre la sévérité des châtiments infligés au contrevenant…"

[460] Revelation 22:15.

[461] Philostratus, *Life of Apollonius* VII, 11.

ments were severe; according to the later *Opinions of Paulus*, "those guilty of the magic art (*magicae artis conscios*) be inflicted with the supreme punishment, i.e., be thrown the beasts or *crucified* (emphasis added)."[462]

Under Roman law some forms of sorcery were considered *lèse majesté* and were punishable by death. The performance of exorcisms, to say nothing of resurrecting Lazarus, whose appearance in Jerusalem advertised Jesus' power and drew a substantial crowd of supporters,[463] "blatantly and publicly defied the emergent Jewish standards of ritual boundaries,"[464] and certainly would have qualified as sorcery. From the standpoint of Roman law it is essential to understand that agents of the state "repressed certain forms of magic and unsanctioned religious practices, especially when deemed potentially subversive" and this was particularly true of "wonder workers."[465] According to Philostratus, who recorded the feats of the wonder-working Apollonius, magic is "condemned by nature (*φυσει*) and by law (*νομω*)."[466]

Magic and murder by poisoning were associated in legal texts; the Latin *veneficus* might be a *poisoner* or a *magician*, and *veneficium*, like the Greek *φαρμακεια* (pharmakeia), "can refer to spells or to a generalized notion of magic" and the *Lex Cornelia de sicariis et veneficiis*—the *Cornelian Law on assassins and poisoners*, established in 81 BCE—was the principle law under which magicians were prosecuted "because the very name 'poisoner' (*veneficus*) was the same as that for 'magician'...To Romans of the first century CE, magic was the 'ultimate *super-*

[462] Rives, *The Religious History of the Roman Empire: Pagans, Jews, and Christians*, 75, 92, 98.
[463] John 12:9-11.
[464] Kee, *Medicine, Miracle and Magic in New Testament Times*, 74.
[465] Fuhrmann, *Policing the Roman Empire: Soldiers, Administration, and Public Order*, 49.
[466] Philostratus, *Life of Apollonius* VII, 39.

stitio.'"[467] Punishment under the law could include the death penalty, particularly for those of the lower classes. As Heintz points out, the danger of magic lay in part in the direct access it afforded to the supernatural world, the possibility of influence over the stars and gods, making magic a 'super religion' beyond state control and thus dangerous.[468]

Although not typically cited as evidence favoring an accusation of magic, Luke specifies that the charge made against Jesus was "perverting our people"[469] —*διαστρεφοντα το εθνος ημων*— which is perhaps *not* coincidentally the very same term he has Paul use against the *magician* Bar-Jesus: *ου παυση διαστρεφων τας οδους του κυριου*: "will you not stop making crooked the paths of the Lord?"[470]

The second passage cited in support of a charge of sorcery comes from Matthew, and is again voiced by the Jewish authorities to Pilate: "My Lord, we remember that that deceiver said while still alive, 'After three days I will raise myself.'"[471]

It bears repeating that by calling Jesus "that deceiver"—*εκεινος ο πλανος*—Matthew tactfully rephrases the traditional Jewish charge against Jesus. Eitrem noted, "common Jewish people

---

[467] Collins, *Magic in the Ancient World*, 144-147.

[468] Heintz, *Simon "Le Magicien": Actes 8, 5-25 et l'accusation de magie contre les prophètes thaumaturges dans l'antiquité*, 32.

"L'accès direct au monde surnaturel, l'évocation des esprits, la possibilité d'influer sur les cours des astres ou sur la decisions des dieux, la perspective de devenir un avec la divinité, faisaient de la magie dan l'Antiquité une sorte de supra-religion, au-dessus des états..."

[469] Luke 23:2.

[470] Acts 13:10.

[471] Matthew 27:63.

εκεινος ο πλανος ειπεν ετι ζων μετα τρεις ημερας αναστησεται: "that deceiver said while still alive, 'After three days I will raise myself.'"

considered Jesus a μαγος (*magician*, my note),"[472] an assessment confirmed by the Christian apologist Justin Martyr: "But those who saw the things he did said it was magical illusion (φαντασια μαγικην), daring to call him a magician (μαγον), and a deceiver of the people (λαοπλανον)."[473] The term φαντασια (phantasia), from which comes our *fantasy*, then as now carried connotations of unreality, the imaginary, in short, *illusion*. The charge that Jesus was in effect an illusionist and therefore a λαοπλανος, or *people deceiver*, made him a μαγος, a *magician*. The charge that Jesus deceived the people was not new in the 2nd century when Justin composed his apology. The pagan critic Celsus apparently based his charge that Jesus practiced magic, at least in part, on information provided by a Jewish informant.[474] Indeed Origen denies that Jesus was a sorcerer but calls "heretical" Christians "frauds and sorcerers" (πλανοι και γοητες).[475]

To substantiate their claim of practicing magic, the Jewish authorities cite Jesus' prediction: μετα τρεις ημερας αναστησεται, "after three days I will raise myself." If construed as the middle voice—the middle voice in Greek indicates what the subject does to or for himself—a very natural reading, εγειρομαι means *I will raise myself*. However, all translators, accepting the claim that God raised Jesus from the dead, render the passage, *I will be raised*, reading the verb as passive. In defense of the apparent charge made by the Jews, it must be pointed out that *Jesus clearly foretold that he would raise himself from the dead*:

> In response the Jews said to him, "What sign are you showing us that you are doing these things?"
>
> In reply Jesus said to them, "Destroy this temple and in three days I will raise it."[476]

---

[472] Eitrem, *Some Notes on the Demonology in the New Testament*, 41.

[473] Archambault, *Justin: Dialogue avec Tryphon*, LXIX, 7 (volume I, 336-338).

[474] Origen, *Contra Celsus* II, 52.

[475] Ibid, VII, 40.

[476] και εν τρισιν ημεραις εγερω αυτον: "and in three days I will raise it."

> Then the Jews said, "This temple was built in forty-six years and in three days you will raise it?" But he said that about the temple of his body.[477]

"Instead of displaying another sign on the spot, Jesus promises one—it will be his greatest and will give the best apology imaginable for his death. That he is to accomplish his own resurrection is virtually unique in the N[ew]T[estament]. If there was any doubt that he had been alluding to his own death (and resurrection), it is dispelled by the formula, *in three days*."[478]

The gospel of John is quite explicit on this point:

> This is why the Father loves me, because I lay aside my life in order that I might take it up again. No one takes it from me, but I lay it aside of my own volition. I have the authority to lay it down and I have authority to take it up again. This is the order I received from my Father.[479]

It is crucial to note the claim of *authority*: *εξουσιαν εχω θειναι αυτην και εξουσιαν εχω παλιν λαβειν αυτην*, "I have the authority to lay it down, and I have the authority to take it up again." As will be shown in a following chapter, Jesus' authority is consistently linked to the working of miracles.

After this surprising announcement the Jews respond: *δαιμονιον εχει και μαινεται*, "He has a demon and he's raving!"—a charge, as we will see, that Jesus is a magician. The contrast is clear: Jesus claims to have *authority*, his opponents claim he has a *demon*. Both are claims that Jesus can perform amazing works of

---

477 John 2:18-21.

478 Miller, *The Complete Gospels*, 187 (footnote on John 2:19).

479 John 10:17-18.

power, the question, as the context reveals,[480] concerns *the source of Jesus' power.*

The gospel of Mark contains very similar wording regarding the death and resurrection of the Son of Man: *μετα τρεις ημερας αναστησεται*, "after three days he will raise himself."[481] After the first such prediction Mark notes that the disciples did not understand what Jesus' was talking about and were afraid to ask.[482] But if Jesus 'merely' predicted that a divine agency would raise the Son of Man from the dead as the Old Testament prophets had raised people from the dead and as Jesus himself raised people from the dead, what was there to misunderstand? To the best of my knowledge there is no text within normative Judaism that speaks of a person raising *himself* from the dead.

The remarkable notion that Jesus could raise himself from the dead is mentioned in a letter of Ignatius, an early martyr, composed around the beginning of the 2nd century. Writing against the Docetist heresy, which claimed that Jesus was a spirit that only appeared to suffer in the flesh, Ignatius says, "He suffered all these things on our account that we might be saved, and he truly suffered *as also he truly raised himself*—*ως και αληθως ανεστησεν εαυτου*.[483] That raising oneself from the dead is exactly the sort of thing a magician might do is confirmed by Hippolytus' accusation that Simon Magnus made precisely such a claim.[484]

Christianity's opponents knew of this remarkable prediction. Origen felt obligated to repeat it in his defense against Celsus, but ascribed it to "false witnesses" who testified at Jesus' trial:

---

480 John 10:19-21.

481 Mark 9:31.

482 Mark 9:32.

483 Ignatius, *Ad Smyrnaeos*, II.

484 Tuzlak, *Magic and Ritual in the Ancient World*, 419.

> At last, two came forward and stated, "This man said, 'I can tear down the temple of God and in three days build it up.'"[485]

Nevertheless, Origen clearly believed that Jesus "*quickly departed from the body* (*ταχα ...εξεληλυθεν απο του σωματος*) that he might keep it intact and that his legs might not be broken like those of the robbers crucified with him" while revealing in the same context that Celsus "equated [Jesus'] wonders with sorceries" (*κοινοποιειν αυτα προς τας γοητειας*).[486] That Celsus believed the resurrection to be an act of magic is clear: "[Jesus] foretold that after dying he will raise himself (*αναστησεται*)," and offers the claim as a case of "exploiting others *by deceit* (*πλανη*)." Accordingly, Jesus appears post mortem to "a woman in a frenzy" (*γυνη παροιστρος*) "and some others under the same spell" (*και ει τις αλλος των εκ της αυτης γοητειας*).[487]

The term *πλανος* (planos) as an adjective is used elsewhere in the New Testament in relation to spiritism—*προσεχοντες πνευμασιν πλανοις και διδασκαλιαις δαιμονιων*: "turning to deceptive spirits and teachings of demons..."[488] After a lengthy analysis of the passage in Matthew, Samain concluded, "...by the epithet *πλανος*, Matthew refers to a man who has won over the crowd not only by his doctrines and his words, but also by his activities and his wonders, that is to say, a magician."[489] In a seminal essay, Aune characterizes Samain's evidence as "an iron-clad case

---

[485] *δυναμαι καταλυσαι τον ναον του θεου και δια τριων ημερων οικοδομησαι*: "I can tear down the temple of God and in three days build it up." *Contra Celsum, Præfatio* I.

[486] Origen, *Contra Celsum* II, 16.

[487] Ibid, II, 54-55. *Γυνη παροιστρος* could be translated "a woman in estrus" (from *οιστραω*, *to be in a frenzy* or "in heat").

[488] 1 Timothy 4:1.

[489] Samain, *Ephemerides Theologicae Lovanienses* 15:458-459.

My translation of: "pour...l'épithète de *πλανος* Matthieu désigne un homme qui a séduit la foule, non seulement par sa doctrine et ses paroles, mais aussi par ses gestes prodiges: c'est à dire un magician."

for understanding the charge of imposture as an accusation that Jesus performed miracles by trickery or magical techniques."[490] "The allegations that Jesus was a magician and that he was a false prophet were known at the time the evangelists wrote. Matthew knew the double form of the accusation. John (certainly) and Luke (probably) were aware that Jewish opponents of Christian claims allege that Jesus was a false prophet who led God's people astray."[491]

The Jewish charge against Jesus also appears in Coptic sources: "when [John] came up to the temple a pharisee by the name of Arimanios confronted him and said to him, 'Where is your master, the one you followed?' And [John] said to him, 'He returned to the place from whence he came.' The *pharisee* (**ⲡⲉⲫⲁⲣⲓⲥⲁⲓⲟⲥ**) said to him, 'This Nazarene *led you astray* (**ⲡⲗⲁⲛⲁ**) …"[492]

Celsus described Jesus as *θεομισους ην τινος και μοχθηρου γοητος*, "a worthless sorcerer, hated by God."[493] Such charges were widely known even in Jesus' day and must obviously be taken seriously. Given Origen's response, it appears Celsus linked Jesus' execution to a charge of sorcery: "That it is perfectly obvious the accounts written about Jesus' suffering have nothing in common with those most miserable men dispatched *on account of sorcery* (*δια γοητειαν*) or on some other grounds is clear to everyone."[494] Well, perhaps not all *that* clear.

In the *Acts of Thomas* the terms *μαγος*, *magician*, and *πλανος*, *fraud*, are applied to the apostle Thomas and the terms are equated: *ηκουσα γαρ οτι ο μαγος εκεινος και πλανος τουτο διδασ-*

---

490 Aune, *Aufstieg und Niedergang der Römischen Welt* II, 23.2, 1540.
491 Stanton, *Gospel Truth? New Light on Jesus and the Gospels*, 160.
492 Giversen, *Apocryphon Johannis*, 46-47.
493 Origen, *Contra Celsum*, I, 71.
494 Ibid, II, 44.

κει, "for I heard that magician and fraud teaches this..."[495] Deception and magic are firmly linked in Revelation where a curse against "Babylon," widely understood to stand for Rome, says in part, "all the nations *were deceived by your sorcery* (*εν τη φαρμακεια σου επλανηθησαν*)...in her was found the blood of the prophets and saints..."[496]

> "To begin with the terminology used in speaking of itinerant magicians: in Greek they continue to be classified as *agyrtai* or begging holy men, although sometimes they are also called *ageirontes*, a participle from the same root as *agyrtes* that means 'those taking up a collection,' and sometimes yet again as *planetai*, 'wanderers or vagabonds,' or *planoi* [plural of *πλανος*, *my note*], the deeply ambiguous term that means primarily 'one who creates delusions in the minds of other men,' then 'sorcerer,' but that may also have connotations of vagabond or wandering beggar; the term *laoplanos*, 'one who deludes the masses,' is also found."[497]

That *πλανος* referred to apocalyptic prophets is clear from Josephus who describes *πλανοι γαρ ανθρωποι και απατεωνεη*, "men, fakes and deceivers" who led crazed multitudes into the wilderness promising that there God would give them "signs of deliverance."[498] Significantly, the same authorities who accuse Jesus of controlling demons also say "he deceives the crowd"—*πλανα τον οχλον*.[499] That magical works of power and apocalyptic predictions inflicted damage on Jesus' reputation long after his death is certain. The gospel of John refers to Jesus' miracles as "signs" (*σημειον*) as opposed to "works of power" (*δυναμις*), likely because of the association of the latter term with magic,[500]

---

495 *Acts of Thomas*, 96.
496 Revelation 18:23-24.
497 Dickie, *Magic and Magicians in the Greco-Roman World*, 224-225.
498 Josephus, *Jewish Wars* II.229.
499 John 7: 12, 20.
500 Plumer, *Biblica* 78: 350-368.

and the apocalyptic content of Jesus' preaching has nearly disappeared from the fourth gospel.

That Paul and his companions were regarded *ως πλανοι*: "as impostors"[501] in certain circles may acknowledge that they were charged with practicing magic—Paul's relation to magicians is the subject of a subsequent chapter.

The Jewish historian Josephus, in a passage which is likely authentic, refers to Jesus as *παραδοξων εργων ποιητης*, "a performer of amazing works," which as Van Voort notes "can be read to mean simply that Jesus had a reputation as a wonder-worker,"[502] but would also be consistent with a charge of practicing magical feats, and raising oneself from the dead would seem to qualify if anything would. The Babylonian Talmud contains similar accusations:

> The master said, "Jesus the Nazarene practiced magic and deceived and led Israel astray."
> "And a herald went forth before him 40 days: Jesus the Nazarene is going forth to be stoned because he practiced sorcery and instigated and seduced Israel (to idolatry)."[503]

Regarding Christian censorship of Jewish references to Jesus, Cohn concludes, "My submission is that the true reason for suppressing the passages was that Jesus was represented in them as an enticer to idolatry and a sorcerer…As a consequence, every report in the Talmud of a trial for either of those crimes that could by any construction be linked up with Jesus was methodically obliterated."[504]

---

501 2 Corinthians 6:8.

502 Van Voort, *Jesus Outside the New Testament*, 89.

503 Schäfer, *Jesus in the Talmud*, 35, 64.

504 Cohn, *The Trial and Death of Jesus*, 306.

Denunciation of Christians for practicing magic continued for over two centuries following Jesus' death. Morton Smith's observations in this regard merit an extended quote:

> ...These persecutions require explanation both because of their frequency and because of the general tolerance throughout the Roman empire for cults of oriental gods and deified men. Occasional exceptions to this tolerance might be explained by peculiar local circumstances; but the consistent opposition to Christianity evidently resulted from something characteristic of the new religion. What was it? The common answer is, the Christians' refusal to worship other gods. But other worshippers of Yahweh—the Jews and the Samaritans—also refused to worship other gods, and they were not generally persecuted. Consequently, the Christians had to explain the persecutions as inspired either by the demons or by the Jews who, they said, denounced them to the authorities...But for what could the Jews denounce them? Certainly not for refusing to worship other gods—that was the hallmark of the Jewish faith generally...What they were accused of was the practice of magic and other crimes associated with magic: human sacrifice, cannibalism, and incest...Magic figures conspicuously in charges against Christians from the second century on...Moreover, as the passages from Eusebius show—and they could be paralleled by many more from Irenaeus, Hippolytus, and Epiphanius—the Christians made considerable use of this charge against one another. Presumably they knew what they were talking about.[505]

A brief quotation from Eusebius suffices to reinforce Smith's point:

---

[505] Smith, *Clement of Alexandria*, 234.

> Formerly [the Devil] had used persecutions from without as his weapon against [the church], but now that he was excluded from this he employed *wicked men and sorcerers* (πονηροις και γοησιν), like baleful weapons and ministers of destruction against the soul, and conducted his campaign by other measures, plotting by every means that *sorcerers and deceivers* (γοητες και απατηλοι) might assume the same name as our religion..."[506]

In summary, we have accumulated evidence that practicing magic was the charge brought against Jesus by the Jewish authorities. The terms κακοποιος, *evildoer*, and πλανος, *fraud*, are terms well attested in the vocabulary of magic, and πλανος is specifically equated with μαγος, *magician*. Outside the New Testament, Justin concedes that Jesus was called a *magician*, μαγος, and Celsus calls Jesus a γοης, a *sorcerer*. Within the writings of Luke, the term διαστρεφω, to *pervert*, *twist* or *mislead*, is used, perhaps inadvertently, both of Bar Jesus and Jesus and a similar word set, πλαναω, to *mislead*, and λαοπλανος, *one who misleads people*, are used of Jesus. Besides the terminology, we have the accusation, explored at greater length in a subsequent chapter, that Jesus practiced magic by controlling Beelzeboul, the prince of the demons, the "Beelzeboul controversy." The prediction of self-resurrection is also the mark of a magician.

And finally, there is the legal situation Jesus created as an apocalyptic prophet who performed miracles, attracted crowds, and in doing so opened himself to the charge of magic and deviant religious practices. As the governor of a Roman province, Pilate's brief was to keep the peace and maintain order, ensuring that magician/prophets, such as those reported by Josephus, would be dealt with quickly and harshly.

The Jewish authorities, who were in fear of the crowds Jesus attracted according to all four gospels, knew precisely the charge

---

[506] Eusebius, *Ecclesiastical History* IV, 7.

that would move Pontius Pilate to action. Indeed, Jesus' confrontation with the temple authorities appears on the best evidence to have been a premeditated act of self-immolation. Given recent history, the following description of Jesus' action, written in 1977, assumes a chilling currency: "In a country seething with frustration and discontent, martyrdom increasingly seemed to Palestinians a glorious fate."[507]

[507] Grant, *Jesus*, 140.

CHAPTER 4: RESURRECTION OR GHOST STORY?

If what happened when the Jewish leaders turned Jesus over to the Roman authority was predictable, what happened after the Roman authority turned Jesus over to history was simply amazing.

Like other New Testament stories, the accounts of the resurrection are riddled with contradictions large and small. Although it is claimed that Jesus' disciples removed his body and buried it,[508] in a passage in Acts the apostle Paul—who appears to have known little about the historical Jesus—clearly states that "those living in Jerusalem and their rulers...asked Pilate to put him to death, even as they fulfilled all the things written about him, and taking him down from the gibbet, they laid him in a tomb."[509] Paul, in his previous incarnation as Saul, was an avid persecutor of the early church[510] and so may have known for a fact that the authorities that had Jesus executed were the ones who then removed the body from the cross and disposed of it. Reimer suggests that Paul may have had some relationship with the temple police in his role of "enforcing Jewish religious law…in a punitive fashion, initiating policy, enforcing it with considerable zeal, and casting judgment against those caught."[511]

Whatever the case, the empty tomb was not at first a symbol of Jesus' victory over death, but a problem that required explana-

---

[508] John 19:38.

[509] Acts 13:27-29.

[510] Acts 7:58-8:1.

[511] Reimer, *Miracle and Magic: A Study in the Acts of the Apostles and the Life of Apollonius of Tyana*, 65-66.

tion and the early church explained the problem by creating resurrection stories. However, the gospel stories of the resurrecttion, like the infancy narratives already examined, raised more questions than they answered and, moreover, were only one of several possible theological solutions. Kirby lists four plausible scenarios other than the traditional empty tomb: "Jesus was left hanging on the cross for the birds," the Romans dumped the body in a mass grave, the Jewish authorities buried the body, or the body was buried by the disciples and remained in a tomb.[512] The Roman authorities might have had several motives for keeping Jesus' body out the reach of his disciples. The magical use of relics is discussed at some length in a later chapter, but as a crucified criminal, Jesus' body, the crucifixion nails, and even the wood of the cross would have been tempting targets for theft. Once the Christian practice of taking post mortem remains to use as relics became known to the Romans, "some governors used soldiers to keep the believers from taking the bodies and then took the further step of rendering the bodily remains entirely inaccessible."[513] Significantly, the gospel of Matthew reports that the Jewish authorities expressed concern that Jesus' disciples would come by night to steal the body and claim that Jesus had raised himself.[514]

It is in connection with the disposition of Jesus' body that Crossan describes "the hierarchy of horror" that entailed not only the loss of life and possessions, but even the "destruction of identity" that included the destruction of the body of the criminal, in some cases even the killing of his family, and "the final penalty," to be unburied, having no tomb to memorialize him, no grave that might be visited. The worst penalties included being burned to death, thrown to the beasts, and crucifixion, which in the last case "the body was left on the cross until birds and beasts of

---

[512] Kirby, *The Empty Tomb: Jesus Beyond the Grave*, 233

[513] Fuhrmann, *Policing the Roman Empire: Soldiers, Administration, and Public Order*, 187.

[514] Matthew 26:62-66.

prey had destroyed it." Crossan concludes, "I keep thinking of all those other thousands of Jews crucified around Jerusalem in that terrible first century from among whom we have found only one skeleton and one nail. I think I know what happened to their bodies, and I have no reason to think Jesus' body did not join them."[515]

Jesus' post mortem appearances fall generally into three categories: visions, epiphanies, and apparitions, but the distinctions are not always maintained, nor are the details wholly consistent. For example, the account of Jesus' appearance to Saul on the road to Damascus, reported in three places in Acts,[516] differs in detail with each retelling. According to the first report, the men with Paul hear a voice but see no one,[517] and in the second the men see a light but do not hear a voice.[518] In the first account, Paul alone falls to the ground,[519] but in the third retelling, all the men fall to the ground.[520]

Soon after his conversion, Saul (aka Paul) again sees Jesus, but under different circumstances:

> It happened that after returning to Jerusalem, while I was praying in the temple, I came to be in a state of ecstasy, and I saw him saying to me, "Hurry and leave Jerusalem at once because they will not accept your testimony about me."[521]

Jesus' appearance to Paul in the temple is an ecstatic vision, but his manifestation on the road to Damascus has characteristics of

---

[515] Crossan, *Who Killed Jesus?* 160-161, 183.
[516] Acts 9:1-19, 22:6-16, 26:12-18.
[517] Acts 9:7.
[518] Acts 22:9.
[519] Acts 9:4.
[520] Acts 26:14.
[521] Acts 22:17-18.

post-resurrection epiphanies: light, voices, glowing raiment,[522] supernatural entities, and natural upheavals.[523] Visions during prayer are well documented,[524] and as Strelan observes, "That [Paul's] prayer included an ecstatic vision is not at all unusual ...It is quite likely that Temple prayer had rhythm and a repetitive element. In addition, it is possible that the body moved in harmony with the rhythm of the prayer. Such a method of praying is often mantra-like and can induce a hypnotic, ecstatic state."[525]

The term εκστασις (ekstasis), which literally means "to be outside oneself," is the obvious source of *ecstasy*. An altered state of consciousness is apparently in view, and the word is often translated *trance*. Peter also sees a vision while in a state of ecstasy.[526]

Throughout the Mediterranean world even the dead were expected to be up and around by early morning, a belief that persists even today in the form of Easter sunrise services. "The funeral was finished and the slow process of death completed when the soul finally departed at the coming of dawn..."[527] "The 'Spell for Coming Forth by Day'...draws the parallel between the sun's passage from night to day, and the deceased's emergence from the tomb to the daylight."[528]

A text often cited as the first report of Jesus' post-resurrection appearances comes to us from a letter written by Paul:

> For I passed on to you as of first importance what I also received, that Christ died for our sins according to

---

522 As at Matthew 28:3, Luke 24:8.

523 Matthew 28:2, 5.

524 Daniel 9:20, for example.

525 Strelan, *Strange Acts*, 180.

526 Acts 10:10-11.

527 Vermeule, *Aspects of Death in Early Greek Art and Poetry*, 21.

528 David, *Religion and Magic in Ancient Egypt*, 84.

> the scriptures, and that he was buried, and that he was raised on the third day according to the scriptures, and that he appeared to Cephas,[529] then to the twelve, then he appeared to more than five hundred brothers at one time, the greater number of whom remain until now, but some have fallen asleep [in death].
>
> Then he appeared to James, then to all the apostles. Last of all, he appeared even to me, as to one born before his time.[530]

However, the claim that Jesus appeared to 500 witnesses at one time is the sort of exaggeration one would expect from a later apocryphal account and the fact that none of the gospels, although written later than 1 Corinthians, report this remarkable confirmation of the resurrection, almost certainly marks the passage as an interpolation inserted into the text after Paul's death. "A simple comparison of the Gospels and 1 Corinthians 15 shows that the two traditions cannot be reconciled."[531]

Robert Price has proposed that the chain of connectives—"*that* Christ died...*that* he was buried...*that* he was raised...*that* he appeared..."—is the relic of an early liturgical confession, i.e., not written by Paul,[532] which if true, would make the gospel of Mark the oldest report of the resurrection:

> When the Sabbath had passed, Mary the Magdalene and Mary the mother of James and Salome bought spices so that they might go and anoint him, and very

---

[529] The usual words meaning to "see" are *βλεπω* (blepō) and *θεωρεω* (theōreō), but here Paul repeatedly uses forms of *οραω* (horaō), a verb often employed in the New Testament for preternatural visions and similar experiences. The related noun, *οραμα* (horama), usually denotes *vision* in the sense of "supernatural experience."

[530] 1 Corinthians 15:3-8.

[531] Riley, *Resurrection Reconsidered: Thomas and John in Controversy*, 89.

[532] Price, *Journal of Higher Criticism* 2/2: 69-99.

> early in the morning on the first day of the week, the sun having risen, they went to the tomb. They were saying to one another, "Who will roll the stone away from the door of the tomb for us?"
>
> Looking up, they saw that the stone—which was extremely large—had been rolled away. And entering the tomb, they saw a young man clothed in a white robe, sitting off to the right, and they were alarmed. But he said to them, "Do not be alarmed. You are seeking Jesus of Nazareth who was crucified. He is not here. He has been raised. Look at the place where they laid him! But go tell his disciples and Peter that he goes ahead of you into Galilee. You will see him there just as he told you."[533]
>
> And after they left, they fled from the tomb, for trembling and panic[534] seized them. And they said nothing to anyone because they were afraid.[535]

Three days in the tomb reflects the Jewish belief that the soul remained in the vicinity of the tomb for three days following burial.

The account contradicts our expectations for several reasons, most clearly because the women do not actually see Jesus, but a young man usually assumed to be an angel. Moreover, there is no sense of reassurance—the women flee the tomb in panic, too frightened to speak of their experience. Later manuscripts of the gospel of Mark append several spurious endings designed to improve on the original conclusion, a conclusion many readers apparently found to be theologically deficient.

---

[533] Contradicting Acts 1:4 where the disciples are ordered to stay in Jerusalem.

[534] Another occurrence of *εκσταασις*, which I have rendered *panic*. The Greeks believed the sight of the nature divinity Pan induced irrational fear, hence our word.

[535] Mark 16:1-8.

The writers of Matthew and Luke were also dissatisfied with Mark's ending and set about repairing it, introducing a number of new difficulties in the process. Matthew appropriates the youth's words from Mark,[536] but in his retelling the women are not struck silent from fear but run joyfully to inform the apostles that Jesus has risen, being met by Jesus on the way.[537] Matthew's expansion has the eleven remaining apostles go to Galilee where they receive the commission to make disciples of all nations, but, we are told, "*some doubted.*"[538]

The doubt of some of the apostles clearly troubled the early church—the resurrection and glorification of Jesus was already the keystone in the arch of Christian belief as Paul explains to the Corinthians: "If Christ has not been raised, your faith is useless. You are still in your sins and those who have fallen asleep in Christ are truly dead. If in this life only we have hoped in Christ, we alone among all men are the most pathetic. But now Christ has been raised from the dead, the beginning of the harvest of those who have fallen asleep in death."[539]

When Luke set about removing the last element of doubt about the reality of Jesus' resurrection, he created a startling narrative shift: the appearances of the risen Christ begin to take on the characteristics of classic ghost stories. Prince, who has published a comparison of the features of Luke's account with classical ghost stories, finds the stories in Luke incorporate a mixture of classical features and concludes, "the method at work in Luke 24 is an attempt to disorient the reader in order to reconfigure the traditions known to the author and reader in light of the disciples' extraordinary experience of the resurrected Jesus."[540] It appears to me that this conclusion begs the questions of how

---

[536] Matthew 28:5-7.
[537] Matthew 28:9-10.
[538] Matthew 28:17.
[539] 1 Corinthians 15:17-20.
[540] Prince, *Journal for the Study of the New Testament* 29:297.

extraordinary ghost stories seemed in antiquity—ghost stories are extraordinary by definition—and whether the disciples were any more confused than moderns when ghosts exhibited contradictory traits, being physical and yet not physical. In fact, Prince cites a number of examples of ghosts that were corporeal but changed appearance at will, exhibiting a well-known spectral tendency to polymorphism, and engaged in various physical activities including sexual intercourse.[541] In her discussion of the spirits of the dead in ancient Egypt, Adams concludes, "Textual allusions or inferences would seem to point in favour of both of these visible types of manifestations of the dead [*spirit* and *shadow*, my note] as being totally human in form."[542]

Few ancient people appear to have believed that the physical body would persist after death or be restored to life without recourse to magic. Yet the disembodied dead could talk, walk, eat and drink, and food offerings and libations were brought to tombs even in cases in which the body had been cremated—following his self-immolation, Peregrinus was reported to be seen walking around dressed in white.[543] It would appear the dead could exist in various modes or states (to use modern terminology) and could change modes at will. The phantom or *ειδωλον* (eidōlon)—from *ειδος*, *what is seen*, a *form* or *shape*—is the reflected image of an eternal reality, the *ψυχη* (psuchē), or *soul*. The phantom, which is the reflection of a deathless entity, could be considered more real than the corruptible body.[544]

What the earliest Christians believed is not entirely clear. A text adduced as prophetic[545] is quoted in Acts: "my flesh will dwell in hope…because you will not abandon my soul in Hades or

---

541 Ibid, 294.

542 Adams, *Current Research in Egyptology 2006*, 3.

543 Lucian, *On the Death of Peregrinus*, XXXXX

544 Riley, *Resurrection Reconsidered: Thomas and John in Controversy*, 49.

545 Psalm 16:9-10.

allow your Holy One to see corruption."[546] "My flesh will dwell in hope" (*η σαρξ μου κατασκηνωσει επ' ελπιδι*) presents us with a curious verb, *κατασκηναω*, based on *σκηνη* (skēnē), *tent.* It means *to encamp*, but is also used of birds alighting in trees. The body is seen as a tent in which the soul temporarily shelters, but the gist of the passage suggests that the body, or some form of body, would be preserved. Paul taught that there are "heavenly bodies"—*σωματα επουρανια*—which seem to be the same as a "spiritual body" (*σωμα πνευματικον*).[547]

The longest of the gospel stories concerns the stranger that two disciples meet on the road to Emmaus. As they walk with him, they repeat the details of the story of the women at the tomb and the vision of angels. Jesus, who they have been prevented from recognizing, then explains all the prophecies relating to himself in the Old Testament. Finally, as they eat the evening meal together, Jesus blesses the bread, breaks it, and hands it to them. The account of the appearance comes to this jarring conclusion, a conclusion particularly unsettling because of the tight association between invisibility and magic: "Their eyes were opened and they recognized him and he became invisible to them."[548] The disciples are vouchsafed a fleeting glimpse of the real Jesus.

This is the only specific mention of disappearance in connection with the resurrection—*και αυτος αφαντος εγενετο απ' αυτων*, "and he became invisible to them"—and the only occurrance of *αφαντος* (aphantos) in the New Testament. The preposition *απο* (apo) in the construction *απ' αυτων* is often used with verbs of concealment and separation, and could be taken to imply that Jesus' manifestation became invisible to them *as he left*, i.e., dematerialized in some way. The Greek magical papyri preserve this spell: "Arise, demon from the realm below...whatever I may

546 Acts 2:27.

547 1 Corinthians 15:40,44.

548 Luke 24:31.

command of you, I, [Name],[549] in that way obey me...if you wish to become invisible, just smear your forehead with the mixture and you will be invisible for however long you want."[550] The wording of the spell, *αφαντος γενεσθαι*: "to become invisible," duplicates the phraseology of Luke's story.

Luke was not unaware of the ghostly nature of this story. Indeed, the next account he relates appears designed to prove that the stranger on the road to Emmaus was not a ghost:

> But while they were talking about these things, he stood in their midst and said to them, "Peace be with you!" But they were alarmed and became afraid, thinking they were seeing a spirit. And he said to them, "Why are you terrified, and why do doubts arise in your hearts? Touch me and see, because a spirit does not have flesh and bones as you see I have." And saying this, he showed them his hands and feet.
>
> But even in their joy they did not believe him, and while they were wondering, he said to them, "Do you have anything here to eat?" And they gave him a piece of fish. And he took it and ate it in front of them.[551]

In this passage Jesus proves his corporeal nature to his disciples by having them touch him and by eating food in their presence. But the disciples wonder—as well they might—how a body of flesh and bones has suddenly appeared from nowhere. A rather similar case is related in Apuleius' story of the miller slain by a crone who turns out to be a ghost.[552] Of this story, Ogden observes, "The fact that the ghost could touch the miller's arm

---

[549] The Greek *ο δεινα* (ho deina), which I translate [*Name*], is a placeholder indicating where the name of the magician or the subject of the incantation is to be inserted into the text as the occa-sion requires. The term is very common in the spell books.

[550] Preisendanz, *Papyri Graecae Magicae*, I, 14.

[551] Luke 24:36-43.

[552] Apuleius, *Metamorphosis* IX, 29-31.

suggests that it had a solid form, but the fact that it could then disappear from a locked room suggests, perplexingly, that by contrast it was ethereal."[553]

The 4th century church historian Eusebius quotes an ancient variant of the Emmaus story: *εφη αυτοις λαβετε ψηλαφησατε με και ιδετε οτι ουκ ειμι δαιμονιον ασωματον*, "He said, take, touch me and see that I am not a disembodied demon..."[554] "Demon" is a common word for "ghost" in magical works and literature of the era, but in this context might reflect a Christian belief that ghosts were evil spirits pretending to be dead people. The textual variant quoted by Eusebius is of great antiquity. An epistle of Ignatius, written at the beginning of the 2nd century preserves it verbatim:

> For I know and I believe him to have been in the flesh after the resurrection, when he came to those with Peter and said to them, "Take, touch me and see that I am not a bodiless demon,"[555] and immediately they touched him and believed...but after the resurrection he ate and drank with them as made of flesh, although spiritually united with the Father.[556]

Ignatius' explanation hardly clears up the problem of the ghost, however. Jesus is *ως σαρκικος*, "as made of flesh," *καιπερ πνευματικως ηνωμενος τω πατρι*, "although spiritually united with the Father." One suspects that, like Paul, Ignatius is having his cake and eating it too. In any case, the disembodied demon/ghost logion "is clearly a free saying with a long history" known to Ignatius, Jerome, who believed it came from the lost *Gospel According to the Hebrews*, and Origen, cited in its Latin version,

---

[553] Ogden, *Night's Black Agents: Witches, Wizards and the Dead in the Ancient World*, 70.

[554] Eusebius, *Ecclesiastical History* III, 36.

[555] *λαβατε ψηλαφησατε με και ιδετε οτι ουκ ειμι δαιμονιον ασωματον*, "take, touch me and see that I am not a bodiless demon..."

[556] Ignatius, *Ad Smyrnaeos*, 3.

"Non sum demonium incorporeum." Riley concludes, "Both Luke and Ignatius have drawn on a common source. Their source sought to demonstrate a material resurrection body by means of physical proofs."[557]

Interestingly, Jesus' appearances tend to occur at night or in the intervals between day and night, i.e., "between times" typically associated with works of sorcery.[558] It is clear from the frequent mention of lamps in the magical papyri that night was the propitious time for magic. On this feature of the magician's work, Eitrem noted,

> Lamp or lantern magic (Lampenzauber) plays a major role here as generally in Egyptian magic—for light, the nocturnal sun, was something to be exploited. The night with its horde of dead spirits and eerie ways—the night through which the sun god navigated in his vessel to reach the east through the dark kingdom of the underworld while the moon shone or the heavens were starry—offered the magician the best opportunity for exercising his art or arts.[559]

The nocturnal workings of the magicians were, in part, a simple reflexion of physiology: "In general the association between sleep, death, dreams, and night was tight."[560] Matthew clearly considered dreams to be of supernatural origin,[561] and the world of the New Testament, a world before the glow of artificial light nearly banished darkness, was a world pullulating with works of sorcery. Ancient sources preserve terms such as *νυκτιπλανος*, *roaming by night*, and *νυκτοπεριπλανητος*, *wandering around by night*, that refer to the activities of magicians. "Alongside public

---

[557] Riley, *Resurrection Reconsidered: Thomas and John in Controversy*, 95-96.

[558] Matthew 28:1; Mark 16:2; Luke 24:29; John 21:4.

[559] Eitrem, *Magika Hiera*, 176.

[560] Ogden, *Greek and Roman Necromancy*, 77.

[561] Matthew 2:12, 19, etc.

Dionysiac festivals there emerge private Dionysos mysteries. These are esoteric, they take place at night, access is through an individual initiation, *telete*."[562] "It seems that the magos had a little bit of everything—the bacchantic (i.e. ecstatic) element, the initiation rites, the migratory life, the nocturnal activeties."[563]

Jesus' nocturnal appearances in the gospel of John retain this spectral quality. Twice Jesus appears in the disciples' midst even though the doors are locked—the verb *κλειω* (kleiō) means *to lock, to shut with a key*—*κλεις* (kleis), *key*. Translations that render the verb as simply *to shut* fail to fully convey the idea that the doors were locked, not merely closed, and that in spite of that fact, Jesus "came and stood in their midst."

> So being the evening of that day, the first of the week, and the doors having been locked where the disciples were for fear of the Jews, Jesus came and stood in their midst and said to them, "Peace to you!" and having said this, showed his hands and side to them. Consequently the disciples rejoiced at seeing the Lord.
>
> And after eight days his disciples were again indoors and Thomas was with them. Jesus came, the doors having been locked, and stood in their midst and said, "Peace to you!"
>
> Then he said to Thomas, "Put your finger here, and look at my hands, and reach out your hand and stick it into my side, and be not unbelieving, but believing."
>
> Thomas exclaimed, "My Lord and my God!"
>
> Jesus said to him, "You have seen me and believed. Happy are those who not having seen yet believe."[564]

---

[562] Burkert, *Greek Religion: Archaic and Classical*, 291.

[563] Luck, *Witchcraft and Magic in Europe: Ancient Greece and Rome*, 104.

[564] John 20:19-20, 26-29.

In these various manifestations Jesus exhibits traits of a *revenant*, an embodied ghost that appears once or for a brief period of time following the death of the subject[565] and performs bodily functions such as speaking and eating, displays pre-mortem wounds, is associated with an empty tomb, and vanishes suddenly without leaving any physical trace, all of which are characteristics noted by Debbie Felton, who has produced a particularly productive analysis of the ancient Greco-Roman ghost story.[566] As noted by Finucane, "...late classical tradition attributed various activities to ghosts, such as informing, consoling, admonishing, and pursuing, the living."[567] Vermeule's observation regarding ghosts is pertinent to Jesus' appearances: "wounding the flesh means wounds in the shade below..."[568] Celsus noted that after he died, Jesus appeared only to his own followers, "and even then as a ghost" (*και ταυτα σκιαν*).[569] The Greek *σκια*, *shadow*, is used in other contexts in a magical sense as discussed in a subsequent chapter.

It is well known that people of antiquity thought certain classes of the dead particularly likely to become ghosts: the *αωρος* (aōros), the *prematurely dead*, the *αγαμος* (agamos), the *unmarried*, the *αταφος* (ataphos), the *unburied*, and the *βιαιοθανατος* (biaiothanatos), the *dead by violence*. It is clear that Jesus could be numbered among at least three of these groups, all of whom share a commonality identified by Johnston: "Those who died before completing life were understood to linger between categories, unable to pass into death because they were not really finished with life."[570] A person who fell into one or more of the categories mentioned above was considered *ατε-*

[565] Evans, *Field Guide to Ghosts*, 19.
[566] Felton, *Haunted Greece and Rome*, 7, 14, 17, 23-26, 28.
[567] Finucane, *Ghosts: Appearances of the Dead and Cultural Transformation*, 25
[568] Vermeule, *Aspects of Death in Early Greek Art and Poetry*, 49.
[569] Origen, *Contra Celsum* III, 22.
[570] Johnston, *Restless Dead: Encounters Between the Living and the Dead in Ancient Greece*, 149.

λεστος (atelestos), *unfulfilled.* Based on 1st century belief, Jesus had all the makings of an angry, restless ghost.

It is now apparent that in at least some cases even an aborted or miscarried fetus could be used as a power source for binding spells. Although such use "is a new form of curse" not previously noted in the extant magical papyri, its absence "teaches us that the magical papyri, while immensely rich documentation for ritual practices in Roman Egypt, should not be taken as in any way exhaustive."[571] A recently published analysis of burials that include the presence of nails as apotropaic devices concludes, "a considerable percentage of the nails discussed here derive from infants' burials; infants are one of the categories of particularly dangerous dead."[572]

It is possibly significant that the Greek of Luke's gospel reveals a higher social register than that of Matthew or Mark—the historiographic preface to Luke's gospel, in keeping with official histories of the era, "indicates that the author has done extensive research."[573] If that is the case, it is not unlikely that the writer was also familiar with accounts of ghosts included in secular histories and the popular *paradoxa*, collections of uncanny and bizarre events that quite naturally included ghost stories. Phlegon of Tralles' story of the newly dead Philinnion who returns to have sex with her family's guest can be cited as a particularly famous example. A fragment of an ancient novel, included among the Greek magical papyri, alludes to a "handsome phantom"—*καλον ειδωλον*—that appears to a woman, apparently one of many, who had fallen for a 'phantastic' body.[574]

---

[571] Frankfurter, *Greek, Roman, and Byzantine Studies* 46: 42.
[572] Alfayé Villa, *Magical Practice in the Latin West*, 450.
[573] Ehrman, *The New Testament: A Historical Introduction to the Early Christian Writings*, 115.
[574] Preisendanz, *Papyri Graecae Magicae* XXXIV, 20-21.

The disappearance, return, and re-disappearance of the famous dead is not limited to the story of Jesus. Here, according to Plutarch, is how the career of Romulus was reported to have ended:

> ...Romulus was perceived to transform suddenly, and no part of his body or shred of clothing was seen. Some speculated that the senators, gathered in the temple of Hephaistos, rose up against him and killed him, and distributed pieces of his body to each to carry away hidden in the folds of his clothing. Others believe it was neither in the temple of Hephaistos, nor when the senators alone were present that he disappeared, but when he held an assembly around the so-called Marsh of the Goat. Suddenly wonders strange to describe occurred in the air, incredible changes, the light of the sun faded, and night fell, not gently or quietly, but with terrible thunder and gusts of wind driving rain from every direction, during which the great crowd scattered in flight, but the influential men huddled together with one another. When the tempest had passed and the sun broke out and the mass reassembled there was an anxious search for the king, but the men in power neither inquired into the matter nor investigated it, but loudly exhorted all of them to honor and worship Romulus as a man imbued with divinity, a god favorably disposed to them rather than a worthy king. The mass of people, believing these things, left rejoicing with high hopes to worship him. However, some bitterly contested the matter in a hostile way, and accused the patricians of foisting a stupid story on the people, being themselves the perpetrators of murder.
>
> At this point, a man from among the patricians, high born, reliable and most esteemed, a trusted intimate of Romulus himself, a colonist from Alba, Julius Proculus, went into the forum and swore by the most sacred emblems that as he traveled along the road he saw Romulus approaching him face to face, handsome and

> strong as ever, decked out in bright, shining armor. He himself, struck with fear at the sight, said, "O king, what were you thinking, subjecting us to unjust and evil accusations, the whole city an orphan in tears, weeping for having been abandoned?" Romulus answered, "It pleased the gods, Proculus, that I be with men for just so long a time, and having founded a city of superlative glory, dwell again in heaven. Farewell, and proclaim to the Romans that if they practice self-control with manliness, they will achieve the very heights of human power. And I will be your propitious daemon, Quirinus."[575]
>
> These things seemed believable to the Romans, based on the character of the man who related them and because of his oath, besides feeling some participation in divine destiny, equal to possession by the gods. No one objected, but all set aside suspicion and opposition and prayed to Quirinus, calling upon him as a god.
>
> ...Romulus is said to have been fifty-four years old, in the thirty-eighth year of his rule when he disappeared from among men.[576]

If Luke sought, consciously or not, to imitate the genre of the classical ghost story or other fabulous 'histories' in framing his accounts of Jesus' post-resurrection appearances, his technique might at the very least have set a precedent for the author of the gospel of John. Alternatively, of course, it is possible that the accounts of Luke and John were not influenced by Greco-Roman literary conventions, in which case we are confronted with a primitive New Testament tradition that contains examples of independently drawn ghost stories. A somewhat similar account

---

[575] *ευμενης εσομαι δαιμων* Κυρινος: "I will be your propitious daemon, Quirinus." Quirinus, the deified Romulus, together with Jupiter and Mars, forms the Capitoline Triad, the gods of the state cult. At a later date, the manly Quirinus and Mars were dropped in favor of Juno and Minerva.

[576] *Plutarch's Lives* I, 27.5—28.3, 29.7.

is given of the wonderworker Apollonius of Tyana, who urged his friends to distance themselves from him while he awaited trial before the paranoid Emperor Domitian and expect his appearance. "'Alive,' asked Damis, 'or how?' 'As I myself believe, alive, but as you will believe, risen from the dead.'" And after he makes his appearance still alive, this is the reaction of his disciples: "Whereupon Apollonius stretched out his hand and said, 'Take hold of me, and if I evade you, then I am indeed a ghost come to you from the realm of Persephone...But if I resist your touch, then you shall persuade Damis also that I am both alive and that I have not abandoned my body.' They were no longer able to disbelieve, but rose up and threw themselves on his neck and kissed him."[577]

The gospel of John implies that Jesus could disappear and reappear at will, although it does not specifically state that this ability was supernatural. After the healing at Bethzatha, Jesus "slipped away" (*εξενευσεν*) into the crowd,[578] and when the authorities sought to arrest him, Jesus "eluded their grasp," or literally "went out from their hand" (*εξηλθεν εκ της χειρος*).[579] After proclaiming that he was not yet destined to die, Apollonius "disappeared (*ηφανισθη*) from the courtroom."[580]

The polymorphic Jesus.

An additional point of interest is the gospel tradition that Jesus appeared post mortem in various physical forms. In addition to his appearance as a stranger on the road to Emmaus,[581] he appears on the shore of the Sea of Galilee, again initially unrecognized.[582] In the century that follows, the apocryphal gospels and

---

577 Philostratus, *The Life of Apollonius of Tyana* VII, 41, VIII, 12.

578 John 5:13.

579 John 10:39.

580 Philostratus, *Life of Apollonius of Tyana,* VIII, 5.

581 Luke 24:15-16.

582 John 21:4.

acts tell of additional appearances of Jesus in the form of "an old man, a youth, a boy...in the form of Paul...in the form of Andrew...To Drusiana he appears in the form of John, and of a young man...to John he appears as an old man, to James, who was with John, as a youth...and to a young married couple on their wedding night he appears as Thomas...The world of the apocryphal acts...is, in many ways, the Hellenistic world in which magic and sorcery were quite at home."[583] In the *Apocryphon of John*, a gnostic reworking of Revelation, Jesus appears to the apostle as a youth, an old man, and a servant; "there was a likeness with multiple forms in the light, and the forms appeared through each other and the likeness had three *forms* (ⲘⲘⲞⲢⲪⲎ)."[584]

According to Origen, Jesus was polymorphic even in life: "Jesus, being one, had more than one reflection (*επινοια*) and to those who saw him he did not appear in the same way...he was not always present *nor did he always appear* (*ουδε...αει εφαινετο*) even to the apostles themselves...before his Passion he was clearly visible to the multitude, although not always, but after his Passion he no longer appeared in the same way..."[585] To the pagan mind, there would be little to distinguish Jesus from any other divinity, Hermes or Hekate, for instance, who manifest in various forms, but perhaps that was exactly the point. "Another element common to Hellenistic magical beliefs was the power of a magician to turn himself...into another form, i.e., metamorphosis."[586]

> Klōthō and Lachesis and Atropos are you, Three-Headed, Persephonē and Megaira and Allēktō, Many Formed ..."[587]

---

[583] Goldin, *Aspects of Religious Propaganda in Judaism and Early Christianity*, 167-168.

[584] Wisse, *The Nag Hammadi Library in English*, 99.

[585] Origen, *Contra Celsum* II, 64-66.

[586] Goldin, 155.

[587] Preisendanz, *Papyri Graecae Magicae* IV, 2796-2798.

"Many Formed"—*πολυμορφε*—describes the expected attribute of many supernatural entities. One may compare Lucian's reference to Hekate, *πολυμορφον τι θεαμα*, "some polymorphous wonder," who changes from a woman to a bull to a puppy.[588] In the following spell—titled a "prayer" (*ευχη*) since *prayers* and *spells* are not distinguished in magical books—the moon goddess is *πανμορφον και πολυωνυμον*, "in every shape and many named":

> Prayer: I invoke you, double-horned Mēnē, in every shape and many named, whose form no one knows for certain except the One who made the entire world, Iaō, the One who formed you into the twenty-eight shapes of the world…"[589]

In the apocryphal *Acts of Thomas*, a demon is addressed as *ο πολυμορφος* (polumorphos), "the many-formed, who reveals himself as he wishes, but cannot change his nature…" In its next two occurrences, the same term, *polymorphos*, is used of the risen Jesus[590] and in the *Acts of John*, Jesus is described as "a unity within *many faces*"—*πολυπροσωπον*.[591] Lalleman, who has written a valuable discussion of polymorphism in the apocryphal Acts, points out that "Polymorphy in the narrow sense is not found in texts that are older than the [Acts of John] and the [Acts of Peter] (second century AD)"[592] but notes a tradition of shape-shifting in the spurious ending of the gospel of Mark which says, "Afterward, when two of them went walking into the country, *he appeared in another form*," *εφανερωθη εν ετερα μορφη*.[593]

---

588 Lucian, *The Lover of Lies*, 14.

589 Preisendanz, *Papyri Graecae Magicae* VII, 756-757.

590 *Acts of Thomas*, 44, 48, 153.

591 *Acts of John*, 91.

592 Lalleman, *The Apocryphal Acts of John*, 111.

593 Mark 16:12.

Not all early Christians believed in a bodily resurrection. The fragmentary gospel of Peter, mentioned previously, describes Jesus' death and departure rather differently from the canonical gospels:

> And the Lord cried out, "My power, O power, did you abandon me?"[594] And when he said this, he was taken up.[595]

What these discrepancies demonstrate is that during the formative period, Christian sects may have explained why Jesus died and what happened to him next in wildly divergent ways. Apologist scholars have proposed a number of supposedly objective criteria by which the resurrection stories can be positively judged as representing real history. But as Hector Avalos has pointed out in a devastating critique of such methods, the very same criteria could be applied with positive results to full-bodied apparitions of another gospel character, the Virgin Mary.[596] Yet oddly enough, no evangelical scholars seem to take sightings of Mary seriously, although many hundreds of witnesses over the course of centuries testify to the reality of such events.

---

594 *η δυναμις μου η δυναμις κατελειψας με*: "my power, O power, did you abandon me?"

595 *Gospel of Peter*, 5:5.

596 Avalos, *The End of Biblical Studies*, 191-194.

CHAPTER 5: MAGICAL PALESTINE

For many centuries Palestine has been a military and cultural crossroads, traversed by the Egyptians as well as their rivals to the north and east. Armies of Hittites, Assyrians and Babylonians marched through the troubled land on missions of conquest, momentary events in the millennia of war and commerce that stirred the great mixing bowl of the eastern Mediterranean, blending the material and the numinous, assimilating both the military forces of earthly kingdoms and the powers of a vast spirit realm, "a pleroma of divine forces."[597]

Whether the Israelites were invaders from Egypt, as claimed by the Old Testament, or an indigenous group already present within Canaan—the land between the Mediterranean Sea and the Jordan River—cannot be determined with certainty. Sometime in the Late Bronze Age, approximately 1200 years BCE, their sacred book tells that the Hebrews embarked on a genocidal campaign against various competing tribes, a protracted conflict justified on religious grounds. The book of Judges leaves a vivid record of this war of extermination:

> Then they utterly destroyed all in the city, both men and women, young and old, oxen, sheep, and asses, with the edge of the sword...And they burned the city with fire, and all within it; only the silver and gold, and the vessels of bronze and of iron, they put into the treasury of the house of the LORD...And all who fell that day, both men and women, were twelve thousand, all the people of Ai...And Joshua took Makkedah on that day, and smote it and its king with the edge of the sword; he utterly destroyed every person in it, he left none remain-

---

[597] Lesses, *Harvard Theological Review* 89:59.

> ing…and the LORD gave [Libnah] also and its king into the hand of Israel; and he smote it with the edge of the sword, and every person in it…and the LORD gave Lachish into the hand of Israel, and he took it on the second day, and smote it with the edge of the sword, and every person in it…And Joshua passed on with all Israel from Lachish to Eglon…and every person in it he utterly destroyed…Then Joshua went up with all Israel from Eglon to Hebron; and they assaulted it, and took it, and smote it with the edge of the sword, and its king and its towns, and every person in it; he left none remaining…[598]

To this litany of death the account happily adds the cities of Debir, and the towns of the Negeb where Joshua "left none remaining, but utterly destroyed all that breathed as the LORD God of Israel commanded," and to those glories were soon added the cities of Gaza and Goshen,[599] followed by a long list of others. What survivors remained the Israelites put to forced labor.[600] Aware that religions of truth are invariably supported by falsified histories, one might grant the possibility that the genocidal frenzy partially described above may have been more a priestly wish list[601] than a factual account. In any event, we are on historically solid ground when the Old Testament concedes,

> …the people of Israel dwelt among the Canaanites, the Hittites, the Amorites, the Perizzites, the Hivites, and the Jebusites; and they took their daughters to themselves for wives, and their own daughters they gave to their sons; and they served their gods.[602]

---

[598] Joshua 6:21, 24, 8:25, 10:28, 30-32, 34-36 (RSV).
[599] Joshua 10:38, 40-43.
[600] Judges 1:28, 30, 33.
[601] Compare Psalm 137:9: "Happy shall he be who takes your little ones and dashes them against the rock!"
[602] Judges 3:5-6.

And learned their magic.

It is now suspected that the abominations of the Canaanites listed in Deuteronomy,[603] including child sacrifice by burning, "were most probably originally Israelite" practices.[604] This conclusion is supported by the story of Jephthah's daughter, vowed as a burnt offering,[605] and by the story of Isaac, who was to be offered up by burning.[606] The Old Testament contains abundant evidence of genocide, specifically including children, foundation sacrifices, and the offering of the firstborn.[607] Modern scholars are inclined to believe that the rhetoric against the 'abominations of the Canaanites' was designed to cover horrific practices among the Israelites themselves: "the Hebrew Bible hardly affords a unanimous voice on what distinguishes the domains of magic and religion, let alone how one is to recognize a Canaanite over against an Israelite."[608]

The previously mentioned Valley of Hinnom had unsavory associations that dated from the remote past; the area is the likely site where the apostate king Solomon built an altar to Moloch, a 'Canaanite' deity associated with child sacrifice by burning.[609] As pointed out by Schmidt, "Isa[iah] 30:33 clearly connects Yahweh and Tophet, and if no such connection was intended in this allusion to Assyria's destruction, then one would have expected some disclaimer to that effect. In any case, the sacrifice of the first born to Yahweh and the Molek sacrifice were possibly related, if not one and the same cult." It is possible "that Molek was Yahweh's chthonic aspect or an independent netherworld

---

[603] Deuteronomy 18:10-14.

[604] Lange, *Legal Texts and Legal Issues*, 398.

[605] Judges 11:31-35.

[606] Genesis 22:2.

[607] Exodus 22:29-30, Leviticus 27:28-29, Deuteronomy 2:34, Numbers 37:17-18, Joshua 6:21, 1 Kings 16:34, 2 Kings 16:3, 21:6, Psalm 106:38, Isaiah 57:5.

[608] Schmidt, *Magic and Ritual in the Ancient World*, 242.

[609] 1 Kings 11:4-8, 2 Kings 16:2-4, 2 Chronicles 28:1-4.

deity of the Yahwistic cult."[610] Römer has made a case that Moloch was the chthonic title of Yahweh, that passing infants through the fire, like human sacrifice in other contexts, was done for divinatory purposes, and that the pronunciation "molek" (Moloch) derived from a derogatory vocalization of 'melek' which was a title used of Yahweh[611]—the Hebrew מלך (m-l-k) can be read "Molek" (Moloch) or "melek," *king*, depending on the vowels supplied. After reviewing a number of Old Testament passages, particularly Ezekiel 20:26 (NIV), "I defiled them through their gifts—the sacrifice of every firstborn—that I might fill them with horror so they would know that I am the Lord," Mark Smith concludes, "child sacrifice was a Judean practice performed in the name of Yahweh."[612]

> Every stroke the Lord lays on them with his punishing club will be to the music of timbrels and harps as he fights them in battle with the blows of his arm. *Topheth* (תפתה) has long been prepared; it has been made ready for *the king* (מלך) [of Assyria, *my note*]. Its fire pit has been made deep and wide, with an abundance of fire and wood; *the breath of Yahweh, like a stream of burning sulfur* (נשמה יהוה כנחל גפרית בערה), sets it ablaze.[613]

In this passage the נשמה (neshamah), *breath*, of Yahweh becomes "a hot wind kindling a flame,"[614] directed against Yah-

---

[610] Schmidt, *Magic and Ritual in the Ancient World*, 248-249.

[611] Römer, "Les Interdits des Practiques Magiques et Divinatoirs dans le Livre de Deutéronomie (Dt 18,9-13)" in *Magie et Divination Dans Les Cultures De L'Orient*, 77-87.

"J'ai essayé de monter ailleurs que la pronunciation 'molek' provient d'une vocalisation pejorative de 'melek' qui n'est rien d'autre dans ce contexte qu'un titre pour Yahvé…(77-78).

[612] Smith, *The Early History of God: Yahweh and Other Deities in Ancient Israel*, 132.

[613] Isaiah 30: 32-33, *NIV* with slight modification.

[614] Brown, Driver & Briggs, *Hebrew-English Lexicon*, 675.

weh's rival, the *king* (melek) who will be cast into the *tophet*, the sacrificial pit. "In this text there is no offense taken at the tophet, the precinct of child sacrifice."[615] Regarding the "two witnesses," Revelation says "and if anyone wants to do them harm, *fire issues forth from their mouths* (πυρ εκπορευεται εκ του στοματος αυτων) and consumes their enemies."[616] Similarly, from the magical papyri, "I am the headless demon...strong, who has the deathless fire...I am the one *whose mouth utterly consumes by fire* (ου το στομα καιεται δι'ολου), I am he who begets and destroys..."[617]

Long after the reign of Solomon, the Judean king Josiah led a violent religious reformation movement during which the altars and furnishings of the 'foreign' gods were destroyed, their priests killed, and the grounds of their holy sites desecrated by the burning of human bones.[618]

Magicians in the Old Testament.

Wonder-workers are featured with some frequency in Hebrew scripture, but the exact details of their performances—which are very rarely described—are a matter of dispute. In any case, Grabbe's observations would appear to apply generally to any period in the thousand years leading up to Jesus' era:

> The esoteric arts were widely practiced...What we today would call "magic" was also a widespread feature of popular religion in antiquity...however, we have to be careful what we are talking about: in many cases it represented a perfectly respectable craft, such as healing and exorcism...Exorcism and control of the spirit world

---

[615] Smith, *The Early History of God*, 133.
[616] Revelation 11: 3, 5.
[617] Preisendanz, *Papyri Graecae Magicae* V, 154-155.
[618] 2 Kings 22:1 – 23:25.

> were acceptable practice in Jewish society...such skills were a common feature of the miracle worker.[619]

That magical practice formed a part of normative Yahwist religion is hardly in question. A leper can be cleansed through a complex ritual which includes, but is not limited to, placing the blood of a sacrificial lamb on the tip of the right ear, the right thumb, and right great toe of the man to be healed, followed by an application of oil which must be poured into the palm of the left hand of the priest, and sprinkled seven times with the tip of the right forefinger, after which procedure the remaining oil is to be applied to the leper's right ear, thumb and great toe, and so on.[620] A house can be cleansed of leprosy by killing one of two small birds in a clay vessel over running water, and sprinkling the walls of the house seven times with bird blood using a wand of cedar and hyssop bound together with scarlet thread. The living bird is then set loose, presumably to carry away the disease.[621] Christian apologists who regard the elaborate rites of the Egyptian magical papyri as preposterous might gain some perspective on the matter through a careful reading of the divinely inspired spells and ritual magic of Leviticus. As Bohak points out in a comprehensive and indispensible work on Jewish magic, as far as divination was concerned, "the prohibitions here are not so much on certain *practices* as on certain *practitioners* ...it seems quite clear than neither magic nor divination are forbidden *per se*...elsewhere in the Hebrew Bible this implicit distinction is made patently clear..."[622] He then cites the example of Saul, who consults the "witch" of En Dor only after failing to get a response from authorized channels,[623] and the case of Ahaziah, rebuked for consulting Baal instead of Yahweh.[624]

---

[619] Grabbe, *Judaism From Cyrus to Hadrian*, II, 520.

[620] Leviticus 14: 10-20.

[621] Leviticus 14: 48-53.

[622] Bohak, *Ancient Jewish Magic: A History*, 14.

[623] 1 Samuel 28:6, 15.

[624] 2 Kings 1:2-6, 16.

According to Deuternomy, there were not only augurs and soothsayers, diviners and sorcerers, but also spell-casters, necromancers, mediums, and people who sacrificed their own children in "the land of promise."[625] The ubiquitous practice of magic in Palestine notwithstanding, an appreciation of its full extent and nature is impeded by several obstacles, the primary one being the perishable nature of most artifacts from the world before plastic. "Jews in the Talmudic period doubtless wrote amulets on papyrus, cloth, and other less durable materials, but apart from an Aramaic papyrus fragment from Oxyrhynchus these have not survived."[626] The preservation of organic material in Egypt is primarily the result of a single phenomenon: dry climate. The artifacts left to us in Palestine and adjacent areas are predominantly inorganic: stone, fired clay, metal, and scrolls if secured in jars and concealed in desert caves. Nevertheless, some such artifacts have survived, including two silver amulets that put the priestly blessing[627] to apotropaic use. These amulets, discovered in a tomb dating from the Second Temple era, are dated to the 7th or 6th century BCE.[628] Besides the inevitable loss of perishable materials, "much of the magical activity was conducted orally,"[629] and could leave no tangible record unless the oral tradition of magic were eventually written down. *Amulets*, from לחש (lachash), meaning *whisper*, *incantation*, are mentioned in Isaiah and the textual evidence suggests the presence of "a regular profession of enchanter."[630]

Regarding the contention that ancient Palestinian Judaism was 'contaminated' by the magical practice of neighboring peoples, Naveh and Shaked have this to say:

---

[625] Deuteronomy 18:9-14.

[626] Schürer, *The History of the Jewish People in the Age of Jesus Christ*, III, Part I, 355.

[627] Numbers 6:22-27.

[628] Bohak, *Ancient Jewish Magic*, 30.

[629] Ibid, 66.

[630] Spoer, *Journal of Biblical Literature* 23: 97.
Compare Isaiah 3:3, 20, Jeremiah 8:17, Ecclesiastes 10:11.

> The *Hekhalot* literature uses the techniques of magic in order to acquire secret knowledge concerning the heavenly world...This literary tradition has its roots in Palestine. Some of its early manifestations are present in the Dead Sea Scrolls...Our present concern is however with the factual statement that magic was less prominently present in Palestine than in Babylonia, which proves to be wrong...Palestine and Mesopotamia had two separate traditions, each with its own style and set of formulae. When however formulae from the two geographical areas converge, it may be invariably established the origin of the theme is Palestinian, rather than Babylonian ...Jewish incantation texts very often make use of biblical verses. This phenomenon is clearly visible in all varieties of Jewish magic, in the Mesopotamian bowls, the Palestinian amulets, as well as the magic material from the Cairo Geniza, and is also widely attested in late mediaeval and modern Jewish magical practice.[631]

As a general rule, magic appears to have been a characteristic of the lower social strata. In the past as today, the members of the higher social orders worked their will through wealth and influence and accordingly felt less need of recourse to supernatural agencies, at least while things were going well. However, as the case of Saul and the ghost caller at En Dor illustrates, the powerful resorted to magic if nothing else availed. The members of the lower classes in antiquity were as a rule not only poor, but also illiterate, so their beliefs and practices were not widely celebrated in writings by their own hand, writings that might have hypothetically survived to serve as sources for our enlightenment. As a result, the magical workings of common folk were unlikely to leave a written record or a permanent residue of evidence for archaeologists to recover. As pointed out by Bo-

---

[631] Naveh & Shaked, *Magic Spells and Formulae: Aramaic Incantations of Late Antiquity*, 19-22.

hak, if magical ritual consisted primarily of verbal activity with some manipulation of common materials, but no writing, it would leave no trace of its existence, a situation compounded by the absence of amulets used in exorcism during this period.[632]

Additionally, the magical practices of the popular religion among the Israelites were in tension with the official cult, which was generally identified with the temple and its priesthood. Unapproved practices were periodically suppressed, at times violently, and associated texts, implements, and sacred sites were destroyed, establishing a practice of vandalism that became Christian policy towards pagan documents and temples. The documents of the official cult, our Old Testament, tend to seriously minimize disapproved popular practices and even when mentioned little or no description is provided. Nevertheless, the evidence for magical practice in the Middle East is so pervasive that a recently published study of an Aramaic adjuration of Beelzebub from the Dead Sea Scrolls states, "The era of the Second Temple was a magical time. A wealth of indirect evidence proves that, on the popular level, magic was often of greater practical significance than were many aspects of the Law of Moses...The [Dead Sea] scrolls include more magic texts than was previously realized even by the few privy to the whole collection...A rich literature of magic and incantation texts has survived from Akkadian sources, and, mutatis mutandis, its formulas and phraseology can sometimes be recognized in the magic texts produced during the long period when Aramaic dominated Mesopotamia."[633]

The activities of popular belief are nearly always under-represented in official histories. How many modern denominational histories mention that many church members regularly consult horoscopes? Certainly many Christians must, or why else would nearly every newspaper in an overwhelmingly Christian country

---

632 Bohak, *Ancient Jewish Magic: A History*, 116-118, 137-138.

633 Penny & Wise, *Journal of Biblical Literature* 113: 627-629.

contain a section devoted to them? How many Christians say, "Bless you!" if someone sneezes, or sit for tarot readings, or knock on wood, play with the once ubiquitous Ouija boards, cross their fingers for luck, avoid black cats, or engage in any number of other superstitions? And where in the official histories might one find documentation of any of these very ordinary events? The *locus classicus* of necromancy in the Old Testament is related as a detail of the downfall of a king and his dynasty, not as part of a story about one of the thousands of commoners who must have made similar inquiries of spirit mediums.

Evidence for the true extent of magical practice in the remote past is therefore necessarily thin due to the ravages of time and climate, destruction due to suppression, the secrecy which often accompanied magical ritual—and may even have been understood as a condition for its success—and the fact that the sheer banality of much of what we might deem magical elicited little or no mention. The official proscription of magical practitioners in Israel was almost certainly an incentive for men interested in practicing de facto magic to represent their activities as something else. Nevertheless, the evidence for magic, exorcism in particular, is fairly extensive. Twelftree, for example, cites the (1) Qumran scrolls, (2) writers such as Josephus and Justin Martyr, (3) rabbinical references, and (4) magical bowls as evidence for the widespread practice of exorcism among the Jews.[634]

Official history, meant to present individuals and their cultures in the best light, typically censors unwanted details. The result is a shaping of narrative like that visible in the New Testament: the magical details of exorcisms reported by Mark are censored in the gospel of Matthew, and accounts of exorcism itself are completely absent from the gospel of John. That a similar pro-

---

[634] Twelftree, *A Kind of Magic: Understanding Magic in the New Testament and its Religious Environment*, 63-67.

cess occurred during the composition and transmission of the Old Testament is not unlikely. "Magic flourished among the Jews despite strong and persistent condemnation by the religious authority. Healing by this means was especially common, sickness being widely diagnosed as caused by malevolent invading spirits which could only be driven out by the appropriate incantations and spells...The story of how Tobias, on the advice of the angel Raphael, expelled the demon who threatened to ruin his wedding night, must surely reflect actual, contemporary magical practice (Tobit 6:3-9, 17-18; 8:1-3)...Josephus, Ant. Viii 2, 5 (46-48), gives a sharply observed account of an exorcism, which he himself witnessed, performed by a Jew called Eleazar in the presence of Vespasian and his officers."[635]

Various sorts of miracle workers are mentioned in the Old Testament, but their job descriptions are never specifically detailed. Instead, we are left to feel our way through the imperfect evidence of etymologies, words in cognate languages and the context of the Hebrew and Aramaic terms themselves. In fact, the Hebrew Old Testament presents the reader with a profusion of terms related to magic and its practitioners. The stem כשף (k-sh-ph), depending on the vocalization, may be read kesheph, *magic*, kashshaph, *magician*, or kashaph, *to pronounce a spell.* The מכשפים (mekashshaphim) are the sorcerers of Exodus[636] who turn their rods into serpents. The Egyptian sorcerers are accompanied by "wise men," חכמים (khakamim)—from חכם (khakam), *wise*—although it is probable that the terms for "wise man" and "sorcerer" were synonymous, "sorcerer" being a definition of "wise man." That the "wise men" were magicians of some sort is clear from the derogatory use of חכמים (khakamim) in Isaiah: "who foils the signs of false prophets and

[635] Schürer, *The History of the Jewish People in the Age of Jesus Christ*, III, Part 1, 342.

[636] Exodus 7:11.

makes fools of diviners, who overthrows the learning of the wise and turns it into nonsense."[637]

It is probable that the term מכשף (mekhasheph) derives from Sumerian kašapu, a type of sorcerer who brought misfortune in its many forms and was therefore "condemned by the government and subjected to severe penalties for carrying on [his] trade."[638] The feminine form, מכשפה, mekhashephah, is the "witch" of Exodus 22:17 (KJV)—"Thou shalt not suffer a witch to live"—historically one of the deadliest scriptural injunctions ever written.

The book of Daniel[639] lists several types of practitioners, the מכשפים (mekashshaphim), *sorcerers*, the אשפים (ashshaphim) —plural of אשף (ashshaph), *enchanter* or *conjurer*—and the חרטמים (khartummim), *magicians*—from חרטם (khartum), *magician*. The word חרטם, *magician*, is likely derived from the word חרט (kheret), *stylus*, reflecting the close association in the ancient mind between magic and writing, an association preserved even yet in the double meaning of "spell," and *grimoire*, derived from *grammar*. Similarly, אשף (ashshaph), *conjurer*, is almost certainly derived from אשפה (ashpah), *quiver* or *arrow case*. The connection becomes clear when read in the context of the time: "For the king of Babylon will stop at the fork in the road, at the junction of the two roads, to seek an omen: He will cast lots with arrows, he will consult his idols, he will examine the liver."[640]

The אשף (ashshaph) is an official who appears to have received official status and support, probably not unlike the astrologers who frequented the Reagan White House or the court magicians familiar to the Babylonians and Romans. It is generally

---

637 Isaiah 44:25 (NIV).

638 Davies, *Magic, Divination and Demonology*, 68.

639 Daniel 5:7,11.

640 Ezekiel 21:21 (NIV).

agreed that the Hebrew term is an Assyrian loan word (ešipu), and that it encompassed fortune telling as well as exorcism.

The קסם (qosem), *diviner* by sortilege, is often associated with the נביא (nabi), *prophet* as at Jeremiah 14:14 and 27:9 where false prophets are linked to diviners and other magical practitioners. It is possible that the קסמים (qosemim), *diviners*, foretold the future by lots, "seeking an oracle by arrows, according to an ancient custom of mixing arrows and letting one be taken out at random,"[641] whereas the prophets specialized in ecstatic states and trances.[642]

Finally, one must draw particular attention to the term נחש (nakhash), *serpent*, and the derived term לחש (lakhash), which depending on how it is vocalized, means *amulet*, or hissed *incantation*—or "whispered prayer"[643]—and מלחש (melakhesh), *charmer* of snakes.[644] The לחשים (lekhashim), of Isaiah 3:20, variously (mis)translated *armlets*, *ankle bracelets* or *earrings*, were in any case charms worn as amulets.[645] The diatribe against adulterous Israel contains a veiled reference to amulets worn as facial jewelry and necklaces: "Let her remove the adulterous look from her face and the unfaithfulness from between her breasts," a allusion that becomes clear as the text continues: "I will punish her for the days she burned incense to the Baals; she decked herself with rings and jewelry, and went after her lovers, but me she forgot, declares the Lord."[646]

Serpent imagery assumes importance in gnostic speculation based in part on the copper serpent made by Moses that by the

---

[641] Davies, *Magic, Divination and Demonology*, 45.
[642] Römer, *Magie et Divination dans les Cultures de l'Orient*, 78.
[643] Isaiah 26:16.
[644] Yahweh threatens the Israelites with snakes that cannot be charmed (Jeremiah 8:17) in a verse that combines the similar words for "charm" and "snake."
[645] Brown, Driver & Briggs, *Hebrew and English Lexicon*, 538.
[646] Hosea 2:2, 13 (NIV).

time of Hezekiah had received both a name, נחשתן, Nekhushtan, and adoration and was for that reason destroyed,[647] and in some traditions, the serpent that revealed knowledge becomes a hero. The use of serpent imagery in magic, the *ouroboros*, is well known. "Since the serpent represented an evil spirit, and even the devil, לחש (lakhash) came to mean a charm against any demon, and the מלחש (melakhesh) a charmer against any and every evil spirit..."[648]

Another category of magical practitioner that assumes major importance over time are the כשדים (kasdim), *Chaldeans*, generally regarded as court astrologers. By the time of Jesus, "Chaldean" or "Babylonian" had become a synonym for "magician" across the Greco-Roman world. "Abraham" becomes a name to conjure with in the magical works in part, no doubt, because Abraham came from Ur of the Chaldeans,[649] a source of Babylonian magic, even as Jesus as a child had allegedly gone to Egypt, another source of powerful magic. "The Jews were renowned throughout the Roman world for their skill in magic arts" and because of their contact with the Persians and Chaldeans, "served as the indirect means by which knowledge of certain formulæ spread throughout the area of the Dispersion."[650]

Only a few terms I have felt to be particularly relevant are explored here—happily a magisterial assessment of the evidence

---

[647] 2 Kings 18:4.
[648] Davies, *Magic, Divination and Demonology*, 52.
[649] Genesis 11:31; Acts 7:4.
[650] Guignebert, *The Jewish World In the Time of Jesus*, 240.

by Ann Jeffers is available.[651] However, as noted by Bohak, "most of these terms admit of no certain translation."[652]

Necromancy in the Old Testament.

Preeminent among the Hebrew terms for necromancy is **אוב** (ōb), a word that occurs in the expression **באל אוב**, (baal ōb), "ghost-master." The etymology of the word *ōb* is murky, but a case can be made for a reference to calling up ghosts by means of a pit into which libations were poured. By metonymy the term could apply to the pit itself, the ghost that emerged from it, or the necromancer who called the spirit up.

A related term, **שאל אוב** (shoel ōb), is generally translated "one who consults an ōb." The Greek translation of the Hebrew bible, the *Septuagint*, regularly translates ōb as *εγγαστραμυθος* (engastramuthos), a word that, if defined solely by its components, means "belly speech." Some translators render it by its Latin equivalent, "ventriloquist," perhaps in an attempt to explain the calling up of ghosts as the trick of voice projection. However, there is little evidence in the Hebrew Bible or in any other source that suggests that the ancients thought mere voice projection was the explanation for necromancy.

A term which often occurs with *ōb*, **ידעני** (yiddoni), is clearly derived from a stem meaning *to know*—**ידע** (yada). Davies conjectured that the word pair is a hendiadys, meaning basically "a ghost that knows."[653] Jeffers agrees, noting "the spirit so return-

---

651 Jeffers, "Diviners, Magicians and Oracular Practitioners," in *Magic and Divination in Ancient Palestine and Syria*, 25-123.

Davies' *Magic, Divination, and Demonology*, 40-59, contains a still useful discussion of nearly all the terms used for magic in the Hebrew Bible.

652 Bohak, *Ancient Jewish Magic: A History*, 15.

653 Davies, *Magic, Divination and Demonology*, 89.

ing is knowledgeable and therefore able to answer the questions of the inquirer."[654] Schmidt also concludes that the yiddoni are "ghosts who have superior knowledge of the affairs of the living."[655] After a survey of the interpretive options, Tropper says the term ōb "signifies persons rather than objects," likely "deified ancestral spirits" that were conjured up in necromantic rites for interrogation about the future.[656]

Regarding the Akkadian counterpart to the ritual partially described in 1 Samuel 28, during which Saul consults the ghost of Samuel, Hoffner notes "the wholly chthonic orientation of the procedure," which included nocturnal performance, silver (the color of the moon), and the use of black sacrificial animals.[657] In the Old Testament account,[658] Saul goes by night to the woman —"a mistress of necromancy"[659] with the request that she bring up the ghost of the prophet Samuel. Saul had previously killed such practitioners, driving them from "the land." Regarding the account of Saul and the "witch" of En Dor, Lewis notes "that necromancy was widespread throughout Israelite society and not just in Canaanite enclaves...the Deuteronomistic legal material...attests to laws against necromancy from which we infer that such practices existed and were flourishing to the extent that they were considered a threat to what emerges as normative Yahwism.[660]

The Old Testament has little to say about the details of necromantic procedure, perhaps because they were already familiar. However, hints appear here and there. Isaiah seems to connect the summoning of ghosts with times of national distress—just as in the case of Saul: "And I will encamp against you round

---

[654] Jeffers, *Magic and Divination in Ancient Palestine and Syria*, 172.
[655] Schmidt, *Israel's Beneficent Dead*, 154.
[656] Tropper, *Dictionary of Deities and Demons in the Bible*, 1524-1530.
[657] Hoffner, *Theological Dictionary of the Old Testament*, I, 132.
[658] 1 Samuel 28:7.
[659] Brown, Driver and Briggs, *Hebrew and English Lexicon*, 15.
[660] Lewis, *Cults of the Dead in Ancient Israel and Ugarit*, 113, 126.

about, and will besiege you with towers and I will raise siege-works against you. Then deep from the earth you will speak, from low in the dust your words shall come; your voice shall come from the ground like the voice of a ghost, and your speech shall whisper out of the dust.[661]

This reference from Isaiah may be compared with the instruct-tions in the *Sepher Ha-Razim* for the magician who wishes "to speak with the spirits." He is to go to a place of public executions "and call out there in a singsong, whimpering way." If his conjure is successful, he will see opposite him "a column of smoke."[662]

References to the practice of consulting ghosts are sprinkled throughout the Old Testament,[663] and the fact that there were laws against it indicates that it was both sufficiently frequent and widespread to cause concern to the gatekeepers of the official religion. And though the legal passages of the Hebrew Bible rail against necromancy, the Old Testament "does not attempt to discredit the efficacy of the practice."[664]

The tombs of the dead are well known in the Old Testament:

> At Hebron, the burial place of Sarah and Abraham,[665] the chiefs made a covenant[666] and Absalom paid his vows.[667] It was a "city of refuge"[668] and a city of the priests...[669] At Ramah, the burial place of Rachael,[670]

---

[661] Isaiah 29:3-4.
[662] Morgan, *Sepher Ha-Rasim*, 39.
[663] Leviticus 19:31, Deuteronomy 18:11, 1 Chronicles 10:19, Isaiah 8:19.
[664] Lewis, *Cults of the Dead in Ancient Israel and Ugarit*, 117.
[665] Genesis 23:19.
[666] 2 Samuel 5:3.
[667] 2 Samuel 15:7, 12.
[668] Joshua 20:7.
[669] Joshua 21:11.

there was a holy stone upon her grave. On the grave of Deborah below Bethel there stood a tree known as *Allôn-bākhûth*, 'the holy tree of weeping.'[671] The burial place of Miriam was *kadesh*, 'the sanctuary.'[672] Shechem, the burial place of Joseph,[673] was the site of a holy tree called "the oak of the oracle," or "the oak of the diviners,"[674] of a holy stone,[675] of an altar,[676] and of a temple.[677] It was also a city of refuge.[678] Of similar character as sanctuaries were probably the graves of the heroes Tola, Jair, Ibzan, Elon, and Abdon.[679]

The Book of Kings records with equal care the burial places of the kings of Judah. Ezek. 43:7-9 shows clearly that in his day these were seats of worship. The words "whoredom" and "abomination" that he applies to them are the ones that are commonly used by the prophets for the cult of strange gods...This change from "holy" to "unclean" can be explained only as due to a growing consciousness that the ancient sanctity of tombs was inconsistent with the sole authority of Yahweh...That this is the correct interpretation of the taboo is shown (1) by the fact that it is called "uncleanness for a spirit" (*nephesh*),[680] which shows that the uncleanness does not come from the corpse but from the spirit associated with it; (2) by the fact that priests, who are specially connected to the worship of Yahweh, are allowed to "defile

---

[670] Genesis 35:19; 1 Samuel 10:2; Jeremiah 31:15.

[671] Genesis 35:8.

[672] Numbers 20:1.

[673] Joshua 24:32.

[674] Genesis 12:6; Deuteronomy 11:30; Judges 9:37.

[675] Joshua 24:26.

[676] Genesis 12:7; 22:9.

[677] Judges 9:4, 46.

[678] Joshua 20:7.

[679] Judges 10:1-5; 12:8-15.

[680] Leviticus 21:1, 11; 22:4; Numbers 5:2; 6:6, 11; 9:6; Haggai 2:13.

> themselves for a spirit" only in a few exceptional cases,[681] and that nazarites are not allowed to defile themselves[682] at all.[683]

Other oblique references to a cult of the dead are also found. Jeremiah refers to cutting the flesh and hair as funerary rites and connects the practice to the service of foreign gods.[684] The bones of dead holy men were credited with miraculous power—a dead man who touched Elisha's bones was instantly raised[685]—and we find a passing mention of necromantic incubation, of those "who sit in tombs, and spend the night in secret places,"[686] a probable reference to "all night vigils in tombs, presumably in order to receive an oracle from the dead."[687]

There is evidence that necromantic procedure survived over an incredible period of time, spreading from ancient Mesopotamia to Palestine and Egypt[688] where evidence of such rites persists in the magical papyri. Faraone has argued that Greek necromancy, divining with the use of skulls and corpses, "originally evolved out of a Mesopotamian and Semitic cultural milieu":

> Various comments in the Mishnah show, moreover, that divination by skulls undoubtedly survived among the post-exilic Jews down into the late antique period. The Tractate Sanhedrin of the Babylonian Talmud, for example, discusses the two kinds of necromancer: "both

---

[681] Leviticus 21:1-4, 11.
[682] Numbers 6:6.
[683] Paton, *Spiritism and the Cult of the Dead in Antiquity*, 251-252.
[684] Jeremiah 16:6, 11-12.
[685] 2 Kings 13:20-21.
[686] Isaiah 65:4.
[687] Lewis, *Cults of the Dead in Ancient Israel and Ugarit*, 175.
[688] Ritner, "Necromancy in Ancient Egypt," *Magic and Divination in the Ancient World*, 89-96.

> him who conjures up the dead by soothsaying, and one who consults skulls."[689]

Although consulting the dead is mentioned as early as Homer's *Odyssey*, it is possible that "necromancy invaded the Graeco-Roman world from the Semitic Orient." Paton cites the practice of wallowing in the dust,[690] sitting in the dust,[691] and putting dust on the head[692] as a "symbolic act of communion with the dead."[693]

The discovery of "incantation bowls" dating from the early Christian era in the area of the Tigris-Euphrates has led to considerable speculation about what these vessels were thought to achieve. The spells are generally written in a descending spiral pattern from the rim to the bottom on the interior of the bowl and the vessel buried in an inverted position. At times pictures of demons are included, usually at the bottom of the bowl. Some have suggested that they are genie-in-the-bottle 'demon traps' that captured unwary spirits lured inside and held by the incantation. Others have proposed that they represent the evolution of skull necromancy, others that they are talismanic, meant to capture magical power and hold it in place. In any event, McCullough concluded that "the inscribed bowl was an innovation in magical technique which came into vogue only in the early Christian centuries" and further noted "its use by Christians, Jews, and Mandaeans indicates that its popularity was quite extensive."[694]

---

689 Faraone, *Mantikê: Studies in Ancient Divination*, 258, 277.

690 Jeremiah 6:26; Esther 4:3.

691 Isaiah 26:19; 47:1; 52:2; Job 2:8.

692 Joshua 7:6; 1 Samuel 4:12.

693 Paton, *Spiritism and the Cult of the Dead in Antiquity*, 150, 250.

694 McCullough, *Jewish and Mandaean Incantation Bowls*, xii-xv. Isbell, *Corpus of the Aramaic Incantation Bowls*, 14, rejects the 'demon trap' hypothesis, but appears to favor the notion of the bowls as substitutes for skulls.

Holy men and prophets.

The closest to a magical generalist in the Old Testament is the איש אלהים (ish elohim), the "man of God." The powers of the *ish elohim*, of which Elijah and Elisha are the preeminent examples, are wide ranging: he knows details of both the present and future,[695] he heals and causes disease,[696] he produces food by magic,[697] raises the dead,[698] calls down fire from heaven,[699] and spends forty days in the desert.[700] The New Testament parallels to the career of Jesus and the apostles are so obvious that they may be passed over for the present without further comment. It is essential to note, however, that "the most characteristic feature of the man of God…[is] his great powers,"[701] not his humanitarianism. Concerning the performance of powerful works by such "men of God", Bohak notes that

> …the range of techniques they employ to perform their feats is quite impressive: in some cases, a simple verbal command or a short prayer is all it takes; in others, they use bodily movements and gestures...and in many cases they use various implements, devices and materials, be it a garment, a staff, a plate with some salt, a piece of wood, a pinch of flour, or the water of the Jordan river ...in some cases it is God Himself who instructs Moses on which ingredients to use to perform miracles, be it some soot from a furnace to get a plague going (Ex 9.8-

Morony, *Prayer, Magic, and the Stars in the Ancient and Late Antique World*, 83-109, provides a discussion of the incantation bowls.

695 2 Kings 4:14-17.

696 2 Kings 5:3; 8:7-13; 5:25-27.

697 1 Kings 17:15-16.

698 1 Kings 17:19-24.

699 1 Kings 18:38.

700 1 Kings 19:4-8.

701 Bohak, *Ancient Jewish Magic*, 22.

10) or a piece of wood to cure a bitter water source (Ex 15.25).[702]

To the *ish elohim* may be added the חבר חבר (hōbēr-heber), or *spellcaster* who is proscribed in Deuteronomy along with other magical practitioners. Of this enigmatic figure, associated with knot tying as symbolic of magical binding, Jeffers says, "...the [hōbēr-heber] would be a person who binds his victims by the use of words, mutterings, incantations, curses...The translation 'spell-binders', or 'weaver of spells"' seems to me to convey best the idea of binding through oral activity."[703] Römer proposes that the term הבר הבר may have included magical protection from adverse spells, or counter-magic.[704]

The notion of magical binding, well attested in the New Testament, is discussed at some length in a subsequent chapter. However, the connection was noted over a century ago: "It is not impossible that Christ's words to the disciples, "What things soever you shall *bind* on earth shall be *bound* in heaven: and what things ye shall loose on earth shall be loosed in heaven" (Matt. xviii.18), were suggested by this magical practice, known in His time and in His country as in all times and lands."[705]

Binding was so fundamental to the practice of magic that representations of magical knots were included in Egyptian tombs and bound in the wrappings of mummies.[706]

The term נביא (*nabī*), "prophet," is used to designate a function of the "man of God" type. Abijah is such a prophet. He not only sees through the disguise of Jeroboam's wife, he foretells the death of her child as part of a curse against the males of

---

702 Ibid, 26.

703 Jeffers, *Magic and Divination in Ancient Palestine and Syria*, 32, 35.

704 Römer, *Magie et Divination*, 81.

705 Davies, *Magic, Divination, and Demonology*, 57.

706 Brier, *Ancient Egyptian Magic*, 88, 193-194.

Jeroboam's house.[707] A *nabī* "hears" events such as rain which is yet to fall,[708] and troops before they arrive[709] and performs healings at a distance,[710] ordering the leper Naaman to wash himself a magical seven times in the Jordan River. The *nabī* can strike a man with blindness,[711] pronounce a curse of death,[712] and his clothing possesses magical power,[713] all of which are duplicated in the works of power of Jesus and his apostles.

Regarding the list of evil practices of Manasseh in 2 Kings 21, an indictment that includes erecting altars to Baal, child sacrifice, divination, and consulting ghosts and familiar spirits, Grabbe remarks, "...this stereotyped list is a useful source for the types of things probably fairly widely practiced in Israel at one time or another."[714] The function of prophets in the Old Testament includes activities that millennia later are known functions of "cunning people" in other cultures, activities as relatively mundane as finding lost objects[715] or strayed animals.[716] The fact that such activities do not receive more attention in the books of the Old Testament is no more surprising than the omission of kitchen witches from the history of the Anglican Church.

The numerous parallels between Old Testament accounts and identical reports in the New Testament strongly support the contention that a common magical culture persisted both for a considerable span of time and over a significant area and that Jesus and the primitive Christians, particularly those with Jew-

---

[707] 1 Kings 14:6, 11-13.

[708] 1 Kings 18:41.

[709] 2 Kings 6:32.

[710] 2 Kings 5:8-14.

[711] 2 Kings 6:18.

[712] 1 Kings 1:17.

[713] 2 Kings 2:14.

[714] Grabbe, *Priests, Prophets, Diviners, Sages*, 124.

[715] 2 Kings 6:5-7.

[716] 1 Samuel 9:20.

ish roots, worked within that magical culture and employed its common techniques.

The *Sepher Ha-Razim.*

Regarding the era in which Jesus lived and in which early Christianity arose, Stone has this observation: "In general, the Hellenistic age was characterized by an interest in the occult, and magic played a great role in the world of that time. The Jews, it seems, were prominent among the magicians of this era, and there were considerable Jewish elements in Graeco-Roman magic."[717] We now have clear evidence that Jewish magicians of the time collected their spells in books.

The ספר הרזים, *Sepher Ha-Razim*, or *Book of Mysteries*, is a collection of Hebrew magical spells reconstructed by Mordecai Margalioth from fragmentary documents discovered in the Cairo *genizah*. Margalioth's original work appeared in 1966, and an English translation by Michael Morgan, the translation referenced in the present work, appeared in 1983.[718] Janowitz points out a number of similarities between the formulæ of the *Book of Mysteries* and the Greek magical books, including the organization of magical recipes, "swearing and adjuring" as magical ritual, the use of angelic helpers, recitations of hymns, and invocation of spirits of the dead that "were thought to linger near their graves."[719] The language of the *Sepher Ha-Razim*, "the thoughtful composition of a well-educated Jewish author," is

---

[717] Stone, *Scriptures, Sects and Visions: A Profile of Judaism from Ezra to the Jewish Revolts*, 82.

[718] It is likely that a further refinement of Margolioth's impressive work will emerge from the work of current scholars examining additional genizah fragments as well as later manuscripts. (Bohak, *Ancient Jewish Magic*, 170).

[719] Janowitz, *Icons of Power: Ritual Practices in Late Antiquity*, 85-95.

the work a man at home in the world of Greco-Egyptian magic; it likely dates from the 7th century.[720]

Characterized by Lapin as "a particularly baroque example of a shared cultural world,"[721] the spellbook is divided into seven sections, each corresponding to an angelic sphere of activity, each level associated with a list of angelic names the magician could invoke, 704 of them, more or less, in short, a seven-tiered magical bureaucracy. The seven heavens of the *Sepher Ha-Razim* "immediately reminds one of the many related discussions in ancient Jewish literature" as well as "Paul's enigmatic reference to a visit to the third heaven".[722] "The simple man, driven by his impulses and instructed by his authoritative Scriptures and by the tradition that angels exist…turns to these angels and spirits for assistance. He has been reassured many times that the Lord is nigh; but angels and ministers of grace, and demons, are nigher."[723] The assistants who come to the aid of magician using the *Sepher Ha-Razim* are never characterized as anything but angels: "For him they are all not divinities but angels, in other words, ministers and emissaries of the Supreme God. The magician is very careful not to slip. Even Helios...is not the Greek sun god for the magus but only the 'angel Helios.'"[724] Of the Greek magical papyri Ciraolo notes, "After the gods, the παρεδροι [*assistants*, my note] are most frequently identified as αγγελοι [*angels*, my note] and δαιμονες [*demons*, my note] of an unspecified character."[725]

[720] Bohak, *Ancient Jewish Magic: A History*, 173-175.

[721] Lapin, *Religious and Ethnic Communities in Later Roman Palestine*, 14.

[722] Bohak, *Ancient Jewish Magic*, 172.

Paul's boast of having ascended to the third heaven, "paradise," appears in 1 Corinthians 12:2-4.

[723] Golden, *Aspects of Religious Propaganda in Judaism and Early Christianity*, 131.

[724] Ibid, 135.

[725] Ciraolo, *Ancient Magic and Ritual Power*, 283.

The majority of scholars date the *Sepher Ha-Razim* from the late 3rd to mid-4th century CE, but the magic it contains likely reflects much earlier formulas. That similar collections predated the spells found in the Cairo *genizah* is nearly certain: "4Q560 [part of the Dead Sea Scrolls, *my note*] is probably the remnants of a recipe book containing the texts of amulets, which a professional magician would have copied out and personified for a client's use. The client would then have worn the amulet, encased in a container, as a charm against the demons who cause the illness which it enumerates…Belief in demons was probably widespread in late Second Temple Judaism, but it should be noted that there is a particularly close affinity between the demonology of the Scrolls and the demonology of the New Testament."[726]

The notion of seven ascending spheres of angelic powers, based on the seven known planets, was clearly a shared concept across the Middle East as this Chaldean incantation indicates:

> …the seven gods of the vast heavens,
> the seven gods of the great earth,
> the seven gods of the igneous spheres,
> the seven gods, these are the seven gods,
> the seven malevolent gods,
> the seven malevolent phantoms,
> the seven malevolent phantoms of the flames, in
> the heavens seven, on the earth seven…[727]

As the sophistication of the *Sepher Ha-Razim* indicates, Jewish magic was not simply folk religion, but a sustained intellectual effort on the part of "learned experts who mastered a specialized body of knowledge and consulted many different sources."[728]

---

726 Alexander, *The Dead Sea Scrolls After Fifty Years*, II, 345, 351.
727 Lenormant, *Chaldean Magic: Its Origin and Devolopment*, 17.
728 Bohak, *Ancient Jewish Magic: A History*, 36.

The *Book of Enoch*.

The clear presence of evil in a world created by a supposedly just God is the problem addressed by *theodicy*, the defense of God's benevolence in the face of overwhelming evidence to the contrary. In the apocalyptic literature of Second Temple Judaism, evil is explained by positing a rebellion of spirit entities, an explanation carried forward in some detail by a collection of writings known as *1 Enoch*.

1 Enoch is a composition of five "books," each book thought by experts to have been compiled in turn from various long-lost sources. *Book One*, frequently called *The Book of the Watchers*, tells how fallen angels called εγρηγοροι (egrēgoroi)—source of the English *egregore*—or *Watchers*, taught heavenly secrets to mankind. *The Book of the Watchers*, likely written in the 3rd century BCE and therefore "available for reading by the time of Jesus and the early church,"[729] is a haggadic expansion of the story of the antediluvian angels who succumbed to their passions for human women as recounted in Genesis.[730] Enoch himself enjoyed an elevated reputation based on the legend that he had been "taken away" by God after living for 365 years[731]—a year for each day of the solar calendar.

The text, first known in the West only by reputation, was discovered in an Ethiopic translation by explorer James Bruce in 1773. The theory that *1 Enoch* was first composed in Aramaic is supported by the discovery of eleven Aramaic fragments of 1 Enoch among the texts of the Dead Sea Scrolls, the oldest fragment tentatively dated from the 2nd century BCE. Additionally, five Greek exemplars of *1 Enoch* as well as Latin copies are

---

[729] VanderKam, *The Jewish Apocalyptic Heritage in Early Christianity*, 33.

[730] Genesis 6:1-4.

[731] Genesis 5:23-24.

known to exist. As is the case with all ancient documents with multiple attestations, the wording varies from source to source.

1 Enoch is quoted verbatim in Jude 14,[732] referenced an additional three times in an early Christian text known as the *Letter of Barnabas*, and Enoch's faith is commended in the book of Hebrews,[733] evidence that it enjoyed canonical status not only among many Jews, but in at least some sects of the early church. The mention of Jesus' descent into the underworld to preach to the "spirits in prison"[734] is also believed to reflect the influence of *1 Enoch*.[735] The influence of Enoch extends beyond references in early Christian writing: "Enoch is arguably the most important evidence of the Hebrew and pre-Christian roots of Gnostic doctrines...eight of the Qumran manuscripts contained apocrypha of Enoch."[736]

For present purposes *1 Enoch*[737] is of interest owing to its description of three seemingly unrelated technologies: cosmetics, metallurgy, and magic:

> It happened in those days that the sons of men were being multiplied and they fathered daughters, beautiful in the bloom of youth. The angels, sons of heaven, gazed upon the girls and lusted after them, and said to one another, "Come on, let's pick out women for ourselves from mankind and we will father children for ourselves."
>
> And Semaxas, who was their leader, said to them, "I fear that perhaps you will not want to perform this deed, and I alone will be the one to pay for this great sin."

---

732 1 Enoch 1:9.

733 Hebrews 11:5.

734 1 Peter 3:19.

735 VanderKam, 35, 62-63.

736 Mastrocinque, *From Jewish Magic to Gnosticism*, 55-56.

737 My translation is based on the Greek text.

They all answered him, "We will all swear an oath and *bind ourselves with a curse* (αναθεματισωμεν παντες αλληλους) not to turn back from this intention until it be accomplished and we complete this deed." Then they swore all together and bound themselves with a curse.

In the days of Jared, two hundred of them in all descended on the peak of Mount Hermon, and they called the mountain "Hermon" because on it they swore and bound themselves with a curse.

And these are the names of their leaders: Semiaza, he was their chief…

And they began to take women for themselves, each of them, picking out women for themselves, and they cohabited with them and were defiled by them, and *they taught the women potions* (εδιδαξεν αυτας φαρμακειας) and *enchantments* (επαοιδας) and *rootcutting* (ριζοτομιας) and revealed the use of herbs to them.

And they became pregnant, and gave birth to great giants…

Azael taught the men to make short swords and long shields and round shields and breastplates, and secretly disclosed the lessons of the angels to them, the metals and how to work them, bracelets and adornment, eye shadow and the beautifying of the eyelids, all sorts of precious stones and the dyeing of cloth. And much wantonness resulted, and they fornicated, and were beguiled and befouled in all their ways.

Semaxas taught enchantments and root cutting, Armaros, *the reversal of spells* (επαοιδων λυτηριον), Rakiel, astrology, Kokiel, the meaning of signs, Sadiel, stargazing, Seriel, drawing of the moon.

As mankind was destroyed, the cry rose to heaven.[738]

At this point, several observations can be made. It initially seems odd that the efficacy of magic is rarely if ever denied in either

---

[738] *1 Enoch* 6:1-7; 7:1-2; 8:1-4.

the Old or New Testament. Denial of the supernatural is so ingrained in the modern mind that it is nearly instinctive, but the author and readers of *1 Enoch* knew that the working of magic, like the working of metals, had been revealed from heaven, only without divine authorization. One could no more deny the effectiveness of potions and enchantments than the superiority of swords and shields over sticks and stones, or the allure of darkened eyes, richly colored cloth, or precious stones.

A strict division of labor is also evident: cooking up potions, like cooking generally, appears to be the work of women. On the other hand metallurgy, whether the forging of weapons or the manufacture of wrist and ankle bracelets, is the work of men.

The Book of the Watchers introduces us to another trait of magical religion: deep affection for the term *mystery.*

> And you see all that Azael did, who taught all wickedness on earth, and uncovered *the eternal mysteries* (*τα μυστερια του αιωνος*), the [mysteries] in heaven which men are making it their goal to learn…
> …so that all the sons of men may not die off because of *the whole of the mystery* (*εν τω μυστηριω ολω*) enjoined by the Watchers and revealed to their sons…[739]

A mystery—*μυστηριον* (mustērion)—is a secret doctrine, always *supernaturally revealed* as the above context shows, a divine secret that surpasses human understanding and would therefore remain forever beyond human discovery except for its revelation. The New Testament puts the word into the mouth of Jesus—"to you it has been given to known the mystery of the kingdom"[740]—as well as his apostles.[741] Inner doctrines, secret

[739] *1 Enoch* 9:6; 10:7.

[740] Matthew 13:11.

[741] 1 Corinthians 15:51, for example. The term is particularly favored by Paul and his school.

teachings, revelations vouchsafed to an elect, are common notions in both magic and ecstatic religion. The secret books in the Egyptian "House of Life," a scribal repository, "were not revealed to outsiders since knowledge, in particular secret knowledge, was dangerous if it fell into the wrong hands. To reveal the secrets of sacred books to non-initiates was to desecrate them, to lessen their power and efficacy…the notion of secret connotes efficacy. Secret knowledge was powerful and prestigious."[742] Secrecy figures importantly both in magical practice and in primitive Christianity.

The Book of the Watchers is of interest on yet another count, the origin of demons. After the giant offspring of the Watchers and their concubines die in the Deluge, "wicked spirits issued from their bodies."[743] A reason for the continued hostility of such demons toward humans is also given: "They will rise up against the sons of men and women because they issued forth from them."[744] This exegetical expansion on the Genesis story reveals the origin of the demons: they are the spirits of the **נפלים** (nephilim),[745] invisible remnants of the offspring of angels and humans, a hybrid version of the angry ghost known in the Qumran texts as "spirits of the bastards" who, being of partly human descent, "have an affinity with humans, which allows them to penetrate the human body. Indeed, it may be implied that, as disembodied spirits roaming the world, like the human 'undead,' they particularly seek embodiment, with all its attendant problems for the one whom they possess."[746]

---

[742] Nordh, *Aspects of Ancient Egyptian Curses and Blessings: Conceptual Background and Transmission*, 145-146.

[743] 1 Enoch 15:9.

[744] 1 Enoch 15:12.

[745] Genesis 6:4.

[746] Flint & VanderKam, *The Dead Sea Scrolls After Fifty Years*, II, 333, 339.

The story of the Nephilim or גברים (gibborim), *mighty ones*,[747] which the *Septuagint*, a Greek translation of the Hebrew Bible renders *γιγαντες*, *giants*, "was of fundamental importance in the development of Gnosticism, because it showed the Lord repenting of his creation and willing to save only the few spiritual men…"[748] Some Christians conceived of Yahweh as synonymous with the *δημιουργος* (dēmiorgos) of Platonic speculation, the "Demiurge" or *craftsman*, who had created the imperfect, evil physical world below as a failed imitation of a perfect, eternal, spiritual realm above. The story of the fallen angels and their offspring indicated to the dualists that the true God, the spiritual God to whom the elect hoped to ascend, had "repented" of the flawed creation[749] of the Demiurge and set about to destroy it. Dualistic theology that regarded the created world as an intrinsically evil sham world in which the enlightened were temporarily trapped, and its creator as a lesser god, caused certain early Christian sects to reject the Old Testament as the revelation of the lesser god Yahweh. The enemy of that lesser god, the serpent, accordingly became a heroic figure in the myth of some early Christian sects.

Annette Yoshiko Reed notes the several uses early Christians made of *1 Enoch*:

> Christian traditions about Satan's role in inspiring "heretics" are here harmonized with early Enochic traditions about the fallen angels teaching magical and divinatory arts to humankind, and it is the very assumption of an inexorable link between "heresy" and "magic" —two categories often used to denounce perceived deviance from ritual and religious norms—that makes this equation possible.

---

747 Genesis 6:4.

748 Mastrocinque, *From Jewish Magic to Gnosticism*, 66.

749 Genesis 6:6.

> ...Proto-orthodox Christians could critique those who adopted such practices without addressing the issue of their efficacy. If anything, the association with demonic spirits helped to explain how astrologers and diviners could predict the future, how magicians and pagan priests could heal, and how oracles from pagan temples could prove true—even as the intrinsically demonic nature of these practices formed the basis for an argument about why they should be avoided at all costs.[750]

Magic in the era of Jesus.

As noted by David Aune in a seminal essay, "The matrix of early Christianity was a Palestinian Judaism which had been permeated by Hellenistic influences to such an extent that any rigid distinction between Palestinian and Hellenistic Judaism must be regarded as untenable."[751]

The extent to which Jesus was influenced by magical practices outside the Jewish milieu is impossible to assess completely. There was a strong Hellenistic[752] presence in Galilee in Jesus' day—the Decapolis, a league of ten Greco-Roman cultural enclaves, is mentioned in the gospels[753]—but the precise antecedents of Jesus' own wonder-working powers cannot be determined. However, the gospel of Mark repeatedly mentions how quickly his fame as an exorcist spread through Galilee and beyond.[754] Herod Antipas had heard of his exploits[755] and other

---

750 Yoshiko Reed, *Fallen Angels and the History of Judaism and Christianity*, 177, 181.
751 Aune, *Aufstieg und Niedergang der Römischen Welt*, II. 23.2, 1519.
752 Hellenization "means only to express indigenous concepts and traditions in Greek, not to transform traditions and concepts according to a Greek mold..." Graf, *Magic in the Ancient World*, 5.
753 At Mark 5:20, for example, where the mention is made in the context of a report of an exorcism.
754 Mark 1:28, 45, 3:7-8, 5:20.

exorcists were quick to use his name.[756] It is clear that soon after his appearance, "Jesus" had become a name to conjure with.

It seems incredible to think that this osmotic transfer of fame and knowledge flowed only in one direction. As pointed out by Lapin, magical techniques were a commodity characterized by "broad geographical and chronological spread" across "a shared cultural world."[757] Exorcism was a quintessentially Jewish technique[758] that rapidly spread throughout the Roman world and the early Christians enjoyed a reputation as exorcists. The Roman Celsus said the Jews, "worship angels and are devoted to sorcery, *in which Moses has become their instructor* (*ο* Μωυσης *αυτοις γεγονεν εξηγητης*)."[759] The "instructor" or *εξηγητης* (exēgētēs)—from which *exegete*—was an interpreter of omens, oracles and dreams. Such was the fame of Moses the magician that a lesser magician assumes his identity while performing a rite: "I call you, *The Headless* (*τον ακεφαλον*), who created heaven and earth, who created night and day, you who created light and darkness…*I am Moses your prophet* (*εγω ειμι* Μουσης *ο προφητης σου*), to whom you have delivered *your mysteries* (*τα μυστηρια σου*) that Israel completely observes…"[760] It is nearly certain that much of the Jewish material in the magical papyri was imported by *pagan* magicians—Morton Smith made a strong case for that understanding[761]—but it also seems clear that distant echoes of half-forgotten Jewish magic linger in these predominantly pagan texts. The magical name *βασυμ* (basum) is tossed into the mix with more usual powerful names such as Ι*σακ*, "Isaac," Σ*αβαωθ* (Sabaōth), [Lord] "of Hosts," Ι*αω* (Iaō), Greek

[755] Mark 6:14.

[756] Mark 9:38.

[757] Lapin, *Religious and Ethnic Communities in Later Roman Palestine*, 14.

[758] Aune, *Aufstieg und Niedergang der Römischen Welt*, II, 16.3, 2108.

[759] Origen, *Contra Celsum* I, 26.

[760] Preisendanz, *Papyri Graecae Magicae* V, 97, 109-110.

[761] Smith, "The Jewish Elements in the Magical Papyri," *Studies in the Cult of Yahweh*, 2, 242-256.

for "Yahweh," and Ιακωπ, a slightly dog-eared "Jacob."[762] The unintelligible βασυμ likely represents the Hebrew בשמ (be-shem), *in the name*, which "implies knowledge, at some time, of Hebrew spells in which spirits were commanded 'in the name' of some power."[763]

To what degree Galilee had been populated by non-Jews is a matter of debate.[764] Matthew refers to "Galilee of the Gentiles,"[765] but the reference is to a passage in Isaiah[766] that Jesus has supposedly fulfilled and therefore should not be taken as an accurate description of a real state of affairs. Even though peasant Jews and Gentiles in Galilee may have maintained a state of segregation,[767] the purity of Galilean religious practices was evidently considered suspect, particularly in Judea, the center of the temple cult. Hence the challenge, "Are you also from Galilee? Search and see that no prophet is to arise from Galilee!"[768] Both the textual and archeological evidence for an extensive Gentile presence in Jesus' home territory are ambiguous, but it is unnecessary to posit a direct connection of any kind between Jewish and Gentile magicians since the broad outlines of magical practice were evidently quite similar all around the Mediterranean and had likely been so for centuries.

Regarding the magical texts recovered from the Cairo *geniza*, Gager notes that they "reveal how widespread such beliefs and practices were in the Jewish communities of the ancient world and how broadly this material circulated, crossing linguistic,

---

[762] Preisendanz, *Papyri Graecae Magicae* IV, 1376.

[763] Smith, *Studies in the Cult of Yahweh*, 2, 249.

[764] The most complete recent investigation is Chancey's *The Myth of a Gentile Galilee* to which the reader is referred.

[765] Matthew 4:15.

[766] Isaiah 9:1.

[767] Compare John 4:9, for example.

[768] John 7:41-42, 52.

chronological, cultural, and religious boundaries."[769] Confounding expectations based on the prohibitions of the Old Testament, magic was widely practiced and "in no way limited to apostate Jews, or to some religiously lax strata of Jewish society."[770]

The archaeological evidence suggests that extensive cross-pollination of magical belief and practice was the rule in the Mediterranean world of Jesus' day, examples of this mindset being the magical amulets written in Aramaic which have been recovered from various sites and the frequent presence of incantation bowls in what is now Iraq. In any event, it is certain that Jesus knew of and used common magical techniques because the gospels of Mark and John record them in some detail, and the connection between Palestine and Egypt, which the ancients regarded as the cradle of magic, had been strong for over 1000 years before the birth of Jesus. As noted by Johnston, "We increasingly realize that religious practices and ideas traveled fluidly across cultural boundaries; it profits the Assyriologist to compare notes with the Hellenist, the scholar of Judaism with the Egyptologist, and so on."[771]

The similarities between Jewish and Egyptian magic are often remarkable:

> The Egyptian word *heka*, which we translate as 'magic', was one of the forces which the creator-god had used in order to bring the world into existence. Creation was a development of the spoken word, and magic was the

---

[769] Gager, *Curse Tablets and Binding Spells from the Ancient World*, 107.

Jewish practice forbids the destruction of any text in which the divine name has been written. Worn out scrolls were therefore retired to a storage area called a *geniza* that was located in or next to the synagogue.

[770] Bohak, *Ancient Jewish Magic: A History*, 11.

[771] Johnston, *Religions of the Ancient World: A Guide*, 142.

> principle through which a spoken command was turned into reality, but magic could be achieved through acts and gestures as well as speech.[772]

As will become apparent in the following chapters, Jesus used "acts and gestures as well as speech" in the performance of his powerful works and the wording of his speech often finds striking parallels in both the Greek and Hebrew magical papyri recovered from Egyptian sites. That the magical practices mentioned in the Old Testament continued in some form into the time of Jesus may be suspected from various allusions in the New: veneration of the dead through the decoration of tombs[773] is an example and repetition of prayer a "magical" number of times—"When you pray, do not say the same thing over and over..."[774]—is another. That the weight of sin can be lifted by the repetition of a prescribed number of Hail Marys and Our Fathers is an atavistic survival of this frankly magical notion. "In the case of the nails found in or by Jewish tombs of the Second Temple Period in Palestine, Hachili and Killebrew have argued that they are a custom taken over from Greek usage. This cannot be shown directly, but they cite some (much) later Rabbinical texts that speak of placing iron objects between or inside tombs to protect them against harmful spirits...nails found in late-antique tombs...are now generally understood...as apotropaic amulets."[775] Belief in the magical attributes of nails, discussed at greater length in a subsequent chapter, appears to have been common in Jesus' era.

This brief survey of magic in Jewish Palestine barely skims the surface of the available literature; it has left aside for the moment discussion of the sophisticated speculative systems based on the מרכבה (merkabah), *chariot-throne*, imagery found in

---

[772] David, *Religion and Magic in Ancient Egypt*, 283-284.

[773] Matthew 23:27, 29.

[774] Matthew 6:7.

[775] Alfayé Villa, *Magical Practice in the Latin West*, 444.

Ezekiel 1:4-26 and the היכלות (heykalōt), *palaces*, mysticism that conceived the heavens as a multi-tiered realm of seven firmaments through which the souls of the righteous ascended to the throne of God. Merkabah mysticism, which began at least a century before the birth of Jesus and became fully developed in the Hellenistic age, had much in common with gnostic thought, and its richly evolved angelology, like that of gnosticism, laid an extensive foundation for magical praxis. Although it is difficult to find traces of such mystical speculation in the words of Jesus, it is certain that the adjuration of angels and divine names from the Hebrew canon spread into magical texts and influenced the beliefs of several early Christian sects. However, since the purpose of this chapter is to establish some context in which to place the wonder working of Jesus, further consideration of the mystical/magical uses of Hebrew divine names will be reserved for a later chapter. The Christian apologist Origen speculated that circumcision itself provided magical protection to the Jewish people from "some hostile angel" (*τινα πολεμιον...αγγελον*) that had the power to injure those not circumcised.[776]

[776] Origen, *Contra Celsum* V, 48.

CHAPTER 6: JESUS THE MAGICIAN

"...Jesus' opponents accused him of black magic, an accusation which stands as one of the most firmly established facts of the Gospel Tradition."[777] We know of this accusation because it is reported—*repeatedly*—by the gospels.[778] "There are sound reasons for concluding that even in his own lifetime Jesus was labeled 'magician' by his opponents.[779] For more than two centuries after his death, Christian apologists were still defending Jesus from the charge of sorcey and according to the apocryphal Acts, likely composed in the late 2nd to early 3rd century, Jesus' followers were repeatedly accused of malicious magical practice. The culture of the Middle East, where magic was pervasive, can be linked to early Christianity, where magic was very much at home, by the wonder-working apocalyptic prophet from Nazareth.

There are numerous similarities between the works and words attributed to Jesus and the spells and incantations of roughly contemporaneous magical documents. The magical papyri, preserved in Egypt by the vicissitudes of geography and weather, are written in a mixture of Greek and Coptic with generous contributions from Hebrew. In addition to the papyri, inscribed amulets (*lamellae*) of gold and silver, gem stones with magical images and text, and engraved lead curse tablets (*tabellae defixionum*) preserve magical texts. It is now recognized that

---

[777] Plumer, *Biblica* 78: 357.

[778] Mark 3:22, 6:16, John 8:48, 52, 10:20, Matthew 9:34, 10:25, 12:24, 27.

See Stanton, *Gospel Truth? New Light on Jesus and the Gospels*, 156-163.

[779] Stanton, *Jesus of Nazareth Lord and Christ*, 178.

"many magical texts can now be assigned to relatively early periods (ca. second century B.C. to early first A.D.)"[780] Against the objection that the papyri and similar sources were written too late the reflect the time of Jesus, I would offer this observation by Trachtenberg:

> However unorthodox in principle, magic is perhaps the most tradition-bound of cultural forms...As we have had occasion to note, magic is the most conservative of disciplines—like the law it clings to archaic forms long after they have lost currency.[781]

Even though the majority of Christian scholars refuse to regard Jesus as a magician, Crossan quite cheerfully applies that label to him: "The more ordinary term for what they describe is *magician*, and I prefer to use it despite some obvious problems. The title *magician* is not used here as a pejorative word but describes one who can make divine power present *directly through personal miracle* rather than *indirectly through communal ritual.* Despite an extremely labile continuum between the twin concepts, magic renders transcendental power present concretely, physically, sensibly, tangibly, whereas ritual renders it present abstractly, ceremonially, liturgically, symbolically...if, in the end, the title magician offends, simply substitute thaumaturge, miracle worker, charismatic, holy one, or whatever pleases, but know that we speak of exactly the same activity in any case, namely, personal and individual rather than communal and institutional access to, monopoly of, or control over divine power."[782]

Unlike people of today, most people of antiquity made no clear distinction between religion and magic, or between medicine and magic, and to impose such distinctions on records from the past is not only anachronistic, but precludes real comprehension

---

[780] Kotansky, *Greek Magical Amulets: The Inscribed*, I, xvii.
[781] Trachtenberg, *Jewish Magic and Superstition*, 75, 81.
[782] Crossan, *The Historical Jesus*, 138.

of what rituals of healing, exorcism, cursing, and divination may have meant for the participants: "...the neat distinctions we make today...did not exist in antiquity except among a few intellectuals."[783] "In Republican Rome, as in Archaic Greece, magic was never thought as something special and radically different from religion or medicine."[784] The reader should understand that *magic* might apply to nearly any ritual behavior that involves speaking or performance, and that when a term like *sorcery* is used, it means something like "religion that works."

The sources of our very incomplete knowledge deserve a brief comment. The oldest magical texts known to us are the pyramid and coffin texts from Egypt, but to what extent these texts still reflected any popular practice in the time of Jesus is uncertain. We also know something of the magic of ancient Mesopotamia, and the Old Testament contains numerous references to sorcery, some of which have been considered. That leaves the Greek magical papyri that are roughly contemporaneous with Jesus' era and have the added advantage of preserving traces of the magic performed by and for common people.

Most of our historical sources, however, were critical of magical practice and may have been preserved down through the Christian centuries for that very reason.[785] Even in pre-Christian times magicians were regarded with suspicion and their books considered dangerous, and under the Christian regime, the pagan cultus became magic by definition and persecution of practitioners of magic intensified. "...the systematic destruction of the magical literature over a long period of time resulted in the

---

[783] Betz, *The Greek Magical Papyri in Translation*, xli.

[784] Meyer & Mirecki, *Ancient Magic and Ritual Power*, 41.

[785] That is certainly true of Lucian, whose mockery of philosophers and their schools as well as Greek religious practice ensured the survival of his writings despite his occasional caustic remarks about Jesus and Christians.

disappearance of most of the original texts by the end of antiquity."[786]

Moreover, the official histories were composed by members of the upper echelon of a stratified society that regarded the magic of the lower classes much as they regarded the people themselves, with a mixture of condescension, fear, and contempt. As Frederick Cryer notes, "In hierarchically ordered societies there is vastly more magic at the bottom of society than there is at the top...It is also full of the elite disdain for the welter of popular superstition that the masses below advocate."[787]

The implications of these negative attitudes toward magic for an understanding of the New Testament are potentially enormous. As has already been noted, Jesus, his disciples, and the majority of those to whom he preached, were drawn from the working class, notable as a group for their susceptibility to the machinations of sorcerers. Moreover, the evening celebrations of the Christians were identified by pagan critics as "secret and nocturnal rites," conducive to conspiracy, for that reason alone suspicious.[788] So when the time finally came to present Jesus and his miracles to the greater Greco-Roman world, there would be plenty of incentive to downplay the magical elements of his performances and that is exactly what we find when examining certain gospel accounts.

The sorcerer and his works.

Several terms were used of magicians during the period during which the New Testament was being composed. Some of the terms encountered in our sources are based on *μαγος* (magos),

---

[786] Betz, *The Greek Magical Papyri in Translation*, xl.

[787] Cryer, *Witchcraft and Magic in Europe: Biblical and Pagan Societies*, 116-117.

[788] Benko, *Pagan Rome and the Early Christians*, 11.

from which we derive *magician*, *magic* (*μαγεια*) and *magical* (*μαγικος*). Of these men Luck notes, "It seems the *magos* had a bit of everything—the bacchantic (i.e. ecstatic) element, the initiation rites, the migratory life, the nocturnal activities."[789]

The term *γοης* (goēs), related to the Greek term for *wailing*, carried connotations of *fraud* in addition to *sorcerer*, and *φαρμακευς* or *φαρμακος* (pharmakos), the obvious source of words like *pharmacy*, could mean either *sorcerer* or *poisoner*. The word for *potion* or *spell*, *φαρμκον* (pharmakon), could also mean *poison*, and *φαρμακεια* (pharmakeia) naturally included *poisoning* as well as *spellcasting*, accounting in part for magic's dubious ancient reputation and illegality. "...references to *veneficium* throughout Roman literature, and to *φαρμακον* in Greek literature, are often ambiguous. The potions were powerful; whether that power was for good or for evil depended on the outcome of each specific case."[790] Often translated "spells," *φαρμακον* covers both magical potions and medicines since medicine and magic were very often the same thing.[791]

Prophets, *soothsayers*, or *oracles* are covered under to term *μαντις* (mantis), and *enchanters* and *readers of omens* generally fall under the term *επαοιδος* (epaiodos), which literally means "one who chants over." Although these are the most common terms, they hardly cover the Greek vocabulary for magic. Fritz Graf defines the *αγυρτης* (agurtēs) as "an itinerant and beggar priest"[792] associated particularly with the worship of Cybele—in response to which I would merely point out that Christian religious orders, such as the Dominicans and Franciscans, that lived by collecting alms are typically known as *mendicants*, not as beggars. The role

---

789 Luck, *Witchcraft and Magic in Europe: Ancient Greece and Rome*, 104.

790 Janowitz, *Magic in the Roman World: Pagans*, Jews, and Christians, 12.

791 See particularly Faraone, *Ancient Greek Love Magic*, 88-89, 112-115.

792 Graf, *Magic in the Ancient World*, 22.

of gender variance and homoeroticism in connection with the priests of Cybele is well-established,[793] additional motivation for itinerant wonder working Christian missionaries to distance themselves from their pagan counterparts. Another term is *ριζοτομος* (rhizotomos), or "rootcutter," the forebear of the herbalist or "kitchen witch."

A complete description of the *γοης* (goēs) and the nature of his type of sorcery—*γοετεια* (goeteia), "the invocation of the dead" —has been given by Johnston. The *goēs* is a man who raises the dead through wailing, a typically female role as indicated by depictions on funeral vases, but is also associated by ancient writers with initiation into mystery cults, protecting the living from the wrath of angry ghosts, and enchantments and incantations, both written and sung.[794] "Aeschylus also shows us, on the stage, the magic mourning that can call up the dead. The name of such mouring is *γοος*, which gives us the origin of the word *γοητεια*, meaning magic...the *γοος* is a sort of *νεκυομαντεια*, necromancy."[795] Graf defines the *goēs* as "a man who combines healing, weather magic, and the calling up of dead souls..."[796] The *goēs* "attracts the attention of the dead through songs and spells, exchanges messages with them, temporarily resurrects them; the necromantic counterpart of the poet."[797] But there are "no Greek terms that correspond precisely to the distinction that has been drawn between sorcery and witchcraft,"[798] and a number of Greek terms I have not mentioned encompass the territory of the English word *magic*.

"Thoth was said to be the inventor of both magic and writing and he was the patron deity of scribes...Thoth was linked in myth with two potent images of power used in magic, the sun

---

793 Conner, *Blossom of Bone*, 99-131.
794 Johnston, *Restless Dead*, 103, 105-123.
795 de Romilly, *Magic and Rhetoric in Ancient Greece*, 13.
796 Graf, *Magic*, 33.
797 Vermeule, *Aspects of Death in Early Greek Art and Poetry*, 17.
798 Greenfield, *Byzantine Magic*, 120.

eye and the moon eye...The image of the Thoth baboon beside a *wedjat* eye occurs on magic wands as early as the twentieth century BC."[799] Indeed, the connection between magic and writing is commemorated in the double meaning of the English word "spell." None of the terms for magician necessarily excludes other functions. Graf describes the γοης-αγυρτης-μαγος as "the itinerant specialist who practices divination, initiation, healing, and magic."[800] It is unlikely that these terms were used in any consistent way by the people of the era to distinguish between "specialists" in magical practice,[801] all of whom were working in what Hans Dieter Betz has felicitously called "the energy jungle,"[802] the human dependency on universal forces conceived under the rubric of divinities of varying rank.

The New Testament uses a number of words for powerful works: δυναμις (dunamis), *power*, from which *dynamite* was coined, and by extension, *powerful work*, *miracle*. Δυναμις is what flows like current from Jesus when a miracle is performed: "I felt the power leaving me..."[803] In reference to Acts 1:8 where Jesus tells his disciples they will receive power (δυναμις) "when the holy spirit falls upon you"—επελθοντος του αγιου πνευματος εφ' υμας—Strelan points out "Clearly what Jesus was promising was something overwhelming and radical in its effect."[804]

There is also τερας (teras), *portent*, *omen*, or *prodigy*, the basis for our medical term *teratology*, the study and classification of birth defects. The ancient Mediterranean cultures considered the birth of deformed animals and humans to be ill omened and employed priests—the τερατοσκοπος (teratoskopos), *omen inspector*—who specialized in the interpretation of such dark

---

[799] Pinch, *Magic in Ancient Egypt*, 28-29.
Within the Greek system, Hermes is assimilated to Thoth.

[800] Graf, *Magic*, 49.

[801] Dickie, *Magic and Magicians in the Greco-Roman World*, 12-15.

[802] Betz, *The Magical Papyri in Translation*, xlvii.

[803] Luke 8:46.

events. Regarding the impending plagues upon Egypt, the *Septuagint* has Yahweh say to Moses, "Behold all the portents I have placed in your hands!"[805] Other terms include *αποδειξις* (apodeixis), *display*,[806] and *θαυμα* (thauma), *wonder*.[807] The apparent avoidance of *thauma* and its cognates may signal a reticence to associate Jesus with *thaumaturgy*, or "wonder working" which was common in the pagan world. Indeed Lucian uses *θαυματοποιος* (thaumatopoios), *conjurer* and the derived verb *θαυματοποιεω*, *to perform wonders*, to describe the religious fraudster Peregrinus.[808]

The most common word for a work of wonder in the gospel of John is *σημειον* (sēmeion), *sign*, of which there are a magical seven: water into wine, healing a fever, a healing at Bethzatha, feeding a multitude, the translocation of a boat, healing a blind man, and the raising of Lazarus.[809] In addition to its seven signs, the gospel also records seven witnesses that say Jesus has been sent from God or is "the Son of God": John the Baptist, Nathanael, Peter, Jesus himself, Martha, Thomas, and the author of the gospel.[810] There are also seven "I am" sayings: "I am the bread of life," "the light of the world," "the good shepherd," "the resurrection and the life," "the way, the truth, and the life," "the true vine," and "before Abraham, I am".[811] These groupings are not coincidental; seven is the most thoroughly attested magical number. The composition history of the gospel of John

---

805 Exodus 4:21.

806 Not common: "in a *display* of spirit and power" (1 Corinthians 2:4).

807 Used only once in the New Testament in an exclamation: "And no wonder!" (1 Corinthians 11:14).

The related adjective, *θαυμασιος* (thaumasios), is used once as a collective noun: "When the chief priest and scribes saw *the wonderful things* (*τα θαυμασια*) that he did…" (Matthew 21:15).

808 Lucian, *The Passing of Peregrinus* (Περι της Περεγρινου τελευτης), 17, 21; *The Runaways* (Δραπεται), 1.

809 John 2:1-11, 4:46-54, 5:1-48, 6:1-14, 6:15-21, 9:1-41, 11:1-57.

810 John 1:34, 1:49, 6:69, 10:36, 11:27, 20:28, 20:31.

811 John 6:35, 8:12, 10:11, 11:25, 14:6, 15:1, 8:58.

is a matter of conjecture; the dating of the magical formulas in papyri is insecure and it is therefore not possible to establish a dependent relationship.[812] Nevertheless both the number seven and the similarity in phrasing are highly unlikely to be coincidental.

"I am" sayings are frequent in the magical spells: "I am the Great One, the One who sits in heaven..."[813] "I am the One upon the lotus, having power, the Holy God..."[814] "I am Abraxas..."[815] Or, "Come to me Isis, because I am Osiris, your consort brother..."[816] "I am" sayings are common in late Egyptian religion—"for I am Horus, son of Isis"[817]—and in the Old Testament, the source of the most famous of the I am sayings:

> God said to Moses, "I am who I am. This is what you are to say to the Israelites: 'I am has sent me to you.'"[818]

The Hebrew expression of Exodus 3:14, אהיה אשר אהיה (ehyeh asher ehyeh), which means approximately, "I will be what I will be," formed the basis of endless mystical and magic speculation on the nature of Yahweh and was considered among Jewish magicians a powerful name with which to conjure.

Variations of the "I am" formula appear in Revelation: *Εγω ειμι το Αλφα και το Ω λεγει κυριος ο θεος ο ων και ο ην και ο ερχομενος ο παντοκρατωρ*, "I am the Alpha and the Omega says the Lord God, the One who is and who was and who is coming, the Almighty,"[819] "I am the Alpha and the Omega, the beginning

---

[812] Ball, *'I Am' in John's Gospel*, 24-27.
[813] Kotansky, *Greek Magical Amulets*, 183-184.
[814] Daniel & Maltomini, *Supplementum Magicum* I, 18.
[815] Ibid, I, 36.
[816] Kotansky, 362.
[817] Griffith & Thompson, *The Demotic Magical Papyrus of London and Leydon*, IX, 22-23.
[818] Exodus 3:14 (NIV).
[819] Revelation 1:8.

and the end" (η αρχη και το τελος)[820]—significantly, the witch goddess Hekate is also "the beginning and the end" (αρχη και τελος).[821] After an analysis of the beginning and end motif in Revelation, Thomas concluded that John was creating an anti-magical polemic, "indicating that Jesus Christ was superior to Hekate."[822] The "I am" formula predictably finds its way into a Coptic spell: **ⲁⲛⲟⲕ ⲡⲉ ⲥⲏⲑ ⲡϣⲏⲣⲉ ⲛⲁⲇⲁⲙ**, "I [am] Seth, son of Adam."[823]

...and the angels began serving him.

With the exception of the signs and wonders reported by the gospel of John, Jesus' miracles are predominantly exorcisms and healings, and they begin immediately after his return from the wilderness:

> It happened in those days that Jesus came from Nazareth of Galilee and was baptized in the Jordan by John. And at once, while he was coming up out of the water, he saw the heavens being ripped open and the spirit descending into him like a dove. And a voice came out of the heavens: "You are my son, the beloved. In you was I pleased."
>
> At once the spirit drove him out into the wilderness and he was in the wilderness for forty days, being tempted by Satan, and he was with the wild animals and the angels began serving him.
>
> After John had been arrested, Jesus came into Galilee proclaiming the good news of God, saying, "The allot-

---

[820] Revelation 21:6.

[821] Preisendanz, *Papyri Graecae Magicae* IV, 2836.

[822] Thomas, *Magical Motifs in the Book of Revelation*, 98-99.

[823] Worrell, *The American Journal of Semitic Languages and Literature* 46: 242.

> ted time has run out and the kingdom of God has almost arrived! Repent and believe in the good news!"
>
> ...
>
> They came to Capernaum and as soon as the Sabbath came, he entered the synagogue[824] and taught. They were astounded by his teaching, for he was teaching them as one having authority and not like the scribes.
>
> Now in their synagogue there was a man with an unclean spirit and he shouted out, "What have we to do with you, Jesus of Nazareth? Did you come to destroy us? I know who you are! The Holy One of God!"
>
> Jesus rebuked it,[825] saying, "Shut up and come out of him!" The unclean spirit convulsed him and screamed with a loud voice and came out of him.
>
> They were all amazed and they were asking one another, "What is this? A new teaching with authority! He commands the unclean spirits and they obey him!" Immediately the report about him spread through all the surrounding region of Galilee.[826]

The mere association of the Jordan with miracle guarantees its appearance in magical spells: "For a discharge or flow of blood: As Elijah, about to cross the Jordan River on foot, raised his staff with commands that the Jordan be like dry land, so also, lord, you must drive the disease from N. child of N..."[827]

Exorcism and healing were central to Jesus' career; the first powerful work recorded by Mark, the earliest gospel, is an exorcism. Porterfield counts 72 instances of miracles in the canonical gospels; forty-one refer to specific events, and in ten crowds

---

824 "A common feature of the Jewish synagogues of all periods is their use as places of healing..." Bohak, *Ancient Jewish Magic: A History*, 314.

825 *επετιμησεν αυτω ο* Iησουη: "Jesus rebuked it..."

826 Mark 1:9-15, 21-28.

827 Meyer & Smith, *Ancient Christian Magic: Coptic Texts of Ritual Power*, 267.

of witnesses are mentioned. "These forty-one episodes involve a variety of different literary forms, an indication of their independent origins."[828] In short, Jesus' wonder working is thoroughly attested, the most basic feature of his career, and cannot simply be minimized by appeal to some larger meaning to his "ministry."

Several features of Mark's opening account merit further comment, particularly the use of the terms *spirit* and *angel*. By the time of Jesus, Jewish speculation about the power of angels was well established and the seven post-exilic archangels, probably imported into Judaism from Babylonian magic, were beginning to appear in the Jewish canon as in Daniel (12:1) where Michael makes an appearance. The familiar "-el" ending of angelic names derives from **אל**, *El, God*, which appears in dozens of words and phrases such as **עמנואל**, Emmanuel, *God is with us*.[829] Matthew uses the title (Εμμανουηλ), and translates it—"God (*ο θεος*) is with us"—to make sure the reader makes the connection.[830] The angelic names incorporate *El as a name within a name*, therefore *twice as powerful in a magical sense* "for with the transference of the divine name to the angels it is believed that the power of the one owning the name is also transferred."[831] To invoke the angel is to simultaneously invoke God. The Hebrew names for the angels incorporate phrases: Michael, **מיכאל**, *Who* [is] *like El?*, Gabriel, **גבראל**, *El* [*is*] *my strength*, or Raphael, **רפאל**, *El heals*.

As recorded by Mark, the spirit that has descended—literally speaking—*into* (*εις*) Jesus immediately drives him out into the wilderness: *ευθυς το πνευμα αυτον εκβαλλει εις την ερημον*, "at once the spirit drove him out into the wilderness..." The verb translated "drove him out"—*εκβαλλω* (ekballō)—is used of

[828] Porterfield, *Healing in the History of Christianity*, 20.
[829] Isaiah 7:14.
[830] Matthew 1:23.
[831] Spoer, *Journal of Biblical Literature* 23: 99.

driving out unclean spirits in its very next occurrence: *και δαιμονια πολλα εξεβαλεν*, "...and he *cast out* many demons."[832] The notion of spirits driving the possessed into the wilderness is found outside the gospels. Prior to exorcizing a pederastic ghost from a good-looking boy, Apollonius is informed by the boy's mother that "the demon" (*ο δαιμων*) habitually "drives him out into the deserted places"—*αλλ' εις τα ερημα των χωριων εκτρεπει*. And as in the case of Jesus, whom Satan challenges "Throw yourself down,"[833] the ghost in possession of the woman's son "threatened her with steep places and precipices."[834]

The language used of Jesus' initiatory experience is the same as that used for spirit manipulation, and it is probably for that reason that both Matthew and Luke not only changed the verb, but also recast it in the passive voice when using Mark's account. The synoptics have Jesus "led" by the spirit: *ο Ιησους ανηχθη εις την ερημον υπο του πνευματος*: "Jesus was led up into the desert by the spirit" (Matthew 4:1); *και ηγετο εν τω πνεματι εν τω ερημω*: "and he was led by the spirit into the desert" (Luke 4:1). "Certainly this Pneuma of God is no innocuous spirit. According to Mark i.12, the Spirit 'drove him out into the desert...In Matt. and Luke the miraculous experience of Jesus on this occasion is tuned down: Jesus is 'conducted by the Spirit...'"[835] However, even this change does not manage to erase the magical vocabulary. Jesus was "led" by the spirit—from *αγω*, *to lead*—even as speechless idols once led the Corinthians into error—*ηγεσθε απαγουμενοι*, "you were led astray."[836] An *αγωγη* (agōgē), an erotic *attraction spell*, leads or drives the desired subject toward the beneficiary of the spell, and the word can also mean "forcible seizure, carrying off, abduction."[837]

---

[832] Mark 1:34.
[833] Matthew 4:6.
[834] Philostratus, *The Life of Apollonius of Tyana* III, 38.
[835] Eitrem, *Some Notes on the Demonology in the New Testament*, 65.
[836] 1 Corinthians 12:2.
[837] Liddell, Scott & Jones, *A Greek-English Lexicon*, 18.

It is therefore little wonder that Matthew and Luke also saw fit to amend the text of Mark which has the spirit descending *into* Jesus: to *πνευμα ως περιστεραν καταβαινον εις αυτον*, "the spirt descending like a dove into (*εις*) him."[838] Matthew changed the preposition to *επι*, "upon"—*το πνευμα...ερχομενον επ' αυτον*: "the spirt...alighting on him"[839] and so did Luke.[840] The Greek magical papyri contain very similar wording for being filled with spirit: *ενπνευματωσον αυτον θειου πνευματος*, "fill it with spirt, divine spirit..."[841]

The descent and ascent of birds as proof of connection with supernatural forces is also known from the magical texts: the descent of the falcon is a *sign*—*σημειον*, *sign*, the same term used in the gospel of John for Jesus' miracles—that the magician has been heard.[842] In another spell, spoken to the sun, the sign that the magician has been heard is the descent of "a falcon into the tree"—*τω ιεραξ επι το δενδρον.*[843]

> After saying these things three times, there will be this sign of divine communion—but you, armed by having a magical soul, do not be afraid—for a falcon from the sea swoops down and strikes your form with its wings, indicating you should arise...say, "I have been united with your holy form, I have been empowered by your holy name."[844]

According to the satirist Lucian, as Peregrinus immolates himself on the pyre a vulture ascends heavenward from the flames,

---

838 Mark 1:10.
839 Matthew 3:16.
840 Luke 3:22.
841 Preisendanz, *Papyri Graecae Magicae* IV, 967.
842 Ibid, I, 65.
843 Ibid, III, 273.
844 Ibid, IV, 209-217.

proclaming loudly with a human voice (*μεγαλη τη φωνη*),[845] "I'm off to Olympus!"[846] and Celsus claimed the descent of the dove in the gospel story was "an apparition" (*το φασμα*).[847] It is well known that birds were linked to magical performance, particularly to divination, *auspicium ex avibus*, either by their songs or by their pattern of flight. Greek has a rich vocabulary related to augury by birds, the augur was an *οιωνοσκοπος* (oiōnoskopos) or *οιωνιστης* (oiōnistēs). All ancient Mediterranean societies considered birds to be messengers of the gods, but obviously a few individuals like Lucian harbored doubts.

The significance of the report that Jesus "was with the wild animals"—*μετα των θηριων*—is clear when placed in the cultural context of his era. Semitic people of the Middle East regarded the desert and mountain peaks as the natural homes of demons.[848] "In Egypt, all things associated with the liminal world of the frontier or periphery were demonized."[849] The "howling creatures" that fill the ruins of Babylon, where shepherds refuse to graze their flocks,[850] reappear in the Qumran scrolls where "they are taken as names for some kind of demon,[851] and the לילית (lilith) that will inhabit the ruins of Edom along with wild animals[852] is widely regarded as a reference to a night demon. It is possible that the wild beasts in question were understood to be demons.[853] When a plague begins to rage in Ephesus, the terrified citizens summon the miracle worker Apollonius who reveals the demonic source in the guise of a beggar.

---

[845] Compare John 11:43 where Jesus cries out *with a loud voice* (*φωνη μεγαλη*) to summon Lazarus from the tomb.

[846] Lucian, *The Passing of Peregrinus* (Περι της Περεγρινου Τελευτης), 39.

[847] Origen, *Contra Celsum* I, 41, 43.

[848] Lenormant, *Chaldean Magic: Its Origin and Development*, 31.

[849] Schmidt, *Magic and Ritual in the Ancient World*, 258.

[850] Isaiah 13:20-21.

[851] Alexander, *The Dead Sea Scrolls After Fifty Years*, II, 335.

[852] Isaiah 34:14.

[853] Williams, *Journal of Theological Studies* 57: 42-56.

Stoned to death, the body of the demon, its eyes "full of fire," is transformed into a "beast" (θηριον), in the shape of a huge dog.[854] One might also cite an amulet that begins, "I adjure you by the living God, that *every spirit* (παν πνευμα) and *ghost* (φαντασμα) and *every beast* (παν θηριον) begone from this woman's soul..."[855]

On Atonement Day, the High Priest will take two goats, one for sacrifice to Yahweh, and another, over which the sins of the people are confessed, for עזאזל (azazel). The goat for Azazel is then led "into the wilderness" by a man who must subsequently bathe and wash his clothing before rejoining the community.[856] This is an example of an αποπομπη (apopompē) ritual in which an animal or its image "is removed from the area of human habitation, much as a live scapegoat is driven out."[857] Given this background, where better to meet the Prince of Darkness face to face than the desert wilderness where only the moan-ing of the wind and the cries of nocturnal birds and beasts break the eerie silence? Yet significantly, Jesus meets *both* the Tempter *and* the angels of God during his time in the desert.

The association of demons with wild animals is also a feature of the magical spellbooks. Regarding the multiple functions of a magical assistant, the spell promises, "he sets [you] free from many evil demons and he stops wild beasts..."[858] Although "demons and wild animals"—δαιμονας και θηρας—are associated in the papyri, the nature of the connection is not specified. It is probable that vicious wild animals were considered to be the embodiment of demons[859] "Mark seems to suggest that Jesus has now entered into an ancient mythic struggle between God and

[854] Philostratus, *The Life of Apollonius of Tyana* IV, 10.
[855] Kotansky, *Greek Magical Amulets*, 383.
[856] Leviticus 16:8-26.
[857] Faraone, *Talismans and Trojan* Horses, 43.
[858] Preisendanz, *Papyri Graecae Magicae* I, 116.
[859] Williams, *Journal of Theological Studies* 57: 42-56.

the demonic monsters of chaos."[860] Ehrenreich points to an impressive series of correlations between carnivorous animals and carnivore deities, citing "Jehovah's furious appetite for animal offerings and his obsessive demands for foreskins, which may have been a substitute for human sacrificial victims" as one of various examples.[861] Origen believed that demons possessed wild animals and that some relationship (*κοινωνια*) existed between the forms (*ειδος*) of demons and the shapes or forms of animals.[862]

The שדים (shedim), the *demons* of the Old Testament, are false gods,[863] but other entities operate in a gray zone of supernatural cause and effect. The infamous שטן (satan), *Satan*, sometimes appears to be the shadow side of Yahweh, "an objectification of the dark side of God."[864] In one place we are informed that Yahweh incited David to take a census,[865] but in another, that it was Satan,[866] and the angel sent to thwart the prophet Balaam is also a "satan" or *opposer*.[867] "Often when quoting Mark, Luke—who seems to be writing to a predominately Gentile audience—changes the term *unclean spirit* (*πνευμα ακαθαρτον*) to "the more familiar Hellenic term *δαιμονιον* [demon, *my note*]...At 4:33, he changes Mark's 'unclean spirit' to 'spirit *of an unclean demon*' (*πνευμα δαιμονιου ακαθαρτου*)." As noted by Paige, *πνευμα* (pneuma), *spirit*, used for beings of intermediate rank, is a Jewish, not pagan, usage. [868]

---

[860] Werline, *Experientia*, I, 62.

[861] Ehrenreich, *Blood Rites*, 73.

[862] Origen, *Contra Celsum* IV, 92, 93.

[863] Deuteronomy 32:17, Psalms 106:37.

[864] *The Dead Sea Scrolls After Fifty Years*, II, 342.

[865] 2 Samuel 24:1.

[866] 1 Chronicles 21:1.

[867] Numbers 22:32.

[868] Paige, *Harvard Theological Review* 95: 435.
Compare Mark 1:23-27, Luke 4:33-3y; Mark 6:7, Luke 9:1; Mark 5:1-18, Luke 8:26-38; Mark 9:17-27, Luke 9:37-42.

Modern people, conditioned by countless depictions of *putti*, the pudgy cupids that reappear in the classical revival of the Quattrocento, have lost touch with the understanding of spirit entities that existed in antiquity. Christianity corrupted the term *demon*, giving it a permanent connotation of evil, a tactically useful move since Christians could then condemn pagan oracles and healing shrines "without addressing the issue of their efficacy."[869] *Angel—αγγελος* (angelos)—has been similarly distorted from its original sense. In classical Greek, the word *angel* meant *messenger*, and the related *αγγελια* (angelia), *report* or *message*.) In Greek culture, a person's *daemon* functioned in much the same way as the modern *guardian angel*. In the context of theurgy, demons were creative powers that emanated from the gods according to Iamblichus.[870] "...by the time of the early Hellenistic philosophers, there already existed a perfectly good and ancient term that was used for what we would call a "spirit": *ο δαιμων* [*the demon*, my note], and its more popular diminutive form to *δαιμονιον*. In philosophical writings, the daimonia serve as divine intermediaries, communicating messages from the gods to humans and carrying prayers from humans to the gods. The *daimonia* may be good or evil; the term might even signify ghosts."[871] Prior to burning himself to death, Peregrinus invokes his mother's "daimons" (*τους μητρωους...δαιμονας*), her guardian spirits.[872]

The word *angel* still has a fairly wide application even in the New Testament. Paul, for example, refers to an undisclosed physical malady as "an angel of Satan,"[873] and some early Christians advocated the worship of angels,[874] and it is likely the

[869] Reed, *Fallen Angels and the History of Judaism and Christianity*, 181.

[870] Clarke, *Iamblichus*: *De mysteriis*, 82-83.

[871] Paige, *Harvard Theological Review* 95: 427.

[872] Lucian, The Passing of Peregrinus (Περι της Περεγρινου Τελευτης), 37.

[873] *αγγελος σατανα*: "an angel of Satan" (2 Corinthians 12:7).

[874] Colossians 2:18.

angels in question were regarded as rulers of one of the seven heavens. As "an intermediary between the worlds of gods and men," even the chthonic goddess Hecate is repeatedly called an "angel."[875] Gerhard Kittel, noting the frequent use of angel in Greek magical curse tablets, says, "There are chthonic as well as heavenly αγγελοι ["angels," *my note*]."[876] Of the angels that appeared to Jesus in the wilderness we are told: "Then the Devil departed and, Look! *angels came and began to serve him*" (αγγελοι προσηλθον και διηκονουν αυτω).[877]

The angels in Mark's account first appear after Satan challenges Jesus to perform magic, transforming stones into bread and flying into the air. It is only after Jesus asserts his *own* authority that the angels come and begin to serve him. To this Luke adds the specific content of the temptation, using the vocabulary of magic:

> Leading him up, the Devil showed him all the kingdoms of mankind in a flash, and the Devil said to him, "I will give you *all this authority* (την εξουσιαν ταυτην απασαν) and all their glory because *it has been handed over to me* (εμοι παραδεδοται) and I give it to whomever I wish.[878]

The New Testament reflects an assumption that worldly wealth and power is under the control of demonic forces—the chthonic god Pluto is πλουτοδοτης, "giver of riches," because precious metals come from his subterranean realm. When a boy plagued by a demon successfully repels it by means of a magical ring, the demon cries out, "Take away the ring...and I will give you all the world's silver and gold!"[879]

---

[875] Rabinowitz, *The Rotting Goddess*, 22.
[876] Kittel, *Theological Dictionary of the New Testament*, I, 75.
[877] Matthew 4:11.
[878] Luke 4:5-6.
[879] *Testament of Solomon* I, 12.

After the angels began to serve him, "Jesus returned to Galilee *in the power of the spirit*"—*εν τη δυναμει του πνευματος*—"and word of him spread through all the surrounding region."[880] Who these angels were can be further confirmed from the ancient Hebrew spell book, the *Sepher Ha-Razim*. Although it was composed at least three centuries after the death of Jesus, it is likely to contain material which is similar if not identical to the spells and adjurations of Jesus' day: "The intense conservatism of magic, the theory being that formulae and rituals retain their virtue only if reproduced without deviation, is a well-documented fact...there would appear to be grounds for reading back (with due caution) the later material into the earlier period."[881]

Supernatural magical assistants are always referred to as angels in the magical formulas of the *Sepher Ha-Razim*; reading this text back into the context of the 1st century provides an important clue to the identity of the angels that began to serve Jesus after his test in the wilderness. Various angels are also known from the Greek magical papyri, likely imported there from Jewish spell books since they bear Hebrew names such as Michael and Gabriel—*Γαβριελ πρωταγγελε*: "Gabriel, first among angels."[882] A gold tablet, found in 1544 among the grave goods in a tomb, was engraved with the names of Michael, Gabriel, Raphael and Ouriel, "the standard archangelic tetrarchy...widely found in Jewish and Christian literature and in magical texts..."[883]

In point of fact, *angel* and *spirit* are not carefully distinguished in the New Testament. Philip, for example, hears a message "from an angel of the Lord" which is apparently the same as "the spirit."[884] In the case of Mary, "holy spirit" appears to be

---

880 Luke 4:14.

881 Schürer, *History of the Jewish People in the time of Jesus Christ*, III, Part 1: 344, 345.

882 Preisendanz, *Papyri Graecae Magicae* I, 300-305.
See Lesses, *Harvard Theological Review* 89: 41-60.

883 Kotansky, *Greek Magical Amulets*, Part I, 26.

884 Acts 8:26, 29.

synonymous with "power."[885] The Pharisees ask concerning Paul, "What if a spirit or angel spoke to him?"[886] In Acts it would appear that "the holy spirit" has become identified with "the spirit of Jesus."[887] To further the confusion, people are not only struck mute by demons[888] but by an angel in the case of Zechariah[889] and an angel strikes Herod with a loathesome disease.[890]

Georg Luck: "An essential part of the magician's training consisted in acquiring a *paredros* (*παρεδρος*, *my note*), i.e. an 'assistant' (daemon). This acquisition is a step toward complete initiation…"[891] Morton Smith: "the report that after the temptation the angels served Jesus attributes to him the success magicians strove for—to be served by supernatural beings."[892] "After the gods, the *παρεδροι* (plural of *παρεδρος*, *my no*te) are most frequently identified as *αγγελοι* (angels) and *δαιμονες* (demons) of an unspecified character. These two types of beings occur frequently in the Greek magical papyri."[893] Παρεδρος (paredros), *associate*, is equivalent to the Latin *famulus* and the English *familiar* (spirit). "The peculiar rôle of the angels, heavenly counterparts of all earthly phenomena, as well as the direct servants and emissaries of God, closest to His ear, rendered powerful indeed the man who possessed the secret of bending them to his will." [894] In Lucian's story of Pancrates the magician, the broom

---

[885] Luke 1:35.
[886] Acts 23:9.
[887] Acts 16:6-7.
[888] Mark 9:17.
[889] Luke 1:20.
[890] Acts 12:23.
[891] Luck, *Witchcraft and Magic in Europe: Ancient Greece and Rome*, 108.
[892] Smith, *Jesus the Magician*, 105.
[893] Leda Jean Ciraolo, *Ancient Magic and Ritual Power*, 283. Ciraolo's "Supernatural Assistants in the Greek Magical Papyri" is an invaluable resource.
[894] Trachtenberg, *Jewish Magic and Superstition*, 25.

of the original sorcerer's apprentice becomes a *paredros* or magical servant when a spell is pronounced over it.[895]

A curious term, *ευπαρεδρος* (euparedros), which is translated "undivided devotion" in the *Revised Standard Version*, is found in 1 Corinthians 7:35. Regarding the word, Smith observed,

> Such a "familiar"—to use the old English term—might play a role in the magician's life not dissimilar to that of "the spirit" in Paul's. That Paul recognized the similarity is shown by his recommendation of celibacy on the ground that it would free the Christian from distractions and make him *euparedros* for the Lord—well suited to be joined to Jesus as a *paredros*. In modern terms, the lack of normal sexual satisfaction is likely to lead to compensatory connections with spirits, hence the requirement of celibacy by many shamanistic and priestly groups.[896]

"astounded by his teaching."

The nature of Jesus' "teaching" in this case must be defined by the context of his actions: today we expect *enlightenment* to result from teaching, but the reaction of the villager of Jesus' day was *amazement*: *και εξεπλησσοντο επι τη διδαχη αυτου*, "and they were astounded by his teaching."[897] Davies remarks on the "state of near conceptual chaos regarding the message of Jesus the Teacher," noting that New Testament experts who examine

---

For further comments on angels as assistants to initiated magicians, see Graf, *Magic in the Ancient World*, 90-91, 117.

[895] Lucian, *The Lover of Lies*, 35.

[896] Smith, *Harvard Theological Review* 73: 244.

[897] Mark 1:22, 27, 2:12, 4:41, etc.

the content of Jesus' message "end up with something every time, but something different every one."[898]

Davies regards Jesus as a healer intermittently possessed by another persona, the "spirit of God." While his book is full of interesting insights, Davies flatly denies that Jesus practiced magic: "Jesus' reported use of ad hoc placebo devices such as spitting and the application of mud is not magic."[899] Davies cannot make the case that the procedures used by Jesus were "ad hoc," much less that they functioned as placebos. There was nothing ad hoc about the use of spittle in magic; it was universal magical praxis, and to exchange "placebo" or "magic" does no more than switch terms. To say that placebos work—and it is clear that they do—is no more clarifying than to say magic works—and it seems clear that on some occasions it does. There is certainly nothing in the gospels to suggest that Jesus had anticipated the findings of modern psychology by two millennia and was cleverly using the placebo effect to produce cures—"the sudden cessation of hysterical symptoms."[900] Jesus and his early followers claimed to be casting out demons, not engaging in sleight of mind.

Regarding Jesus' "teaching," Smith noted that "...Jesus' legal teachings are of dubious historicity, and, for what they are worth, indicate that such legal teaching as he did was mostly *ad hoc*...there is no reason to suppose that the [teaching] derived from legal theory, and no consistent legal theory is attributed to him in the gospels or in any other New Testament book.[901]

Paul, the chief spokesman for proto-orthodox Christianity, apparently cared little and knew less about Jesus' ethical teaching.

---

[898] Davies, *Jesus the Healer: Possession, Trance, and the Origins of Christianity*, 13-15.
[899] Ibid, 104.
[900] Smith, *Jesus the Magician*, 8.
[901] Ibid, 23.

As we will see in another chapter, he built his following, not on the message of Jesus, which he scarcely mentions, but on practices of spirit possession, specifically possession by Jesus' spirit.[902] At the level of the most primitive tradition "teaching" and "prophecy" were tightly linked to the performance of magic.

It is clear from the magical papyri that successful works of magic resulted in amazement: *ην και δοκιμασας θαυμασεις το παραδοξον της οικονομιας ταυτης*, "once you have tested it, you will be amazed by the marvel of this magical operation."[903] Once the "the magical characters"—*οι χαρακτηρες* (charaktēres), a magical sigil-like symbol written on papyrus or inscribed on metal—have been put to use the magician is assured, "you will be astounded" (*εκπλαγησει*). [904] The reaction to New Testament magic is typically amazement[905] and fear,[906] just as in the case with pagan magic: *και θαυμασεις*, "and you will be amazed."[907] "…stressing the astonishing efficacy of recipes is a common feature both in magical and medical texts. *Θαυμαζω* and its derivatives are the words usually employed…"[908] The superior efficacy of their miracle working, *the guarantor of truth*, was the constant boast of early Christians. Beginning at the latest with the book of Acts, Christian writers brag non-stop about the power of Christian versus pagan magic. To be amazed by Christian miracle is the first step to conversion; the teaching of the gospel comes later.

---

[902] As at Galatians 4:6-7, for example.

[903] Preisendanz, *Papyri Graecae Magicae* IV, 233.

[904] Ibid, VII, 921.

[905] Matthew 9:33; Luke 5:26; Acts 13:12.

[906] Mark 4:41; Acts 19:17.

[907] Preisendanz, *Papyri Graecae Magicae* XXXVI, 76.

[908] Daniel & Maltomini, *Supplementum Magicum* II, 134.

Meyer & Smith report a similar tendency in Coptic/Egyptian spells, "testifying to the excellence or efficacy of the ritual." *Ancient Christian Magic: Coptic Texts of Ritual Power*, 17.

Jesus' actions everywhere conform to those of a magician. "In Mark 1:24 the demon cries out to Christ, 'I know who you are' continuing with the holy name as proof of recognition. This is a magical formula well attested in the [magical] papyri...This is rather similar to the girl with the oracular spirit in Acts 16.17 who greets Paul and his friends with the warning exclamation, 'These men are servants of the most high God' just before the spirit is exorcized."[909] Janowitz: "In the first centuries in order to unmask a daimon and drive it from somebody's body the officiant himself had to have more-than-human status...Divine names...function similarly to signatures and signature guarantees in our culture, which are understood to be legally binding representations."[910] "...the names are the source of power by which human beings can enforce their will upon the gods or angels."[911]

As a layman, Jesus' authority to preach is based on *exorcism*, not formal preparation. As noted previously, the crowd declares Jesus to be a prophet *after* he performs signs. As Jesus himself said of his public, "Unless you see signs and wonders, you will never believe."[912] Some have interpreted Jesus' extended time in the wilderness as having shamanistic overtones consistent with a vision quest, but due caution should be exercised in this regard; there is no evidence for an exact equivalent of shamans in the Middle East.[913] Nevertheless, Lewis notes, shamans are masters of spirits[914] and the Jesus of the gospels is nothing if not a master of spirits.

---

909 Hull, *Hellenistic Magic and the Synoptic Tradition*, 67-68.
910 Janowitz, *Magic in the Roman World*, 36, 40.
911 Lesses, *Harvard Theological Review* 89: 52.
912 John 4:48.
913 Dickie, *Magic and Magicians in the Greco-Roman World*, 13.
914 Lewis, *Ecstatic Religion*, 56.

"with authority and not like the scribes."

Mark tells us that Jesus taught with "authority" and "not like the scribes." The scribes were a literate class charged with both copying and interpreting the laws of Moses and they worked to be self-supporting so as to impose no financial burden on the population. They were the men to whom questions of religious observance might be referred, and they were deeply respected, a respect indirectly acknowledged in Mark.[915] It is not possible that they had *no authority.*

The word Mark uses for *authority* is εξουσια (exousia); it refers particularly to "the belief that some people have supernatural powers as a gift."[916] In Jesus' case the accounts make clear that the authority in question had nothing whatever to do with interpreting the laws of Moses. Jesus had the power to command demonic spirits. Hull notes that of the ten instances of εξουσια in Mark, only one is *not* connected with exorcism or healing, and concludes, "The people do not admire Jesus for his learning but for his power over the demons."[917] Mark himself clearly defines what the *authority* in question meant: "*He commands the unclean spirits and they obey him.*" As Lenormant observed, "the sorcerer...subjected the demons to his orders."[918] Significantly, Satan offered Jesus εξουσια, "authority," which Jesus refused (Luke 4:6).

That Jesus' *authority is the power to command spirits* is specified by Luke: "And they were all overcome with wonder and began say- ing to one to another, 'What *oracle* (λογος) is this that *with authority and power* (εν εξουσια και δυναμις) he commands the unclean spirits and they leave?"[919] The polysemous term λογος

---

[915] Mark 12:38.

[916] Luck, *Witchcraft and Magic*, 99.

[917] Hull, *Hellenistic Magic*, 165. The exceptional use of exousia is found in Mark 13:34, where the reference is apocalyptic.

[918] Lenormant, *Chaldean Magic: Its Origin and Development*, 60.

[919] Λυκε 4·36.

(logos), which I have translated "oracle," can mean *word, speech* or *oracle* in this context, and is used in the magical papyri to mean *spell.* In any case, Jesus' authority is *the power to cast out demons,* a power he can transmit to others: "After calling the twelve together, *he gave them power and authority* (*εδωκεν αυτοις δυναμιν και εξουσιαν*) over every demon and to cure diseases…[920]

Some of the methods by which Jesus commands obedience from unclean spirits are revealed in this account of an exorcism:

> After he got out of the boat, immediately he encountered coming out of the tombs a man controlled by an unclean spirit. He lived among the tombs since no one was able to bind him even with a chain. He had been bound with chains and shackles many times, but he snapped the chains apart and broke the shackles in pieces, and no one was strong enough to restrain him.[921]
>
> He screamed day and night in the tombs and in the hills, lacerating himself with stones.
>
> When he saw Jesus from far away, he ran and fell at his feet and screamed out in a loud voice, "What have I to do with you, Jesus, son of the Most High God? I beg you in God's name do not torture me!"
>
> Because Jesus had said to it, "Come out of the man, unclean spirit!" and asked him, "What is your name?"
>
> He said, "Legion is my name, because we are many."[922] He entreated him not to banish them from the region. There was a large herd of pigs grazing on the hill and the demons begged him, saying, "Send us into the pigs so that we can enter them." He gave them per-

---

[920] Luke 9:1.

[921] *ουδεις εδυνατο αυτον δησαι*: "no one was able to restrain him…" (Mark 5:3). See below for discussion of the term *δεω*, *bind.* The failure to "bind" the man may imply previous failed exorcisms as well as physical restraints.

[922] "…the demon's utterance of its name signals its defeat." (Ogden, *In Search of the Sorcerer's Apprentice*, 132).

> mission and the unclean spirits came out and entered the pigs and the herd of about two thousand pigs stampeded over the cliff and into the sea and drowned in the sea.[923]

Mark's account has a number of points in common with the manipulation of demons and ghosts described in ancient sources —that the demons in question may have included ghosts is suggested by the report that the afflicted man "lived among the tombs." The transfer of the demons from the man into the pigs is an ancient technique: "Much of the magician's art consisted in his ability to transfer a spiritual power from its abode into some object under his control."[924]

When being cast out, the demons typically scream—"the unclean spirit *screamed with a loud voice* (φωνησαν φωνη μεγαλη) and came out of him"[925]—or beg not to be tortured—"crying out with a loud voice" (κραξας φωνη μεγαλη) the demon pleads, "I beg you by God do not torture me!" (ορκιζω σε τον θεον μη με βασανισης).[926] As Apollonius stares down a ghost (ειδωλον) that has possessed a man, it screams "like those being branded or stretched on the rack,"[927] and confronting "one of the vampires" (μια των εμπουσων) masquerading as a man's bride, "the phantom (το φασμα) appeared to shed tears and pleaded with him *not to torture it* (μη βασανιζειν αυτο) or to force it to confess what it was."[928] The threat of torture is also known from the magical papyri: "God of gods, King of kings, now compel a kindly demon, a giver of oracles, to come to me *lest even more severe tortures be applied...*" (ινα μη εις χειρονας βασανους ελθω).[929] In short, the exorcisms of the gospel of Mark conform

[923] Mark 5:2-13.

[924] Thompson, *Semitic Magic: Its Origins and Development*, 142.

[925] Mark 1:26.

[926] Mark 5:7.

[927] Philostratus, *Life of Apollonius*, IV, 20.

[928] Ibid, IV, 25.

[929] Preisendanz, *Papyri Graecae Magicae*, II, 53-55.

exactly to the standard magical practice of the age. "Sorceres" (*οι γοητες*), Philostratus observes, perform their wonders by "torturing restless ghosts (*βασανους ειδωλων χωρουντες*), or barbaric sacrifices or incantations..."[930]

The exorcisms of the New Testament are nearly identical in many details with an exorcism described by Lucian:

> Everyone knows of the Syrian from Palestine, the master of his art, and how he receives many moonstruck, frothing at the mouth and eyes rolling, and he sets them aright and sends them away sound of mind...standing beside them as they lie there, he asks from whence [the demons] have come into the body. The madman himself is silent, but the demon answers in Greek or a barbarian [language] from whence and how he entered the man. By adjuring, or if the spirit does not obey, threatening, he drives out the demon.[931]

The "Syrian from Palestine" is a Jewish exorcist. It is not impossible that Lucian had Jesus himself—renowned for casting out demons—in mind when composing his story of the Jewish exorcist and that he and his audience were enjoying a joke at Christian expense. "This passage enraged pious scholiasts who saw it as yet another of Lucian's blasphemies."[932]

Several lines of evidence suggest this conclusion. As noted above, Lucian appears to have been well acquainted with Christians and considered them figures of fun. In connection with Peregrinus' fling with Christianity, Lucian says of Jesus, *τον δε ανεσκολοπισμενον εκεινον σοφιστην αυτον προσκυνωσιν*, "and

---

[930] Philostratus, *Life of Apollonius*, V, 12.

[931] Lucian, *The Lover of Lies*, III, 16.

[932] Jones, *Culture and Society in Lucian*, 48.

"It is possible this parody was inspired by some gospel story..." (Smith, *Jesus the Magician*, 57.)

worshipping that crucified sophist himself,"[933] a remark dripping with contempt that also aroused the wrath of later Christian commentators.[934] The *sophist, σοφιστης*, in Lucian's story is a *fraud*, and *σοφιστης* (sophistēs) could be used as a synonym for *γοης* (goēs),[935] *deceiver* or *sorcerer*. The Greek term for sophist is used here with much the same force as the negative connotation of "jesuitical." Lucian calls Peregrinus—who he compares to Jesus, "the man who was crucified in Palestine (*τον ανθρωπον τον εν τη Παλαιστινη ανασκολοπισθεντα*)"—a *prophet* (*προφητης*), a *leader of a religious cult* (*θιασαρχης*) and even a *συναγωγευς*, *one who calls an assembly*, or *leader of a synagogue*, and clearly considered both Peregrinus and Jesus to be *frauds* or *sorcerers* (*γοης*) and *tricksters* (*τεχνιτης ανθρωπος*), sleight of hand artists.[936]

An unfortunate vinedresser named Midas is bitten by a snake and carried *in extremis* on a stretcher out of the field. At the suggestion of a helpful bystander, a "Chaldean," who is also called a "Babylonian," is summoned. The Chaldean pronounces an incantation (*επωδη*) over the bite. Midas, now completely restored, then picks up his cot and returns to work to the amazement of the bystanders—"we were amazed" (*ημεις δε εθαυμαζομεν*).[937] A similar story from the gospel of Mark concerns a paralytic brought to Jesus for healing. Due to the density of the crowd that has gathered, it proves impossible for the four men carrying the cot to approach Jesus through the door, so they break a hole in the roof and lower the cot down to Jesus through the hole. The result of Jesus' healing miracle is described as follows: "He got up, took his mat and walked out in full view of them all. This amazed everyone (*εξιστασθαι παντας*) and they praised God, saying, 'We have never seen anything like this!'"[938] The

---

[933] Lucian, *On the Death of Peregrinus*, 13.
[934] Ogden, *In Search of the Sorcerer's Apprentice*, 133.
[935] Liddell & Scott, *A Greek-English Lexicon*, 1410.
[936] Lucian, *On the Death of Peregrinus*, 11, 13.
[937] Lucian, *The Lover of Lies* (*Φιλοψευδης η απιστων*), 12-13.
[938] Mark 2:12 (NIV).

pick-up-your-cot-and-walk story was widely circulated; it is repeated by the gospel of John,[939] written near the end of the 1st century or afterward, and if Lucian had heard it, it is likely he found the tale an irresistible target for parody, inserting a variant into *The Lover of Lies*. The supposition that Lucian had Jesus specifically in mind is made more attractive by Lucian's inclusion of magicians who amaze crowds,[940] fly through the air,[941] walk on water,[942] and bring a rotting corpse to life.[943]

The reference to the wild man from the tombs as "demon-possessed"—*θεωρουσιν τον δαιμονιζομενον καθημενον*, "they saw the demon-possessed man sitting…"[944]—introduces a term, *δαιμονιζομαι* (daimonizomai) well known from the magical papyri: "*If you say the name to the demon-possessed* (*εαν δαιμονιζομενω ειπης το ονομα*) while putting sulfur and asphalt under his nose, instantly [the demon] will speak and go away…"[945]

Names to conjure with.

The demand that the demon tell its name is standard magical praxis: "The invocation of angelic names in Jewish magic may be regarded as in part the parallel to the pagan invocation of many deities, and in part as invocation of the infinite (personified) phases and energies of the one God. Both Jewish and pagan magic agreed in requiring the accumulation of as many names of the deity or demon as possible, for fear lest no one name exhaust the potentiality of the spiritual being conjured."[946]

---

939 John 5:9.
940 Matthew 9:33; Luke 5:26; Acts 13:12.
941 Matthew 4:6.
942 Matthew 14:25, 26.
943 John 11:39.
944 Mark 5:15.
945 Preisendanz, *Papyri Graecae Magicae*, XIII, 243-244.
946 Trachtenberg, *Jewish Magic and Superstition*, 86-87.

The names of spirit entities are central to magical working; they function as "the reservoir of heavenly power."[947]

It is of interest that healing and raising people from the dead also involves calling them by name. Several examples can be cited, that of Aeneas, a paralytic,[948] Tabitha, who is dead,[949] and particularly, Lazarus.[950] In the case of Lazarus, who has been dead for four days, the miracle raises not only a corpse, but an interesting question: to whom or to what is the command to come forth addressed? To the body that has begun to decay?[951] The soul? A ghost?

The casting of the demons into the swine represents another common magical procedure involving the transfer of an evil spirit into an inanimate or living object, a technique sometimes known in the literature as *envoûtement.* "Sumerian incantations against evil demons describe how an animal, usually a goat or pig, was offered as a substitute for the sick person. The purpose of the ritual was the transference of the disease or demon from the man to the animal…the demon was conjured to leave him and take possession of the animal instead."[952]

The centurion's slave boy.

We are given some further insight into the nature of Jesus' authority by the story of the centurion's slave boy.

---

947 Lesses, *Harvard Theological Review* 89: 52.
948 Acts 9:33-34.
949 Acts 9:40.
950 John 11:43.
951 John 11:17, 39.
952 Marie-Louise Thomsen, *Witchcraft and Magic in Europe: Biblical and Pagan Societies*, 71-72.

> As he entered Capernaum, a centurion came to him, entreating him, "Lord, my boy is lying at home paralyzed, suffering terribly."
>
> Jesus said to him, "I will come and heal him."
>
> The centurion replied, "Lord, I am not worthy for you to step under my roof, but say a word and my boy will be healed. For I, too, am a man with authority, having soldiers under my command, and I say to this one, "Go!" and he goes, and to another, "Come!" and he comes, and to my slave, "Do this!" and he does it."[953]

The point of the story is that the centurion intuitively understands Jesus' command of the spirits to be the same as his command of his soldiers, and for this insight is rewarded with the healing of his boy. The wording of the pericope of the centurion and his boy—*τω δουλω μου ποιησον τουτο και ποιει*: "to my slave, '*Do this,*' *and he does it*"—is nearly identical to that of the Greek magical papyri where the magician commands his spirit assistant: *λεγε αυτω ποιησον τουτο το εργον και ποιει παραυτα*: "say to him, "*Do this task, and he does it* immediately…"[954] Jesus can say the word and summon 12 legions of angels, 72,000![955] Elijah enjoyed similar angelic support in the form of heavenly armies.[956]

> No spirit of the air that is joined to a powerful assistant will draw back into Hades, for all things are subordinate to him, and if you wish to do something, merely speak his name into the air and say, "Come!" and you will see him standing near you. Say to him "Do this task," and he does it immediately, and having done it, he will ask, "What else do you wish, for I am hurrying into the sky." If you have no orders at that moment, tell him, "Go,

---

[953] Matthew 8:5-9.

[954] Preisendanz, *Papyri Graecae Magicae*, I, 182.

[955] Matthew 26:53.

[956] 2 Kings 6:16-17

> Lord," and he will leave. In this way you alone will see the god, nor will anyone except you alone hear his voice when he speaks.[957]

The text of Matthew reflects nearly identical imagery from the *Sepher Ha-Razim*: "...to declare the names of the overseers of each and every firmament...and what are the names of their attendants...and to rule over spirits and over demons, to send them (wherever you wish) so they will go out like slaves..."[958] Jennings and Liew conclude:

> What is stunning is that both the centurion and the Pharisees are basically embracing the same assumptions: authority works only *within* chains of command. Just as a centurion can order the coming and going of soldiers and servants under his command, the ruler of demons can cast out demons under its rule. What then is the centurion implying about Jesus' identity? He believes that Jesus can order the coming and going of the demon that has been "torturing" his boy-love with paralysis, because he believes that Jesus is the commander or the ruler of that and other demons. In other words, not only are the centurion and the Pharisees in agreement about how authority operates, they further concur on the identity of Jesus as a commanding officer in the chain of demonic beings.[959]

The word *παιδιον* (paidion) used of the enigmatic boy carried sexual connotations, and homosexual relations with slaves were apparently common. "Male and female slaves were quite simply sexually available to their masters at all times—whether children, adolescents or adults—and also available to those to whom their owners granted rights...In essence, a slave was ex-

---

[957] Preisendanz, *Papyri Graecae Magicae*, II, 179-189.

[958] Morgan, *Sepher Ha-Razim*, 17-18.

[959] Jennings & Liew, *Journal of Biblical Literature* 123: 485-486.

cluded from the very category of manhood, perpetually retaining—despite his physical characteristics—the character of a child."[960] The slave, along with women and boys, is in "a catch-all category that might best be labeled *unmen*..."[961] In his classic study of childhood, deMause sketches the situation: "The child in antiquity lived his earliest years in an atmosphere of sexual abuse...Boy brothels flourished in every city, and one could even contract for the use of a rent-a-boy service in Athens...men kept slaves boys to abuse, so that even free-born children saw their fathers sleeping with boys. Children were sometimes sold into concubinage."[962]

The story of the centurion's boy and its redaction give us a nearly perfect example both of the ambiguity of the Greek vocabulary and of the editing and rephrasing to which the New Testament material has been subjected. In any case it is clear that even if the *Sitz im Leben* of the story has been blurred, the point made about authority is retained.

The stronger overcomes.

The notion that superior authority encompasses the idea of superior strength agrees entirely with Jesus' own characterization of exorcism: the strong are overcome and bound by the stronger:

> "How can Satan cast out Satan? If a kingdom divides against itself, that kingdom cannot stand, and if a house divides against itself, that house will not be able to stand. So if Satan rises up against himself and becomes

---

[960] MacDonald, *New Testament Studies* 53: 95, 106. MacDonald also points out that from a Christian perspective *total* obedience of children and slaves was expected (Colossians 3:20, 22).

[961] Anderson & Moore, *New Testament Masculinities*, 69.

[962] deMause, *The History of Childhood*, 43.

> divided, he cannot stand. To the contrary, his end has come."
>
> "No one can enter the strong man's house to plunder his possessions unless he first binds the strong man, and then he plunders his house."[963]

The *strong man* metaphor—*την οικιαν του ισχυρου*: "the strong man's house..."—is also known from the magical papyri: *εγω ειμι ο ακεφαλος δαιμων ισχυρος ο εχων το πυρ το αθανατον*: "I am the headless demon...the mighty one who has the unquenchable fire..."[964]

The claim being made is that Jesus is stronger than "the strong man," able to bind him and take away his possessions.[965] On this passage Grundmann says: "The mission of Christ means that the *ισχυτερος* ["stronger," *my note*] comes, that he binds the *ισχυρος* ["strong"] when he has entered his house, and that He robs him of his spoil. This is how the exorcisms are to be understood."[966]

As Garrett notes in connection with the metaphor of plunder, "whenever Jesus exorcises or heals, he takes spoil from Satan's kingdom and adds it to God's own...he as 'the stronger one' is entering and plundering the domain of the conquered Satan."[967] The gospels consistently represent Jesus as operating from a position of superior strength in regard to demons. "The exorcist mentioned by Mark, ix.38-39, introduced the very name of Jesus into the stock of *ισχυρα ονοματα* ["powerful names," *my note*] and formulae which he—like other Jewish conjurors—probably had at his command for the explusion of demons ...This indeed very surprising concession on the part of the

---

963 Mark 3:23-27.

964 Preisendanz, *Papyri Graecae Magicae* V, 146-147.

965 Compare Matthew 3:11, "The one coming after me is *stronger* than I..."

966 Grundman, *Theological Dictionary of the New Testament*, III, 401.

967 Garrett, *The Demise of the Devil*, 45.

Lord implied that his *ονομα* ["name," *my note*] worked *ex opere operato*, like other 'strong names' of traditional magic."[968]

In keeping with his authority, the gospels speak of Jesus *rebuking* demons. The verb in question, *επιτιμαω* (epitimaō), is variously translated *rebuke*, *warn*, *reprimand*, or *reprove*, and it is used not only for exorcism, but also for healing and for the performance of weather magic. In addition to demons,[969] Jesus "rebukes" the wind,[970] a fever,[971] and the apostle Peter—where the wording, "Get away from me, Satan,"[972] has the character of an exorcism. Exorcism is subjugation by force.[973] Horsley argues that the "term signifies something far stronger than a 'rebuke,' something more like 'vanquish' or 'destroy'"[974] and the question of the demons, "Have you come to destroy us?"[975] supports that conclusion.

"he put his fingers in his ears, spit, and touched his tongue..."

A brief account in the gospel of Mark reveals some additional magical elements of Jesus' healing technique:

---

[968] Eitrem, *Some Notes on the Demonology in the New Testament*, 4-5.

[969] *επετιμησεν δε ο Ιησουη τω πνευματι τω ακαθαρτω και ιασατο τον παιδια*: "Jesus rebuked the unclean spirit and the boy was healed." (Luke 9:42). Compare Luke 4:41.

[970] *και διεγερθεις επετιμησεν τω ανεμω*: "and arising, he rebuked the wind." (Mark 4:39).

[971] *επετιμησεν τω πυρετω και αφηκεν αυτην*: "he rebuked the fever and it left her." (Luke 4:39).

[972] *επετιμησεν Πετρω και λεγει υπαγε οπισω μου σατανα*: "he rebuked Peter and said, 'Get away from me, Satan!'" (Mark 8:33). Compare the language of Matthew 4:10: *λεγει αυτω ο Ιησους υπαγε σατανα*: "Jesus said to him, 'Get away, Satan!'"

[973] Kee, *New Testament Studies* 14: 232-246.

[974] Horsley, *Experientia*, I, 53.

[975] Mark 1:24.

> They brought a deaf mute[976] to him and they entreated him to lay his hand upon him. Taking him away from the crowd to a private place, he put his fingers in his ears, spit, and touched his tongue, and looking up into the sky, he groaned and said, "Ephphatha!" that is, "Be opened!"
>
> Instantly his ears were opened, and the bond that held his tongue was loosed and he spoke normally.[977]

The several steps in this healing ritual—"he put his fingers in his ears, spit, and touched his tongue, and looking up into the sky, he groaned,"—*και αναβλεψας εις τον ουρανον εστεναξεν*, "and looking up into the sky, he groaned"—find very close parallels with similar rituals in the magical papyri: "Facing the sun, speak seven times into your hand, and spit once, and stroke your face..."[978] "*Looking into the air* (εις αερα βλεπων), holding your hand over your heart, say Ū, *looking into the sky* (εις τον ουρανον βλεπων), holding both hands on your head, say, Ō..."[979] Compare "And when you finish reciting this adjuration twenty-one times, look upwards and you shall see something like a flame of fire..."[980] On Egyptian magical procedure: "The healer would sometimes accompany these incantations with a ritual which involved carrying out a series of acts and gestures upon the patient..."[981] "Whilst healing this man, Jesus put his fingers into the man's ears...in other biblical contexts the finger appears as the symbol of God's power. In this latter use it may

---

[976] Mute because the demon possessing him is mute (Matthew 9:32; Luke 11:14).

[977] Mark 7:32-35.

[978] Preisendanz, *Papyri Graecae Magicae*, III, 422-423.

[979] Ibid, XIII, 831, 832.

[980] Bohak, *Ancient Jewish Magic*, 171, quoting from the *Sepher Ha-Razim*.

[981] *Religion and Magic in Ancient Egypt*, 286.

have connections with magic and exorcism, and there are many parallels in the magical literature."[982]

Spittle was a well-known magical substance. In the *Satyricon*, we are told how a witch used spit to cure Encolpius' erectile dysfunction: "The old woman pulled a string made from threads of different colors from her dress and tied it around my neck. Then she took some dirt, mixed it with her spittle, and with her third finger made a mark on my forehead..."[983]

Essentially the same technique is used by Jesus to cure blindness: "Spittle is used in three of the miracles. In John 9.6 paste is made from the spittle of Jesus and clay is smeared on a man's eyes; in Mark 8.23 and 7.33 spitting is used in cases of blindness and dumbness...All races of antiquity attached magical significance to spittle. The Pyramid Texts (late third millennium BC) speak of Atum spitting out Shu, the air, in the act of creation...The Epidaurus inscriptions describe miraculous cures wrought by the lick of sacred snakes and dogs within the temples of Asclepius..."[984] And from Lenormant: "...at the moment he spat he made a compact with the demon..."[985] Achtemeier observes that "saliva...was effective in cures, especially of the eyes..."[986] The use of spittle in Egyptian magical praxis has been described in detail by Ritner,[987] who notes regarding "the magical applications of spittle" (89) that "Egyptian practice will have coincided with certain healing miracles of Jesus, though the direct influence of Egyptian methodology has been strongly suggested" (90). Ritner also notes that spittle came to be regarded in the early church "as a bodily relic" (91). "Spittle, like every secretion of the body and, indeed, the πνευμα ["breath,"

982 Hull, *Hellenistic Magic and the Synoptic Tradition*, 82.

983 Quoted by Luck, *Arcana Mundi*, 89.

984 Hull, *Hellenistic Magic*, 76-77.

985 Lenormant, *Chaldean Magic: Its Origin and Development*, 63.

986 Achtemeier, *Aspects of Religious Propaganda in Judaism and Early Christianity*, 153.

987 Ritner, *The Mechanics of Ancient Egyptian Magical Practice*, 74-92.

or "spirit," *my note*] itself, is by itself a vehicle of *δυναμις* ["power"] and ambivalent—in Palestine as elsewhere…On the whole the spittle of *θειοι ανδρες* ["divine men"] was preeminently powerful."[988]

Lucian turns the magical use of spittle to comic effect in his story of Menippus the Cynic, who, disillusioned by philosophers, traveled to Babylon to make the acquaintance of "one of the Magi...a Chaldean wise man of supernatural skill...who muttered indistinct incantations to invoke certain spirits (*τινας επικαλεισθαι*)...and after the incantation, he spat (*αποπτυσας*) three times in my face."[989]

Tipei, a dogmatically apologetic writer, concedes, "The use of spittle in healing brings together medicine, miracle, and magic. There are cases when the use of spittle has unambiguous magical functions." After presenting pages of references that support this observation, he nevertheless concludes, "Whatever its signifycance in the healing practice of Jesus, the use of spittle had no magical connotations."[990] Others are less eager to ignore the evidence: "Finally, Jesus as a popular first-century Jewish magician in the tradition, say, of Elijah and Elisha, may well be different from the professional magicians who owned those magical papyri, but that should be established by comparing their actions, not presuming their motives."[991]

As far back as 1927, Campbell Bonner noted, "*στεναζω* ["groan," *my note*] and *αναστεναζω* ["cry out"] are words which have mystical and magical associations, and that the action denoted by them may be considered as a conventional part of the

---

[988] Eitrem, *Some Notes on the Demonology in the New Testament*, 56, 58.

[989] Lucian, *Menippos or The Descent into Hades* (Μενιππος η νεκουμαντεια), 6-7.

[990] Tipei, *The Laying On of Hands in the New Testament*, 143-145.

[991] Crossan, *The Historical Jesus*, 310.

mystical-magic technique."[992] Such details of magical technique are typically omitted by Matthew and Luke, who also chose to delete any mention of healings *that take place in stages* such as the healing of the blind man recorded in Mark 8:22-26. For example, Elijah raises a dead boy after lying on him three times.[993]

Matthew and Luke edit Mark's exorcism stories to remove "features that might suggest a magical association for Jesus' miracles. The deep sighs of Jesus and his pronouncing of foreign phrases in Mark have been removed by these evangelists precisely because they seem to fit so well into a magical tradition of healing."[994] Groaning and wailing are techniques for summoning spirit powers: "Having said these things, make sacrifice and *back away, wailing loudly as you finish* (*αναστεναξας αναποδιζων καταβηθι*) and [the goddess] will come immediately."[995] "Sighing or groaning…may also confirm the contact with the deity or demon invoked, or intensify an *αγωγη* [attraction spell, *my note*]."[996] The stories of healing and exorcism recounted in the gospels of Mark and John reveal well-known elements of magical practice including the use of spittle, a word of power or *vox magica*, as well as sighing and gestures: "From other stories in the New Testament, Greco-Roman and rabbinic texts we can reconstruct a fairly standard repertoire of exorcistic techniques. These included looking upwards, sighing or groaning, making hand gestures (such as making the sign of the cross), spitting, invoking the deity and speaking "nonsense" words or letter strings. Sometimes the demon was commanded to speak as a way of demonstrating both his presence in the human body and the practitioner's control over him."[997]

---

[992] Bonner, *Harvard Theological Review* 20: 172.
[993] 1 Kings 17:21.
[994] Cotter, *Miracles in Greco-Roman Antiquity: A Sourcebook*, 177.
[995] Preisendanz, *Papyri Graecae Magicae* IV, 2491-2492.
[996] Eitrem, *Some Notes on the Demonology in the New Testament*, 54.
[997] Janowitz, *Magic in the Roman World*, 39.

The invocation Jesus uses as a part of his technique of exorcism also has close parallels in the magical papyri as the comparison below illustrates:

> Seeing the crowd bearing down on him, Jesus rebuked the unclean spirit, saying to it, "I order you, speechless and deaf spirit, get out of him, and may you never come back into him!"
>
> Shrieking and convulsing him horribly, it came out and left him like a corpse so that most of them said, "He's dead!" But Jesus, taking him by the hand, raised him and stood him upright.[998]

> Excellent ritual for casting out demons.
> Spell to be recited over his head:
> [*Coptic gloss inserted into Greek text.*]
> I order you, demon, whoever you are, by this god...Get out, demon, whoever you are, and stay away from [*Name*]! Now, now! Quickly, quickly! Get out, demon...![999]

As Geller points out, "Jesus' specific exorcism formula, 'Go out from him and never enter him again'—*εξελθε εξ αυτου*: "get out of him..."—can also be identified in contemporary magical literature."[1000] The language reflects a widely known formula for exorcism used by Jesus among others: *εξελθε δαιμων οστις ποτ' ουν ει*: "get out, demon, *whoever you are*...!" The exorcist is supposed to fill in the name or characteristics of the particular demon—"whoever you are"—in question, which is why Jesus says, "I order you, *speechless and deaf spirit*, get out of him..."

The textual history of this spell presents some difficulties: an Old Coptic gloss has been inserted into the Greek text. The

---

998 Mark 9:25-27.

999 Preisendanz, *Papyri Graecae Magicae*, IV, 1229-1246.

1000 Geller, *Journal of Jewish Studies* 28: 145.

Coptic reads: "Hail, God of Abraham; hail, God of Isaac; hail, God of Jacob; *Jesus Chrēstos,*"—ⲒⲎⲤⲞⲎⲤ ⲠⲒⲬⲢⲎⲤⲦⲞⲤ—"the Holy Spirit, *etc...*" The Greek *χρηστος* (chrēstos), which becomes the Coptic loan word ⲬⲢⲎⲤⲦⲞⲤ, means *good, auspicious* or *true, trustworthy.* Based on recent discoveries from the papyri it is nearly certain that *χρηστος* was a variant spelling of *χριστος*, *Christ,* and that "Christ" is meant to form part of a magical spell. Several lines of evidence support this conclusion. Working from the Oxyrhynchus material, Blumell cites a letter from "Heras, a Christian" in which the Greek wording, *Ηρας χρηστιανος*, preserves the spelling found in the magical text. The variant spelling made sense to ancient writers because "it was taken to have an association with the adjective *χρηστος* (good) since the *iota* of *χριστιανος* is periodically replaced by an *eta.*"[1001] It is also noteworthy that the spelling *χρηστιανος* is found at Acts 11:26 and 26:28 in no less an ancient authority than the Codex Sinaiticus. As pointed out by Meyer and Smith, "Only in these Coptic words are there Christian elements in this text."[1002]

Morton Smith: "These uses of Jesus' name in pagan spells are flanked by a vast body of material testifying to the use of his name in Christian spells and exorcisms...The attestations are confirmed by a multitude of Christian amulets, curse tablets, and magical papyri in which Jesus is the god most often invoke-

---

[1001] Blumell, *Lettered Christians: Christians, Letters, and Late Antique Oxyrhynchus,* 37, 39.

As Blumell has documented, there are in fact no less than four spellings of "Christian" in the materials recovered from Oxyrhychus: *χριστιανος*, *χρηστιανος*, *χρησιανος*, and *χρητιανος*, although in most cases the religious identity of the writer is uncertain because self-referential use cannot be clearly demonstrated (pg 38).

See particularly Shandruck, *Bulletin of the American Society of Papyrologists* 47: 205-219 which gives a detailed assessment of the evidence.

[1002] Meyer & Smith, *Ancient Christian Magic: Coptic Texts of Ritual Power,* 43.

ed..."[1003] To cite but one example, the Coptic abbreviation for "Christ," ⲡ̅ⲭ̅ⲥ̅, "the Christ," is known from "a perfectly Jewish magical text."[1004]

It is worth noting that in the accounts of both Matthew and Luke, the procedural details of the exorcism of the deaf and dumb spirit, as well as the description of the dramatic physical effects, have been stripped away, leaving us with these insipid versions:

> So Jesus rebuked the unclean spirit and the demon came out of him and the boy was healed in that very hour.[1005]

> As the boy approached, the demon threw him down in convulsions, so Jesus rebuked the unclean spirit and healed the boy and returned him to his father.[1006]

I propose that these are particularly clear examples of the way in which the exorcisms have been "edited"—*cleaned up* would be more accurate—to make them more "miraculous" and less "magical," thereby rendering Jesus more palatable to a sophisticated audience. Similar editorializing continued with the apocryphal gospels and acts following Jesus' death: "Almost as if to disprove any charge against the apostles as sorcerers or magicians, the apocryphal acts never describe their miracles in such as way as even to hint at the use of herbs or incantations, or magical devices...this is the most obvious example of anti-magical polemic in the way a miracle is performed, the intention is symptomatic of other accounts of miracles..."[1007]

[1003] Smith, *Jesus the Magician*, 63.

[1004] Bohak, *Bulletin of the American Society of Papyrologists* 36:35-36.

[1005] Matthew 17:18.

[1006] Luke 9:42

[1007] Achtemeier, *Aspects of Religious Propaganda in Judaism and Early Christianity*, 169.

However, an alternative reading of Mark 9:25-27 must be acknowledged. According to this reconstruction of the history of the text, the core idea 'Jesus rebuked the demon and it left' was the basic form of the text of Mark from which Matthew and Luke copied. In short, the gospel of Mark used by Matthew and Luke lacked the exorcistic formula, "I order you, speechless and deaf spirit, get out of him, and may you never come back into him!" This reading of the texts assumes that the exorcistic formula represents a later addition to Mark, i.e., it could not have been *deleted* by Matthew and Luke since it was never in the earlier form of the gospel in the first place.

The pericope under discussion is one of a number of well-known instances in which Matthew and Luke differ from Mark at points where they appear to be using Mark as a source. It is possible that Matthew and Luke copied from a shorter form of the gospel of Mark which is now lost to us. This theory assumes that in the first century the text of Mark existed in two or more forms. Since we have no manuscript of any gospel from the first hundred years after their composition, the theory of multiple co-existing forms of the gospels cannot be confirmed, but it is not in any way inconsistent with the available evidence.

The plausibility of this reconstruction of events is supported by Koester's observation that the exorcistic formula does not really match the demonic manifestation: if specific demons were held responsible for specific diseases, then why is a demon of *deaf-mutism* being adjured in a case of *seizure*? "Apparently, the redactor shows little interest in the healing of the disease. Rather, he wants to describe the effect of a powerful exorcism and thus introduces the following action of Jesus which has no parallel whatever in Matthew and Luke."[1008]

[1008] Koester, *Gospel Traditions in the Second Century*, 24.

Regardless of how the history of the text is reconstructed—I happily admit that my proposal is at least as speculative as any other—the evidence of the text shows that early Christians could describe the details Jesus' exorcism in the same language as that of the magical papyri and that such a description became incorporated into the officially approved records of the church. "Details of some of the healing stories in Mark indicate a magical context just as details of the exorcisms seem to. The healing of the deaf mute in Mark 7:32ff. is perhaps the clearest case."[1009] In any event, the inclusion of the exorcistic formula is evidence that formulae of exactly this kind were already in use among Christians when the gospel was composed and that its insertion (or retention) in the gospel of Mark served to validate such use.

Although the healings and exorcisms are held up as evidence of Jesus' divine status, the details of their performance evidently became an embarrassment to elements within the later church—they portray a Jesus who might be regarded merely as one among many itinerant wonder-working holy men. By this point theology was already moving steadily away from the historical Jesus whose flaws, particularly his reputation as a magician, were being papered over even as his official résumé was being prepared. As Hull notes, "Matthew has a suspicion of exorcism. We have seen how though the messianic authority over the evil spirits is maintained, almost all details of techniques are omitted. This is because exorcism was one the main functions of the magician. The magic consisted in the method; Matthew retains the fact without the method, trying in this way to purify the subject."[1010] Keck also notes "the Matthean reluctance to celebrate the signs of present salvation, which in Paul, Luke-Acts, and John are signaled by the enabling presence of the Spirit...if for Paul, Luke-Acts, and John the presence of the Spirit is char-

---

[1009] Hull, *Hellenistic Magic*, 73.
[1010] Ibid, 139.

acteristic of Christian life, for Matthew it is reserved for a truly exceptional situation."[1011]

The author of Matthew anxiously eliminated all references to magical technique, including the *voces magicae*: "and he cast out the spirits *with a word*,"[1012] but the *word* is never specified. It should be noted that λογος (logos), *word*, frequently occurs as a text heading in the magical papyri where it means *spell*. Ironically, it would be conceivable to translate the passage in Matthew, "he cast out the spirits *with a spell*." But in fact, Matthew reports only one word spoken to a demon, and twenty-three words spoken by demons, whereas Luke records nine words spoken directly to demons, and three more indirectly, as well as thirty-four words spoken directly by demons to Jesus.[1013]

It will come as no surprise that modern Christian apologists draw the very conclusions that Matthew, the chief editor of the exorcism stories, intended:

> Mark reports Jesus' prayer consisting of a single word, "Ephphatha (be opened)" (7:34)—which stands in the sharpest possible contrast with the extended invocations and formulas of the magical texts...As in the first story, there is no hint of elaborate invocation of angelic powers or of therapeutic procedure.[1014]

This line of argument, which seeks to exonerate Jesus of charges of magical practice, begins by assuming that Jesus' word was a "prayer," not an "invocation" or a "formula"—the text of the gospel nowhere calls Jesus' words a "prayer," but specifies not only that Jesus groaned and looked up to the sky, i.e., behavior consistent with magical technique, it tells us that Jesus took the

---

1011 Keck, *The Social World of the First Christians*, 152-153.
1012 Matthew 8:16.
1013 Hull, *Hellenistic Magic*, 130.
1014 Kee, *Religion, Science, and Magic*, 136.

man aside, put his fingers into his ears, spit, and touched the man's tongue, all of which conform to "therapeutic procedure," or as Tipei might say, 'medicine, miracle, and magic come together.' Even if *ephphatha* had been specifically called a *prayer*, the magical element would clearly exist. Spells in the magical papyri are quite regularly called *ευχαι* (euchai), *prayers*, as anyone who is the least bit familiar with the subject knows.

A spell in the *Sepher Ha-Razim* instructs the magician "fall upon your face to the earth and *pray this prayer* (תפלה, my note)."[1015] "Part of this incantation is a prayer (literally called 'prayer'—*tefillah* in Hebrew) to the god Helios..."[1016] Texts dating from well after the composition of the gospels do not blush to call spells *prayers*: the Coptic spell known as the *Prayer of Mary* uses the Greek loan word *προσευχη*, *prayer*, that is carried over into Coptic, (ⲡⲣⲟⲥⲉⲩⲭⲏ). Regarding the "taxonomic status" of the spell, the late Marvin Meyer observed, "the ritual power of the magical spell becomes practically indistinguishable from the ritual power of the Coptic Church, and Christian prayer and Christian invocation of ritual power seem to be two sides of the same coin. Or maybe even the same side."[1017] Accused of the ritual sacrifice of a young boy for divination, Apollonius replies, "They pretend that I massacred him despite his pleas and cries, and that after immersing my hands in the blood of this boy, I *prayed* (*ευχεσθαι*) to the gods to reveal the truth to me."[1018]

Cautioning against using the elaborate formulae of the magical papyri "as the benchmark for ancient magic," Twelftree comments, "even the longer elaborate magical papyri dedicated to exorcism are essentially highly eclectic compilations of shorter, simpler texts. This indicates that the simpler forms are likely to

---

1015 Morgan, *Sepher Ha-Razim*, 71.

1016 Schäfer, *Envisioning* Magic, 37.

1017 Meyer, *Prayer, Magic, and the Stars in the Ancient and Late Antique World*, 66, 67.

1018 Philostratus, *The Life of Apollonius of Tyana*, VIII, 7.

be the earliest."[1019] Even scholars who tend strongly toward the apologetic concede that the gospel accounts have been edited. "Matthew excised not only the more blatant thaumaturgical traits but even whole incidents, such as the stories of the healing of the deaf mute (Mark 7:31-37) and of the blind man near Bethsaida (Mark 8:22-26), both of which might lend themselves to magical interpretation…Luke seems to have made an intentional effort to distance Jesus and church leaders from magical notions."[1020] As Smith noted, "That Jesus is not represented by the Gospels as using long spells is insignificant. Once a magician 'had' his spirit, he need only command it and it would instantly obey. Here too, the Gospels represent Jesus as a successful magician would have represented himself."[1021] Brenk, in his discussion of the demonology of the Imperial Period, observes that "the holy man in the Graeco-Roman period disdains magical formula, such disdain being a sign of his power...he can accomplish his object with one wonder-working word."[1022] In fact, we have Jesus' own word on the subject as reported by the evangelist: *τα εργα α εγω ποιω εν τω ονοματι του πατρος μου*, "the works that I do *in the name of my father*,"[1023] "corresponding," as Eitrem admits, "to his disciples' later exorcising in [Jesus'] own name."[1024] That the *works* in question were works of magic is confirmed by the context: "But many among them began to say, 'He has a demon and he's raving'" (*δαιμονιον εχει και μαινεται*).[1025]

David Aune's observation on the question of *voces magicae* merits an extended quote:

[1019] Twelftree, *A Kind of Magic*, 75.
[1020] Kee, *Religion, Science, and Magic*, 143.
[1021] Smith, *Clement of Alexandria*, 235.
[1022] Brenk, *Aufstieg und Niedergang der Römischen Welt*, II.16.3: 2113.
[1023] John 10:25.
[1024] Eitrem, *Some Notes on the Demonology in the New Testament*, 11.
[1025] John 10:20.

> The brevity of [Jesus'] exorcistic formulae has led some scholars to contrast them with the long adjurations of the magical papyri...Aside from the not unimportant observation that such a contrast is quantitative, not qualitative, it should be noted that most of the magical papyri come from the third through the fifth centuries A.D. during the great *Blütezeit* of Graeco-Roman magic; it appears the older the magical forms, the shorter and more precise are the formulas...The short authoritative commands of Jesus to demons in the gospel narratives are formulas of magical adjuration.[1026]

There is no clear distinction between spell casting and prayer in the magical papyri: "To the Greeks, a magician not only uttered spells, he also prayed to the gods: Plato, for one connects the *επωιδαι* (spells) and the *ευχαι* (prayers) of the magician...I count five instances where *ευχη* [prayer, *my note*] occurs as an actual title of a spell..."[1027] Because there is no real distinction between religion and magic in the 1st century, there is correspondingly no real difference between prayers and spells. The attempt to impose a difference by writers such as Kee may be dismissed as a clumsy apologetic maneuver that simply refuses to see what is inconvenient.

A second claim is that the "evangelists" carefully distinguish between exorcism and healing, so that whatever may be said about the exorcisms, Jesus' healings at least cannot be read as magical. This distinction is also quite patently false; the "rebuke" of a fever in Luke 4:38, for example, employs the vocabulary of exorcism and weather magic. Wahlen, who takes the position that exorcism and healing are separate categories, nevertheless notes it "is decisive that here we have a healing depicted in terms of an exorcism." In his discussion of the terminology of exorcism in

---

[1026] Aune, *Aufstieg und Niedergang der Römischen Welt*, II.23.2: 1531-1532.

[1027] Graf, *Magika Hiera*, 188, 189.

Mark, Wahlen states, "The exorcisms in Mark, unlike in Matthew or Luke, are consistently distinguished from the healing of disease," but concedes that in Luke 9:42, based on the exorcism story in Mark 9:25-27, "by casting out the demon, Jesus is said to have healed (*ιασθαι*) the child..."[1028] Matthew says of a man possessed by a demon that Jesus *healed* him"—*εθεραπευσεν αυτον*.[1029] Bell also admits that exorcisms "can be difficult to distinguish" from healings and that the distinction is "not always clear."[1030]

The remains of a 4th century amulet show that Christians of that era considered healing to encompass not only interventions against fever, chills, and disease, but also possession and witchery:

> Christ was born from the Virgin Mary and was crucified under Pontius Pilate and was buried in a tomb and was raised on the third day and will come again from the heavens...Jesus who once healed every debility of the people and every disease, Savior Jesus, we believe you once went into the house of Peter's mother-in-law who had a fever and touched her hand and cast the fever out from her and now we call upon you, Jesus, heal also now your servant girl, who wears your great name, from every disease and from every fever, and from fever with chills and from migraine and from bewitchment and from every wicked spirit in the name of the Father, and the Son, and the Holy Spirit, *etc.*[1031]

1028 Wahlen, *Jesus and the Impurity of Spirits in the Synoptic Gospels*, 88, 154, 164.

1029 Matthew 12:22.

1030 Bell, *Deliver Us from Evil*, 78.

1031 Daniel & Maltomini, *Supplementum Magicum*, 31.

Meyer & Smith cite an amulet in which Silvanus "prays" to be delivered from "the demon of witchcraft" as well as from "every disease and every infirmity." *Ancient Christian Magic: Coptic Texts of Ritual Power*, 42.

The plea for healing—*Ιησου οτι εθεραπευσες τοτε πασαν μαλακιαν*—"Jesus that once healed every debility..." employs the language of exorcism—*και αφηκεν αυτην ο πυρετος*—"and cast the fever out from her" as well as healing "bewitchment and every evil spirit"—*και απο πασης βασκοσυνης και απο παντος πνευματος πονηρου*. Jesus' servant girl—"who wears your great name"—will accordingly fold the papyrus spell and suspend it around her neck as an amulet. The text is an example of a *historiola*, a short recitation of a biblical miracle designed to produce an analogous magical effect, a practice that was very common in both Jewish and Christian magic.[1032] A healing spell in Coptic treats disease, magic, and demons as essentially synonymous: "you must take away from him all sickness and all illness and all magic and all potions and all mishaps and all pains and all male spirits and all female spirits."[1033] Another papyrus amulet of Christian provenance combines an invocation to Jesus with *voces magicae*:

> Amulet of Jesus Christ the Helper against fever:
> Quick, quick, heal John, son of Zoē.
> SARIX, AORKACH, RHOUGACH, CHIOSNĒCH, KOCH[1034]

Spellwork, Christian or otherwise, makes no distinction between demons, ghosts, diseases or other sources of suffering: "An amulet,[1035] a bodyguard against demons, against ghosts, against every sickness and misfortune, inscribed on a leaf of gold or silver...[1036] There is likewise no clear distinction between healing and exorcism in either Judaism, the New Testament, or

---

[1032] See particularly Bohak, *Ancient Jewish Magic*, 413, and Meyer, *Magic and Ritual in the Ancient World*, 415, for *historiolae* invoking the Virgin Mary.

[1033] Meyer & Smith, *Ancient Christian Magic: Coptic Texts of Ritual Power*, 119.

[1034] Daniel & Maltomini, *Supplementum Magicum*, 28.

[1035] An *amulet*, *φυλακτηριον*, from *φυλαξ*, *guard*.

[1036] Preisendanz, *Papyri Graecae Magicae* VII, 580.

early Christianity: "The book of Tobit contains two prayers used as part of a 'spell' to drive away a demon named Asmodeus ...in order to 'heal' (*ιασασθαι*) both Tobit and Sarah (v.17). This healing takes the form of 'setting her free' (*λυσαι*) from the demon (v. 17)."[1037]

The evidence of the gospels is perfectly clear on this point: "and there were certain women who had been healed (*τεθεραπευμεναι*) of evil spirits and infirmaties (*πνευματων πονηρων και ασθενειων*)..." The passage was purportedly by Luke,[1038] a doctor,[1039] who might be presumed qualified to have known the difference between exorcism and healing if there was one.

Less attention has been paid to the passage in John 20:22 that describes another magical technique by which the resurrected Jesus passes power to his disciples: "And saying this, he blew and said to them, 'Receive holy spirit.'" The magical papyri contain very similar wording to that found in John: *ενπνευματωσον αυτον θειου πνευματος*, "infuse it with spirit, divine spirit..."[1040] Blowing is a well-attested magical technique in our sources. Celsus compared Christian miracles, described as "the work of sorcerers"—*τα εργα των γοητων*—the street magicians "who drive demons out of men, and blow away diseases—*και νοσους αποφυσαντων*—and call up the souls of the heroes..."[1041] "He blew"—*ενεφυσησεν*—in the gospel of John is exactly duplicated in Lucian's story of the "Babylonian" snake charmer who calls out all the vipers from the vineyard: "he blew on them—*ενεφυσησε μεν αυτοις*—and they were instantly burned up by the breath and we were amazed."[1042] Lucian, who wrote satirical pieces for public performance, obviously considered it a given that his audience would be familiar with such magical techni-

[1037] Werline, *Experientia*, I, 68.
[1038] Luke 8:2, compare Acts 10:38.
[1039] Colossians 4:14.
[1040] Preisendanz, *Papyri Graecae Magicae* IV, 967.
[1041] Origin, *Contra Celsum* I, 68.
[1042] Lucian, *Lover of Lies*, 12.

ques as blowing as well as the expectation that onlookers would be "amazed." Blowing could naturally be combined with other magical techniques: "Then he proceeded to tie seven knots upon the string. Before drawing each knot hard he blew upon it... there is an allusion to the mischief of 'those who puff into knots,' and an Arab commentator on the passage explains that the knots refer to women who practice magic by tying knots in cords, and then blowing and spitting upon them."[1043] Tertullian may be cited as a further witness to this magical technique: "From our naming the name of Christ...So at our touch and *breathing*...[the demons] leave at our command..."[1044] The apocryphal Christian gnostic work, *The Apocryphon of John*, reflects this widely used magical technique: "And they said to Yaltabaoth, 'Blow into his face the spirit which is the power of his mother.'"[1045]

Raising the dead.

No discussion of magical technique would be complete without mention of the procedure used by Jesus and Apollonius to raise the dead. Philostratus records such a miracle attributed to Apollonius, who asked the victim's name, and "*laying hold* (*προσαψαμενος*) of her, with some secret spell (*τι αφανως επειπων*) he awoke the young woman from her apparent death and the girl spoke and returned to her father's house."[1046] Jesus raises a little girl in similar fashion: "and *laying hold* (*κρατησας*) of the girl's hand, he said to her, *talitha koum*, which being translated is 'little girl,' I tell you, 'get up,' and immediately the little girl stood up and walked."[1047] In each case physical contact is made with the victim, a spell is pronounced—in Mark the spell, *ta-*

[1043] Thompson, *Semitic Magic: Its Origins and Devolpment*, 168.
[1044] Benko, *Pagan Rome and the Early Christians*, 116.
[1045] *The Apocryphon of John*, 19.
[1046] Philostratus, *Life of Apollonius*, IV, 45.
[1047] Mark 5:41-42.

litha koum (*ταλιθα κουμ*), is specified—and the victim awakes and gives proof of life by speaking or walking. Other accounts closely conform to this pattern. The story of Peter raising Dorcas records a somewhat mangled version of the *talitha koum* formula, *ταβιθα* (tabitha) *αναστηθι*. When the magical words are pronounced, Dorcas opens her eyes.[1048] The gentile author of Acts, writing about 64 C.E., mistakenly takes *ταλιθα* for the proper name, Tabitha, reflecting the imperfect oral transmission of the early Christian tradition, a process consistent with the transmission of magical lore generally. "...non-Jewish practitioners who invoked these divine names often had no sense of their original meanings...most or all of which had no connection whatsoever with the language from which the original word had been taken."[1049]

In other biblical accounts physical contact is necessary for the dead to come to life. In one case, Elijah lies face-to-face, palm-to-palm, on a dead child[1050] and in another a dead man revives when he touches Elijah's bones.[1051] To raise the son of the widow, Jesus touches the litter on which the dead man is carried, and as proof of life he speaks and Jesus gives him to his mother.[1052] When Paul raises Eutychus, he falls upon him and embraces him.[1053]

Binding and loosing, locking and unlocking.

The story of the deaf mute introduces the metaphor of binding and loosing—*και ελυθη ο δεσμος της γλωσσης αυτου*, "and the

[1048] Acts 9:40.
[1049] Bohak, *Prayer, Magic, and the Stars*, 71.
[1050] 2 Kings 4:34.
[1051] 2 Kings 13:20-21.
[1052] Luke 7:14.
[1053] Acts 20:10.

bond that held his tongue was loosed..."[1054] The concept of binding was basic to 1st century magical practice: the verb and noun set is *δεω* (deō), *bind*, and *δεσμος* (desmos), *bond*. Büchsel: "[*δεω*] is used of supernatural binding in L[uke] 13:16 and also in A[cts] 20:23."[1055] "The Talmud calls the amulet קמיע, [qimeh, *my note*] a word which comes from קמע, *to bind*, and points to the manner in which it was carried out..."[1056]

A closely related set, *καταδεω* (katadeō), *tie down*, and *καταδεσμος* (katadesmos), *binding spell*, were used of magical spells designed to restrain the actions or choices of others. A charm directed against a woman named Aristo says, "...I seized and bound her hands and feet and tongue and soul...may her tongue become lead..."—*εγω ελαβον και εδησα τας χειρας και τους ποδας και την γλωσσαν και την ψυχην...η γλωσσα αυτης μολυβδος γενοιτο*.[1057] The victim's tongue 'becomes lead' to prevent her speaking.

Regarding binding and the imagery of knots, Lenormant described this procedure: "...next he holds over this symbolical image a cord which he has prepared with this intention, making a knot in it to signify that he is acting with resolution and persistence, that at the moment when he spat he made a compact with the demon who acted as his associate in the operation ..."[1058] Magical binding is very extensively attested; "Illness and death: it is these two elements of the magico-religious complex of 'binding' which have had the widest currency almost all over the world..."[1059] "...running throughout all antiquity we find the idea that a man can be 'bound' or 'fettered by demonic influences. It occurs in Greek, Syrian, Hebrew, Mandaean, and

[1054] Mark 7:35.
[1055] Büchsel, *Theological Dictionary of the New Testament*, II, 60.
[1056] Spoer, *Journal of Biblical Literature* 23: 97.
[1057] Horsley, *New Documents Illustrating Early Christianity* 4, 45.
[1058] Lenormant, *Chaldean Magic: Its Origin and Development*, 63.
[1059] Eliade, *Images and Symbols*, 92-124.

Indian magic spells."[1060] "In the book of Daniel (5:12, 16) the ability 'to loose knots' is listed as one of the magician's accomplishments."[1061] Gager reports a curse tablet that refers to "this impious, accursed, and miserable Kardelos...bound, fully bound, and altogether bound..."[1062] "'I have bound for thee a cord.' It is probable that this rite of binding a cord before the god belongs to the great body of sympathetic magic that plays so important a part in Babylonian sorcery. The spell was in all probability regarded as binding only so long as the cord remained knotted."[1063] "And who could deny that the song of the Erinyes is a magic song? It is called *υμνος δεσμιος*, a binding song, just as the magical formulas were generally called *καταδεσμα*."[1064]

These references hardly exhaust the discussion of knots and magical binding in the ancient Middle East.[1065] The metaphor of binding is also used in Jesus' argument with the Pharisees regarding the source of his powers over the demons.[1066] In Acts, Paul says, "I have been bound by the spirit."[1067] "Binding and loosing are common technical terms in magical practices in which people are bound by spirits or released from them."[1068] Because sickness and possession are not clearly differentiated in the gospels, identical language is often used in connection with both healing and exorcism:

[1060] Deissmann, *Light from the Ancient East*, 304.

[1061] Trachtenberg, *Jewish Magic and Superstition*, 127.

[1062] Gager, *Curse Tablets and Binding Spells from the Ancient World*, 71.

[1063] King, *Babylonian Magic and Sorcery*, 22.

[1064] de Romilly, *Magic and Rhetoric in Ancient Greece*, 13.

[1065] Thomsen, *Witchcraft and Magic in Europe: Biblical and Pagan Societies*, 37-38.

[1066] Matthew 12:22-32.

[1067] Acts 20:22.

[1068] Strelan, *Strange Acts*, 94.

> "And this woman, a daughter of Abraham, *who Satan bound* (*ην εδησεν ο σατανας*) for—just imagine! Eighteen years! *Was it not fitting that she be loosed from this bond* (*ουκ εδει λυθηναι απο του δεσμου τουτου*) on the Sabbath day?"[1069]

Satan himself will be bound in turn: *και εδησεν αυτον χιλια ετη*: "and bound him for a thousand years." (Revelation 20:2) The notion of binding and loosing is extended both in the New Testament and the magical books to *locking* and *unlocking*, particularly of the realm of the dead.

> I will give you the keys of the kingdom of the heavens and whatever *you bind on earth* (*δησης επι της γης*) *will be a thing that has been bound* (*εσται δεδεμενον εν τοις ουρανοις*) in the heavens and whatever you may loose on earth will be a thing loosed in the heavens.[1070]

In Revelation, the risen Christ says to John, "Do not fear! I am the First and the Last, the Living One, and I became dead, and look! Now I am living for the ages of the ages *and I have the key of death and of Hades*"—*και εχω τας κλεις του θανατου και του αδου*.[1071] The *key* is a frequent topos in eroto-magical charms and the dead can be released through the good offices of the chthonic gods: "O Anoubis, Keybearer (*κλειδουχε*) and Guardian, send up to me in this very hour these phantoms of the dead to be my attendants..."[1072] Aune's discussion of the chthonic goddess Hekate, who is called *κλειδουχος* and *κλειδοφορος*—

[1069] Luke 13:16

[1070] Matthew 16:19. In the corresponding formula in Matthew 18:18, the power to bind on earth and heaven has been extended to *all* the disciples: Αμην λεγω υμιν, οσα εαν δησητε επι της γης..., "Truly I say to you (plural), whatever things you (plural) bind..."

[1071] Revelation 1:18.

[1072] Preisendanz, *Papyri Graecae Magicae* IV, 1469.

"Keybearer"—in the magical papyri is particularly recommended.[1073]

Antinous, the lover of the Emperor Hadrian, drowned in the Nile in 130 CE, possibly in self-sacrifice for the ailing emperor, and Hadrian established a cult for his worship.[1074] It is estimated that he was by that time in his late teens, hence dead well before his time, and like others prematurely dead, available for the workings of magicians. In an Assyrian list of those who produced restless ghosts we find "He whom the bank of a river hath let perish, and he hath died."[1075] "Antinous was automatically identified with that other young god of myth who had died in the Nile and been resurrected, conquering death and bringing life to the earth—Osiris…The holy Nile had long conferred sanctity and immortality not just on Osiris but on all those mortals it took to itself by drowning. Only the priests of the Nile could touch the corpses of those so sanctified by drowning…" We know that Antinous was venerated in at least 40 cities, in at least a dozen there were cults specific to him, and in seven games were held in his honor. Some 2000 statues of him were produced, including one of great fame recovered from Eleusis.[1076] Like Osiris, Dionysus, Hermes, and Jesus, Antinous became a psychopomp, a guide of souls.

[1073] Aune, *Apocalypticism, Prophecy, and Magic in Early Christianity*, 353-361.

[1074] Hadrian's fascination with prophecy is attested by the magical papyri where his name is mentioned in connection with the magician Pachrates. (*Papyri Graecae Magicae* IV, 2447-2455).

[1075] Thompson, *Semitic Magic: Its Origins and Devolpment*, 19.

[1076] Lambert, *Beloved and God: The Story of Hadrian and Antinous*, 2, 3, 105, 125.

Antinous as Osiris.

Necromancy using the famous dead was common in Egypt, and "extended to nonroyal spirits as well, particularly those whose death by drowning assimilated them to the god Osiris."[1077] According to Egyptian legend, Seth drowned Osiris, husband of Isis, the goddess of magic, in the Nile. Osiris, "the divine Drowned,"[1078] becomes a gatekeeper of the world of the dead and drowning in the Nile results in magical identification with him. According to the spells of the *Leyden Papyrus* a scarab beetle is to be drowned before being bound to the body of a boy clairvoyant (IV, 34,35), and a hawk is drowned in a jar of wine (XXV, 33).

The notion that drowning assimilates the victim to Osiris and thus empowers him comes to an absurd conclusion in the famous cat spell of the magical papyri in which a cat is drowned to create an empowered ghost. "Come to me (*δευρο μοι*)," the magician commands "the cat-faced god" (*ο αιλουροπροσωπος θεος*) "because I call upon you, *holy spirit* (*ιερον πνευμα*)." Sprinkling the holy water used to drown the poor cat, the magician intones, "I conjure you…ghost of the 'enspirited' cat (*τον δαιμονα του αιλουρου πνευματωτου*)…cat-faced angel (*αιλουρο-*

[1077] Ritner, *Magic and Divination in the Ancient World*, 94.

[1078] Griffith, *The Leyden Papyrus: An Egyptian Magical Book*, VI, 12.

προσωπος αγγελος)..."[1079] Setting aside the cruelty of this bizarre ritual, we are left to confront the pervasive belief in the power of ghosts to accomplish magic or "miracles," the power of "spirits" or "angels," whether of sacrificed animals or humans, to grant wishes for the living. There is nothing, on a purely theoretical level, to differentiate the invocation of the spirit of a drowned cat from a prayer directed to the ghost of a crucifed criminal, Jesus serving as a possible example, in the mind of a 1st century subject who believes in the power of the dead.

The murdered Osiris, like the executed Jesus, has the keys of Hades, and therefore the power to release the ghost of Antinous. It is evident that the Christian understanding of Jesus' powers shares much common ground with Greco-Egyptian necromancy: resurrected gods have the keys to the realm of the dead. Jesus the Keybearer has joined the ranks of the chthonic deities like those adjured in this erotic attraction spell:

> I entrust [this binding spell] to you, *underworld gods and infernal goddesses* (θεοις καταχθονιοις και θεαις καταχθονιαις) Pluto Yesmigadōth, and Kourē Persephonē, Ereschigal and Adonis, also called Barbaritha, and chthonic Hermes Thoth and mighy Anoubis Psēriphtha *who holds the keys down to Hades* (τας κλειδας εχοντι των καθ' αδου) *and underworld ghosts of men and women prematurely dead* (και δαιμοσι καταχθονιοις αωροις τε και αωραις), youths and maidens, year after year, month after month, day after day, night after night, hour after hour. I command all the ghosts of this place, assist this daemon...[1080]

As part of his praxis the magician can assume the identity of Hermes and control him through the manipulation of his cultic objects: "*Hermes, Chief of magicians, the Elder* (μαγων αρχη-

[1079] Preisendanz, *Papyri Graecae Magicae* III, 1-2, 50, 91.
[1080] Daniel & Maltomini, *Supplementum Magicum*, 46.

γετης Ερμης *ο πρεςβυς*), I am father of Isis...I have hidden this, your symbol, your sandal, *and I hold your key* (*και κλειδα κρατω*)...I speak the sign, the bronze sandal of the Tartaros Keeper, wreath, key, herald's wand,[1081] iron magic wheel[1082] and black dog..."[1083] Αρχηγετης (archēgetēs) can also mean *founder*, reflecting the legend that Hermes/Thoth was the inventor of writing and magic. "The papyri present the new syncretistic Hermes as a cosmic power, creator of heaven and earth and almighty world ruler (*παντοκρατωρ, κοσμοκρατωρ*). Presiding over fate and justice, he is also lord of the night and of death and its mysterious aftermath..."[1084]

The term *παντοκρατωρ* (pantokratōr), *almighty*, is used once in the letters of Paul[1085] and eight times in Revelation[1086] where its use parallels its occurrence in the magical papyri, typically combined with divine names derived from Hebrew: "Iaō, Sabaōth, Adōnai...I conjure you by the almighty living god...Adōnai... Iaō" (Ιαω Σαβαωθ Αδωναι...*ορκιζω σε κατα του παντοκρατορος θεου ζωντος*...Αδωναι...Ιαω).[1087] "*Hermes, almighty* (*παντοκρατωρ*), in the heart, circle of Selene...Hither to me, He of the spirit realm, invisible, *almighty* (*παντοκρατωρ*), creator of the gods...hither to me, He who never mourned his own brother, Seth. Hither to me, fire-bright spirit...[1088]

Significantly, "the Christian Fathers singled out the cult of Antinous for particular attack, presumably because it in some way

---

[1081] *κηρυκιον* or *κηρυκειον*, the wand of Hermes, the *caduceus*.

[1082] *ρομβος σιδηρους*, the *rhombus, magic wheel* or *bullroarer*, a divice spun on cords or whirled to create the sound of wind, summons the numina.

[1083] Preisendanz, *Papyri Graecae Magicae* IV, 2290-2294, 2334-2337.

[1084] Fowden, *The Egyptian Hermes: A Historical Approach to the Late Pagan Mind*, 25.

[1085] 2 Corinthians 6:18.

[1086] Revelation 1:8; 4:8; 11:17; 15:3; 16:7, 14; 19:6; 21:22.

[1087] Preisendanz, *Papyri Graecae Magicae* IV, 1539-1555.

[1088] Ibid, VII, 668, 960-964.

competed with their own..."[1089] The pagan Celsus accused certain Christian sects of unmentionable rites "much darker than those of the Egyptian Antinous" (*κατα σκοτον πολυν των Αντινου του κατ' Αιγυπτον*) which likely involved an implied accusation of homosexuality. In any case, the Christian apologist Origen does not address the specifics of Celsus' charge but concedes that Jesus and Antinous were being compared: "As regarding Antinous, being set alongside our Jesus..."—*Περι δε των κατα Αντινουν παραβαλλομενον ημων τω Ιησου*[1090]—a comparison that may have been common among pagans, given the commonalities between the two self-sacrificed gods.

The metaphor of locking and unlocking, opening and closing, so common in the magical papyri, is also prominent in the book of Revelation, the most overtly magical of the New Testament books. The risen Jesus is "The One who has the key of David, who opens and no one locks and who locks and no one opens" —*ο εχων την κλειν Δαυιδ ο ανοιγων και ουδεις κλεισει και κλειων και ουδεις ανοιγει.*[1091] Even as the magician *holds* Hermes' key—*και κλειδα κρατω*, "and I hold [your] key..."—Jesus is "the One *holding* the seven stars in his right hand"—*ο κρατων τους επτα αστερας εν τη δεξια αυτου.*[1092]

Other terms such as *φιμαω* (phimaō), *muzzle*, *silence*, *shut*, are used magically in both the New Testament and the magical spells: "And after he woke up, he rebuked the wind and said to the sea, 'Be silent! *You have been muzzled* (*πεφιμωσο*)!'"[1093] This strange command finds a close parallels in the spellbooks: "...on the back of the sheet of metal [write]: EULAMŌ SISIBABAIĒRSESI PHERMOU CHNOUŌR ABRASAX utterly subject, completely enslave, *muzzle the soul* (*φιμωσον την ψυχην*), the breath of life

---

[1089] Lambert, *Beloved and God*, 139.
[1090] Origen, *Contra Celsum* V, 63.
[1091] Revelation 3:7.
[1092] Revelation 2:1.
[1093] Mark 4:39.

of [Name] because I command you by the fearsome Necessity..."[1094] "Say the spell seven times. ERMALLŌTH, ARCHIMALLŌTH. *Silence the mouths* (φιμωσατε τα στοματα) of those [who speak] against me..."[1095] "...they will silence my adversary (φιμωσουσιν τον αντιδικον εμου)..." [1096] "...silence (φιμωσον), subordinate, enslave [Name]..."[1097] Spells to "muzzle" opponents are attested from Jewish synagogues: "both the Meroth synagogue and the small synagogue in Bar'am produced bronze lamellae with spells intended to 'muzzle' the opponents of the clients who procured them."[1098] To *silence* or *muzzle* in these contexts is to restrict the action, even as the oxen that turned the grindstone are muzzled to prevent them from eating the falling grain,[1099] and the prophets who "stopped the mouths of lions"[1100] were restraining their actions, not literally silencing them. A spell to subject and restrain a victim is a φιμωτικον (phimōtikon), a *restraining spell.*[1101]

It nearly goes without saying that magical spells included incantations to release prisoners from literal chains—"the god *is an aerial spirit* (πνευμα εστιν αεριον)...*he frees from bonds* (λυει δε εκ δεσμων) a person chained in prison, *he opens doors* (θυρας ανοιγει)..."[1102]—just the sort of magical deliverance described in Acts in which an angel releases Peter from his chains and leads him out of prison past *two guards stationed in front of the door* (φυλακες τε προ της θυρας) and through an *iron gate* (την πυλην την σιδηραν) that magically opens of its own accord.[1103]

[1094] Preisendanz, *Papyri Graecae Magicae* IX, 8-10.
[1095] Ibid, XXXVI, 164-165.
[1096] Audollent, *Defixionum Tabellae* (Insula Cyprus), 22:43.
[1097] Preisendanz, *Papyri Graecae Magicae* VII, 968.
[1098] Bohak, *Ancient Jewish Magic: A History*, 318.
[1099] 1 Corinthians 9:9.
[1100] Hebrews 11:33.
[1101] Preisendanz, *Papyri Graecae Magicae* VII, 396.
[1102] Ibid, I, 96-101.
[1103] Acts 12:3-10.

We find a slyly mocking reference to the ability of magicians to break literal bonds in Apollonius' hearing before the paranoid Emperor Domitian: "If you think me a wizard, how will you ever fetter me? And if you fetter me, how can you say that I am a wizard?"[1104] Such was the magical power of Apollonius that he could escape his bonds "without so much as a prayer, or even speaking."[1105] With reference to breaking fetters through magic, Origen says "Peter also was bound (δεδομενος) in prison and *after an angel loosed his bonds* (αγγελου λυσαντος τους δεσμους), he escaped...and Paul...*though bound was loosed by divine power* (δεδομενος ελυθη θεια δυναμει) when *the prison gates were opened* (θυραι της φυλακης ηνοιχθησαν)...and *some sorcerers* (γοητες τινες) break chains and open doors by spells (επωδαις) so that [Celsus] would compare the feats recounted about sorcerers with our scriptures."[1106] Celsus, had he still been alive, might have said, "If the shackle fits..."

The Beelzeboul controversy.

In the 1st century it was well known that people with supernatural gifts often exhibited unnatural behavior, an observation reflected in this account from Mark:

> He came home and a crowd gathered again, so much so that they were not even able to eat a meal. His family went out to restrain him when they heard about it, because they were saying, "He's out of his mind!"
>
> The scribes who came down from Jerusalem were saying, "He has Beelzeboul!" "He casts out the demons by the ruler of the demons."

[1104] Philostratus, *The Life of Apollonius of Tyana* VII, 34.

[1105] Ibid, VII, 38.

[1106] Origen, *Contra Celsum* II, 34. The references are to Acts 12:7 and 16:26.

> Calling them together, he made an analogy: "How can Satan cast out Satan? If a kingdom divides against itself, that kingdom cannot stand, and if a house divides against itself, that house will not be able to stand. So if Satan rises up against himself and becomes divided, he cannot stand. To the contrary, his end has come."
>
> "No one can enter the strong man's house to plunder his possessions unless he first binds the strong man, and then he plunders his house."
>
> "Truly I say to you, every error and blasphemy will be forgiven the sons of men, but whoever blasphemes against the holy spirit will have no forgiveness for all ages, but is guilty of everlasting sin"—because they were saying, "He has an unclean spirit."[1107]

The verb *εξιστημι* (existēmi) can refer to states of confusion or amazement or to insanity, but there is certainly nothing in the context to suggest that Jesus was either so confused or so amazed—*ελεγον γαρ οτι εξεστη*: "because they were saying, 'He's out of his mind!'"—that his family felt they needed to restrain him. The related noun, *εκσταασις* (ekstasis), which has already been mentioned, is commonly regarded as referring to a state of trance or frenzy. Concluding a discussion of the "agitation" associated with Jesus' miracles and the textual tampering apparent in Mark 1:41 to conceal this feature of his healing, Eitrem says, "We have to interpret the cure of the leper as *originally* effected by an ecstatic Jesus by the expulsion of a demon or foul spirit."[1108] "Magicians who want to make demons obey often scream their spells, gesticulate, and match the mad in fury."[1109]

As Levison points out in discussing the rise and demise of Saul (1 Samuel 10-19), "several correspondences between the evil spirit of God and the good spirit of God suggest that they are to

---

[1107] Mark 3:20-30.

[1108] Eitrem, *Some Notes on the Demonology in the New Testament*, 53.

[1109] Smith, *Jesus the Magician*, 32.

be understood as similar in nature."[1110] The spirit sent to Saul is in *both* cases the רוח אלהים, the *ruakh elohim*, the *spirit* or *breath of God*, and/or the רוח יהוה, the *ruakh Yahweh*, the *spirit* or *breath of Yahweh*,[1111] which *rushes upon* (צלח)[1112] Saul, causing him to "prophesy"—"The Spirit of the Lord will come powerfully upon you, and you will prophesy with them; and you will be changed into a different person"[1113] or to "rave"—"The very next day a tormenting spirit from God overwhelmed Saul, and he began to rave in his house like a madman."[1114] The same verb, נבא, *naba*, used both of Saul's prophesying *and* raving, means *to prophesy*, particularly "in the ecstatic state" or "in frenzy."[1115] Levison concludes that "the loss of mental control was valued as integral to the prophetic experience,"[1116] an observation that echoes the evaluation of the Jews who witnessed Jesus' ecstatic performance: "He is demon-possessed and raving mad."[1117]

To Jesus' family it may have appeared that he had taken leave of his senses but the religious authorities saw it differently: Βεελζεβουλ εχει: "He has Beelzeboul," a πνευμα ακαθαρτον εχει: "He has an unclean spirit." The Jewish authorities believed Jesus to be in control of a demon—"an unmistakably Palestinian demon, impossible to attribute to 'the Hellenistic church'"[1118]—basing their belief on his erratic behavior. The claim that Jesus controlled demons led to his rejoinder concerning blasphemy

---

1110 Levison, *The Spirit in First Century Judaism*, 36.
1111 1 Samuel 10:6,10; 11:6; 16:13-15,16; 18:10.
1112 "the Spirit…rushed upon him," Brown, Driver & Briggs, *Hebrew and English Lexicon*, 852.
1113 1 Samuel 10:6 (*New International Version*).
1114 1 Samuel 18:10 (*New Living Translation*).
1115 Brown, Driver & Briggs, *Hebrew and English Lexicon*, 612. English translations of the passages quoted use "prophesy" and "rave" interchangeably to translate the same Hebrew word (נבא).
1116 Levison, *The Spirit in First Century Judaism*, 36.
1117 John 10:20 (NIV).
1118 Smith, *Jesus the Magician*, 32.

against the holy spirit and his question, "If I cast out demons by means of Beelzeboul by what means do your sons cast them out?"[1119] Significantly, Jesus nowhere denies being able to manipulate a spirit—which is after all the *sine qua non* of the miracle-working holy man—but replies that the spirit in question is the spirit of God, not an unclean spirit, or in Christian parlance, the Holy Spirit, not an unholy spirit. The notion that spirits perform miracles is reflected in the apocalyptic books of Jesus' time: "And I saw…out of the mouth of the false prophet three unclean spirits like frogs. They are the spirits of demons that perform signs"—*εισιν γαρ πνευματα δαιμονιων ποιουντα σημεια.*[1120]

Jesus' success as an exorcist appears to have been beyond dispute. No one questioned it. "All they could do was cast doubt on the power behind such exorcisms."[1121] However, Mark's reference to Jesus as being "out of his mind" was too extreme for both Matthew and Luke—there is no trace of this part of the story in either of their gospels, and as noted elsewhere, exorcism itself proved too incriminating for the writer of John; there is no mention of exorcism in the fourth gospel. According to Twelftree, exorcism passes without mention in the gospel of John because "the Fourth Gospel portrays Jesus as relying on no other source of power-authority outside himself in performing miracles."[1122] The Fourth Gospel thereby evades the question, "Tell us, by what authority are you doing these things?"[1123]

Crossan underscores the tension that must have existed between Jesus and the temple authorities: "In all of this the point is not really Galilee against Jerusalem but the far more fundamental dichotomy of magician as personal and individual power against

---

[1119] Matthew 12:27.

[1120] Revelation 16:13, 14.

[1121] Bell, *Deliver Us from Evil*, 84.

[1122] Twelftree, *In the Name of Jesus: Exorcism Among Early Christians*, 193.

[1123] Luke 20:2.

priest or rabbi as communal and ritual power. Before the Second Temple's destruction, it was magician against Temple, thereafter magician against rabbi...If a magician's power can bring rain, for what do you need the power of temple priesthood or rabbinical academy?"[1124] But in this contest of authority, of exactly what did the accusation consist?

That the expression "He has Beelzeboul" should be taken in the *active*, rather than passive sense, was pointed out by Kraeling: "In the relations of men and demons there are two basic possibilities, either the demon has a man in his possession, or a man has a demon under his control...in the second the demon is the servant and the man a magician."[1125] Kraeling's observation is confirmed by the nearly identical wording of Revelation 3:1 where the glorified Christ is called "*the One who has the seven spirits of God*"—*ο εχων τα επτα πνευματα του θεου*—"and the seven stars"—*stars* which are identified in the context as angels.[1126] On the meaning of *having* the seven spirits, Hanse says, "These seven spirits are thought of as autonomous beings, and they are to be equated with the seven angels which stand before God...What does it mean that Christ "has" them? It obviously means that He has authority over them, that He can command them..."[1127] The belief that magicians drove out one demon with the help of a demon more powerful yet is reflected by the Christian historian Eusebius who alleged that Apollonius "drives out one demon with the help of another" and explains one of Apollonius' famous exorcisms as having been accomplished

---

[1124] Crossan, *The Historical Jesus*, 157-158.

[1125] Kraeling, *Journal of Biblical Literature* 59: 153.

[1126] Revelation 1:20.

[1127] Hanse, "εχω" in *The Theological Dictionary of the New Testament*, II, 821.

The *Exegetical Dictionary of the New Testament* says of εχω in Revelation 3:1, "It probably means that [Christ] has sovereignty over these powers." (II, 95).

"with the help of a more important demon."[1128] Eusebius is using the same charge against Apollonius and the Jewish authorities used against Jesus.

Yet Hanse interprets the identical expression in Mark 3:22 in a passive sense, that of possession *by* a demon, an inconsistency that seeks to avoid the implication that Jesus worked magic through the control of demons. David Aune: "...the rise of the Biblical theology movement was accompanied by a strong reaction against the notion that ancient Mediterranean magic could have influenced early Christianity in any substantial way. The authors of many of the articles in the '*Theologisches Wörterbuch zum Neuen Testament,*' [the German predecessor of *The Theological Dictionary of the New Testament, my note*] most of whom consider themselves Biblical theologians, write as if they were involved in a conspiracy to ignore or minimize the role of magic in the New Testament and early Christian literature."[1129]

The accusation by the Jewish leaders is not that Jesus is possessed *by* a demon, but rather that he is the magician *par excellence* because he has bound Beelzeboul himself, the prince of demons, to his service and works his miracles as a result of exercising that control. It is nonsense to acknowledge that Jesus has authority over demons and in the next breath claim that one possesses him. Demonic possession means that the man is controlled by the demon, not that the demon is controlled by the man. "...it marks the proper distance between John the Baptist and Jesus when John is said to 'have a demon' (Matt. xi.18) but Jesus is said to 'have Beelzebub' (Mark iii.22)."[1130] Jesus' magic is more powerful than John's because Jesus controls a more powerful demon. Jesus is the Prince of magicians as

---

[1128] Eusebius, *The Treatise of Eusebius*, XXVI, XXXI (Conybeare, *The Life of Apollonius of Tyana*, II, 551, 567).

[1129] Aune, *Aufstieg und Niedergang der Römischen Welt*, II, 23/2, 1508.

[1130] Eitrem, *Some Notes on the Demonology in the New Testament*, 4.

Beelzebub is the "Prince of demons."[1131] It appears that the Beelzeboul controversy was still alive and kicking well into the 3rd century when it is mentioned by Origen.[1132]

Nearly identical usage—"I have him"—is found in the papyri in a necromantic spell to retain power over the ghost of a man killed violently, a favorite category of ghost for working sorcery:

> I beseech you, Lord Helios, listen to me [Name], and grant me the power over *this spirit of a man killed violently* (τουτου του βιοθανατου πνευματος) from whose tent[1133] I hold [a body part]. *I have him with me [Name], a helper* (εχω αυτον μετ' εμου [του δεινα] βοηθον) and avenger for whatever business I desire.[1134]

"I have him with me—εχω αυτον μετ' εμου—"I control his spirit that serves me as a helper." The *helper*, βοηθος (boēthos), a spirit entity, is used of Jesus at Hebrews 13:6, Κυριος εμου βοηθος, "the Lord, my helper." That *the magician controls the demon* is the whole point of Jesus' question, "How can one enter a strong man's house and seize his belongings *unless one first binds the strong man*?"[1135] Jesus is not only claiming to loose those bound by Satan, but to bind demons to his will, an authority he can transmit to others.[1136] After a thorough review of the evidence intrinsic to the gospel accounts, Samain construed "to have a demon" in the active sense, i.e., *to have control of the demon*: "Christ is the master of Beelzeboul and he controls him to the point of using him to perform his exorcisms…Christ is

---

1131 Luke 11:15.

1132 Origen, *Contra Celsum* II, 9.

1133 σκηνη, *tent*, the body as a covering of the soul, hence a corpse. Compare 2 Corinthians 5:4, "to be in the tent," i.e., alive in a body.

1134 Preisendanz, *Papyri Graecae Magicae* IV, 1947-1954.

1135 εαν μη πρωτον δηση τον ισχυρον: "unless one first binds the strong man…" (Matthew 12:29).

1136 As at Luke 13:16. Compare Matthew 10:1, 16:19 (what is bound on earth is bound in heaven).

alleged to be a magician: joined with the ruler of the demons, he compels him, by using his name, to perform the miracles he wants, particularly exorcisms; no spirit, no demonic power can resist him...*Δαιμονιον εχει* ["He has a demon," *my note*] therefore means that Jesus is a false prophet, a magician."[1137]

Samain's conclusion agrees completely with the analysis of a much earlier writer, the Christian apologist Origen, who above all other writers from antiquity, provides us with an explanation of how exorcism and magic were thought to work:

> Once we concede that it is consistent with the existence of *magic and sorcery* (*μαγειαν και γοητειαν*), *made active by evil demons* (*ενεργουμενην υπο πονηρων δαιμονων*) that are invoked, *spellbound by magical charms* (*περιεργοις θελγομενων*), *submitting to practitioners of sorcery* (*ανθρωποις γοησιν υπακουοντων*)...[1138]

Demons *are compelled* by Christian exorcists as well as pagan magicians, forced to submit by incantations in the case of magicians, or the powerful name of Jesus in the case of Christian exorcists: "Did we not cast out demons *in your name* (*τω σω ονοματι*) and perform many powerful works *by your name* (*τω σω ονοματι*)?"[1139] The demons are "spellbound" (*θελγομενων*) by a *force majeure*, specifically the *knowledge of their name*, induced "to do the wishes of the one invoking them."[1140] "It was thought

---

[1137] My translation of: "le Christ est maître de Béelzéboul et le domine au point de l'employer pour opérer ses exorcismes...uni au chef des demons, il le forcerait, possédant son nom, à opérer les prodiges qu'il veut et spécialement les exorcismes; nul esprit, nulle puissance démoniaque ne lui résiste...*Δαιμονιον εχει* signifie donc encore que Jésus est un faux prophète magician." *Ephemerides Theologicae Lovanienses* 15: 468, 470, 482.

[1138] Origen, *Contra Celsum* II, 51.

[1139] Matthew 7:22.

[1140] Thee, *Julius Africanus and the Early Christian View of Magic*, 373.

that demons, like dogs, would obey if you called them by their names."[1141]

That having a demon under one's control is very different from being possessed by a demon is reflected both in the language of the New Testament and in the terminology of the magical papyri. A particular verb—*δαιμονιζομαι* (daimonizomai)—"to be possessed by a hostile spirit"[1142] is consistently reserved for those tormented by demons and *even his opponents never apply it to Jesus in the New Testament.*[1143] In response to the accusations that Jesus is employing an evil spirit to accomplish his miracles, the crowd correctly states, *ταυτα τα ρηματα ουκ εστιν δαιμονιζομενου*, "These are not the words of a possessed man!"[1144] Samain also noted, "It is true that *δαιμονιζομενος* [possessed by a demon, *my note*] is never used to describe a magician."[1145] The verb is used of those under the control of a demon, not of a man in control of one. This use is also noted by Paige: "The evangelists never use the familiar 'neutral' or good terms of religious possession known from Plato and other writers…They always use the verb *δαιμονιζομαι* in its very late (first century onwards) and probably Jewish/Christian sense, 'to be afflicted with or possessed by demons' (e.g., Mark 1:32-34), even when the evil entity is described in the pericope as a 'spirit'…"[1146]

Jesus is never represented as being among the demon-possessed, those who have *lost control of themselves*—*δαιμονιζομενους και σεληνιαζομενους και παραλυτικους*, "demon-possessed and moonstruck and paralyzed."[1147] Of such tragic figures Trach-

---

[1141] Smith, *Jesus the Magician*, 33.

[1142] Danker's *Greek-English Lexicon*, 209.

[1143] *δαιμονζομαι* occurs 13 times in the gospels and nowhere else in the New Testament.

[1144] John 10:20-21.

[1145] Samain: "Il est vrai que *δαιμονιζομαι* ne se rencontre jamais pour designer un magician." *Ephemerides* 15:482.

[1146] Paige, *Harvard Theological Review* 95: 427-428.

[1147] Matthew 4:24.

tenberg observed, "Demons who have taken possession of a human body exercise such complete control over it that the personality and the will of the victim are extinguished."[1148] Such unfortunates have most emphatically not been placed in command of spirits, whereas Jesus is everywhere presented in the gospels as operating from a position of superior strength vis-à-vis the demons. Jesus' authority—his *exousia*—"means a mysterious superhuman force whereby demons were controlled and afflictions miraculously healed."[1149]

We should be perfectly clear on this point: *pace* Howard Clark Kee, the scribes nowhere "charge that [Jesus] can control the demons because he is himself controlled by their prince, Beelzebub," a situation that would for all intents make Jesus into a puppet of Satan.[1150] To the contrary, their charge is that *Jesus is in control of Beelzeboul*: "He casts out demons *by the ruler of the demons*." The charge of the scribes is that Jesus is a magician so powerful that he can bind even the Prince of Demons to his service, making Jesus the Prince of Magicians. Jesus even gives others authority to expel demons.[1151] How could that happen if Satan had control of Jesus?

As noted previously, erratic or strange behavior was long associated with exorcistic ritual, prophecy, and wonder working generally. In a hostile encounter with Jewish holy men, this very power was turned against Saul as described in the account of his hunt for his rival, David.

> Saul was told, "David is at Naioth in Ramah." Then Saul sent messengers to take David. When they saw the company of prophets in a frenzy, with Samuel standing

[1148] Trachtenberg, *Jewish Magic and Superstition*, 51.
[1149] Starr, *Harvard Theological Review* 23: 303.
[1150] Kee, *Religion, Science, and Magic*, 138.
[1151] Luke 9:1.

> in charge of them, the spirit of God came on the messengers of Saul and they also fell into a prophetic frenzy.
>
> When Saul was told, he sent other messengers, and they also fell into a frenzy. Saul sent messengers again the third time, and they also fell into a frenzy.
>
> Then he himself went to Ramah. He came to the great well that is in Secu; he asked, "Where are Samuel and David?" And someone said, "They are at Naioth in Ramah." He went there, toward Naioth in Ramah; and the spirit of God came upon him. As he was going, he fell into a prophetic frenzy, until he came to Naioth in Ramah. He too stripped off his clothes, and he too fell into a frenzy before Samuel. He lay naked all that day and all that night. Therefore it is said, "Is Saul also among the prophets?"[1152]

The bizarre behavior that accompanied Jesus' own miracle working is the subject of this telling passage in the gospel of John:

> Again a division of opinion occurred among the Jews because of these words. Many of them were saying, "He has a demon and he's raving! Why listen to him?"
>
> Others said, "These are not the words of a possessed man! Is a demon able to open the eyes of the blind?"[1153]

In this text "raving" translates the verb *μαινομαι* (mainomai), and given the context, it is clear that Jesus' opponents are not simply accusing him of talking nonsense, but are pointing to Jesus' raving as evidence of magical ritual—*δαιμονιον εχει και μαινεται*: "He has a demon and he's raving!" The nominal form, *μανια* (mania), which occurs as a description of the frenzy of the Bacchic rites, refers specifically to violent behavior that accompanied possession. In either case, it is important to note that the

---

[1152] 1 Samuel 19:20-24, *NRSV*

[1153] John 10:19-21.

word simply designates behavior, and not its cause or motive. In point of fact, the ancients distinguished between different types of ecstatic experience; appearances were not necessarily accurate indicators of how ecstasy *functioned.*[1154] "The words which the Greeks used to describe such phenomena are varied and inconsistent...These various expressions can neither be reconciled systematically nor distinguished in terms of an evolution in the history of ideas; they mirror the confusion in the face of the unknown. The most common term is therefore *mania*, frenzy, madness."[1155] Lucian addresses raving as a magical technique in his exposé of Alexander of Abonoteichos. Even allowing for the skeptical description of Alexander's actions, the reader easily detects the presence of magical praxis: "feigning madness, he sometimes filled his mouth with foam..."[1156]

At no point do Jesus' opponents deny that he casts out demons. It is only Jesus' method that is open to question, but whether accomplished by the spirit of God or by Beelzeboul, the prince of demons, the results are formally identical: the demons leave when commanded. It must also be emphasized, however, that *for the exorcist*—unlike the prophet—*raving functions as a mimetic technique,* not a symptom of passive possession. Whereas the prophet raves as a sign of possession, the magician raves to establish control. For the magician, raving is an enactment, sacred theater. Unlike the prophet, who courts possession through music, dance, and dream, the role of the magician is active—magic is about taking control of and manipulating power. Lewis, in his extensive discussion of possession phenomena, points out the distinction between involuntary possession and "a spirit possessed (voluntarily) by a person...controlled trance, the essential requirement for the exercise of the shamanistic vocation...the shaman 'possesses' his spirits..."[1157] This explanation

---

[1154] See Shaw, *Theurgy and the Soul*, 231-236.
[1155] Burkert, *Greek Religion*, 109-110.
[1156] Alexander the False Prophet (*Αλεξανδρος η ψευδομαντις*), 12.
[1157] Lewis, *Ecstatic Religion*, 54-55.

accords completely with the New Testament description of Jesus: he is the master, not the slave, of spirits and ghosts.

The "son of David."

Jesus is frequently called the "son of David," a title usually interpreted as a reference to the kingdom of Israel of which Jesus is the promised heir.[1158] However, a different explanation has been proposed.

It is notable that the term "son of David" is very frequently used in the context of healing and exorcism, particularly in the formula, "Son of David, take pity on me!"[1159] Jesus is so addressed by the Canaanite woman whose daughter he exorcises,[1160] and after the exorcism of a blind and deaf man, which exorcism is characterized as a healing, the crowd asks, "Can this be the son of David?" In response to this question, the Jewish leaders reply that Jesus *casts out demons* by the power of Beelzeboul, the prince of demons,[1161] i.e., he is not the "son of David." The final occurrence of the title is part of the acclamation of the crowds in the temple at Jerusalem, "Hosanna, Son of David," which is said in recognition that Jesus is a prophet, a wonder-worker who cures the blind and lame.[1162]

The context of the gospels firmly connects the "son of David" with exorcism. As has been noted by various scholars,[1163] the son

---

[1158] As at Luke 1:32-33.

[1159] Mark 10:47-48, Matthew 9:27, 20:30, Luke 18:38-39.

[1160] Matthew 15:22.

[1161] Matthew 12:22-24.

[1162] Matthew 21:11.

[1163] See particularly Duling, whose article "Solomon, Exorcism, and the Son of David" provides a thorough summation of the evidence that *son of David* acknowledged Jesus' magical skills. *Harvard Theological Review* 68:235-252.

of David was, in fact, *Solomon,*[1164]—"the great exorcist and magician of antiquity, the forerunner of the exorcistic activity of Jesus, and the genius of later Christian magic and divination."[1165] "David and Solomon, whose roles were not those of miracle workers in the canonical books of the O[ld] T[estament], came later to be regarded as exorcists. Whatever may have been the reason for the reinterpretation of the role of many ancient heroes—it seems *not* to have been the Greco-Roman influence—the Jewish traditions furnished a wealth of material of their own for such reinterpretations."[1166] "David, as an early Jewish exorcist himself anticipating Solomon of later lore, is able to ward off the spirit by singing and playing the kinnor."[1167]

There is substantial evidence that Solomon's magical abilities were already celebrated in Jesus' lifetime. The *Wisdom of Solomon,* which was probably composed in the Jewish community in Alexandria, Egypt, a century or more prior to Jesus' birth, reflects the belief that Solomon's fabled wisdom consisted of both manifest and occult knowledge. Solomon's wisdom, extolled in 1 Kings,[1168] "surpassed…all the wisdom of Egypt," a land known in antiquity as the cradle of magic. Of Solomon the Septuagint reports, "and his songs were five thousand," a considerable improvement over the 1005 mentioned in the Hebrew bible. Regarding the possible purpose of these songs, it may be recalled that when Solomon's father David played the harp, the evil spirit sent from God left Saul.[1169]

The **Σοφια Σαλωμων**, the *Wisdom of Solomon,* was included among the apocryphal books of the *Septuagint,* the Greek trans-

---

[1164] Matthew 1:6.

[1165] Rainbow, *Harvard Theological Review* 100: 249.

[1166] Koskenniemi, *Journal of Biblical Literature* 117: 465. See also Alexander, *The History of the Jewish People in the Age of Jesus Christ,* III, Part I, 375-379.

[1167] Kotansky, *Ancient Magic and Ritual Power,* 257.

[1168] 1 Kings 4:29-34.

[1169] 1 Samuel 16:14-23.

lation of the Hebrew Bible made in Alexandria, Egypt, for the Greek-speaking Jews of the Diaspora. That *Wisdom* was known to the earliest Christians is virtually certain: Romans 9:21 is very likely a close paraphrase of *Wisdom* 15:7. Of Solomon's many gifts, *Wisdom* has this to say:

> For he gave me faultless knowledge of the things that are, to know the structure of the world and the conjuring of elemental spirits, the beginning, end, and midpoints of time, the manner of the change and transitions of the seasons of the year, the orbits and position of the stars, the natural qualities of animals and passions of beasts, the power of spirits and designs of men, the varieties of plants and powers of roots, both that which is hidden and visible I know.[1170]

The elemental spirits in question—*συστασιν κοσμου και ενεργειαν στοιχειων*: "the structure of the world and the conjuring of the elemental spirits…"—refers to spiritual powers thought to control the world, the "*demons* or *tutelary spirits* of nature."[1171] The term *στοιχειον* (stoicheion), *elements*, in reference to superhuman spirit powers occurs several times in the writings of Paul and his school.[1172] The "power of the spirits" refers to demonic spirits as in Mark 1:27. "Some translators obscure these facts; they write, e.g., 'the power of the winds', when the context shows that daemons are meant. Josephus certainly understood the passage in this way."[1173]

Solomon's accomplishments receive further elaboration in Josephus' *Antiquities of the Jews*, where it is said of him,

---

[1170] *Wisdom* 7:17-21.

[1171] Abbott-Smith, *A Manual Greek Lexicon of the New Testament*, 418.

[1172] Galatians 4:3, 9, Colossians 2:8.

[1173] Luck, *Witchcraft and Magic in Europe: Ancient Greece and Rome*, 117.

> God allowed [Solomon] to learn the art of casting out demons for the benefit and healing of men and the formulation of incantations by which sicknesses are healed and he left behind the ways of performing exorcisms...[1174]

In this brief passage from the *Antiquities*, the *ωδαι*, *songs*, of the *Septuagint* have become *επωδαι*, *incantations*: *επωδας τε συνταξαμενος*: "and the formulation of incantations..."

Solomon's mastery of the demons is made explicit: *την κατα των δαιμωνιων τεχνην*: "the art of casting out demons..." literally, "the art against the demons..." It is from Josephus that we first hear of Solomon's signet ring—which Solomon received from Michael the archangel[1175]—the ring the exorcist Eleazar uses to expel a demon in the presence of no less a person than Vespasian, the future Caesar.[1176] Solomon's fame is on a rising trajectory from the *Antiquities*, through the *Testament of Solomon* of late antiquity, to the well-known grimoires of the present such as the 17th century *Clavicula Salomonis*. A group of early apotropaic amulets depict a horseman, identified as Solomon, spearing a recumbent female figure, the demon Lilith. The iconography of Solomon the Cavalier spread beyond Jewish circles, becoming the Christian icon of Saint George and the dragon.[1177] "Solomon's control of demons was a matter of pride for Josephus...is often reported in Rabbinic literature, and is the subject of a romance preserved in several Greek versions, The Testament of Solomon."[1178]

[1174] *τροπους εξορκωσεων κατελιπεν*: "he left behind the ways of performing exorcisms..." Josephus, *Antiquities* VIII, 45.

[1175] *Testament of Solomon* I, 6.

[1176] Josephus, *Antiquities* VIII, 46-49.

[1177] Alexander, *The Cambridge History of Judaism*, III, 1076-1078.

[1178] Smith, *Jesus the Magician*, 79.

The answer to the question, 'Who is this that he commands the winds and demons?'[1179] is answered when, *in the context of exorcisms,* the New Testament proclaims of Jesus, "Something greater than Solomon is here!"[1180] An early tradition related to the control of demonic power, rather than kingship, is probably in sight and the title "Son of David" is a veiled reference to Jesus' success as an exorcist and healer. The identification of the title with the Messiah who comes from the line of David is a latter interpretive gloss that shifts the focus away from magical practice.

It is possibly for this reason that Mark, who also used the term, felt no need to concoct a story placing Jesus' birth in Bethlehem, the city of David. For the primitive tradition that Mark represented, "son of David" means simply "successor to Solomon" with all that implies.

...but when they saw him walking on the sea...

This relatively brief survey omits other magical stories about Jesus such as walking on water,[1181] solar phenomena such as three hours of darkness, and resurrection en masse.[1182] It will come as no surprise to the reader to learn that similar celestial events are the norm in pagan legend and magic.[1183]

[1179] Matthew 8:27, Mark 1:27, Luke 8:25.

[1180] Matthew 12:22-32, 42, Luke 11:14-23, 41.

[1181] Mark 6:49; Matthew 14:26.

[1182] Mark 15:33; Matthew 27:45, 51-54; Luke 23:44-45.

[1183] See, for example, Collins, *Religious Propaganda and Missionary Competition in the New Testament World*, 207-227.

Solar magic and walking on water appear in magical spells: *Papyri Graecae Magicae* XXXIV, 1-10.

CHAPTER 8: A DARKER SORCERY

Given the quintessentially Christian view that connects sorcery with all that is evil, it is quite surprising to find Jesus performing acts that incorporate dark magical elements. It is even more surprising to find some of these accounts clustered in the gospel of John, widely held to be the most heavily 'spiritualized' gospel.

> As he passed by, he saw a man blind from birth. His disciples asked him, "Rabbi, who sinned, this man or his parents, so that he was born blind?
>
> Jesus answered, "Neither this man nor his parents sinned, but it happened so that the works of God might be manifest in him. We must perform the works of the one who sent me while it is day. A night approaches when no one can act. While I am in the world, I am the light of the world."
>
> When he had said this, he spit on the ground, made a paste from the spittle, and smeared the paste on the man's eyes and said to him, "Go wash in the pool of Siloam," which interpreted means Sent. Then he went and washed and came back seeing.
>
> Consequently the neighbors and those who had previously seen that he was a beggar said, "Isn't this the man who sat and begged?" Others said, "That's him!" But others were saying, "No, it's someone like him." The man was saying, "It's me!" So they said to him, "So how were your eyes opened?"
>
> The man answered, "The man called Jesus made a paste and smeared it on my eyes and said to me, 'Go to

> Siloam and wash,' and then I went and washed and received my sight."[1184]

This episode, like the version in Mark which differs from it in that it requires *two* applications of spit to be effective,[1185] is not conventionally miraculous. Indeed, it fairly reeks of magic: one must do *this*, then *this*, and next *this* to accomplish *that*. The common perception is that Jesus simply speaks and his miracles occur, but as this account shows, that is not the case. These accounts describe exactly the sort of ritualistic step-by-step behavior associated with the performance of magic.

The smallest details of Jesus' miraculous healings find their way into magical amulets with somewhat bizarre results. The pick-up-your-cot-and-walk story related in John 5:1-14 finds an echo in an amulet written for "your handmaid Joannia"[1186] in which Jesus has become "the God of the sheep pool"—*ο θεος της προβατικης κολυμβηθρας*[1187]—in a somewhat mangled reference to the pool of Bethesda that was located near a sheep market.

Regarding the healing of the blind man, Crossan notes: "The magic features of that process are also emphasized by the private nature of the cure 'out of the village.' The concluding injunction not to reenter the village may well be Markan redaction, another of those injunctions to silence that indicate the danger of misunderstanding Jesus' miracles. But the opening separation is part of the traditional story, and it underlines the dangerously deviant nature of magical healing."[1188]

[1184] John 9:1-11.

[1185] Mark 8:22-26. Compare 1 Kings 17:21: Elijah lies on a dead child three times to resuscitate him.

[1186] Meyer & Smith, *Ancient Christian Magic: Coptic Texts of Ritual Power*, 40-41.

[1187] Hunt, *The Oxyrhychus Papyri*, VIII, 252.

[1188] Crossan, *The Historical Jesus*, 325.

So powerful is Jesus' magic that even his clothing takes on talismanic power:

> There was a woman who had suffered from a flow of blood for twelve years, and she had endured many treatments by many doctors and spent everything she had and received no benefit, but had become even worse off.
>
> Having heard about Jesus, she came up from behind him in the crowd and touched his clothing, for she kept saying, "If I just touch his clothes, I will be healed." And immediately her flow of blood dried up and she perceived in her body that she was healed of the affliction.
>
> Suddenly realizing in himself that power had gone out of him, Jesus turned around in the crowd and said, "Who touched my clothes?" His disciples said to him, "You see the crowd pressing in on you and yet you say 'Who touched me?'"
>
> He looked around to see who had done it, but the woman, knowing what had happened to her, came trembling with fear and fell down before him and told him the whole truth. But he said to her, "Daughter, your confidence has healed you. Go in peace and be healed of your affliction."[1189]

Predictably, Matthew's reworking of the story shortens it by excising details, with the result that the healing is no longer impersonal, i.e., *magical*, in nature: in Matthew's version Jesus knows he has been touched and turns and heals the woman.[1190] But as Twelftree points out, "*δυναμις* [power, *my note*] works immediately and impersonally, responding to the contact of any believing person without the knowledge or approval of Jesus."[1191]

[1189] Mark 5:25-34.

[1190] Matthew 9:20-22.

[1191] Twelftree, *In the Name of Jesus: Exorcism Among the Early Christians*, 137.

Both Matthew and Luke are careful to specify that the bleeding woman, who was ritually unclean,[1192] touched only the *fringe* or *tassel* of Jesus' garment.[1193] The fringe or tassel on the four corners of the garment marked the wearer as an observant Jew,[1194] and the fact that longer tassels signified greater holiness[1195] and that whoever touched the tassels of Jesus' robe were healed *ex opere operato*,[1196] indicates the impersonal nature of the healing. Even a scholar who leans toward the apologetic must admit the "automatic" nature of this healing, a trait which marks it as clearly magical.[1197]

Similar magical healing is featured prominently in later Christianity; any contact with an article associated with a saint, "living or, more often, dead," might result in a cure. The saint's clothing, "the straw on which he had slept," his tomb and bits or dust chipped from it, images, relics, or water used to wash his corpse, even wine poured over relics, was "administered to patients in tiny amounts."[1198]

The story of the woman with the hemorrhage has provoked some interesting observations by John Hull that may be summarized as follows: the woman exhibits no particular interest in or knowledge of Jesus' mission or his person, she knows the healing power is available independent of Jesus' will, the impersonal nature of Jesus' power is known to himself, the woman, and the evangelist, the power, like electricity, flows automatically to another if their touch is deliberate and they have confidence in its efficacy, the power in Jesus is also in the garment,

---

1192 Leviticus 15: 25-27.

1193 Matthew 9:20, Luke 8:44.

1194 Numbers 15:25-27.

1195 Matthew 23:5.

1196 Mark 6:56.

1197 Kee, *Medicine, Miracle and Magic in New Testament Times*, 118.

1198 Wilson, *Saints and Their Cults: Studies in Religious Sociology, Folklore, and Hitory*, 19.

Jesus notices the flow of power, not the touch, and Jesus does not find the woman's action blameworthy.[1199]

Jesus' power is such that other exorcists, unknown to him or his disciples, cast out demons using his name[1200]—"clearly an example of a professional magical use"[1201]—a practice that continues after his death.[1202] Matthew has Jesus himself predict that lawless men would cast out demons, prophesy and perform miracles in his name,[1203] clearly in response to the use of Jesus' name by figures of whom the early Christians disapproved. Regarding the unknown exorcist of Mark 9:38, Schäfer notes, "...using the powerful name of Jesus had nothing to do with believing in Jesus...the magical use of the name of Jesus worked automatically, no matter whether or not the magician believed in Jesus."[1204] "...the fact that some of Jesus' deeds appeared to rescind the action-consequence principle in an illegitimate way, that is, in a way not based on appealing to God's forgiveness, opened the way for suspicion that they were magical in nature."[1205]

Borrowing a phrase from theology, various commentators have remarked that the miracles of both Jesus and other exorcists and healers appear to work *ex opere operato*, i.e., by the mere fact of performance, not by the merit of the performer. In a fashion similar to the benefit of a sacrament, the efficacy depends upon the willingness to receive the benefit, not on the status of the one performing the ritual. Indeed, Jesus' disciples possess such power that not only can contact with articles of their clothing heal, but *even their shadow falling across the sick effects a cure.*[1206]

1199 Hull, *Hellenistic Magic and the Synoptic Tradition*, 109-110.
1200 Mark 9:38-39.
1201 Ibid, 72.
1202 Acts 19:13.
1203 Matthew 7:21-22.
1204 Schäfer, *Jesus in the Talmud*, 60.
1205 Holmen, *A Kind of Magic*, 55.
1206 Acts 5:12-16, 19:11-12.

Šedina notes the common belief that "things which once were connected preserve this relationship even after they have been separated." Material artifacts or places are conduits of power, "a person and any separate part of his or her body, such as hair or nails" or "used pieces of clothing or an imprint of the body, at a place where a particular person slept," a linkage that extended to "the divine or demonic powers and their natural names."[1207]

These accounts reveal an attitude toward working miracles that shares the same basic assumption as working magic: power is *value-free* and hence available to those who master the techniques required to access it. Techniques can be taught, and power transferred from one practitioner to another. In fact, the gospel of Mark specifies that Jesus taught his disciples—including Judas?—the techniques of exorcism,[1208] and it is this understanding of the impersonal nature of the energy involved that motivated Simon to offer to pay Peter for his miraculous powers.[1209]

> Any magical operation presupposes that some sort of energy is available in the universe which can be used by the operator. The modern anthropologists call it *mana*, the Greeks called it *dynamis* [δυναμις, *my note*], "power," or *charis* [χαρις, *my note*], "grace," or *arete*, [αρετη, *my note*][1210] "effectiveness." In a polytheistic society, it was only natural that the one Power took on the forms and names of many powers—gods, daemons, heroes, disembodied souls, etc—who were willing, even eager, to work for the *magos.*[1211]

1207 Šedina, *Listy filologické*, 136, 1-2, 20.

1208 Mark 9:28-29.

1209 Acts 8:18-19. The details of this failed transaction are examined in a subsequent chapter.

1210 Hence *aretology*, a *list of virtues*, or in a magician's case, *miracles*.

1211 Luck, *Witchcraft and Magic in Europe: Ancient Greece and Rome*, 105.

"John the Baptist...raised from the dead..."

> And Herod heard of it, for [Jesus'] name became known and they were saying, "John the Baptist has been raised from the dead and because of this the powers are at work in him.
>
> But others said, "He is Elijah," but others, "A prophet, like one of the former prophets." But when Herod heard, he said, "John, the one who I beheaded, has been raised."[1212]

Since Greek does not depend on sentence inversion to indicate a question, the text at Mark 6:16 could also be translated, "But when Herod heard, he said, 'Has John, the one who I beheaded, been raised?'" Various suggestions have been offered for why John was beheaded, including Antipas' desire to see the head as proof of John's death. However, Ross Kraemer has proposed that the gospels emphasize the method of John's death—decapitation—precisely to counter the rumor that Jesus was John raised from the dead:

> *Why is Jesus not John resurrected from the dead?* The Gospel narratives are clear that this identification has been suggested. It would seem to be troubling to followers of Jesus for obvious reasons, namely, that it obscures distinctions between Jesus and John and may even subordinate the former to the latter. The account of John's death in the Gospels, but not in Josephus, provides a functional response to this question. Jesus is not John raised from the dead because John's body and head were severed: only his body was buried by his disciples, while the whereabouts of his head, given to

---

[1212] Mark 6:14-16.

> Herodias, are unknown, thus, implicitly, making his bodily resurrection impossible.[1213]

From a superficial reading of the gospel text, a person might assume that people were speculating that John the Baptist had been resurrected from the dead in much the same way that Lazarus and others were raised—"John the Baptist has been raised from the dead *and because of this the powers are at work* (*και δια τουτο ενεργουσιν αι δυναμεις*) in him." However, Kraeling proposed a much different reading, one not only in accord with the circumstances of the times, but with the vocabulary of the passage:

> Between demons as the servants of magicians, and spirits of the dead used in a similar way there is no basic distinction. Both are beings of the spiritual order, not limited by time or space, and endowed with supernatural powers…What the people and Herod originally said about Jesus' relation to John was that Jesus was using the spirit of John brought back from the dead to perform his miracles for him.[1214]

The broader context of the story establishes that Herod Antipas not only knew and feared John the Baptist as a holy man, but that he had previously protected him. Furthermore, Herod obviously knew John was dead—Herod himself had ordered John's execution and had seen his head delivered on a platter.[1215]

Whoever "they" were that claimed John the Baptist had been raised from the dead, it is clear that they had known John. Why else would they mention him unless they had been in the crowds that went out to be baptized by him and considered him

---

1213 Kraemer, *Journal of Biblical Literature* 125: 343.
1214 Kraeling, "Was Jesus Accused of Necromancy?" *Journal of Biblical Literature* 59: 154-155.
1215 Mark 6:20, 26-28.

a prophet?[1216] And they must certainly have known Jesus and seen him in action. What else would explain their animated speculation about the source of his powers? Why, therefore, should we suppose that the crowds who first flocked to hear John the Baptist and later witnessed the wonders performed by Jesus could not tell that John the Baptist and Jesus of Nazareth were two different people? The gospels agree that John attracted large crowds and that he became very well known. John's fame was such that Jesus used it to trap the temple authorities,[1217] and John sent out disciples to question Jesus.[1218] It strains credibility to suppose that anyone familiar with either man's career thought Jesus could literally have been John raised from the dead, although such confusion might have occurred much later among people who were *not* eyewitnesses to either man's career, people alive at the time the gospels were being composed.

Note carefully how the common people explained Jesus' powers: "John the Baptist has been raised from the dead *and because of this* the powers are at work in him." They did not mean that John had been resurrected, but that his ghost had been raised up for magical purposes. The unquiet ghost—the *νεκυδαιμων* (nekudaimōn)—fell into several categories, the *αωρος* (aōros), the *untimely dead*, the *βιαιοθανατος* (biaiothanatos), the *dead by violence*—"a biaiothanatos, those who have been killed by violence, part of the wider class of the restless dead, who came to be thought of as the typical instruments of malign magic"[1219]—the *αγαμος* (agamos), the *unmarried*, and the *αταφος* (ataphos), the *unburied*, as well as the *αγυναιος* (agunaios), *wifeless*, and the *απαιδης* (apaidēs), *childless*. Regarding the unburied, "The *ατελεσтοι* [atelestoi, "not completed," *my note*] are

[1216] Mark 1:5. Compare Matthew 3:5, Luke 3:7-15, John 1:20-26.
[1217] Matthew 21:24-26.
[1218] Matthew 11:2-6.
[1219] Gordon, *Witchcraft and Magic in Europe: Ancient Greece and Rome*, 176.

the dead that have not received the due rites. Such spirits, like the ones of those that have died by violence or before their time, cannot achieve rest..."[1220] "It was generally believed that the spirit of any human being who had come to an unjust, violent, or otherwise untimely end was of enormous power. If a magician could call up and get control of, or identify himself with such a spirit, he could then control inferior spirits or powers."[1221]

The "untimely dead" figured prominently in later Christianity. Legendary child saints and confessors, including Pancras, Agnes, Vitus, Goswin and Donninus, to name but a few, became the focus of cults that were spread by the "translation" of their body parts and relics from church to church. Even in the Middle Ages they were connected to magical healing: "In several instances the children were suspected by their persecutors of being magicians rather than saints, and of practicing magical arts..."[1222]

In Jesus' day it was widely believed that the ghosts of those who had died before achieving life's goals, particularly by meeting up with a violent end, were earth-bound sources of enormous power. Rabinowitz vividly describes such restless dead: "Needy and dangerous figures waiting in the shadows of existence...particularly those who died young or violently, the unhappy and unsatisfied dead with their restless energy and free-floating rage."[1223] Or as Vermeule expresses it, "...no living person has

---

[1220] Ogden, *Witchcraft and Magic in Europe: Ancient Greece and Rome*, 22.

[1221] Smith, *Jesus the Magician*, 34.

[1222] Wasyliw, *Martyrdom, Murder, and Magic: Child Saints and Their Cults in Medieval Europe*, 57.

[1223] Rabinowitz, *The Rotting Goddess: The Origin of the Witch in Classical Antiquity*, 104

See also *Arcana Mundi*, 165-168; *Magic, Witchcraft, and Ghosts in the Greek and Roman Worlds*, 146-152.

The νεκυια (nekuia), the rite by which ghosts are raised, is pre-Homeric.

the power of even a minor nameless hero, whose power flows simply from the fact that he is dead and angry about it, and cannot sleep still…many heroes die angry…waiting to be avenged for their murders; these are potential actors in ghost stories, dangerous and partly wakeful."[1224] I will make the case that "raising" of the John the Baptist in the gospel of Mark is the earliest record of Christian necromancy, an attempt, in the words of Peter Brown, "to join Heaven and Earth at the grave of a dead human being."[1225] The argument that a form of necromantic practice became central to the function of early Christian miracle and continued in the guise of adoration of the martyrs is made in the material that follows.

We know that spirit manipulation was standard magical praxis in the Middle East a millennium or more before the time of Jesus. "…by associating itself with power over demons Christianity associated itself with magic in the minds of its critics."[1226] Ghosts were often invoked to accomplish magical acts:

> *I command you, ghost of the dead* (εξορκιζω σε νεκυδαιμον), by the powerful and implacable god and by his holy names, to stand beside me in the night to come, in whatever form you had, and if you are able, transact for me [Named] deed, if I command you, now, now, quick, quick...and he will actually stand alongside you in your dreams throughout the night and he will ask you, saying, "Command what you wish and I will do it."[1227]

For similar concerns about the unquiet dead in Mesopotamia, see *Witchcraft and Magic in Europe: Biblical and Pagan Societies*, 79-82.

1224 Vermeule, *Aspects of Death in Early Greek Art and Poetry*, 7, 27.

1225 Brown, *The Cult of the Saints: Its Rise and Function in Latin Christianity*, 1.

1226 Sorensen, *Possession and Exorcism in the New Testament and Early Christianity*, 179.

1227 Preisendanz, *Papyri Graecae Magicae* IV, 2030-2053.

That necromancy was known among the Jews of Jesus' era is certain, as these spells from the *Sepher Ha-Razim* make clear:

> These are the angels that obey (you) during the night (if you wish) to speak with the moon or the stars or to question a ghost or to speak with the spirits...
>
> If you wish to question a ghost; stand facing a tomb and repeat the names of the angels of the fifth encampment ...I adjure you, O spirit of the ram bearer [Hermes, *my note*], who dwell among the graves upon the bones of the dead...[1228]

The "ghost" of the *Sepher Ha-Razim* that one might wish to question is the familiar אוב (ōb) of the Old Testament.[1229]

Regarding a motive for why Jesus might have selected the ghost of John the Baptist above all others as a source of power, this observation by Daniel Ogden bears careful note: "How signify-cant were these categories of dead for necromancy in particular? Often the prime criterion in selecting a ghost for necromancy was the relevance of the individual ghost to the matter at hand. Hence, the ghost exploited was often a dear one...A further category that may have been particularly valued for necromancy was that of the exalted ghost."[1230] Who could have been more relevant to Jesus' career than John the Baptist? He is Jesus' fore-runner, "the voice of one crying in the wilderness," even a relative according to Luke, and of those born of women, who was greater than John?[1231]

[1228] Morgan, *Sepher Ha-Razim*, 36, 38.

[1229] Goldin, *Aspects of Religious Propaganda in Judaism and Early Christianity*, 133.

[1230] Ogden, *Greek and Roman Necromancy*, 226-227.

Kraeling cites the fact that John was a *βιαιοθανατος* in his article and observes that the verb used of raising John is also used in the Greek magical papyri for conjuring spirits of the dead.

[1231] John 1:23, Luke 1:36, Matthew 11:11.

Because the people believe that Jesus has raised the ghost of John, they conclude that "the powers are at work in him"—the powers of darkness.[1232] In several New Testament passages "powers" make a clear reference to spirit entities,[1233] and of the verb translated "be at work in"—*ενεργεω* (energeō)—Bertram notes that in the New Testament "theological or demonological use is predominant;"[1234] the verb is "always used of some principle or power at work."[1235] Both the verb and corresponding noun, *ενεργεια* (energeia), from whence *energy*, are used in the magical papyri for working sorcery.[1236]

In the process of redacting his version of the story, Matthew has Herod say, "*This man is John the Baptist* (*ουτος εστιν* Ιωαννης *ο βαπτιστης*). He was raised from the dead *and that is why the powers are working* (*και δια τουτο αι δυναμεις ενεργουσιν*) in him."[1237] The text makes Herod simply identify Jesus as John, interpreting Jesus as John *redivivus*, but this gloss does not address the question of why the powers would be working in someone because they had been raised from the dead, nor does it contemplate what sort of powers were thought to be involve-ed—the New Testament records no case of special powers accruing to the resurrected. To make sure his reader understands that Jesus is not John's ghost raised from the grave, Matthew has John's disciples come and take the now headless body away, bury it, *and tell Jesus about it.* Jesus then temporarily retires from the scene.[1238]

[1232] Compare Colossians 1:13.

[1233] As at Romans 8:38, 1 Peter 3:22.

[1234] Bertram, *Theological Dictionary of the New Testament*, II, 653.

[1235] Abbott-Smith, *A Manual Greek Lexicon of the New Testament*, 153.

[1236] Muñoz Delgado, *Léxico de magia y religión en los papiros mágicos griegos*, 39.

[1237] Matthew 14:2.

[1238] Matthew 14:12-13.

Luke, on the other hand, produces a Herod who is "completely perplexed,"[1239] at a seeming loss how to even begin to explain Jesus' famous powers. Garrett admits that Luke rephrases "the most damaging part of the account," to avoid the charge of necromancy, but next claims that the evangelists "did not share modern readers' frequent assumption that identity of appearance implies actual identity."[1240]

Garrett does not explain *how* she knows what assumptions the anonymous "evangelists" shared. If their own opinion is to be allowed, it appears the gospel writers believed that 'trees are known by their fruit,'[1241] and it is clear that early Christian groups had little difficulty identifying who was and who wasn't a magician. The frequent alterations and omissions of incriminating details by Matthew and Luke indicate that the writers of those gospels shared *exactly* the assumption that appearance implies "actual identity" an assumption their readers shared. Why report Jesus' healings and exorcisms at all if their performance was not thought to establish something about his identity? And why change or delete Mark's reports of Jesus' performance unless the identity being established by Mark was not to the exact liking of Matthew and Luke?

Garrett's argument also ignores the evidence for Jesus' reputetion among non-Christians—Gentiles regarded Jews as accomplished exorcists and Jesus the Jew as a magician. Evidently his early critics also shared our "modern" assumption that appearances tell us something about identity: "The church fathers, among them Irenaeus, Arnobius, Justin Martyr, Lactantius, and Origen, were keenly aware of the charge—made by Jew and Gentile alike—that Jesus was a magician. In reply to this assertion, these early Christian writers made no effort to distinguish Jesus' actions from those of a wonder-worker...It was a question

---

[1239] Luke 9:7-9.

[1240] Garrett, *The Demise of the Devil*, 3.

[1241] Matthew 7:20.

not of the form of the wonders, but of the relationship of the purported doer to the person speaking or writing."[1242]

Those pondering the source of Jesus' power, then as now, are torn between two possibilities: he is a prophet like one of the prophets of old and his powers come from the spirit of God, or he is a necromancer and the powers at work in him include the ghost of John the Baptist. Herod Antipas appears to lean toward the latter conclusion: "John, the one who I beheaded, has been raised." Little wonder that the origin of Jesus' authority remains an issue up to the end of his life.[1243] The possibility that Jesus may have fit the description of a בעל אוב (baal 'ob), "ghost-master," or a שאל אוב (shoel ob), "one who calls up ghosts," is raised in a previous chapter. In any case, it seems clear enough from the gospel of Mark that the ghost Jesus was accused of calling up was not the Holy Ghost.

Cursing opponents.

Even his enemies everywhere acknowledge that Jesus controlled demons, but the fact that he could send unclean spirits into animals and men has received far less attention.

> After saying this, Jesus became disturbed in spirit and declared, "Most certainly I tell you, one from among you will betray me!"
>
> The disciples looked around at one another, uncertain about whom he was speaking. One of the disciples—the one that Jesus loved—was lying up against Jesus. Simon Peter motioned him to ask him about whom he was speaking, so the disciple leaning against Jesus' chest said to him, "Lord, who is it?"

[1242] Ricks, *Ancient Magic and Ritual Power,* 141.

[1243] Matthew 21:23, Mark 11:28, Luke 20:2.

> Jesus answered, "It is the one I give the morsel of bread that I dip. Then he took the morsel and dipped it and gave it to Judas, the son of Simon Iscariot. And after the morsel, then Satan entered into him.
>
> Jesus said to him, "Do what you are doing more quickly." But none of those reclining with Jesus knew why he said that to him.[1244]

As noted by Smith, this comparative use of *ταχυς* (tachus), *quickly*, appears to echo a frequently attested conclusion to magical spells, *ηδη ηδη ταχυ ταχυ*: *now, now, quick, quick.*[1245] This conclusion is supported by the frequent occurrence of "I am coming quickly" (*ερχομαι ταχυ*) in Revelation.[1246] Regarding the magical use of *ταχυ*, *quickly*, in Revelation Thomas concluded, "Though it is not possible to prove that *ταχυ* definitely was used in the same fashion as it is to be found in later centuries, it seems possible, and currently there are no credible contenders for an alternative source."[1247] This very common closing formula of magical spells, *now, now, quickly, quickly*, "the battle-cry of late antique magicians,"[1248] found its way into both Arabic and Coptic.

As soon as John tells us that Jesus "became disturbed in spirit" we are put on notice of an impending supernatural event. Such "disturbances"—the verb is *ταρασσω* (tarassō)—in the gospel of John always precede miraculous occurrences. When the water of the pool of Bethzatha is "stirred" by an angel, the first sick person in is healed—a sort of divinely-sponsored 'race for the cure' —and when Jesus' soul is "troubled" a heavenly voice is heard. Jesus becomes similarly "disturbed" on first encountering the mourners at Lazarus' tomb and again as he stands before the

---

[1244] John 13:21-28.

[1245] Smith, *Jesus the Magician*, 111.

[1246] Revelation 2:16; 3:11; 22:7,12,20.

[1247] Thomas, *Magical Motifs in the Book of Revelation*, 105.

[1248] Bohak, *Bulletin of the American Society of Papyrologists* 36: 35.

tomb itself—the raising of the beloved Lazarus quickly follows.[1249]

In the case of the final meal with his disciples, Jesus' disturbance of spirit again signals a preternatural event, two of them to be exact. First, Jesus foresees Judas' betrayal.[1250] It should nearly go without saying that the power to read others' minds is a frequent preoccupation of the magical spells: "...let me foresee today the things in the soul of each person..."[1251]

Next Jesus hands Judas over to Satan so that Satan can destroy him. There is a clear precedent for this action: he has previously handed a herd of swine over to the horde of demons that drove the pigs over a cliff to their death—as previously noted, "transference of the disease or demon from the man to the animal" is a well-attested magical technique in the ancient Middle East.[1252] That a man of God could curse others to death, even by invoking the most sacred name of God, is apparent from the case of Elisha who curses the boys who taunt him: "and he cursed them *in the name of Yahweh* (בשם יהוה)."[1253] As a result forty-two of the boys are mauled to death.

As Davies noted over a century ago,

[1249] John 5:7. The longer text found in the *King James Version*, which explains the agitation of the water as the result of an angel, likely originated as a marginal gloss that was later copied into the body of the text.

John 12:27-29, 11:33, 38.

[1250] That Jesus has the power to read thoughts is everywhere stated in John (John 1:47-48, 2:24-25, 4:16-18, 5:42, 6:61, etc.). John even says that Jesus foreknew which of his disciples did not believe and which would betray him (6:64). Compare Mark 2:8.

[1251] Preisendanz, *Papyri Graecae Magicae* III, 265, to cite but one of many examples.

[1252] Thomsen, *Witchcraft and Magic in Europe: Biblical and Pagan Societies*, 71-75.

[1253] 2 Kings 2:24.

> Demons were among the later Jews supposed to be capable of being transferred from one individual to another, or from human beings to animals. We come across this formula in the Talmud: "May the blindness of M, son of N, leave him and pierce the eyeballs of this dog."[1254]

As pointed out by Strelan, the use of animals, particularly dogs, for cleansing and healing was common: "a dog, through contact with an ill person, was thought to contract the disease... Rubbing people with the dead bodies of puppies was thought to cause all harmful and polluting substances to be absorbed by the animal, and thus remove them from the person."[1255] Magical transference might be accomplished through words, gestures, a look, spells, and poppets or "voodoo dolls." "There need not always be a lack of proximity between victim and witch...she causes her victim to incorporate witchcraft by means of food, drink, washing, and ointment."[1256]

The piece of bread that Jesus dips in the bowl and hands to Judas is the equivalent of Judas' kiss of betrayal: it is the sign to the Adversary to approach and take control. Morton Smith: "The notion that a demon can be sent into food so as to enter anyone who eats the food is common."[1257] Jesus betrays Judas to Satan before Judas betrays Jesus to the temple police. In so doing, Jesus is merely following the example set in the Old Testament where God regularly sends evil spirits into those of whom he disapproves.[1258] Regarding "masters of spirits," Lewis asks, "If

---

1254 Davies, *Magic, Divination, and Demonology Among the Hebrews and their Neighbors*, 104.

1255 Strelan, *Biblical Theology Bulletin* 33:149.

1256 Abusch, *Mesopotamian Witchcraft*, 7.

1257 Smith, *Jesus the Magician*, 110

1258 Judges 9:23, 1 Samuel 16:15, 16, 23, 18:10, 19:9.

their power over the spirits is such that they can heal the sick, why should they not also sometimes cause what they cure?"[1259]

The gospel does not say the morsel of bread was offered to Satan, only that "after the morsel, then Satan entered into him" —*και μετα το ψωμιον τοτε εισηλθεν ο Σατανας*.[1260] By now it should come as no surprise to find a close parallel to Jesus' actions in the magical spells, in this case an attraction spell that calls up the gods of the underworld using morsels of bread:

> Leave a little of the bread you did not eat, and breaking it apart, make seven morsels and go to where the heroes and gladiators and men who died violently were slain. Say the spell into the morsels and toss them.
>
> This is the spell to be pronounced into the morsels...[1261]

After the magician says the spell *into* the morsels—*λεγε τον λογον εις τους ψωμους*—the bread forms a conduit for the passage of the spirits and the spell is activated. The notion that powerful entities, good or bad, can be transferred into or out of a subject is the very basis for exorcism as well as hexing a victim. Legend had it that Apollonius came by night to a temple guarded by dogs and prevented their barking "by tossing the dogs scraps he had ensorcelled" and was therefore detained "for being a sorcerer (*ως γοητα*) and a thief."[1262] "The magical principle behind the treatment of diseases can be identified as that of correspondence or symbolic magic, the more important effect being the transfer of the illness into a concrete thing, liquid, person or animal through various rituals. We should also note that

---

[1259] Lewis, *Ecstatic Religion*, 33.
[1260] John 13:27.
[1261] Preisendanz, *Papyri Graecae Magicae* IV, 1392-1395.
[1262] Philostratus, *Life of Apollonius* VIII, 30.

the means used to heal a person can be used to harm him, showing that the forces used in rituals are fundamentally neutral."[1263]

A text of an amulet references the need for protection against ensorcelled food and other forms of magical transmission: "God of Abraham, God of Isaac and God of Jacob, protect Alexandra, daughter of Zoē, *from demons and enchantments* (απο δεμονιων και φαρμακων)...flee from Alexandra, Zoē's daughter...*lest you use potions on her* (φαρμακωσητε αυτην), *either by a kiss* (μητε απο φιληματος)...*or by food* (μητε εν βρωσει), or by drink...*or by the* [*evil*] *eye* (μητε απο οφθαλμου), *or by an article of clothing* (μητε τω ιματιω)...One God and his Christ, help Alexandra."[1264]

The magical papyri and curse tablets supply us with many examples of such black magic. The verb used in the New Testament that is translated "hand over," παραδιδωμι (paradidōmi), is commonly used in magical curse tablets—known as a καταδεσμος (katadesmos) or "tie down" in Greek and as a *defixio* or "nail down" in Latin—to send a person's soul to the gods of the underworld. For example, we find this curse directed against anyone who might disturb a man's grave: παραδιδωμαι αυτον θεοις καταχθονιοις, "...I hand him over to the gods of the underworld."[1265] That Jewish magicians in the time of Jesus used techniques of cursing opponents is evident. In the *Sepher Ha-Razim* we encounter this spell: "I deliver to you, angels of anger and wrath, N son of N, that you will strangle him and destroy him and his appearance, etc..."[1266]

Specific references to Jesus cursing people to death, if such events occurred, have been removed from the gospels, but the fact that Jesus could curse something to death is supported by

---

[1263] Jeffers, *Magic and Divination in Ancient Palestine and Syria*, 235.
[1264] Kotansky, *Greek Magical Amulets*, 278-281.
[1265] Horsley, *New Documents Illustrating Early Christianity* 4:165.
[1266] Morgan, *Sepher Ha-Razim*, 27.

the story of the withered fig tree.[1267] Eitrem noted the moral ambivalence revealed by this story: "Actually an *εξορκισμος* [exorcism, *my note*]—just as a *ορκος* [oath], an *αρα* [curse, execration], or an *αναθεμα* [a thing cursed, bound by a curse]—is ambivalent, it can be used for good or for bad. Ambivalent is also Jesus' own mighty command, as we see from his destructtion of the fig tree near Jerusalem (Mark xi.13): 'May no one ever eat thy fruit any more…'"[1268] After noting the case of Jesus cursing the fig tree, Ritner points out that "the notion of cursing was not alien to the evolving Judeo-Christian traditions" and supports his contention by citing a number of gospel examples.[1269]

The anonymous author of the *Infancy Gospel of Thomas* had no trouble imagining that Jesus could curse people to death. He has Jesus killing other children by magic starting when he is only five years old, as well as crippling and blinding the objects of his infantile temper.[1270] However, an example of an indirect form of cursing to death is given in Matthew 26:24: "Woe to that man through whom the son of man is handed over! Better for him if that man had not been born!" In response to this proleptic countercurse, Judas hangs himself.[1271] Myllykoski notes, "The horrible death of Judas [Acts 1: 18-19, *my note*] can also be considered a divine *Strafwunder*, even though there is no agent mentioned."[1272]

The attitude of early Christians toward their opponents, particularly the nonconformists in their ranks, was hardly an exam-

---

[1267] Mark 11:13, 21-24.

[1268] Eitrem, *Some Notes on the Demonology in the New Testament*, 14-15.

[1269] Robert Ritner, *Ancient Christian Magic: Coptic Texts of Ritual Power*, 185. Specifically Mark 11:12-22; Matthew 21:18-19; Luke 9:5, 10:13-15; Matthew 10:11-15; Acts 18:6.

[1270] *Infancy Gospel of Thomas* 3:3, 4:1-4, 8:3.

[1271] Matthew 27:5.

[1272] Myllykoski, *Wonders Never Cease*, 156.

ple of turning the other cheek. The act of "handing over" common to the New Testament is thoroughly attested curse technique—*ουαι δε τω ανθρωπω εκεινω δι ου ο υιος του ανθρωπου παραδιδοται*, "Woe to that man through whom the son of man is handed over..." Even as Jesus handed Judas over to the Adversary, Jesus' followers exercise the power both to strike people dead on the spot,[1273] as well as hand them over to Satan. The gospels make little effort to conceal the disciples' murderous impulses: "When the disciples James and John saw this, they asked, "Lord, do you want us to call fire down from heaven to destroy them?"[1274] The process of "handing someone over" to demonic forces is a well-documented technique in the magical papyri:

> Next, take [the curse written on papyrus] off *to the tomb of one dead before his time* (*εις αωρου μνημα*), dig down four fingers deep and put it in [the hole] and say:
> "Spirit of the dead, whoever you may be, *I hand* [*Name*] *over to you* (*παραδιδωμι σοι τον δεινα*) so that he may not accomplish [*Named*] action." Then, after burying it, go away. Better you do it when the moon is waning...[1275]

Of this procedure Deissmann remarks, "A person who wished to injure an enemy or to punish an evildoer consecrated him by incantation and tablet to the powers of darkness below...The only difference between Jewish and pagan execrations probably lay in the fact that Satan took the place of the gods of the lower world."[1276]

In his letter to the Corinthians regarding a man in an incestuous relationship, Paul commands the congregation "*to hand such a*

[1273] Acts 5:1-11.
[1274] Luke 9:54 (NIV).
[1275] Preisendanz, *Papyri Graecae Magicae*, V, 332.
[1276] Deissman, *Light from the Ancient East*, 302.

person over to Satan (*παραδουναι τον τοιουτον τω σατανα*) for the destruction of the flesh,"[1277] And in the pseudo-Pauline "pastoral" epistle, two more miscreants are similarly "handed over" to Satan—"Hymenius and Alexander, *whom I handed over to Satan* (*ους παρεδωκα τω σατανα*)..."[1278] As noted by Collins, "The tradition of Greek magic helps explain why the procedure advocated by Paul took the form it did and how the process was expected to work...the passage is quite similar to the thought of the magical papyri. The recalcitrant opponents are to be consigned to a demonic power which will prevent them from doing a type of deed."[1279]

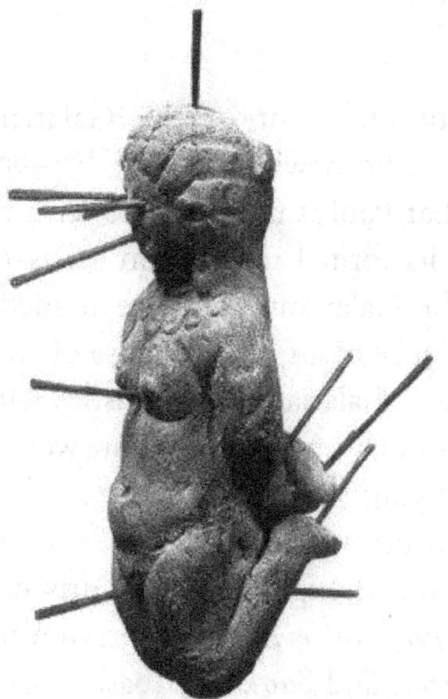

A *κολοσσος* (kolossos), or "voodoo doll" employed for magical binding.

Paul's correspondence even contains curses pronounced upon those who deviate from his gospel: "For even if we, or an angel

[1277] 1 Corinthians 5:5.
[1278] 1 Timothy 1:20.
[1279] Collins, *Harvard Theological Review* 73: 256, 258.

from heaven, proclaim a gospel different from the gospel we preached to you, a curse on him! As we have said before, even now I repeat, if anyone proclaims a gospel contrary to what you received, a curse on him!"[1280] As Betz notes in his commentary, "Galatians begins with a conditional curse, very carefully constructed, cursing every Christian who dares to preach a gospel different from that which Paul had preached...What does this imply for the literary function of the letter? It means that as the carrier of curse and blessing the letter becomes a 'magical letter.' This category is well-known from ancient epistolography."[1281] "Let him be accursed!"—*αναθεμα εστω*—became, as the world soon learned, the typical Christian response to differences of opinion.

Regarding the bewitchment of the Galatian Christians—*τις υμας εβασκανεν*, "who bewitched you?"[1282]—Neyrey says, "It is my hypothesis that Paul is using it [the term for casting the evil eye, *my note*] in its formal sense as an accusation that someone has bewitched the Galatians." In an extended analysis, he goes on to note, "evidence of an intense sense of rivalry, competition, and even jealousy…Galatians fairly bristles with a sense of rivalry and competition."[1283] So the short answer to Paul's question, "Who bewitched you?" is, "*Other Christians.*" In the era in question and for centuries before and after, *βασκανια* (baskania), *jealousy* or *envy*, was thought to be the driving force behind the *βασκανος οφθαλμος*, or *evil eye*. By extension, *baskania* also meant *bewitchment*, and *βασκανος* (baskanos), *slanderer*, *malicious*, and by extension, *sorcerer*.[1284] Christians considered envy to be a basic component of the personality of Satan; in the apocryphal *Acts of Thomas*, the demon is addressed, "O Jealous One, who never rests"—*ο βασκανος ο μηδεποτε ηρεμων*. The term

---

[1280] Galatians 1:8-9.

[1281] Betz, *Galatians*, 25.

[1282] Galatians 3:1.

[1283] Neyrey, *Catholic Biblical Quarterly* 50: 72, 97.

[1284] Liddell & Scott, *A Greek-English Lexicon*, 278.

αβασκαντος (abaskantos), "unharmed by the Evil Eye," is well attested from Christian letters recovered from Oxyrhynchus: "*I greet your children by name, whom may the Evil Eye not harm* (ασπαζομαι κατ᾽ονομα τα αβασκαντα σου παιδια), and I pray for their health and yours in the Lord God." Blumell notes "this phrase [αβασκαντος, *my note*] can be found in other letters where Christian provenance is secure" and points out that Athanasius, the bishop of Alexandria, "felt compelled to devote an entire treatise urging his fellow Christians in Egypt to stop using charms and amulets to ward off malevolent forces, such as the evil eye."[1285]

Paul is accusing rival preachers of casting the evil eye due to envy and the letter to the Galatians functions as a counter-curse against their malign influence. Paul himself had a reputation for sorcery; the *Acts of Paul* records the reaction of the people when Paul is hauled into court for preaching abstinence: απαγαγε τον μαγον διεφθειρεν γαρ ημων πασας τας γυναικας, "Off with the magician! He has corrupted all our wives!"[1286] The church historian Eusebius had to counter the charge that Peter and Paul were "were uneducated men, liars and sorcerers" (ανθρωποι ψευσται και απαιδευτοι και γοητες).[1287]

In the account about Ananias and his wife Sapphira, the apostle Peter performs a "punitive action, which is a typical feature of magic,"[1288] causing the death of both. Ananias, confronted with his dishonesty, drops dead on the spot. Three hours later his wife arrives, reiterates their lie, and is told, "Why did you conspire to test the spirit of the Lord? Now look! The feet of the men who buried your husband are at the door and they will

---

[1285] Blumell, *Lettered Christians: Christians, Letters, and Late Antique Oxyrhynchus*, 57.
[1286] *Acts of Paul*, 15.
[1287] Eusebius, *The Treatise of Eusebius*, II (Conybeare, *The Life of Apollonius*, II, 488).
[1288] Kee, *Medicine, Miracle and Magic in New Testament Times*, 118.

carry you out! Instantly she fell at his feet and expired."[1289] "In contrast to the gospels, *Strafwunder* occupy a very prominent position in the 'Acts of the Apostles' where both Peter and Paul perform them. In the story of Ananias and Sapphira, Peter presides over the death of Ananias (Acts 5:5), who dies without the invocation of a curse, while the death of his wife Sapphira (5:10) is preceded by a curse (5:9) which becomes immediately effective...Elymas the magician is struck blind in consequence of an imprecation pronounced by Paul...In early Christian apocryphal literature, the incidence of *Strafwunder* attributed to both Jesus and the apostles exhibits a marked increase in frequency..."[1290]

The use of magic against opponents continues long after the death of the apostles: "An unworthy woman was paralyzed when she received the eucharist at Paul's hands...and an unworthy lad's hands withered when he took the elements from Thomas...As a result of slapping Thomas, a man dies, as Thomas had predicted he would...Simon is struck dumb when a baby speaks to him with a man's voice, and Simon kills a boy by whispering in his ear...At Peter's prayer, the flying Simon falls and breaks his leg in three places."[1291] Within the canonical gospels and Acts, magical ritualistic behavior is everywhere present: "shake the dust from your feet,"[1292] and "he shook out his clothing."[1293] It bears noting that "shake" and "curse to death" are both derived from the same Hebrew stem, קלל.[1294]

[1289] Acts 5:9-10.

[1290] Aune, *Aufstieg und Niedergang der Römischen Welt*, II.23.2: 1552-1553.

Strafwunder refers to a miracle of punishment. The German *straf* is the basis of the English word *strafe*.

[1291] Fiorenza, *Aspects of Religious Propaganda in Judaism and Early Christianity*, 166.

[1292] Matthew 10:11-15, Luke 9:5, 54.

[1293] Acts 18:6.

[1294] Brown, Driver & Briggs, *Hebrew and English Lexicon*, 886.

The apocryphal Acts both continue and enlarge upon the rich tradition of Christian magical cursing. When Drusiana raises Fortunatus from the dead, the young man denounces her act of necromancy and flees, provoking this curse of incandescent malignancy from the apostle:

> Be thou destroyed from among those who trust in the Lord, from their thoughts, from their mind, from their souls, from their bodies, from their affairs, from their life, from their conversation, from their death, from their business, from their counsel, from the resurrection unto God, from the fragrance of fellowship you share, from their fasts, from their prayers, from the holy bath, from the Eucharist, from food for the body, from drink, from clothing, from love, from abstinence, from self-control, from righteousness, from all these, may you be profaned before God! Hated Satan! Jesus Christ our Lord will destroy you and those who share your character![1295]

The apostle soon announces, "Brothers, some spirit in me foretold"—*πνευμα τι εν εμοι εμαντευσατο*—"that Fortunatus is about to die from the blackness of a snake bite." The young men set out in search of him and find him dead as John has described. Triumphant, the apostle declares, "Your child is delivered, O Devil."[1296]

The posture of Christianity was one of active aggression directed toward opponents, an attitude that crystallized into summary executions during the rule of Constantine, the first emperor to embrace the new religion. As Paul himself correctly observed about the Christian response to opposition, "The kingdom of

---

[1295] Junod & Kaestli, *Acta Ioannis*, 84. The translation of the text is my own.

[1296] Ibid, 86.

God is not about speech, but about power."[1297] "Occasionally the bargain was explicit: acknowledge God or be punished. So an ascetic of Hermoupolis in Egypt reduces a procession of non-Christian worshippers to frozen immobility, right in the middle of the road, through spells; and they cannot regain the use of their limbs until they 'renounce their error.' Or you might defy the ascetic—in this case, Aphraates, in a Syrian city—and by no mere coincidence, straightway you died a horrible death. From that, people 'realized the strength of Aphraates' prayer.'"[1298]

Necromantic sortilege.

In earliest Christianity we find another strong parallel with pagan practice: as the apostles attempt to select a replacement for the traitor Judas, they engage in a séance. They first pray to Jesus to designate a successor and then cast lots—*κληρος* (klēros), *lot*—which fall to Mathias.[1299] This is a straightforward example of necromantic sortilege: "Sanctuaries where divination was exercised regularly, as part of the cult of the god, are known as oracles (L. *oracula*, Gk. *manteia* or *chresteria*). But as noted earlier, an oracle is also the response of the god to a question asked by a visitor to the shrine. The method of divination varied from shrine to shrine. Sometimes the will of the god was explored by the casting or drawing of lots (*kleroi*, *sortes*)—for example, dice or sticks or bones. The word *sortilegus* originally designated a soothsayer who practiced this particular method of divination (*sortes legere* 'to pick up lots'); later by extension, it referred to any type of prophecy or sorcery."[1300]

1297 1 Corinthians 4:20.
1298 MacMullen, *Christianizing the Roman Empire*, 62.
1299 Acts 1:23-26.
1300 Luck, *Arcana Mundi*, 244.

The Christian 'busybodies': sorcery in action.

Early Christians were accused of being "evildoers" and "meddlers" and the charge of "meddling" was serious enough to warrant execution:

> Nor may any of you suffer death as a murderer, or an evildoer, or a thief, or as a meddler in others affairs...[1301]

Obviously the "meddling" involved was a charge serious enough to warrant death: *ως φονευς η κακοποιος η κλεπτης η ως αλλοτριεπισκοπος*: "as a murderer, or an evildoer, or a thief or as a meddler in others affairs…"

The Greek term *αλλοτριεπισκοπος* (allotriepiskopos), which I've translated "meddler in others affairs" merits extended comment. The word occurs only in this passage in the New Testament. It is a compound word composed of *αλλοτριος* (allotrios), meaning *foreign*, or *belonging to another*, and *επισκοπος* (episkopos) *inspector, overseer, guardian*. That being said, it should be noted that the etiology of a word is not the definition of a word, so knowing the elements from which the word was formed does not tell us much about how the recipients of the epistle of 1 Peter may have interpreted the term.

Various attempts, all speculative, have been made to discern the meaning of this word both in the context of the letter of 1 Peter —written pseudonymously decades after Peter's death[1302]—and in the context of the society of the day. Whatever the meaning of such "meddling," it was a capital offense, on par with theft and murder. It seems unlikely that such punishment, however well deserved, was meted out to the local neighborhood busybody or even to officious Christians who considered themselves society's moral guardians. It has been claimed that "It is unne-

---

[1301] 1 Peter 4:15.

[1302] Ehrman, *Forged*, 70-77.

cessary…to propose a more serious form of activity than the one suggested by the English translation equivalents 'meddler' or 'busybody'" which, it is said, was "considered by some to be subversive to the fabric of society."[1303] It seems that to substantiate this assertion one would have to produce some evidence that Roman authorities actually executed busybodies with anything approaching the frequency with which murderers and brigands were dispatched.

The term "meddler" is linked in the passage with the term "evildoer," the same charge brought against Jesus at his trial, discussed in Chapter 4, where it was argued that the "evil" Jesus was accused of doing was sorcery. Elsewhere in the epistle, the writer notes of Christians, *καταλαλουσιν υμων ως κακοποιων*, "they slander you as evildoers."[1304] Like murder and theft, the practice of magic was considered an evil punishable by death and the Romans credited both Jews and Christians—who were not clearly distinguished from Jews—with the practice of magic. As noted by Selwyn, Tertullian translated *κακοποιος* in 1 Peter 4:15 with the Latin *maleficus*, meaning *magician.*[1305] "*Maleficium*, literally a 'crime' or 'evil deed,' becomes increasingly associated with magic until it becomes a synonym for it."[1306]

That the Roman government sometimes prosecuted people engaged in magical practice with a ferocity that approached caricature is clear from the report of the historian Ammianus Marcellinus, who records such an episode of violent persecution: "…for if anyone wore on his neck an amulet against the quartan ague, or was accused by the testimony of the evil-disposed of passing by a grave in the evening, on the ground that he was a dealer in poisons, or a gatherer of horrors of tombs and the vain

---

[1303] Brown, *Journal of Biblical Literature* 125: 549.

[1304] 1 Peter 2:12.

[1305] Selwyn, *The First Epistle of St. Peter: The Greek Text with Introduction, Notes and Essays*, 225.

[1306] Stratton, *Naming the Witch: Magic, Ideology and Stereotype in the Ancient World*, 33.

illusions of the ghosts that walk there, he was condemned to capital punishment and so perished."[1307] The dealer in poisons (*ut veneficus*) was a sorcerer who gathered body parts for necromantic rites during which ghosts were summoned and questioned about the future.

When Marcus Aurelius speaks of *τερατευμενοι* (terateumenoi), *miracle-mongers*, and *γοητες* (goētes), *sorcerers*, it is thought likely that he had Christian exorcists in mind.[1308] A number of Christians were executed under his generally benign rule, including the relentless busybody, Justin Martyr. The term *γοης*, meaning *fraud* or *sorcerer*, or both, occurs only once in the New Testament: "Evil men and *frauds* will give ever worse offense, misleading and being misled."[1309] Paul acknowledges that he and his fellow travelers are treated "as deceivers"[1310]—*ως πλανοι* —a word already noted to carry the added weight of *magician*. Although Paul does not elaborate on the meaning of *planos*, the charges brought against him in a Roman colony following an *exorcism* are suggestive: "These men, being Jews, are creating a disturbance in our city and they advocate rites that are not lawful for us, as Romans, either to view with approval or to perform."[1311] The context of the accusation makes clear that rituals peculiar to Jews—including *exorcism*, a form of magical practice —are being distinguished from Roman rites, which are legal to perform. As in Acts 19:1-20, a contrast is being drawn between Christian and pagan wonder-working and the Christian variety is "not lawful."

Lloyd Pietersen makes the case that *γοης* in 2 Timothy 3:13—"*Evil men and frauds* (*πονηροι δε ανθρωποι και γοητες*) will give ever worse offense, *misleading and being misled*" (*πλανωντες και*

[1307] *Ammianus Marcellinus* XIX, 14.

[1308] Marcus Aurelius, *Meditations* I, 6.

[1309] 2 Timothy 3:13.

[1310] 2 Corinthians 6:8.

[1311] Acts 16:20-21.

πλανωμενοι)—could be better translated "evil men and sorcerers,"[1312] although to my knowledge no English translation does so, and points out that the letter compares the writer's opponents to Jannes and Jambres, two legendary Egyptian sorcerers who opposed Moses' magical plagues.[1313] Further evidence favoring this translation is Philo's nearly identical description of those who employ "enchantments and charms" (*τους επαοιδους και φαρμακευτας*) "and transform rods into real serpents" (*τας βακτηριας εις δρακοντων μεταστοχειουσι φυσεις*). Philo's magicians "are ever more deceived while thinking they are deceiving others"—*συναυξοντες απατον δοκουντες απατοναι* —like pseudo-Paul's evil men and sorcerers who are "misleading and being misled."[1314]

Julian, a Christian who converted to a theurgic form of paganism prior to becoming emperor, said, "I will point out that Jesus the Nazarene, and Paul also, outdid in every respect *all the sorcerers and tricksters*," (*τους πωποτε γοητας και απατεωνας*).[1315] Celsus also described Jesus as a sorcerer. In short, Roman officials regarded Christians as more than merely obnoxious; they were widely suspected of performing nocturnal magical rites. Suetonius said that Christianity was "a new and evil superstition"—*superstitio nova et malefica*[1316]—a charge which carried "connotations of magical practices and sorcery."[1317] As noted previously in the discussion of the Beelzeboul controversy, Jesus' wonderworking undermined authority, a charge also leveled against his followers. Early Christianity not only redefined the *faithful*, it radically redefined authority itself.[1318]

[1312] Pietersen, *Magic in the Biblical World: From the Rod of Aaron to the Ring of Solomon*, 166.

[1313] 1 Timothy 3:8. Compare Exodus 7:10-12.

[1314] Philo, *De migratione Abrahami*, 83.

[1315] Julian, *Against the Galileans*, I, 100.

[1316] Suetonius, *Lives of the Caesars* VI, 16.

[1317] Benko, *Pagan Rome and the Early Christians*, 20-21.

[1318] Kee, *Medicine, Miracle and Magic in New Testament Times*, 73.

Paul was known for works of power, "in word and deed, *by the power of signs and wonders, in powerful works of the spirit*" (*εν δυναμει σημειων και τερατων εν δυναμει πνευματος*)[1319] to quote his own boast, so it comes as little surprise that the apocryphal Acts recall accusations of practicing sorcery leveled against Paul. Bremmer notes Paul's influence in *The Acts of Paul and Thecla*: "Thecla, as the mother vividly described her, 'sticks to a window like a spider...bound by a new desire and fearful passion' [2.9]. The term 'bound' [*δεδεμενη*, from *δεω*, *my note*], as used by Theoclia, recurs later when Thamyris finds Thecla 'bound with him [*συνδεδεμενεν*, a compound of *δεω*, *my note*] in affection' [2.19]. These recurring references to 'binding' suggest a case of erotic magic; they prepare the reader for the later accusation of Paul as a performer of erotic magic."[1320] Paul's words weave a spell over the women of the town. Thecla, who is betrothed, renounces marriage, and her fiancé, Thamyris, brings a complaint against the apostle with the following result: "And the whole crowd shouted: 'Away with the sorcerer! For he has corrupted all our wives.'"[1321]

One of the several editions of the *Acts of Paul* contains the freakish story of Paul and the "baptized lion," an elaboration of Paul's claim to have fought with the beasts in Ephesus.[1322] When Paul's encounter with the lion in the arena fails to end in his dismemberment, the crowd screams, "Away with the magician! Away with the sorcerer!"[1323]

There are several Greek synonyms for *αλλοτριεπισκοπος* that refer to prying into what is off limits. A more common synonym is the noun *περιεργος* (periergos) and the related verb *περι-*

[1319] Romans 15:18.

[1320] Bremmer, *The Apocryphal Acts of Paul and Thecla*, 42.

[1321] Schneemelcher, *New Testament Apocrypha*, II, 357.

[1322] 1 Corinthians 15:32.

[1323] *αραι τον μαγον, αραι τον φαρμακον*: "Away with the magician! Away with the sorcerer!"

Wikgren, *Hellenistic Greek Texts*, 129.

εργοζομαι (periergazomai) that occur in three places in the New Testament. In two cases the context links snooping with an excess of leisure: "We hear that some among you are conducting themselves in a disorderly way, not working, but meddling in other's affairs."[1324] The writer does not specify in what the disorderly behavior consisted, nor does he indicate in what exactly the reprimanded subjects were meddling, but there is no suggestion that the meddling was magical in nature. The second case, part of an advisory on enrolling young widows in congregationally sponsored assistance programs, is part of an early Christian version of *kinder, küche, kirche*: "…they learn to gallivant around from house to house, not only lazy, but prattling and meddlesome, talking about what is not proper…"[1325] Although the writer is sure that such young women with too much time on their hands are up to no good, he does not appear to be accusing them of witchcraft.

It is in the next occurrence of *περιεργος* that we find a meaning pertinent to the text of 1 Peter 4:15. In Acts 19:19 we are told of Christian converts, many of whom were "dabbling in the magical arts,"[1326] who brought their books out and burned them. It is worth asking if the burning of a book might not be considered a sort of counter-curse in itself, but the point being made is the use of the fixed expression *τα περιεργα* (ta perierga), *things about which one should not inquire*, that is, *magical arts*. That *periergos* is a synonym for *magos*, *magician*, is clear from the apocryphal *Acts of Andrew*, where the apostle clearly equates the terms *περιεργος*, *μαγος* and *αλλοτριος*: "God, who harkens not to magicians (*μαγοις μη επακουων*), God, who submits not to sorcerers (*περιεργοις μη παρεχων εαυτον*), God, who remains far from those foreign to him (*ο των αλλοτριων αφισταμενος*

1324 *μηδεν εργαζομενους αλλα περιεργαζομενους*…: "not working, but meddling in others affairs…" 2 Thessalonians 3:11.

1325 *φλυαροι και περιεργοι*…: "prattling and meddlesome…" 1 Timothy 5:13.

1326 *ικανοι δε των τα περιεργα πραξαντων*…: "many of those dabbling in the magical arts…"

θεος)..."[1327] The apologist Origen attempts to distance "orthodox" Christians from "heretics"—"if anyone wishes to learn about *the fictions of those sorcerers*" (*τα πλασματα των γοητων εκεινων*)—whose teachings, imbued with magical elements, are "alien and impious" (*ως αλλοτρια και ασεβη*).[1328]

An extended quote from an official circular of the 2nd century, published in Roman Egypt, sheds some light on what was covered by the term *periergos*:

> [Since I have come across many people] who consider themselves to be beguiled by the means of divination [immediately I thought it essential], so that no risk should follow from their foolishness, to state explicitly here to all to abstain from this misleading curiosity.[1329] Therefore neither through oracles, viz., written documents ostensibly emanating in the presence of the divinity, nor by the means of procession of images or similar trickery, let anyone lay claim to have knowledge of the supernatural, or give himself out as an expert about the obscurity of future events...if anyone is discovered sticking to this undertaking, let him be sure that he will be handed over for capital punishment..."[1330]

In short, there is considerable circumstantial evidence to suggest that the "meddling" against which the readers of 1 Peter were being warned were accusations of practicing magic. In Plutarch's essay on being a busybody, he refers to the goals and activities associated with meddling, goals identical in many cases to those achieved through magic: "...but if meddling in degraded things (*το περιεργον εν φαυλοις τισιν*), like a maggot in

---

[1327] Prieur, *Acta Andreae*, 447.

[1328] Origen, *Contra Celsum* VI, 31, 32.

[1329] *της επισφαλους ταυτης περιεργιας*: "this misleading curiosity..." Perhaps better translated, "this dangerous curiosity," since its practice would lead to execution.

[1330] Horsley, *New Documents Illustrating Early Christianity*, I, 47-48.

dead matter, proves altogether necessary...seductions of women ...compounding of potions (*παρασκευναι φαρμακων*)[1331] ...insinuate themselves into forbidden assemblies, behold sacred rites it is not lawful to see, trample holy ground, and pry into the actions and words of rulers."[1332] A magical spell to induce a woman to have sexual relations—known as an *αγωγη* (agōgē), a spell for attraction—was a common enough form of magic, and to foretell the death of a ruler through divination, a capital crime. Charges of malicious sorcery continued to circulate against Christians for centuries and neither the New Testament documents nor the apocryphal Acts indicate that impression was misplaced. "Christian miracle was cruel and destructive: the saints burned a palace with its inhabitants and murdered the magician...the pagan magician was here a provider of food, and the disciples of St. Paul arsonists and killers."[1333]

Faraone has made a convincing case that fear of prosecution caused necromancers to conceal the use of body parts in ritual, skull necromancy in particular, by substituting *σκυφος* (skufos), meaning *cup*, or *pail*, as a code word for *skull*, and *σκηνος* (skēnos), *tent* for *corpse* in necromantic spells. Nevertheless, a close reading of the text reveals "that the author of the recipe... has no scruples about recommending a form of graveside ritual that involves grasping part of the corpse in ones' hands."[1334] It is clear from various sources that Christian devotion to bodily relics of martyrs was seen as just another magical practice, and a necromantic one at that.

It is primarily through the holes in the narrative seams of the gospels that we catch a fleeting glimpse of Jesus the man, the man condemned to stand forever in the shadow of the Christ. To the office of apocalyptic prophet we may now add a second,

---

[1331] The reference would also cover the preparation of poisons.

[1332] Plutarch, *Moralia* VI, 486-514.

[1333] Kazhdan, *Byzantine Magic*, 79.

[1334] Faraone, *Mantikē: Studies in Ancient Divination*, 256-265.

that of ecstatic wonder worker. Jesus would likely have been regarded by the pagan population of his day as a *γοης* (goēs), or "wailer," a sorcerer, a necromancer, or merely as a charlatan, a fraud. The ancient world was a full of wonder-workers—*θαυματουργος* (thaumatourgos), *thaumaturge*, is only one of many terms we moderns have inherited from it—as ours is of faith healers and smarmy televangelists, and like their modern counterparts, the religious actors of Jesus' day were received with responses that spanned the spectrum from bug-eyed credulity to smirking derision.

It is initially surprising how easily exorcism, magic, and apocalyptic speech flow together in the person of Jesus, breaking through the artificially imposed categories laid down by centuries of theology. In point of fact, we see no distinction in our texts between religion and magic, between prayers and spells, or between healing and magic. In both Mark and John, the magical details of Jesus' workings are reported quite ingenuously, with little awareness of a difference between magic and miracle, whereas Matthew and Luke carefully filter the same details out of their accounts, attempting at every turn to distinguish Jesus from other itinerant healers who prophesy and cure blindness with spittle and mud. But as Mark and John reveal, at the level of the earliest, most primitive tradition, it is a distinction without a difference.

Christian necromancy: from Jesus to the martyrs.

The extent to which the worlds of the living and the dead intersected in antiquity can hardly be overestimated. Earthly life as seen through the lens of the magical texts "seems to consist of nothing but negotiations in the antechamber of death and the world of the dead."[1335] Many children died in infancy, many women died in childbirth, during times of peace nearly all

---

[1335] Betz, *The Greek Magical Papyri in Translation*, xlvii.

people died at home and the task of washing, dressing, carrying out, and buring the bodies fell to family members. In times of plague and famine, death was literally in the streets. Against this background of day-to-day mortality were superimposed violent crime, domestic violence, political assassinations, wars that swept up civilian populations, infanticide, public executions, brawling, and fighting to the death as entertainment. Yet despite the ever-present proximity of the living and the dead, religious practice enforced certain boundaries between their worlds, and transgression of those limits was the very mark of black magic. With the advent of Christianity, however, pagan religious practice was overturned and the boundary between the living and the dead utterly breached.

The case has been made elsewhere[1336] that some within early Christian communities that used the source material of the gospels of Mark and John saw the raising of Lazarus, the "beloved disciple,[1337] as an enacted parable of Jesus' own rising from the dead, an identification that may go back to the generation of the crucifixion. That identity, reinforced by the use of various markers, included particularly linen grave clothes—Jesus is wrapped in linen prior to burial in a garden tomb,[1338] sealed with a stone,[1339] and Lazarus, raised from a tomb sealed with a stone,[1340] appears in Jerusalem during Passover,[1341] and in Gethsemane where Jesus is arrested, Lazarus eludes his captors,[1342] still wearing the sign of his resurrection, his linen shroud.[1343] Morton Smith may have come close to this reconstruction of

---

[1336] Conner, *Jesus the Sorcerer*, 231-256.

[1337] There are six references to the beloved disciple, all occurring late in the gospel of John (13:23; 19:26; 21:7, 20) in which he is *ον ηγαπα* , "the one he loved," or (20:2) *ον εφιλει* "the one he loved."

[1338] John 20:15.

[1339] Mark 15:46.

[1340] John 11:38-39.

[1341] John 12:9.

[1342] John 12:9-11.

[1343] Mark 14:51-52.

events, noting the several parallels between the raising of Jesus and the raising of Lazarus, and in his comments on *περιβεβλημενος σινδονα επι γυμνου*, "wearing a linen cloth over his naked body," he said, "Verbatim in Mk. 14.51...the subject is *νεανισκος τις* ["a certain young man," *my note*]—the young man in a sheet who was with Jesus at the time of his arrest and who, on being seized, fled naked (an episode both Mt. and Lk. chose to omit)...the occurance of the phrase both in the longer ["Secret" Mark, *my note*] and canonical texts of Mark can hardly be explained as an accident of free composition. Either the phrase was a fixed formula in the life of some early church (a baptismal rubric?) or its presence in both texts is evidence of some historical connection."[1344]

The resurrection of Lazarus is presented in John as proof of Jesus' divine calling. Like the figure of Lazarus, who appears late in John's gospel, "a certain young man" appears late in the gospel of Mark—*και νεανισκος τις συνηκολουθει αυτω*, "and a certain young man went along with him."[1345] The verb *συνακολουθεω*, *to accompany*, is used also in Mark 5:37 in the following passage: *ουκ αφηκεν ουδενα μετ αυτον συνακολουθησαι ει μη τον Πετρον*, "he allowed no one but Peter to go along with him." That Mark is using the verb to signal an inner circle of disciples is shown by the fact that it is again Peter, James and John who accompany Jesus to Gethsemane.[1346] Lazarus has joined this inner circle; he is the beloved who at Peter's behest asks who will betray Jesus,[1347] the one to whom Jesus entrusts his mother,[1348] the first male witness to the resurrection,[1349] and the first to identify the risen Jesus in Galilee.[1350] Based on his analysis of the foot washing ceremony in the gospel of John, Neyrey notes that

---

[1344] Smith, *Clement of Alexandria and a Secret Gospel of Mark*, 116.
[1345] Mark 14:51.
[1346] Mark 14:32.
[1347] John 13:23-25.
[1348] John 19:26-27.
[1349] John 20:4.
[1350] John 21:17.

the beloved disciple is "the consummate insider, a true elite," who "acts as Peter's broker and mediator."[1351] Neyrey does not, however, identify the beloved disciple as Lazarus. That his sisters—not his wife and children—send for Jesus when Lazarus falls sick and are his chief mourners when he dies suggest that Lazarus, like Jesus, is unmarried.

Van Hoye also noted the similarity between the young man (νεανισκος) in the garden of Gethsemane and the young man who appears in the empty tomb. The same verb, περιβαλλω, *wrap up in*, is used to describe the linen garment worn by the youth in Gethsemane and the white robe worn by the youth in the empty tomb.[1352] Van Hoye concludes, "There is therefore reason to think that the numerous verbal correspondences which we have noted are not the result of pure chance, but manifest an intention."[1353] The various parallels point to a specific individual known to the primitive community, but unnamed in Mark, but identified by name in John: Lazarus. The enigmatic young man in the garden who ecapes arrest still dressed in his linen shroud. Miles Fowler and Michael Haren have both suggested this identification. Fowler asks, "How would a crowd recognize which person standing among the numerous followers of Jesus is Lazarus? Mark 14:51 provides the answer that there could be no more impressive identification of Lazarus, nor any more vivid symbol of his resurrection, than his wearing a burial shroud."[1354] Haren adds, "The question must arise whether the manifestation of the glory was to be confined to Bethany or whether it was contemplated presenting Lazarus, dramatically and dressed so that he would instantly proclaim the miracle, in Jerusalem itself," and concludes that the appearance of Lazarus

---

[1351] Neyrey, *The Social World of the First Christians*, 208.
[1352] Mark 14:51; 16:5.
[1353] Van Hoye, *Biblica* 52: 406.
My translation of, "Il y a donc lieu de penser que les nombreaux contacts verbaux que nous avons relevés ne sont pas un pur effet du hazard, mais manifestent une intention."
[1354] Fowler, *Journal of Higher Criticism* 5/1: 3-22.

"as a sign of God's power" may have been the factor that caused the Jewish authorites to arrest Jesus.[1355] Some part of the early community clearly understood the raising of Lazarus to be a true example of resurrection:

> Jesus said to her, "Your brother will be raised."
> Martha said to him, "I know he will be raised in the resurrection on the last day."
> Jesus said to her, "I am the resurrection and the life. Those who believe in me will live even if they die."[1356]

The point of the dialog is to establish that Jesus is more than 'the resuscitation and the life' and to prove it, Lazarus is resurrected. In that case, one might suppose the conditions of those raised "on the last day" would apply to Lazarus: "For in the resurrection neither do they marry nor are they given in marriage, but they are like angels in heaven."[1357] "Nor can they still die, for they are like angels and are sons of God, being sons of the resurrection."[1358] A case has been made (Chapter 5) that Jesus' post mortem appearances are apparitions consistent with a "revenant" that retains marks of wounds inflicted in life, polymorphic, and able to appear and disappear at will. The text of John may preserve a trace of a similar tradition in regard to Lazarus:

> And saying these things, *he shouted out with a loud voice* (φωνη μεγαλη εκραυγασεν), "Lazarus, come out here!"[1359]

Jesus is not the only magician on record who shouted loudly enough to wake the dead. Lucian's magus "shrieks" (επεβοατο),

---

[1355] Haren, *Biblica* 79:525-531.
[1356] John 11: 23-25.
[1357] Matthew 22:30.
[1358] Luke 20:36.
[1359] John 11:43.

"bellowing at the spirits" (*παμμεγεθες...ανακραγων δαιμονας*).[1360]

In calling up Lazarus—*Λαζαρε δευρο εξω*, "Lazarus, come out here!"—the text of the gospel uses language remarkably similar to that used in magical spells to summon spirits: "come to me, Kupris"—*δευρο μοι* Κυπρις[1361] or, "I call you, Fawn Slayer, Trickstress, Infernal One, Many-formed, come, Hekate of the three ways—*δευρ'* Εκατη *τριοδιτι*—who has fire-breathing ghosts...[1362] or "Come hither to me—*δευρο μοι*—He of the four winds, almighty god, who blows the spirits of life into men ...[1363] or the invocation of a spirit that is to possess a boy medium: "Come to me, O Lord, borne upon the pure light—*δευρο μοι κυριε επι τω αχραντων φωτι οχουμενος*. Citing another example of the formula found on a divination bowl—*δευρο μοι ο αυτογεννητωρ θεε*, "Come to me, O Self-begotten god"—Daniel and Maltomini note "the phrase *δευρο μοι* is very common in prayers in the magical papyri."[1364] The phraseology of John 11:43 implies Lazarus' spirit is being summoned and if that was the case, was the resurrected Lazarus a revenant, a corporeal ghost? There was speculation about the mortality of the beloved disciple: "So word spread among the brothers that that disciple would not die."[1365]

The dead could be raised by magic: "Raising of a dead body: I command you, spirit winging in air, come in, instill spirit, be empowered, raise up this body by the power of the eternal god and let it walk around this place because I am the one who acts

---

1360 Lucian, *Menippus*, 9.

1361 Daniel & Maltomini, *Supplementum Magicum* 63.

Cyprus (*Κυθηρα*), the legendary site of the birth of Aphrodite from the *sea foam* (*αφρος*), is frequently used as one of her titles.

1362 Preisendanz, *Papyri Graecae Magicae* IV, 2726-2728.

1363 Ibid, XII, 237.

1364 Daniel & Maltomini, *Supplementum Magicum* II, 74.

1365 John 21:23.

with the power of Thauth, the holy god. Say the name!"[1366] Among the many works of sorcerers Lucian mentions "leading up ghosts and calling up the putrid dead"—*δαιμονες αναγων και νεκρους εωλους ανακαλων*.[1367] It is not impossible that Lucian had the Lazarus story in mind; after four days in the tomb, Lazarus had begun to stink.[1368] Jesus, who has the keys of death and the grave, has released Lazarus—*λυσατε αυτον*, "unbind him"—and if the raising of Lazarus was thought to presage the (self) resurrection of Jesus, and the youth in the tomb was Lazarus, an interesting circularity appears: the reality of Jesus' resurrection is proclaimed by the disciple Jesus has raised from the dead: "You are seeking Jesus of Nazareth who was crucified. He was raised. He is not here. Look at the place where they laid him."[1369]

A culture of relics.

Borrowing a term from theology, various commentators have remarked that the miracles of Jesus and other exorcist/healers work *ex opere operato*, i.e., by the mere action of performance, and not due to the merits of the performer. It is this feature of Jesus' miracles that permits strangers to use his name effectively.[1370] Because of the impersonal nature of magic, objects and places once in contact with a person—including the body, its parts, and its blood—could continue to transmit their magical power. As the hymn proclaims, "There is pow'r, pow'r, wonder-working pow'r in the precious blood of the Lamb."[1371] "…the body parts…along with such things as crucifixion nails, were valuable for necromancy…people of the time believed corpses had to be guarded to prevent theft by witches, who used

[1366] Preisendanz, *Papyri Graecae Magicae* XIII, 278-282.
[1367] Lucian, *Lover of Lies*, 14.
[1368] John 11:39.
[1369] Mark 16:6.
[1370] Mark 9:38; Matthew 7:22.
[1371] "Power in the Blood," written around 1899.

body parts in their magic..."[1372] "...the efficacy of the metal could be enhanced by taking the metal's provenance into account: iron linked with the dead, especially the blood of the criminal dead, was believed to possess special potency."[1373]

As one of the untimely dead, Jesus became a source of power. A curse from the papyri says of a ghost, "Osiris will grant your request because you are *untimely dead and childless and wifeless—αωρος και ατεκνος και αγυναις*."[1374] The best evidence is that Jesus was unmarried, childless, dead before his time and dead by violence, and may have been unburied as well if left hanging on the cross or tossed into a lime pit, hence a restless and powerful ghost. The ancient traditions of ascent from the cross and the empty tomb imply a missing body. Shantz observed the connection between texts "colored by and filled with the phenomena of religious ecstacy...identified as signs of possession" and "the arresting image of carrying the death of Jesus in the body" of the believer.[1375]

That miracle-working power adheres to things associated with the miracle worker provides an obvious motive for the preservation of relics associated with saints, particularly body parts —"keeping them safely under the control of the church."[1376] Regarding the habit of collecting such relics, Lane Fox says: "The new Christian attitude to the dead and their relics marked a break in previous religious life. Before long, church leaders were digging up corpses and breaking them into fragments, a type of grave robbery which pagans had never countenanc-

---

1372 Carrier, "The Plausibility of Theft," *The Empty Tomb*, 350-351.
1373 Alfayé Villa, *Magical Practice in the Latin West*, 441.
1374 Daniel & Maltomini, *Supplementum Magicum*, 52.
1375 Shantz, "The Confluence of Trauma and Transcendence," *Experientia*, I, 195, 197.
The reference is to 2 Corinthians 4:10.
1376 Kolenkow, *Aufstieg und Niedergang der Römischen Welt*, II.23.2, 1497.

ed."[1377] This observation, while true of *official* pagan religions, does not hold for necromantic sorcerers or specialists in love spells who, like early Christians, "naturally focused their attention on those objects which afforded immediate contact with the source of powers; the most convenient objects were relics."[1378] Ancient literature is replete with references to the theft of bodies and body parts for magical working.[1379] It has been observed of the early Christian saints that people came seeking "a transfer of supernatural power…as if [the saint] were a talisman…the only thing believed in was some supernatural power to bestow benefits."[1380] The use of personal possessions was basic to spellcasting. Speaking of the items required by "an effective witch, a Syrian by race," the courtesan Bakchis tells her girlfriend Melitta,

> "You'll also need something belonging to the man himself, like clothes or boots or a few hairs, or something of that sort."
>
> "I have his boots."[1381]

Ancient literature references the theft of body parts for magical working. The newly dead have to be guarded from witches in search of ears and noses and they are described grubbing around graveyards and scouring battlefields in search of gruesome trophies.[1382] The *Leyden Papyrus* describes the ingredients of a potion: "You take a little shaving of the head of a man who has died a violent death, together with seven grains of barley that has been buried in a grave of a dead man…"[1383] The magical

---

[1377] Lane Fox, *Pagans and Christians*, 448.

[1378] Geary, *Furta sacra: Thefts of Relics in the Central Middle Ages*, 35.

[1379] Ogden, *Magic, Witchcraft, and Ghosts in the Greek and Roman Worlds*, 140ff.

[1380] MacMullen, *Christianizing the Roman Empire*, 3-4.

[1381] Lucian, *Dialogues of the Courtesans*, 4.

[1382] Ogden, *Magic, Witchcraft and Ghosts in the Greek and Roman Worlds*, 140, ff.

[1383] Griffith & Thompson, *The Leyden Papyrus* XV, 1-2.

value of a piece of "the true cross" would have been instantly appreciated by any necromancer of antiquity who read a spell that advised,

> ...and take wood from a gallows and carve a hammer and strike the eye while saying the spell, "I command you by the holy names..."[1384]

Lucian's Eucrates says, "The Arab gave me the ring made from the iron [nails] of crosses and taught me the spell of many names."[1385] Coptic magical spells used by later Christians invoke "the sufferings...upon the cross," and "the wood of the cross."[1386] Bailliot has published images of nails used in magical ritual that have been recovered by archaeologists, [1387] and Thompson documented instances of the magical use of nails: "The *shêkh* comes and lays his hands on the patient's head and then drives a nail into the wall, thus obviously transfixing the devil therewith" and describes "a house...haunted by spirits and devils who threw stones about, but were finally laid by a holy man pronouncing an incantation and driving a nail into the wall."[1388] The mere sign of the cross assumes magical powers as well: "At every forward step and movement, at every going in and out, when we put on our clothes and shoes, when we bathe, when we sit at table, when we light the lamps, on couch, on seat, in all the ordinary actions of daily life, we trace upon the forehead the sign."[1389]

[1384] Preisendanz, *Papyri Graecae Magicae* V, 75-76.

[1385] Lucian, *Lover of Lies*, 17.

[1386] Meyer & Smith, *Ancient Christian Magic: Coptic Texts of Ritual Power*, 176, 178, 180.

[1387] Bailliot, *Magie et sortileges dan l'Antiquité romaine*, XVII, Figure 35.a.

[1388] Thompson, *Semitic Magic: Its Origins and Development*, 18.

[1389] Benko, *Pagan Rome and the Early Christians*, 118, quoting Tertullian.

The relationship between miracles and martyrs brought Christianity much closer to the attitude of necromantic sorcery than to anything in normative pagan religious belief. "Not only did former cemeteries become centres of population and worship, but a degree of intimacy was sought with the relics of saints that was horrifying to a Roman pagan with traditional ideas about the pollution of death...It is clear that in establishing this new intimacy with the dead, and in fact using it as a basis for public worship, the Christian Church had overthrown a great tabu, and its subsequent success shows that it had gained strength from doing so. A deep well of psychological power may have been tapped..."[1390]

The deep well of power that had been tapped through evocation of the dead would have been instantly recognizable to any pagan sorcerer, and likely accounted for the suspicion with which pagans regarded Christians in their midst, a suspicion, it appears, that was founded on a strong element of fact. Smith noted this similarity: "Christianity was allied with another type of magic, that by which the recalled spirits (*not* resurrected bodies) of executed criminals and of persons who had died unmarried or childless were invoked by the magician. Jesus belonged to all three of these categories."[1391]

"...devotion to the remains of saints can be traced to two fundamental antecedants: the pagan cult of heroes, and the Christian belief in the resurrection of the body."[1392] The Greek ηρως (hērōs), *hero,* is the ghost of a powerful figure, such as a gifted athlete or warrior, or the founder of a city, that has achieved the rank of a minor deity. The cult of the martyrs, like the hero cults prevalent in Greece, quickly became an organizing principle in the early church. The gifting of body parts established chains of patronage that united Christian communi-

---

1390 Merrifield, *The Archaeology of Ritual and Magic*, 81-82.

1391 Smith, *Harvard Theological Review* 73: 243.

1392 Geary, *Furta sacra*, 33.

ties. The Holy Innocents, as Herod's legendary victims came to be known[1393] were an endless source of material for relics "since the number of children was unkown, a limitless supply of relics was thereby made available." Relics "found many commercial applications beyond the initial gift or sale"[1394] within medieval Christianity since they attracted pilgrims with money to sites where bone, blood, and various items of saintly bric-a-brac were venerated. By the time the Coptic magical spells are composed, Herod's victims have undergone a veritable population explosion—"You must send me today your 144,000 whom Herod killed, each of them by name…"[1395]—through conflation of the number of children murdered by Herod with the number of the "bride of the Lamb."[1396] Lest anyone think that being spellbound by the power of relics is merely an ancient superstition that has long since faded into obscurity, it should be noted that as recently as 1968 a relic of "Saint Mark" was "translated" by Pope Paul VI to the custody of Pope Kyrolos and enshrined in Saint Mark Coptic Orthodox cathedral in Cairo.

Ever alert to any possibility of locating relics, the faithful eventually realized that the shorn prepuce of Jesus must not have ascended to heaven with its former owner, set about finding it, and apparently succeeded in doing so more than a few times. "The foreskin of Christ was one of those cash-cow curios that packed in the pilgrims. So much so that it was eventually copied and forged all over Europe. Depending on what you read, there were eight, twelve, fourteen, or eighteen different Holy Foreskins in various European towns during the Middle Ages."[1397]

[1393] Matthew 2:16.

[1394] Wasyliw, *Martyrdom, Murder, and Magic*, 30-31, 39.

[1395] Meyer & Smith, *Ancient Christian Magic*, 118.

[1396] Revelation 14:1.

[1397] Farley, *An Irreverent Curiosity: In Search of the Church's Strangest Relic in Italy's Oddest Town*, 4.

"Jesus Christ, crucified"—raising the spirit of Jesus.

As previously noted, the ghost of a person who had suffered a violent or untimely death, particularly execution, was considered to be a source of tremendous power, an assumption basic to the performance of both necromantic sorcery and primitive Christian miracle. "For Paul, to know Jesus Christ is to manifest the power of Jesus' crucifixion in one's body through spirit possession and performance characterized by possession phenomena."[1398] It was common knowledge that "the souls of those dead by violence" could be raised by sorcerers—"one beheaded or one who has been crucified"[1399] serving as paradigmatic examples. One could make the case that the fact that John the Baptist and Jesus both conspicuously fit this description is anything but coincidental.

Pagan magical praxis included calling upon both *gods* and *ghosts* of the dead to achieve a goal:

> I deposit this binding spell with you, underworld gods, Pluto and Korē and Persephonē and underworld ghosts, men and women dead before their time, virgins and youths, help this demon, whoever he may be. Kamēs, ghost of the dead, raise yourself for me, from the repose that holds you fast. For I command you by the holy name...[1400]

The spell calls up the *δεμονες καταχθονιοις*: literally, "underworld demons," understood to mean "ghosts," as stipulated by the next words. Kamēs, the name of the deceased, should appear where the placeholder "whoever he may be," occurs, but the careless scribe copied it in addition to the dead man's name. The *νεκυδαιμων*, *nekudaimōn*, is a term compounded from *νεκυ*,

[1398] Mount, *Journal of Biblical Literature* 124: 319-320.
[1399] Lucian, *The Lover of Lies*, III, 29.
[1400] Kotansky, *Greek Magical Amulets*, 50.

dead, and δαιμων, *demon* or *ghost*. It is sometimes translated "corpse demon." The *νεκυια* (nekuia) is the rite by which ghosts are raised.

Christian apotropaic spells combine *angels*, *god*, and *the dead*:

> I command you, Michael, archangel of the earth...the Almightly Sabaōth[1401]...I command you and the dead, release Taiollēs...[1402]

"...the invocation of the dead on the part of a Christian is noteworthy, especially in the light of the often-discussed relationship between pagan and Christian cults of the dead..."[1403] It is clear that early Christians, like their pagan contemporaries, credited the dead with magical power—*ορκιζω σε και νεκρους απαλλαξατε* Ταιολλης: "I command you and the dead (*νεκρους*), release Taiollēs"—but Christianity rapidly made public what until that time had been most secret, the use of the dead as conduits of supernatural power. Pagan, Jewish, and Christian spells invoke an army of angels, preeminently Michael—*ορκιζω σε* Μιχαηλ *αρχαγγελε γης*: "I command you, Michael, archangel of the earth"—and Yahweh under his title **צבאות**, *Tsabaōt*, (Lord) "of hosts," or (God) "of the battle array"[1404]—*τον παντοκρατορα* Σαβαωθ: "the Almighty Sabaōth." *Sabaōth* becomes one of the most common powerful names invoked in the magical texts, appearing frequently not only in its Greek transliteration, but in Coptic as well (**ⲥⲁⲃⲁⲱⲑ**).

Another spell against fever—that begins IXς *νικα*, "J[esu]s conquers" and ends *αγιος αγιος αγιος κς* Σαβαοτ, "holy, holy, holy, L[or]d Sabaot"—invokes Michael the archangel, Yahweh

---

[1401] *τον παντοκρατορα* Σαβαωθ: "the Almighty Sabaōth..." Daniel & Maltomini, *Supplementum Magicum*, 25.

[1402] Ibid, 29.

[1403] Ibid, I, 80.

[1404] Brown, Driver & Briggs, *Hebrew and English Lexicon*, 839.

under the title Sabaōth, *the dead*, Abraham, Isaac and Jacob as well as Solomon, and tosses in a few biblical quotations, including a garbled version of the Lord's Prayer, just in case.[1405] The translator, apparently laboring under the impression that Christians then or now know their own scriptures, regards the spell as "syncretistic rather than distinctively Christian," due to the "incoherent manner in which the verses are quoted."[1406] Be that as it may, the spell is as perfect an example as could be hoped for of the notion that *magical power resides in the names of the famous dead.* But we need not venture outside the New Testament for confirmation of this linkage; when Peter and John are arrested, their inquisitors ask, "By what power *or what name* did you do this?"[1407] The answer has already been given: "God raised his servant, Jesus…"[1408] Christians, like their pagan contemporaries, credited the dead with *power*, *δυναμις*, power accessed through the name. Crum cites an amulet, transcribed into Coptic letters from Greek, ⲡⲣⲁⲕⲝⲓⲥ: ⲭⲁⲣⲓⲥ: ⲓ̅ⲏ̅ⲥ̅ ⲭ̅ⲣ̅ⲥ̅ ⲛⲓⲕⲁ ⲥⲧⲁⲩⲣⲟⲩ ⲛⲓⲕⲁ,[1409] "Rite: spell: Jesus Christ, conquer by the cross,[1410] conquer!"

> To gain this advantage, further ancient barriers had to be broken. Tomb and altar were joined. The bishop and his clergy performed public worship in a proximity to the human dead that would have been profoundly disturbing to pagan and Jewish feeling.[1411]

1405 Daniel & Maltomini, *Supplementum Magicum*, 25.

1406 Ibid, I, 80.

1407 Acts 4:7.

1408 Acts 3:26.

1409 Crum, *Catalogue of the Coptic Manuscripts in the British Museum*, 175.

1410 A genitive of instrumentality, "by the cross" (*σταυρου*) as at Philipians 2:8, *θανατου δε σταυρου*, "death [by mean of] a cross."

1411 Brown, *The Cult of the Saints*, 9.

To illustrate of how thin this barrier soon became, note how the suffering, death, and resurrection of Jesus figure in this healing spell, likely derived from primitive liturgy:

> Christ foretold,
> Christ appeared,
> Christ suffered,
> Christ died,
> Christ rose,
> Christ ascended,
> Christ reigns,
> Christ saves Ouibius, who Gennaia bore, from all fever, from all shivering, daily, quotidian, now, now, quickly, quickly![1412]

The connection between Jesus' *violent death by crucifixion* and the *derived power* is everywhere presupposed in the authentic writings of Paul and Luke. The apostles testify to Jesus' resurrection "with great power (δυναμει μεγαλη)": "If δυναμις is understood here as 'miracle working power,' that is, the sort of power that works δυναμεις ('miracles'), then the apostles' role in testifying to the resurrection is not just oral, but linked directly to their miracle working."[1413] As Myllykoski notes, the raising of Jesus "is the foundation miracle for the whole narrative of Acts"[1414]—as is also the case in the gospel of John, which specifies that the spirit will not be given until Jesus is "glorified."[1415] The book of Acts consistently connects the performance of signs and wonders with the risen Jesus, "nailed up and killed by the hands of lawless men."[1416] God raised Jesus "by releasing him from the bonds of death" (ον θεος ανεστησεν λυσας τας ωδινας

[1412] Daniel & Maltomini, *Supplementum Magicum*, 35.
[1413] Reimer, *Miracle and Magic: A Study in the Acts of the Apostles and the Life of Apollonius of Tyana*, 91.
[1414] Myllykoski, *Wonders Never Cease*, 162.
[1415] John 7:39.
[1416] Acts 2:22-23, 43.

του θανατου)[1417] a passage is often mistranslated "pangs of death" (*τας ωδινας του θανατου*). The Hebrew stem חבל (kh-b-l), mistranslated *ωδις* (ōdis), *pangs*, *throes*, in the Greek *Septuagint* can mean *rope*, *noose*, or *bind*, *writhe in pain*, depending on which vowels are supplied. The *cords of death* (מות חבלי) and the *snares of the grave* (שאול חבלי) in the Hebrew text become the "throes of death" (*ωδινες θανατου*) and "pains of the grave" (*ωδινες αδου*) in the *Septuagint* and, since the gospel writers read Greek, not Hebrew, the erroroneous translation "pangs of death" was carried over into the New Testament.[1418] Due to this sequence of faulty translations, the metaphor of *death as a form of binding* is lost to the Christian reader.

Having come proclaiming "the mystery of God," Paul is determined to know nothing "except Jesus Christ and him crucified" and backs up his preaching "*by demonstrations of spirit and power* (*εν αποδειξει πνευματος και δυναμεως*) so that your faith might not be in the wisdom of men, but in the power of God."[1419] In the letter to the "bewitched" Galatians, "Jesus Christ crucified" supplies both "the spirit" and the resulting "performance of powerful works."[1420] The Ephesian Christians will know "the surpassing greatness of his power among us who believe, *according to the working* (*κατα την ενηεργειαν*) of the power of his might, *which he put into operation by raising Christ from the dead*" (*ενεργησεν εν Χριστω εγειρας αυτον εκ νεκρων*).[1421] Of the use of *ενεργεια* ["working," *my note*] in the magical papyri, Kotansky observes that it "generally refers to the (activated) power of magic…the actual 'activating' of a magic spell."[1422] The same pattern of evocation is carried over into the apocryphal Acts: *εγω Ιωαννης εν ονοματι Ιησου Χριστου του σταυ-*

[1417] Acts 2:24.

[1418] A point easily confirmed by consulting any English version of the Tanakh translated from Hebrew.

[1419] 1 Corinthians 2:1-5.

[1420] Galatians 3:1, 5.

[1421] Ephesians 1:19-20.

[1422] Kotansky, *Greek Magical Amulets*, 241.

ρωθεντος επιτασσω σοι, "I, John, command you in the name of Jesus Christ the crucified..."[1423]

In Romans 8:9-10, Paul's language is the terminology of spirit possession: "If anyone does not have the spirit of Christ,[1424] he does not belong to him"—*ει δε τις πνευμα Χιστου ουκ εχει ουτος ουκ εστιν αυτου*—and "if Christ is in you"—*ει δε Χριστος εν υμιν*— duplicates the language of Mark 1:23, "a man in [the power of] an unclean spirit"—*ανθρωπος εν πνευματι ακαθαρτω*. Just as Jesus "raised" John the Baptist from the dead and "because of this the powers are working in him,"[1425] so has the spirit promised by the risen Jesus[1426] come to empower his followers. The *παρακλητος* (paraklētos), the Christian "Paraclete," the one summoned to assist, becomes the Christian version of the *παρεδρος*, the assistant of the magical papyri.[1427] The *παρακλητος*, or *helper*—which is a spirit[1428]—functions in much the same way as the *παρεδρος*, the magical helper, which is a spirit. Significantly, the spirit cannot arrive until after Jesus leaves.[1429] "The death of Christ set the Pneuma free..."[1430]

It is commonly claimed that *παρακλητος*—the Paraclete—means *advocate* in a legal sense, but in a survey of the occurrences of this fairly uncommon word, Grayston found scant evidence for such a meaning. "...the universal conviction in antiquity...that in approaching an important person, for whatever

---

[1423] Daniel & Maltomini, *Supplementum Magicum*, I, 95, quoting the *Acts of John*.

[1424] Like Jesus "has" Beelzeboul (Mark 3:20-30).

[1425] Mark 6:14.

[1426] John 14:16-17.

[1427] *παρακλησις*, a *calling upon*, or *summoning*, is linked in several places to the gift of prophecy (1 Corinthians 14:3, 1 Timothy 4:13-14), a possession phenomenon.

[1428] The *παρακλητος* is *το πνευμα της αληθειας*—"the spirit of truth" (John 16:13).

[1429] John 16:7.

[1430] Eitrem, *Some Notes on the Demonology in the New Testament*, 69.

reason, you need an influential person or group of supporters... the Paraclete is, as it were, an eminent person through whom the petitioner gains favorable access to the Father."[1431] In a later century the Christian martyrs would become "invisible friends" —*αορατος φιλος*—and "intimate companions"—*γνησιος φιλος* —of the faithful not unlike the personal *δαιμων* or *numen* ('guardian angel') of paganism,[1432] and with the passage of time functioned "as advocates pleading causes...as mediators, as go-betweens, as intriguers or wire-pullers at the court of Heaven,"[1433]

Most of the sprits called upon by pagan magicians "are the disembodied former inhabitants of [people]...the *δαιμονες* [*ghosts*, my note] of the deceased," which are also called "an *αεριον πνευμα*, an "aerial spirit"" in the magical papyri.[1434] In Acts, the "holy spirit" is used synonymously with "the spirit of Jesus."[1435] Pagan sorcerers raised ghosts by incantations. How did early Christians raise the spirit of Jesus in order to perform powerful works? Justin Martyr, describing the expulsion of demons in his day, says, "they are exorcized *in the name of Jesus Christ, crucified* under Pontius Pilate"—*εξορκιζομενα κατα του ονοματος Ιησου Χριστου του σταυρωθεντος επι Ποντιου Πιλατου.*[1436] As pointed out by Lietaert Peerbolte, Justin often links the *power* of the name of Jesus with his *crucifixion.*[1437] For the purposes of Christian magic, Jesus' "name" is *Jesus-Christ-crucified.* In fact, there existed such a strong relationship between ghosts and magic that the connection was alleged to have led to ritual murder to create ghosts for necromantic use. Pagans likely saw something that to them seemed very similar to necromancy in Christian rituals such as the eucharist, the talismanic

---

[1431] Grayston, *Journal for the Study of the New Testament* 13: 72, 80.

[1432] Brown, *The Cult of the Saints*, 50-68.

[1433] Wilson, *Saints and Their Cults*, 23.

[1434] Ciraolo, *Ancient Magic and Ritual Power*, 286.

[1435] Acts 16: 6,7.

[1436] *Iustini Martyris Dialogus cum Tryphone*, 118.

[1437] Lietaert Peerbolte, *Wonders Never Cease*, 190-192.

use of relics, and the symbol of the cross, an instrument of execution.[1438]

Relics as "ousia."

Whether a piece of the 'true cross,' the Shroud of Turin, the Church of the Nativity in Bethlehem, the purported place of Jesus' birth, or the Holy Sepulcher, the supposed site of his burial, Christian fascination with objects and places once in contact with Jesus is of ancient vintage.[1439] The merest association with Jesus could render a site magical; a fountain where Jesus washed his feet "consequently possessed the ability to remove all forms of disease from both people and animals."[1440] Jesus' disciples possess such power that not only can contact with articles of their clothing heal, but *even their shadow falling across the sick effects a cure.*[1441]

> The rise of the Christian cult of saints took place in the great cemeteries that lay outside the cities of the Roman world: and, as for the handling of dead bodies, the Christian cult of saints rapidly came to involve the digging up, the moving, the dismemberment—quite apart from much avid touching and kissing—of the bones of the dead, and, frequently, the placing of these in areas from which the dead had once been excluded.[1442]

[1438] Benko, *Pagan Rome and the Early Christians*, 60-63, 118-124.

[1439] See particularly Bentley, *Restless Bones: The Story of Relics.*

[1440] Trzcionka, *Magic and the Supernatural in Fourth-Century Syria*, 131.

[1441] Acts 5:12-16, 19:11-12.

[1442] Brown, *The Cult of the Saints*, 4.

"[Lucilla] had owned a bone of a martyr, and had been in the habit of kissing it before she took the Eucharist...". Ibid, 34.

Only one other group in antiquity besides the Christians was strongly identified with the practice of digging up and dismembering corpses: *witches.*

> But along with these pieces of corpses, certain objects which had been in contact with the body at the moment of death are also in high demand among the sorcerers ...[Apuleius] provides us with specific information regarding their origin: these nails come from gallows, so they have been in contact with a particular category of the dead, those condemned and tortured. That is not without importance; these can form a part of those *biaithanatoi*, the dead who have perished from a violent death...Everything that has been in contact with death and its realm, be it part of a corpse or an object, has, in the final analysis, a special interest for the sorcerer. These materials really represent the *ousia*, magical materials that still have a link with the soul of the deceased from which they come.[1443]

The importance of *ousia*—from *ουσια* (ousia), *substance*, *essence*, or merely *stuff*—for working sorcery is everywhere attested in the magical papyri. Of a spell recorded on papyrus fragment from the 3rd century, Daniel notes, "A lock of hair (the *ousia* of the beloved) was originally attached to the papyrus, and some of

[1443] My translation of: "Mais à coté de ces morceaux de cadavres, certains objets ayant été en contact avec le corps au moment du trépas se trouvent tout aussi recherchés par les sorcières...Une precision quant à leur origine nous est fournie par [Apulée]: ces clous proviennent de gibets, donc ont été au contact d'une catégorie particulière de morts, les condamnés et les suppliciés. Cela n'est pas sans importance; ceux-ci peuvent faire partie de ces biaithanatoi, ces morts qui ont perí de mort violent...Tout ce qui a été en contact avec la mort et son royaume, que ce soit une partie du cadavre ou un objet, a, en fin de compte, un intérêt particulier pour le sorcière." Michaël Martin, *Magic et magicians dans le monde gréco-romain*, 223.

it still remains on the verso."[1444] An *αγωγη*, or *attraction spell*, summons the "underworld gods, Pluto and Kore and Persephone, and ghosts of the underworld, the dead, maidens and youths dead before their time" to assist the magician's spirit helper. The spell must work because "you have the hairs of her head…you have the material"—*εχις* (sic) *τας τριχες της κεφαλης αυτης…εχις την ουσιαν*.[1445]

> *Ουσια μαγικη*, 'magical material', are things taken from the body or clothing of the victim, hair, nail clippings, bits of cloth; some of the actualizations of the recipe show that it was a lock of hair which was used in its application. In the same sense, the sorcerer later has to take ousia of the dead in his hand in order to direct the attention of Helius to this specific nekydaimon; ousia, 'being, essence' thus is a sort of pointer which points to its owner.[1446]

It is clear that body parts were handled during necromantic rituals, a practice much like the intimate contact believers had with Christian relics of the dead:

> Facing the setting sun *while holding material from the tomb* (*εχων ουσιαν του μνημειου*) say: …I summon the ruler of heaven and earth, Chaos and Hades, and the *ghosts of men* (*δαιμονες ανθρωπων*) slain, who once looked upon the light, and even now I beg you, Blessed One, immortal master of the world, if you enter the hidden places of the earth, the Land of the Dead, send this ghost to [Name] from whose corpse *I hold the remains in my hands* (*κατεχω τοδε λειψανον εν χερσιν εμαις*).[1447]

[1444] Franco & Maltomini, *Supplementum Magicum* I, 128.
[1445] Kotansky, *Greek Magical Amulets*, 50.
[1446] Graf, *Envisioning Magic*, 98.
[1447] Preisendanz, *Papyri Graecae Ma*gicae IV, 435, 443-449.

"With relics came miracles." Not only are miracles performed by prophets and apostles, they occur through contact with *inanimate objects* that have been in close contact[1448] with the apostles: "that he forge for you a double iron nail...Bring it to me, dip it in the blood of Osiris..." or "through the name and the nails that were driven into the body of Manuel..." or "I adjure you today by the crown of thorns that was placed upon your head, and the 5 nails that were driven into your body, and the spear thrust that pierced his side, and his blood and water that came forth from him upon the cross."[1449]

"The *telling* of miracles is itself a performative act."[1450] The incantatory retelling of a miracle, a *historiola*, can produce a similar miracle by invoking precedent. Christian miracle is not a clean break from pagan magic and necromancy; it inhabits the same mental world as pagan magic and understands the basis for performing powerful works in the same way. *Ousia* makes the ghost of the one dead before his time magically present, even as the relic of a saint, "such as a blood-soaked handkerchief,"[1451]—"The *Proconsular Acts of Cyprian* tell us that the martyr-bishop's congregation spread cloths and napkins to catch the blood that fell as the saint was beheaded"[1452]—makes the saint magically present, hence the burial of Christian relics beneath altars[1453]

[1448] Acts 19:12.
[1449] Meyer & Smith, *Ancient Christian Magic: Coptic Texts of Ritual Power*, 24, 98, 336.
[1450] Grig, *Making Martyrs in Late Antiquity*, 86.
[1451] Geary, *Furta Sacra*, 34.
[1452] Grig, *Making Martyrs in Late Antiquity*, 87.
[1453] Brown, *The Cult of the Saints*, 37.

Relics are often divided into two categories: *bodily* relics, which are bodies or pieces of bodies, and *brandea*, ordinary objects or substances such as cloth or water, that have come into contact with the bodies of saints or with holy places. *Brandea* were frequently worn around the neck as talismans. Corpses of saints were often moved or "translated," sometimes by theft, and were also broken into pieces, or "parti-

where 'miracles' such as transubstantiation occur. Legend has it that the body of the apostle Peter was buried at the present site of the altar of Saint Peter's basilica in the Vatican.

The earliest record of Christians collecting relics comes from *The Martyrdom of Saint Polycarp* in which the writer describes what happened after Polycarp's body was burned:

> So later we collected his bones, more valuable than the most precious stones, more excellent than gold, and put them aside for ourselves in a suitable place.[1454]

We need only compare the gathering of the bones of Polycarp with Lucian's report of those who rushed to the spot where Peregrinus burned himself to ashes "to gather up some relic of the fire."[1455] In his satire on superstition, Lucian recounts a cure of snakebite achieved by a "Chaldean" magician by the recitation of a spell and the use of "a piece of rock chipped from the tombstone of a dead girl."[1456] Morton Smith noted that an attitude toward miracle that was never far from pagan necromancy pervaded early Christianity:

> The later Christian collection of the remains of martyrs' bodies was suspiciously like magicians' collection of the remains of bodies of executed criminals (the martyrs were legally criminals) whose spirits they wished to control. We have many ancient stories of thefts of dead bodies for magical purposes; the practice was evidently common and may explain the disappearance of Jesus' body and the empty tomb. Be that as it may, the Christians' frequent gatherings around tombs and in cata-

---

tioned," and the parts distributed, the religious version of 'trickle-down' economics.

See particularly Brown, *The Cult of the Saints*, 86-105.

1454 *The Martyrdom of Saint Polycarp, Bishop of Smyrna*, XVIII, 2.

1455 Lucian, *The Passing of Peregrinus*, 40.

1456 Lucian, *The Lover of Lies*, 11.

> combs must have seemed to most pagans an indication of necromancy.[1457]

The 4th century writer Eunapius captures the revulsion of many pagans who witnessed the Christian practice of adoring relics and graves:

> Next they imported the men called "monks" into the holy places, men in appearance, but living like pigs. They publicly engaged in countless evil and unspeakable acts and considered it righteous to despise divine things. Every man in a black robe, resolved to disgrace himself publicly, possessed tyrannical authority, to such an extreme of virtue had humanity been driven...They also settled these "monks" in Canobus, chaining humanity to the service of worthless slaves instead of the real gods. They gathered up the bones and skulls of those apprehended for numerous crimes, men the courts had condemned, and proclaimed them to be gods, wallowed around their tombs, and declared that being defiled by graves made them stronger. The dead were called "martyrs," and some kind of "ministers," and "ambassadors of the gods," these degraded slaves, eaten alive by whips, their ghosts bearing the wounds of torture.[1458]

"Contemporary veneration of saintly relics—with invocations, visions and healings—is 'necromancy' be definition, but not by name."[1459] The witch goddess Hekate, who holds the keys to the grave, "is portrayed as leading packs of dead souls through the night," and Persephone, "the queen of the dead, could release souls when she wished to."[1460] In the new Christian spiritual economy, Jesus, "who is the beginning, the firstborn from the

---

[1457] Smith, *Studies in the Cult of Yahweh*, II, 211.
[1458] Eunapius, *Lives of the Philosophers and Sophists*, 473.
[1459] Ritner, *Magic and Divination in the Ancient World*, 96.
[1460] Johnston, *The World of Ancient M*agic, 86.

dead,"[1461] holds the keys to the abyss.[1462] Regarding Lazarus he commands, "Unbind him and let him go."[1463] Jesus, who has "the name abover every name,"[1464] is the new Christian god of resurrection and magic.

It is clear from the account of Polycarp, probably written in the 2nd century, that Christians had already developed a devotion to corpses that bordered on necrophilia. Pilgrimages to the graves of martyrs could also involve sleeping by the tomb, a continuation of the ancient practice of incubation. "Among the Christians, incubation is done at the shrine of holy men or martyrs. Among many examples: a Jew suffering from sciatica dreamed in the basilica of Saint Domentius in Syria; the saint appeared to him and healed him."[1465]

Pilgrims to the temples of Asklepius, the god of healing, hoped for *εγκοιμησις* (enkoimēsis), the manifestation of the god in a healing or prophetic dream. The temple area where sleepers awaited dreams was the *κοιμητηριον* (koimētērion), the source of our *cemetery*. To achieve a dream, the patient might have to sacrifice a sheep and sleep on its fleece, a practice known as *incubation* from Latin *incubare*, "to lie down on," the source of the English *incubus*. "Incubation must involve, somehow, a magic procedure, for a god is conjured or summoned by some ritual, but it is performed within a religious context, under the supervision of priests who may have had some medical knowledge."[1466] The practice of incubation "continued at some Christian shrines in the East. Western examples may be cited, too, in which patients slept on or by tombs and shrines, or in which the

---

[1461] *ος εστιν αρχη πρωτοτοκος εκ των νεκρων*, "who is the beginning, the firstborn from the dead." Colossians 1:18.

[1462] Revelation 20:1.

[1463] John 11:44.

[1464] Philippians 2:9-10.

[1465] Stroumsa, *Barbarian Philosophy: The Religious Revolution of Early Christianity*, 199.

[1466] Luck, *Arcana Mundi*, 141.

healing saint appeared to them in dreams." The custom of bringing *ex votos*, representations of healed body parts, "a tradition dating back to Neolithic times,"[1467] continued at Christian shrines.

Consulting ghosts, or necromancy—*νεκυομαντεια* (nekuomanteia)—was also an important function of dreams. Daniel Ogden: "It is not surprising that ghosts should have been sought in dreams, since they often visited the living spontaneously in this way," and notes that various Greek characters return to visit the living in their dreams.[1468] As mentioned in a previous chapter, the Israelites "who sit in tombs, and spend the night in secret places"[1469] were likely using graveyards to provoke necromantic visions. Incubation also is a cross-cultural phenomenon: the calling of a "man of high degree" in the Australian aboriginal cultures "may be deliberately sought by sleeping in an isolated place, particularly near the grave of a medicine man or some other enchanted spot."[1470] And of the Scandanavian people: "The *Flateyjarbók* tells of a man who was inspired with the gift of poetry by a dead *skald* on whose howe he slept.[1471] Christians even competed with one another to be interred in churches next to martyr's remains—"burial *apud sanctos*."[1472]

In Matthew's infancy narrative, prophetic warning dreams are sent to Joseph (1:20), to the magi (2:12), again to Joseph a second (2:13), third (2:19), and fourth time (2:22), and later to Pilate's wife (27:19). As noted by Hull, "No less than five dreams surround the divine birth and Messiah goes to his death in the ominous mystery of Pilate's wife's dream…The parousia of the Messiah is also to be accompanied by warning portents. The reference to 'the signal of your coming' and 'the sign that her-

[1467] Wilson, *Saints and Their Cults*, 20-21.
[1468] Ogden, *Greek and Roman Necromancy*, 76.
[1469] Isaiah 65:4.
[1470] Elkin, *Aboringinal Men of High Degree*, 17.
[1471] Jones & Pennick, *A History of Pagan Europe*, 142.
[1472] Grig, *Making Martyrs in Late Antiquity*, 87.

alds the Son of Man' (24:3, 30) are unique to this gospel. So the birth, death and reappearance of Jesus Christ are all authenticcated by signs."[1473] Prophetic dreams are likewise common in the Old Testament.[1474]

Christian fascination with items associated with apostles and saints differed not one whit from pagan belief in the magical power of inanimate things to transmit gifts of the spirit. Lucian tells of the tyrant Neanthus who acquired the mythic lyre of Orpheus under the delusion that the genius of Orpheus resided in the lyre and that with it he could "subdue everyone by spells (*παντας καταθελξειν*) and bewitchment (*κηλησειν*)." Instead, the noise of the lyre summoned a great number of dogs that tore Neanthus to pieces. In Lucian's own time a man paid three thousand drachmas for the lamp of Epictetus, thinking that if he read by its light, he would acquire wisdom. Another man paid a talent for the staff that Peregrinus discarded before jumping into the flames, and Dionysus of Syracuse bought the wax tablets of the poet Philoxenus supposing that he "would be filled with divine inspiration" (*ενθεος εσεσθαι και κατοχος*) by composing on them.[1475]

1473 Hull, *Hellenistic Magic and the Synoptic Tradition*, 116-117.

1474 As at Genesis 3:5-8, 41:7-41, or Daniel 2:1-30 to cite a few examples.

1475 Lucian, *The Ignorant Book Collector*, 12-15.

CHAPTER 10: PAUL'S CULT OF POSSESSION

"The form of early Christianity associated with Paul can be characterized as a spirit-possession cult. Paul establishes communities of those possessed by the spirit of Jesus."[1476] Paul assures the Corinthians—"*because you are zealous devotees of spirits,*" *υμεις επει ζηλωται εστε πνευματων*—"on that account I reveal to you that *no one speaking by a spirit of God* (*ουδεις εν πνευματι θεου λαλων*) says 'Anathema Jesus!' and no one is able to say 'Lord Jesus!' except *by a holy spirit* (*ει μη εν πνευματι αγιω*)".[1477] "The worshippers and the attending spirits form a double assembly..."[1478]

According to Paul, Jesus "was ordained the Son of God *in power* (*εν δυναμει*) owing to [the] spirit (*πνευμα*) of holiness by resurrection from the dead."[1479] "This connection of the Spirit with resurrection was so vivid in Christian minds because their encounter with the risen Jesus brought them the same kind of power that marked Jesus' ministry..."[1480] Given the connection between miraculous power and spirit following Jesus' resurrection, it is worth making a short detour to examine what the New Testament says about "spirit."

The word spirit (*πνευμα*), which occurs nearly 400 times, admits of no single definition nor is it used in a consistent way even within categories. In fact, Christians have been fighting over the theology of the spirit for centuries; in the Middle Ages

---

[1476] Mount, *Journal of Biblical Literature* 124 (2005): 316.
[1477] 1 Corinthians 12:3.
[1478] Thee, *Julius Africanus and the Early Christian View of Magic*, 382.
[1479] Romans 1:4.
[1480] Brown, *Worship* 57 (1983): 225-236.

the Western churches split from the Eastern Orthodox, the Schism of 1014, over a single word, *filioque*, "and the Son," in the phrase *qui ex Patre Filioque procedit*—"that proceeds from the Father and the Son." The Western church confessed the "double procession" of the Spirit, teaching that the Holy Spirit proceeds from *both* the Father and the Son, while the Eastern Orthodox churches teach that the spirit proceeds from the Father alone. The Protestant Reformation was also, in many important ways, a quarrel over the role of the spirit in Christian life, over whether the spirit speaks to Christians through the magisterium of the Church, the apostolic *regula fidei*, "rule of faith," or through the biblical text, *sola scriptura*, "Scripture interprets Scripture."

It is clear, however, that in the New Testament the holy spirit has become conflated with the spirit of Jesus: "prevented *by the holy spirit* (*υπο του αγιου πνευματος*) from speaking the word in Asia," Paul and Timothy attempt to enter Bithynia, "but *the spirit of Jesus* (*το πνευμα* Ιησου) did not allow them."[1481] To the house churches in Rome Paul says, "But you are not in flesh, but *in spirit* (*εν πνευματι*) if indeed [the] *spirit of God* (*πνευμα θεου*) dwells in you. But if anyone *does not have* [the] *spirit of Christ* (*πνευμα* Χριστου *ουκ εχει*), this [person] is not his."[1482] "A [person] joined to the Lord *is one spirit* (*εν πνευμα εστιν*)."[1483] "Because you are sons, God sent forth *the spirit of his Son* (*το πνευμα του υιου αυτου*) into your hearts."[1484] "For I know that because of your entreaties [to God] and imparting of *the spirit of Jesus Christ* (*του πνευματος* Ιησου Χριστου), this will result in my deliverance."[1485] Similar language appears in later documents; the author of 1 Peter attributes the predictions of the prophets of the Old Testament to "*the spirit of Christ in them* (*το εν αυ-*

[1481] Acts 16:6-7.
[1482] Romans 8:9.
[1483] 1 Corinthians 6:17.
[1484] Galatians 4:6.
[1485] Philippians 1:19.

τοις πνευμα Χριστου) when it testified ahead of time about the sufferings of Christ and the glories to follow."[1486] Jesus remains or abides in his followers, "and by this we know that he remains in us, *by the spirit that he gave us* (εκ του πνευματος ου ημιν εδωκεν)."[1487] That receiving the spirit was contingent upon Jesus' resurrection is apparent from this stark declaration in John: "*For as yet there was no spirit* (ουπω γαρ ην πνευμα) because Jesus had not yet been glorified."[1488]

Paul's discourse on the gifts of the spirit is specifically directed to people who had once worshipped the pagan deities—"You know that when you were serving speechless images"—and who were therefore already familiar with such manifestations of spirit possession as ecstatic oracular speech, particularly during rites accompanied by music.[1489] Regarding such ecstatic speech, Paul says:

> ...tongues are a sign, not for believers, but for unbelievers, and prophecy, not for unbelievers, but for those who believe. In the same way, if the whole church comes together and all speak in tongues, and strangers or unbelievers enter, *will they not say you are possessed* (ουκ ερουσιν οτι μαινεσθε)?[1490]

Tongues are a sign for unbelievers because ecstatic speech, already familiar to pagans, is proof that Christians have a spirit—"that religious trances and ecstasy were the manifestation of possession by a god was one of wide currency in Greek and Near Eastern religions."[1491] The pagan who enters a Christian gathering and finds a house full of agitated Christians all raving in-

---

[1486] 1 Peter 1:11.
[1487] 1 John 3:24.
[1488] John 7:39.
[1489] 1 Corinthians 12:2. Note the mention of the flute and lyre in the same letter (14:7).
[1490] 1 Corinthians 14:22-23.
[1491] Esler, *The First Christians in their Social Worlds*, 46.

comprehensibly will come to the conclusion that the speakers are *possessed*, the meaning of *μαινομαι* (mainomai) in this context. Given Paul's near legendary lack of precise expression, whether such possession is to be regarded positively or negatively is uncertain.[1492] Elsewhere Paul mentions his own spiritual transports: "if we are in ecstasy, it is for God, if in our right mind, for you"[1493] and reminds the jabbering masses that he speaks in tongues more than all of them.[1494]

Confronted with raving Christians, the response of the unbeliever, "God is truly *in* you!"[1495] —rendered "God is really *among* you" by the *Revised Standard Version*—reflects the ancient notion of possession, *ενθεος* (entheos), *entered by the god.* The act of spirit possession is consistently described by the metaphor of filling a container: God "will pour out" his spirit[1496] and fill the disciples even as sound fills a house;[1497] their "extravagance of divine power" is contained "in clay vessels."[1498] In the Old Testament, Yahweh promises to 'pour out' the spirit like water,[1499] 'pour it out' on all flesh.[1500] The Jewish writer Philo, a contemporary of Jesus, provides a thinking man's description of possession:

> Whenever [the light of the mind] dims, ecstasy and possession naturally assail us, *divine seizure and madness* (*κατοκωχη τε και μανια*). For whenever the light of God

---

[1492] An exhaustive discussion of this and many other aspects of such speech can be found in Forbes' *Prophecy and Inspired Speech In Early Christianity and its Hellenistic Environment,* 175, ff.

[1493] 2 Corinthians 5:13.

[1494] 1 Corinthians 14:22.

[1495] *οντως ο θεος εν υμιν εστιν*: "God is truly in you" (1 Corinthians 14:25).

[1496] Acts 2:17.

[1497] Acts 2:2,4.

[1498] 2 Corinthians 4:7.

[1499] Isaiah 44:3.

[1500] Joel 2:28, quoted in Acts 2:17.

> shines upon us, human light is extinguished and when the divine sun sets, the human dawns and rises. This is what is apt to happen to the guild of the prophets. At the arrival of the divine spirit, our mind is evicted. When the spirit departs, the wandering mind returns home, for it is well established that that which is subject to death may not share a home with that which is deathless. Therefore the eclipse of the power of reason and the darkness that envelops it *begets ecstasy and inspired madness* (*εκστασιν και θεοφορητον μανιαν εγεννησε*).[1501]

Philo's characterization of possession is aggressive: *εικος εκστασις και η ενθεος επιπιπτει*: "ecstasy and possession naturally assail us." The verb *επιπιπτω* (epipiptō), like other verbs of magic, is a power verb. It means *to fall upon* or *attack*, and is used of disease, accidents and storms. The New Testament equivalent, *επερχομαι* (eperchomai), "when the holy spirit *comes upon* you,"[1502] likewise has violent connotations as already noted. The Jews "came down" from Antioch and provoked the stoning and eviction of Paul,[1503] and Simon prays that the curses uttered by Peter "may not befall me" (*μηδεν επελθη επ' εμε*)[1504] The holy spirit "will come upon" Mary—*πνευμα αγιον επελευσεται επι σε*: "holy spirit will come upon you..."—and "the power of the Most High will overshadow" her. In short, Mary will be taken by force, *seized*. The verb *επερχομαι* is also used in the papyri for magical attacks: *φυλαξατε με απο παντος πραγματος επερχομενου μου*: "defend me from all troubles coming upon me…"[1505]

[1501] Philo, *Quis rerum divinarum heres*, 264-265. *Philo*, volume 4, of the Loeb series is the source of the Greek text.

[1502] Acts 1:8.
See particularly *Strange Acts*, 59-63.

[1503] Acts 14:19.

[1504] Acts 8:24.

[1505] Preisendanz, *Papyri Graecae Magicae* XXXVI, 176.
For the magical use of *επερχομαι*, see *Supplementum Magicum*, I, 38.

That 'an eclipse of the power of reason' resulted in something close to chaos during meetings of the house churches Paul makes explicit when setting out rules that will rein in the wild enthusiasm of the Corinthians:

> So if anyone speaks in a tongue, do so two at a time, or three at most, and in turn, and let one interpret. But if there is no interpreter, keep silent in church. Let each speak to himself and to God. Let two or three prophets speak and let others evaluate what they say. But if another receives a revelation while seated, let the first person be silent. For all can prophesy in turn so that all may learn and all be encouraged. The spirits of the prophets are subject to the prophets, for God is a God, not of pandemonium, but of harmony.[1506]

"The one speaking in tongues speaks not to men, but to God. No one understands, but *he is speaking mysteries* (*λαλει μυστηρια*) by the spirit," speaking in "the tongues…of angels" (*ταις γλωσσαις…των αγγελων*).[1507] Likewise the magican invokes the "immortal, living, honored names," names that "are not declared in articulate speech" by the human tongue (*υπο ανθρωπινης γλωσσης*), and bursts forth in volumes of jibberish: "ĒEŌ OĒEŌ IŌŌ OĒ ĒEŌ OĒ EŌ IŌŌ OĒĒE ŌĒE IĒ ĒŌ OŌ," etc, etc.[1508] "So if the whole church comes together and everyone speaks in tongues, and inquirers or unbelievers come in, will they not say that you are out of your mind?"[1509] Miller: "When God "breaks into human speech, his sounds are the echoes of the alphabet, the vowels...ecstatic prayer...does not sound like normal language but rather like music (as Paul's repeated musical metaphors suggest—gong, cymbal, flute, harp, bugle); it is not intelligible, but

---

[1506] 1 Corinthians 14:27-32.

[1507] 1 Corinthians 14:2, 13:1.

[1508] Preisendanz, *Papyri Graecae Magicae* IV, 605-611.

[1509] 1 Corinthians 14:23 (NIV).

it is rhythmic; and it is also powerful, for it brings manifestations of the Spirit."[1510]

The descriptions of spirit manipulation are strikingly similar: *πνευματα προφητων προφηταις υποτασσεται*, "the spirits of the prophets *are subject to* the prophets" as are the demons: *τα δαιμονια υποτασσεται ημιν εν τω ονοματι σου*, "the demons *are subject to* us in your name."[1511] In Corinth, as in some modern Christian sects, spirit possession, not message, had become the mark of a supposed spiritual elite.

> To each is given the manifestation of the spirit for the common good. To one, speech of wisdom is given through the spirit, but to another, speech of knowledge according to the same spirit. To another, faith by the same spirit, but to another gifts of healing in the spirit, but to another, works of power. To another, prophecy, but to another, distinguishing between spirits, to yet another, kinds of tongues, and to another, interpretation of tongues. But all this operates through one and the same spirit, apportioned to each as it chooses.[1512]

The phrase translated "works of power" in the passage above—*ενεργηματα δυναμεων*, "miraculous powers"[1513]—duplicates the terminology used in the magical papyri where it means *magical powers*: "*The mighty assistant* (*ο κραταιος παρεδρος*) will gladly accomplish these things. But impart them to no one except your own true and worthy son when he asks you for *the magical powers (τα...ενεργηματα)*."[1514] "However often you want to command the greatest god Ouphora, speak and he will comply. You have *the ritual of the greatest and most divine magical working*

[1510] Miller, *Classical Mediterranean Spirituality*, 483, 486.

[1511] Luke 10:17.

[1512] 1 Corinthians 12:7-11.

[1513] Danker, *Greek-English Lexicon*, 335.

[1514] Preisendanz, *Papyri Graecae Magicae*, I, 193-194.

(την τελετηον του μεγιστου και θειου ενεργημματος)."[1515] "Paul, who *talks about* what the magical papyri *do*, has in his first letter to the Corinthians described the basic aspects of alphabetical language."[1516]

That spirit possession was recognized as inherently problematic is shown by the inclusion among the gifts of the spirit of "distinguishing between spirits"—*διακρισεις πνευματων*: literally, "discernment of spirits," the ability of differentiate between works done through the spirit of God and those done through the power of demons. The Christian beloved are admonished, "*Do not believe all the spirits* (μη παντι πνευματι πιστευετε), but test the spirits [to prove] if they are from God, because *many false prophets* (πολλοι ψευδοπροφηται) have gone forth into the world."[1517] Inspiration is deeply ambiguous. Regarding Saul's inspired speech, Levison observes, "First, the preceding instance of Saul's 'prophesying' took place when the *evil* spirit of God rushed upon him (1 Samuel 18:10). Second, the idiom employed to describe the spirit's presence in 1 Sam[uel] 19:19-23, היה על, is employed otherwise in this narrative only of the *evil* spirit (16:16, 23; 19:9). Third, each of the seven prior references, from 16:14 to 19:9, is to the evil spirit, and its presence is so well established that in 16:23 it can be described simply as 'spirit of God,' without the adjective 'evil.'"[1518]

The ambiguous connection between spirit possession and prophecy is perhaps best illustrated by the story of Balaam—the name בלעם (Balaam) is likely derived from בעל (Baal).[1519] When the Israelite horde invades Canaan, Balak, the king of the Moabites, hires Balaam, a powerful wizard, to pronounce a

---

[1515] Ibid, XII, 316-317.

[1516] Miller, *Classical Mediterranean Spirituality*, 486.

Letter strings related to ecstatic speech are discussed at length in a subsequent chapter.

[1517] 1 John 4:1.

[1518] Levison, *The Spirit in First Century Judaism*, 37, footnote 23.

[1519] Numbers 22-24.

curse of execration against Israel as was commonly done in preparation for war, but overcome by the spirit of Yahweh, Balaam proves unable to comply, pronouncing a series of blessings instead. Balaam must speak whatever the spirit of Israel's God puts in his mouth.[1520] The account of the conquest in Joshua mentions that the Israelites killed Balaam, who is there described as הקוסם (ha-qosem), the *soothsayer.*[1521] Depending on how broadly or narrowly one defines magic, this tends to contradict Seland's claim that Balaam "is not explicitly described as a magician" either in the Hebrew Bible or in the *Septuagint*, the Greek translation of the Hebrew Old Testament in general use among Jews in the Diaspora in the era of Jesus.[1522] The Greek translation of Numbers 22:7 specifies that the elders of the various Canaanite tribes "came to Balaam bearing (literally, *in their hands*) the fee for divination" (*τα μαντεια εν ταις χερσιν αυτων και ηλθον προς Βαλααμ*).[1523] It is probable that Balaam escaped an open accusation of magic because "Philo portrays Balaam's oracles as prophecy of the highest order,"[1524] an estimation that likely reflected Jewish opinion in general.

The language used to describe prophetic possession is revealing. The Greek translation of the Hebrew scriptures, a translation in use by both Jews and early Christians, describes Balaam's possession thus: *και εγενετο πνευμα θεου εν αυτω*, "and the spirit of God overpowered him."[1525] The verb *γινομαι* is polyvalent; its most common meaning is simply *to happen* or *become*, but depending on context it can also mean *to fall under the power of* something or someone,[1526] as in this case. It can be used of catastrophic events: "And I beheld him open the seventh seal and a

---

[1520] Numbers 23:12.

[1521] Joshua 13:22.

[1522] Seland, *The New Testament and Early Christian Literature in Greco-Roman Context*, 342.

[1523] Numbers 22:7, *LXX*.

[1524] Seland, 342.

[1525] Numbers 24:2.

[1526] Liddell & Scott, *A Greek-English Lexicon*, 309.

strong earthquake *occurred* (εγενετο) and the sun *turned* (εγενετο) as black as sackcloth made from goat hair and the full moon *turned to* (εγενετο) blood."[1527]

The Jewish writers Philo and Josephus both repeat the Balaam story and relate it in ways that reflect their understanding of prophetic possession, an opinion likely shared by early Jewish Christians. In Philo's retelling, the angel of God tells Balaam, "You will repeat the words I give you without understanding and I will control your organs of speech as required by what is just and advantageous, for I will hold the reins of speech, foretelling everything by your tongue though you do not understand…He went outside and *immediately became possessed* (ενθους αυτικα γινεται), *invaded by a prophetic spirit* (προφητικου πνευματος επιφοιτησαντος) that completely banished his mantic art from his soul. For it is not permissible for *most holy possession* (ιερωτατη κατοκωχη) to share the same place with *magical artifice* (μαγικην σοφιστειαν)."[1528] To this description of Balaam's prophecy, Josephus adds, "So much for the conjuring of *one no longer self-possessed* (ουκ ων εν εαυτω), but *overpowered by the divine spirit* (θειω πνευματι…νενικημενος)…for that [spirit] utters what speech and words it wishes of which none are aware …"[1529] Given these descriptions, it is apparent that spirit possession displaced the mental faculties of the possessed, whether described as a *prophet* (μαντις)[1530] or as a *magician* (μαγος).[1531] It is possible that Josephus "understands the stories of Balaam and Saul similarly as stories in which an angelic spirit overpowered its subject by seizing mental control."[1532] The writer of the gospel describes ecstatic speech in much the same way: "It is not

---

[1527] Revelation 6:12.
[1528] Philo, *De Vita Mosis* I, 48.
[1529] Josephus, *Antiquities of the Jews* IV, 6.
[1530] Philo, *De Vita Mosis* I, 282, ff.
[1531] Ibid I, 276.
[1532] Levison, *The Spirit in First Century Judaism*, 38.

you who are speaking, *but the spirit of your Father that speaks in you,"* (*αλλα το πνευμα του πατρος υμων το λαλουν εν υμιν*).[1533]

The power of music to inspire ecstatic speech is reported in the Old Testament. Elisha, asked to foretell the fate of the army of Judah, requests a musician and, as the instrument is played, is seized "by the hand of the Lord" and begins to prophesy.[1534] The technique of inducing trance through chanting appears to have been common within the primitive Christian community. The *Acts of John*, a work of the late 2nd century, describes how the disciples hold hands to form a circle and chant "Amen" in response to Jesus:

> Glory be to thee, Logos.
> Glory be to thee, Grace. Amen.
> Glory be to thee, Spirit.
> Glory be to thee Holy One.
> Glory be to thee, Glory. Amen.
> We praise thee, Father.
> We thank thee, Light.
> In whom darkness does not reside. Amen.
> And why we give thanks I tell you:
> I will be saved and I will save. Amen.
> I will be loosed and I will loose. Amen.
> I will be wounded and I will wound. Amen
> I will be born and I will bear. Amen.
> I will eat and I will be eaten. Amen.
> I will hear and I will be heard... Amen.
> etc.[1535]

1533 Matthew 10:20.

1534 2 Kings 3:13-15.

1535 Bowe, *Journal of Early Christian Studies* 7: 84-85. I have used Bowe's translation without strictly following her punctuation.

The Greek text of the chant can be found in Junod & Kaestli, *Acta Ioannis*, 94-96.

It is likely that this chant, which is quite a bit longer than the section quoted, employed a steadily increasing tempo and it would seem only natural that those standing in the circle around Jesus would begin to sway in unison or move together in a circular direction. Bowe notes "that its choreography and antiphonal chorus describe a circle dance performed by Jesus and his disciples on the night before his death." The canonical gospels refer to singing as part of the "Last Supper,"[1536] and as Lucian points out, "There is not even one *mystery cult* (τελετην) to be found without dancing..."[1537]

For my purposes the function, not the form, of this text is of greater interest: the repition of "Amen," by the chorus "creates a staccato rhythm in this section which becomes almost mesmerizing."[1538] Examples of similar confession-response, almost certainly derived from liturgy and adapted to magical ends, can be cited:

> Christ was born. Amen.
> Christ was crucified. Amen.
> Christ was buried. Amen.
> Christ was raised. Amen.
> He has awakened to judge the living and the dead.
> You, too, fever with chills,
> Flee from *Kalēs who wears this magic charm* (απο Καλης της φορουσης το φυλακτηριον τουτο).[1539]

Any claim that only Christians sought possession by the "holy spirit" or that the notion of "holy spirit" was a Judeo-Christian invention could not be further from the truth. "This [is] the

[1536] Mark 14:26; Matthew 26:30.
[1537] Lucian, *The Dance* (Περι ορχησεως), 15.
[1538] Bowe, *Journal of Early Christian Studies* 7: 97.
[1539] Daniel & Maltomini, *Supplementum Magicum*, 23.

spell: Come to me, *lord...holy spirit* (*κυριε...αγιον πνευμα*)..."[1540] "...*and may the holy spirit breathe in me* (*και πνευση εν εμοι το ιερον πνευμα*)..."[1541] "Hail, spirit that enters me and convulses me *and leaves me* (*και χωριζομενον μου*) according to the will of god..."[1542] "...continue revealing, truthfully, lord, a waking vision of every action *by the command of the holy spirit* (*προς επιταγην αγιου πνευματος*), the angel of Phoibos..."[1543] "...and immediately the divine spirit enters (*εισερχεται το θειον πνευμα*) ..."[1544]

The connection between prophecy and possession is made again when Elisha sends a young prophet to anoint Jehu as king. The prophet calls Jehu aside, gives him the message, and flees.

> When Jehu came back to his master's officers, they said to him, "Is everything all right? Why did that madman come to you?" He answered them, "You know the sort and how they babble."[1545]

The Greek Old Testament labels the young "madman" with a revealing term, *επιληπτος* (epilēptos), the source of *epileptic*, one *seized* by the hand of God. The connection between song and magic, and between "seizure" and prophecy is also evident in Greek culture: the term for *enchantment* (which itself means "to chant in")—*επωδη* (epōdē)—is literally a *song*—*ωδη* (ōdē)—chanted *over*—*επι* (epi)—the subject of a spell. From this comes the term *επαοιδος* (epaoidos), *enchanter*, a close associate of the *magos*.[1546] Similarly, we find *πυθοληπτος* (putholēptos), literally

---

[1540] Preisendanz, *Papyri Graecae Magicae* III, 392-393.
[1541] Ibid, IV, 510.
[1542] Ibid, IV, 1121.
"Leaves me" as the soul leaves the body; compare Liddell & Scott, *A Greek-English Lexicon*, *χωριζω*, 2016.
[1543] Preisendanz, *Papyri Graecae Magicae* III, 288-289.
[1544] Ibid, I, 284.
[1545] 2 Kings 9:11 (NRSV).
[1546] As at Daniel 2:2, 4:7, for example.

"seized by the python"—the python is a symbol of Apollo, god of prophecy—to describe the ecstatic state entered by the priestess of the god as she utters oracles. The transcultural nature of this general method of divination can be appreciated from the following quotation regarding the Scottish Celts: The Dingwall Presbytery Records tell of the *derilans* who appear to have been officiating priests on the island. Dixon suggests that this title comes from the Gaelic *deireoil*, "afflicted," inferring that the priesthood was composed of people enthused by "divine madness" in the manner of shamans the world over."[1547]

There are substantial differences between the "tongues" described by Paul and the phenomenon described by Luke in the book of Acts. According to Paul, "the open display of the spirit" (*η φανερωσις του πνευματος*)[1548] in Christian gatherings could take various forms including "speech of wisdom"[1549] and "speech of knowledge,"—*λογος γνωσεως*, "speech of *gnosis*," were one to prefer such a reading—both of which are listed separately from "kinds of tongues" and the related gift of "interpretation of tongues."[1550] The context makes clear that tongues conveyed neither wisdom nor knowledge. In fact, Paul's discussion of the gift makes clear that "tongues" were unintelligible:

> The one speaking in tongues speaks, not to men, but to God, for he speaks mysteries by means of the spirit…for if the trumpet sounds but is not clearly heard, who will prepare himself for war? And so with you: if through tongues you are given unintelligible speech, how will it be known what is said? You will be talking into the air…but in church rather I speak five words with my

---

[1547] Jones & Pennick, *A History of Pagan Europe*, 107.

[1548] 1 Corinthians 12:7.

[1549] 1 Corinthians 12:8.

[1550] 1 Corinthians 12:10.

mind that another be taught than a thousand words in a tongue.[1551]

By the time Luke composes Acts near the end of the 1st century or beginning of the 2nd—*mirabile dictu*—the tongues have become recognizable languages, not an utterance of unknown meaning to either speaker or listener.[1552] Regarding speaking while possessed, Esler observes, "[Luke's] presentation of what happened at Pentecost does not encourage confidence in this phenomenon having been current among the group or groups for whom he was writing...Luke is portraying xenoglossy, not glossolalia."[1553] The possessed Christians "call the spirit in the spirit's own language"[1554] and "the spirit itself speaks up [for us] with unintelligible moaning" (*αυτο το πνευμα υπερεντυγχανει στεναγμοις αλαλητοις*).[1555] The adjective *αλαλητος* (alalētos), *unutterable, shouting, wailing*, is derived from *αλαλη* (alalē), *war cry*, the shout with which the frenzy of battle commenced.

The sound of rushing wind[1556] that accompanied the gift of tongues in Acts has parallels with other forms of paranormal phenomena, a point explored by Greg Taylor in an interesting and provocative essay.[1557] The sound of the wind, which indicates the active presence of the numina, was produced by spinning the *ρομβος* (rhombos), or *bullroarer*, during magical rites of mystery or initiation, a technique of spirit raising known to several cultures.

1551 1 Corinthians 14:2, 9, 19.

1552 Acts 2:4-13.

See particularly Forbes, *Prophecy and Inspired Speech In Early Christianity and its Hellenistic Environment*, 47-49.

1553 Esler, *The First Christians in their Social World*, 49.

1554 Smith, *Clement of Alexandria and a Secret Gospel of Mark*, 232.

1555 Romans 8:26.

1556 Acts 2:2.

1557 Taylor, "Her Sweet Murmur: Exploring the Aural Phenomenology of Border Experiences," *Dark Lore*, 15-37.

The early gifts of the spirit are a perfect illustration of the law of unintended consequences. As the Church would soon discover, claims to status by virtue of direct revelation cut both ways, Paul or no Paul. The issue reached crisis proportions with the appearance of Montanus, who initiated a movement of ecstatic prophesying in the late 2nd century. Claiming possession by the Holy Spirit in a manner reminiscent of modern Pentecostalism, Montanus represented himself to be the Paraclete foretold in the gospel of John, and began to foretell the end of the world. Whereas Paul had successfully challenged the central Christian authority in Jerusalem, Montanus did not prove as successful with the ecclesiastical powers in Rome. To rein in this latest outbreak of enthusiasm, the Church moved to make written texts, not private revelations, the final arbiter of Christian teaching, hastening "the invention of scripture"[1558] by the formation of a canon of accepted books. The collection of an approved body of writings, the interpretation of which the Church could control, signaled that henceforth inspired prophets would be appearing more often in frescoes than in person.

John Chrysostom (347-407) said of the spiritual gifts, "the present church is like a woman who has fallen from her former prosperous days and in many respects retains the symbols only of that ancient prosperity; displaying indeed the repositories and caskets of her golden ornaments, but bereft of her wealth."[1559] James Dunn's observations regarding the waning of the spiritual gifts merits extended quotation:

> If Paul's vision of charismatic community under the control of the Spirit of Christ was translated into reality *it was a reality which does not appear to have outlived him* ...In the Pastorals *charisma* has lost its dynamic character. It is no longer the individual manifestation of grace...the vision of the charismatic community has fad-

[1558] Ehrman, *Lost Christianities*, 238.
[1559] Quoted by Thiselton, *The Holy Spirit and Christian Origins*, 221.

> ed, ministry and authority have become the prerogative of the few, the experience of the Christ-Spirit has lost its vitality, the preservation of the past has become more important than openness to the present and future. *Spirit and charisma have become in effect subordinate to office, to ritual, to tradition*—early-Catholicism indeed!... the present becomes in effect only a channel whereby the religion of the past can be transmitted to the future in good order.[1560]

Mystery cults and magic.

Of the many forms of religious experience current in the days of Jesus, the practices of at least five mystery cults are still known to us in some detail. The Eleusinian mysteries, located at Eleusis, a small town about fourteen miles west of Athens, were held in high regard even by skeptics. The cult of Mithras, in which the membership was restricted to males, was popular among the Roman legions. The cult of Isis and Osiris (Serapis) enjoyed a wide popularity, particularly among women. The ecstatic cults of Dionysus and Cybele, or Mater Magna, finish out our brief list.

Μυω (muō), the Greek verbal base from which *mystery* and its cognates are formed in both Greek and English, means *to shut*, in the case of mystery cults, *the mouth*. The initiate's lips were sealed and the oath of secrecy was taken seriously. Rather little is known with any certainty about the inner life of these cults, but it is clear that they shared certain broad characteristics: initiation, reenactment, personal transformation following the revelation of secret knowledge—often called *rebirth*—and particularly in the cults of Dionysus and Mater Magna, ecstatic possession

---

[1560] Dunn, *Jesus and the Spirit: A Study of the Religious and Charismatic Experience of Jesus and the First Christians as Reflected in the New Testament*, 346-349.

by the god.[1561] Meyer: "...the mysteries emphasized an inwardness and privacy of worship within closed groups."[1562] The mystery religions were vehicles of salvation: "Isis was a mistress of magic and a saviour goddess who initiated human beings into the mysteries of everlasting life."[1563] "The symbols (συμβολα), the formulas (συνθηματα)...cannot be understood without the assumptions of magic. Consequently, one must assume that magic was a constitutive element of the mystery cults from their inception."[1564]

Mystery cults, pagan, Jewish, or Christian share two essential traits: mysticism and magic. Luck: "*Mystes*...applies also to the sorcerer who has reached a certain level. *Mysterion* or *telete* [τελετη, *my note*] could designate a high degree of magical knowledge, while telesma [τελεσμα] (hence 'talisman') also means 'amulet,' sometimes also *alexikakon,* [αλεξικακον] 'averter of evil.'"[1565] On the connection between magic and the mystery cults, Graf notes, "It must be concluded that there existed, at the level of ritual, affinities between the mystery cults and magic...Magic in general, as a combination and linked series of different rites, is called *ta musteria* or *hai teletai*, 'mysteries'...the *musterion* also designates magical objects or tools, like a ring or ointment."[1566] Regarding the Merkavah school of Jewish mystics, Schäfer points to "two clearly recongnizable components, one of which is the so-called heavenly journey of the mystic, and the other one the magical adjuration of angels by the mystic" and notes both that "the Hekhalot literature is dominated by all

---

[1561] A discussion of the phenomenon of induced ecstasy, written by Georg Luck, can be found in *Religion, Science, and Magic*, 185-217.

[1562] Meyer, *The Ancient Mysteries: A Sourcebook of Sacred Texts*, 4.

[1563] Jones & Pennick, *A History of Pagan Europe*, 23.

[1564] Betz, *Magika Hiera: Ancient Greek Magic and Religion*, 250.

[1565] Luck, *Witchcraft and Magic in Europe: Ancient Greece and Rome*, 100.

[1566] Graf, *Magic in the Ancient World*, 92, 97.

kinds of magical adjurations" and that "the 'pure' heavenly journey with no or little magic almost does not exist."[1567]

The vocabulary of the mystery cults proved irresistible both to Hellenistic Judaism and to primitive Christianity—both assimilated mystery cult terminology to describe the inner workings of their respective faiths.[1568] The recently published gnostic *Gospel of Judas* appears to have no direct reference to *γνωσις* (gnōsis), *knowledge*, but begins, "The secret word of revelation that Jesus spoke..." (ⲡⲗⲟⲅⲟⲥ ⲉⲧϩⲏⲡ ⲛⲧⲁⲡⲟⲫⲁⲥⲓⲥ ⲛⲧⲁ ⲓ̅ⲏ̅ⲥ̅ ϣⲁϫⲉ), which revelation consists of "mysteries" (ⲉⲙ̄ⲙⲩⲥⲧⲏⲣⲓⲟⲛ).[1569] The promise to reveal mysteries is a favored sales pitch in early Christianity; *The Apocryphon of John*, a "Sethian gnostic" text begins, "The teaching of the Savior and the revelation of the mysteries and the things hidden in silence..."[1570]

Paul's readers are privy to "*my gospel* (*το ευαγγελιον μου*) and the proclamation of Jesus Christ, *the revelation of a mystery* (*κατα αποκαλυψιν μυστηριου*) that has been kept secret for ages past ..."[1571] Indeed all that Paul says is qualified as "mystery,"[1572] "we speak *wisdom of God in a mystery*" (*θεου σοφιαν εν μυστηριω*)[1573]—Paul seems to be veering dangerously close to the "Gnostic" Sophia, *Wisdom*—"eye has not seen, and ear has not heard"[1574] the hidden marvels Paul reveals. Scarcely any aspect of Christianity escapes the label: the kingdom is a mystery,[1575]

1567 Schäfer, *Envisioning Magic: A Princeton Seminar and Symposium*, 39, 40.

1568 Betz, *Magika Hiera*, 250-251.

1569 *Gospel of Judas*, 33, 35, 45.

1570 Wisse, "The Apocryphon of John," *The Nag Hammadi Library in English*, 99.

1571 Romans 16:25.

1572 1 Corinthians 2:1. Compare Colossians 1:26, Ephesians 1:9, 3:3-5.

1573 1 Corinthians 2:7.

1574 1 Corinthians 2:9.

1575 Mark 4:11.

the gospel is a mystery,[1576] the Christian faith is a mystery (*το μυστηριον της πιστεως*),[1577] as is the Christian religion[1578] and the union of Christ and his church "is a great mystery" (*το μυστηριον τουτο μεγα εστιν*).[1579] The will of God is a mystery (*το μυστηριον του θεληματος αυτου*)[1580] and Christ as well (*το μυστηριον του Χριστου*).[1581] The recalcitrance of Israel is a mystery[1582] as are the tedious Christian sectarian conflicts, "the mystery of lawlessness" (*το μυστηριον...της ανομιας*),[1583] which is already at work. The identification of Christianity as just another ancient mystery cult could hardly be better established by its founding documents. One might well ask if Christianity was really a mystery cult or merely a caricature of one.

Nevertheless, as Devon Weins has pointed out, it is a mistake to look for exact correspondence between the pagan mystery cults and Christianity. In spite of shared characteristics such as symbolism, redemption, rebirth, death and rising of a deity, sacramental drama, eschatology, and focus on the fate of the individual, the details of the Judeo-Christian and pagan mysteries were based on different frames of reference. "Alongside the venerators of Isis, Mithra, Cybele, Attis, and company, existed the adherents of a thousand and one other cults and philosophical belief-systems, in a veritable 'rush hour of the gods.' This manifold complexity, this bewildering plethora of religions makes it extremely difficult to reconstruct the actual situation."[1584]

[1576] Ephesians 6:19. Compare Revelation 10:7.
[1577] 1 Timothy 3:9.
[1578] 1 Timothy 3:16.
[1579] Ephesians 5:32.
[1580] Ephesians 1:9.
[1581] Colossians 4:3.
[1582] Romans 11:25.
[1583] 2 Thessalonians 2:7.
[1584] Weins, *Aufstieg und Niedergang der Römischen Welt*, II, 23.2, 1265.

The μυστης (mustēs), the *initiate* into a mystery cult, was typically introduced to the rites by a sponsor, the μυσταγωγος (mustagōgos), or *mystagogue*. The body of secret knowledge revealed to the initiate was usually called τα μυστερια (ta musteria), *the mysteries*. In the cults of Dionysus and Cybele, *possession* by the god was a regular feature of the rites, resulting in εκστασις (ekstasis) or ενθουσιασμος (enthousiasmos)—the obvious sources of our *ecstasy* and *enthusiasm*—altered mental states associated with visions, oracular speech, and frenzied behavior. For the Greeks, the oracle at Delphi with its "pythoness" speaking in a trance exemplified oracular possession.[1585] In the case of the Bacchic rites associated with the worship of Dionysus, the god of wine, the participants entered a state of μανια (mania), a condition of violent frenzy in which live animals were ripped apart and their raw flesh consumed. Female participants in the rites of Dionysus were called *maenads*, which roughly translated, means "crazies." A similar inspired frenzy is recorded of Samson: "and the Spirit of the LORD came mightily upon him, and he tore the lion asunder as one tears a kid; and he had nothing in his hand."[1586]

The Greeks distinguished between four categories of divinely inspired madness: *mantic*, or prophetic, associated with Apollo, the god of prophecy, *poetic*, associated with the Muses, *erotic*, linked to Aphrodite, and *telestic*, from τελεστικος (telestikos), *initiatory*, or *mystical*, having to do with τελετη (teletē), *initiation* into the mysteries, particularly those connected to Dionysus. It has been claimed that the water-to-wine miracle at Cana echoes similar wonders performed by Dionysus. One of Dionysus' many miracles connected with wine were the εφημεροι αμπελοι, *one-day vines*, that flowered and bore grapes in the space of a single day,[1587] a pagan miracle which may have incited

[1585] On the recent archeology, see the recent discussion by John Hale, *et al*, *Scientific American* 289/2: 66-73.

[1586] Judges 14:6, *RSV*.

[1587] Otto, *Dionysus: Myth and Cult*, 98.

the Christian claim, *εγω ειμι η αμπελος η αληθηνη*: "I am the true *vine*."[1588] The cult of Dionysus must therefore be a false one.

The roots of modern theater trace back to the Bacchic initiation rites, the Dionysia held in Athens in honor of Dionysus, at which actors speaking from behind masks gave performances. "The theatrical use of the mask presumably grew out of its magical use: Dionysus became in the sixth century the god of theatre because he had long been the god of masquerade."[1589] Our word *tragedy*—*τραγωδια*, *goat ode*—comes from this source, as does *thespian*—*θεσπις*, *inspired*, having words from the gods. Accompanied by flutes, drums, and cymbals—associated variously with altered mental states, gender variance and homoeroticism[1590]—a chorus of men dressed as satyrs, half-man and half-goat, chanted the dithyramb in unison as the dancing celebrants tossed their heads in a violent, whirling motion, entering a state of ecstatic frenzy. "The pandemonium in which Dionysus himself, and his divine entourage make their entry—that pandemonium which the human horde, struck by his spirit, unleashes—is a genuine symbol of religious ecstasy."[1591]

Dionysus was an ecstatic god of paradox, often portrayed as effeminate: *ο μαινολας Διονυσος και γυναικεια περιβεβλημενος*: "the raving Dionysus and his womanly attire..."[1592] yet whose symbols included the *φαλλος* (phallos), a likeness of the erect penis, a symbol of the generative power of nature, and the *θυρσος* (thursos), the Bacchic wand wreathed with ivy with a pine cone at the tip. "The priest in female clothes is typical of

---

[1588] John 15:1.

[1589] Dodds, *The Greeks and the Irrational*, 94.

[1590] Conner, *Blossom of Bone*, 114-122.

Deissmann quotes from a letter written in Greek during the 3rd century BCE: "And send us also Zenobius the effeminate, with tabret, and cymbals, and rattles." *Light from the Ancient East*, 164.

[1591] Otto, *Dionysus: Myth and Cult*, 92.

[1592] Origen, *Contra Celsum* III, 23.

trance religion...in eastern shamanism the male shaman also cross-dresses as a sign of his separateness from normal life."[1593] The *wand* or *staff*—*ραβδος* (rhabdos)—is a very old magical tool,[1594] well attested in both the Greek magical papyri and in the Greek translation of the Hebrew Old Testament, where, in the story of the confrontation between Aaron and Moses and the magicians of Egypt, Aaron is told: *λαβε την ραβδον και ριψον επι την γην εναντιον Φαραω*: "take your staff and cast it on the ground before Pharoah."[1595] The magical papyri allow Jesus the use of a magical staff or wand,[1596] as does Revelation where Jesus will "herd all the nations with a staff of iron"—*εν ραβδω σιδηρα*.[1597] The iron staff—*κατεχων ραβδον σιδηραν*, "who possess an iron staff"—is both a symbol of authority and a likely phallic reference in an erotomagical spell addressed to the god Min.[1598]

The mystery cults incorporated three fundamental types of observances: (1) *invocations*—the *λεγομενα* (legomena), or "things said," (2) *performances*—the *δρωμενα* (drōmena) or "things enacted," and (3) the *δεικνυμενα* (deiknumena) or "things shown." The New Testament contains several sacred formulas—known in the mystery cults as *συμβολα* (sumbola)—confessions of faith called "Christ hymns," as well as cultic invocations to which some verbal response was probably expected:

> For everything that is brought to light is light. Therefore it is said, "Awake, O sleeper, and rise from the dead and the Christ will shine upon you!"[1599]

1593 Jones & Pennick, *A History of Pagan Europe*, 118

1594 See particularly the wands in the Egyptian collection of The Metropolitan Museum of Art illustrated in Brier's *Ancient Egyptian Magic*, 49.

1595 Exodus 7:9, *Septuagint*.

1596 Daniel & Maltomini, *Supplementum Magicum* I, 32.

1597 Revelation 12:5.

1598 Preisendanz, *Papyri Graecae Magicae* XXXVI, 109.

1599 Ephesians 5:14.

Clement of Alexandria

Titus Flavius Clemens, known as Clement of Alexandria (died circa 215 CE), was almost certainly initiated into one or more of the mystery cults before converting to Christianity.[1600] Clement attempted a synthesis of Christian theology with pagan philosophy—a subject of his *Exhortation to the Greeks*—and revealed how easily Christian doctrine could be expounded in the imagery of the pagan mysteries, as well as how closely magic and mystery cults must have intertwined:

> Let us sweep away then, sweep away forgetfulness of the truth, the ignorance and the darkness, the obstacle that like *a mist* (*αχλυς*)[1601] slips down over our sight. *Let us see a vision* (*εποπτευσωμεν*)[1602] of what is really and truly divine, first of all singing out to Him this cry, *Welcome, Light! Light for us from heaven* (*χαιρε φως φως ημιν εξ ουρανου*)! For us who lie buried in darkness and have been wrapped up in the shadow of death!

[1600] "Christian writers converted from paganism may, of course, have been initiated in their youth and on this ground the evidence of Arnobius and Clemens is a priori superior..." Farnell, *The Cults of the Greek States*, II, 128.

[1601] *αχλυς*, *mist*, or if the reference is to Homer—for Clement was well read—the *film* that forms on the eyes of the dying.

The term had a magical and specifically theurgic connotation in Neoplatonic thought. See Derek Collins, *Magic in the Ancient Greek World*, 128.

Athene removes "the mist" (*την αχλυν*) that dulls men's eyes. (Philostratus, *The Life of Apollonius of Tyana*, VII, 32).

[1602] *εποπτευσωμεν*: "let us see a vision," from *εποπτευω*, *to be admitted* into the highest grade of the mysteries, to become an epopthV, one who has achieved the final grade of the mysteries and seen all that is to be revealed. Similar terminology is used in 2 Peter 1:16.

If, on the one hand, those who have trusted in the sorcerers (Ειθ' οι μεν τοις γοησι πεπιστευκοτες) *receive amulets and enchantments* (τα περιαπτα και τας επαοιδας...αποδεχονται) merely purported to bring deliverance, do you not rather resolve to put on the heavenly [amulet], the Word that saves, and *trusting in the enchantment of God* (τη επωδη του θεου πιστευσαντες), be delivered from passions...[1603]

O the truly holy mysteries (Ω των αγιων ως αληθως μυστηριων)! O pure light! Being enlightened (δαδουχουμαι), I am initiated into the highest mysteries of the heavens and of God (τους ουρανους και τον θεον εποπτευσαι)! I become holy by being initiated (αγιος γινομαι μυουμενος)!

The Lord reveals the mysteries (ιεροφαντει δε ο κυριος) and places his seal upon the initiate when he has believed, and lighting his way, conducts him to the Father, where he is protected for all ages...

These are my mysteries, my Bacchic revelries (ταυτα των εμων μυστηριων τα βακχευματα)! If you desire, be initiated yourself and *you will dance with angels around* (και χορευσεις μετ' αγγελων) the unbegotten and undying and only true God *as the Word of God chants along with us* (συνυμνουντος ημιν του θεου λογου).[1604]

[1603] Johnston: "In accord with theurgy's Platonizing tendencies, these demons were interpreted by the theurgists as the inflictors of corporeal passions that would lure the soul away from its proper pursuits..." *Restless Dead: Encounters Between the Living and the Dead in Ancient Greece*, 137.

[1604] *Clement of Alexandria*: *The Exhortation to the Greeks*, XI, XII. I have used the Greek text of the Loeb edition (242, 244-246, 256), but unless otherwise noted, all translations of Greek sources are my own.

Clement's terminology borrows deeply and promiscuously from the vocabulary of the mysteries,[1605] touching at every point upon the terms and metaphors of the mystery religions. Clement quite ingenuously refers to the heavenly Christ as an *amulet* and salvation as an *enchantment*, describing his Christian faith in the terms of a mystery celebration. His imagery of dancing with the angels deliberately recalls ecstatic rites. MacMullen describes the difficulty the church faced in banning dancing from ritual: "Ambrose of Milan…witnessed his congregation dancing during times of worship. (He seems to mean right inside the churches, but he does not supply details.) He was shocked. Such conduct was pagan."[1606] "You will dance with angels"—*χορευσεις μετ' αγγελων*—uses the nearly technical term *χορευω*, *to dance a round dance* or *choral dance*, "esp[ecially] of the Bacchic chorus or dance."[1607] Clement is Jesus' *χορευστης* (choreustēs), his *ecstatic follower*, and Jesus' mysteries are Clement's Bacchic revelries.

Even Clement's invocation, "Welcome, Light!"—*Χαιρε φως*—duplicates examples known from spells in both Coptic and Greek. "*Hail, Dispenser of fire* (Χαιρε πυρος ταμια)…"[1608] "*Welcome, lord* (Κυριε *χαιρε*), you by whom favor is granted…"[1609] **ⲭⲁⲓⲣⲉ ⲫⲛⲟⲩⲑⲓ ⲁⲃⲣⲁⲁⲙ**, "Hail, God of Abraham…"[1610] A spell for revelation addressed to Apollo addresses him as *πολυφωτιστης*, *all-illuminating*.[1611]

[1605] For an analysis of similar mystery cult language in Clement's *Stromateis*, see Deutsch, "Visions, Mysteries, and the Interpretive Task: Text Work and Religious Experience in Philo and Clement," *Experientia*, I, 83, ff.

[1606] MacMullen, *Christianizing the Roman Empire*, 74.

[1607] Liddell & Scott, *A Greek-English Lexicon*, 1734.

[1608] Preisendanz, *Papyri Graecae Magicae* II, 88.

[1609] Ibid, XII, 183.

[1610] Ibid, IV, 1232.

[1611] Ibid, II, 121.

Mixed with terms from the ecstatic Dionysion cult are terms from the mysteries of Demeter and Kore at Eleusis. The Lord "reveals the mysteries"—*ιεροφαντει δε ο κυριος*—becoming the *hierophant*, the official who reveals the symbols to initiates. Clement is enlightened (*δαδουχουμαι*), a reference to the *δαδουχος*, the *torch bearer*, another feature of the Eleusinian mystery cult. Correspondingly, the spirit invoked by Paul is "a spirit of wisdom and of revelation" (*πνευμα σοφιας και αποκαλυψεως*).[1612] Like the revelations of the mystery cults, the Christian mysteries "are delivered through speech," the *unspeakable* (*τα απορρητα*) mysteries remaining unwritten and undescribed.[1613]

That Clement could speak of Christ in frankly magical terms reflected contemporary Christian thought: "An amulet intended to provide protection against illness and the power of evil" preserves this wording: "for the seal of Jesus Christ is written upon my forehead..."[1614] During Clement's life, it is probable that the Christian movement in Alexandria consisted of "a number of esoteric groups"[1615] in which *gnosis* or divinely revealed knowledge led eventually to perfection.

Although Clement, the head of the catechetical school in Alexandria, was no minor figure, during the 16th century his feast day, December 4th, was dropped from the calendar after his writings came to be viewed as doctrinally tainted, an event which reflected the tendency of the Catholic Counter-Reformation to distance itself from anything that emitted the slightest whiff of heresy or magic. As indicated by the brief excerpts of Clement given above, the forces of Catholic orthodoxy may have been on to something. Clement's writings seem clearly to

---

[1612] Ephesians 1:17.

[1613] DeConick, *Mystery and Secrecy in the Nag Hammadi Collection and Other Ancient Literature*, 12.

[1614] Meyer, *Ancient Christian Magic: Coptic Texts of Ritual Power*, 113, 115.

[1615] Klijn, "Jewish Christianity in Egypt" in *The Roots of Egyptian Christianity*, 173.

reflect an age in which the line between Christian teaching and mystery cult was fuzzy, at the very least so as far as Clement was concerned. It is, however, richly ironic that Clement, one of the earliest Christian apologists, should later be declared heretical by the very religion he sought to defend.

Christianity bears additional striking similarities to both the language and theory of the mystery religions. Betz: "Expansion of mystery cult terms and ideas is evidenced also by the early Christian literature. Paul frequently employs *μυστηριον* (mystery) as a term designating the revelation of the transcendental realities of the divine world and of wisdom, prophecy, history, the after-life and, by implication, the sacraments of baptism and the eucharist as well. Ephesians extends the usage, calling the Gospel itself *μυστηριον* (mystery), something Paul himself did not do. The *agape* relationship between the heavenly Christ and his church on earth is called *το μυστηριον μεγα* (the great mystery). In all probability, Ephesians received this language from Colossians, which more closely reflects Paul's usage. 1 Timothy (3:9, 16) speaks of *το μυστηριον της πιστεως* (the mystery of faith) and *το της ευσεβιας μυστηριον* (the mystery of religion)."[1616] Paul, one of the "assistants of Christ and stewards of the mysteries of God,"[1617] often employs such language: "We speak wisdom among the initiated (*εν τοις τελειοις*)...the wisdom of God in a mystery that has been hidden away..."[1618]

Samuel Angus:

> Common to the Mysteries and Gnosticism were certain ideas, such as pantheistic mysticism, magic practices, elaborate cosmogonies and theogonies, rebirth, union with God, revelation from above, dualistic views, the importance attaching to names and attributes of the

[1616] Betz, *Magika Hiera*, 251.
[1617] 1 Corinthians 4:1.
[1618] 1 Corinthians 2:6.

> deity, and the same aim at personal salvation. As Gnosticism took possession of the field East and West, the Mysteries assumed an increasingly Gnostic character. The dividing line is sometimes difficult to determine.[1619]

Christian metaphors such as rebirth,[1620] being a new creation,[1621] the importance attaching to the name of Christ[1622] and claims of special revelation—including being snatched away to heaven[1623] —are common knowledge and certainly need no reiteration here. "Every serious mystes [initiate into a mystery cult, *my note*] approached the solemn sacrament of Initiation believing that he thereby became 'twice born,' a 'new creature,' and passed in a real sense from death unto life by being brought into a mysterious intimacy with the deity."[1624]

By the end of the first century, the apocalyptic belief of the first generation began to fade into a harsh austerity that would soon lead to an ascetic condemnation of the world, a state of mind predicted by Paul's declaration: "May I never brag except about the cross of our Lord Jesus Christ through which the world has been crucified to me, and I to the world."[1625] Hand in hand with that retreat from the early apocalyptic expectation, the initial charismatic ebullience becomes muted, and the Christian mystical experience is increasingly described in the terms of the mystery cult: "For it was not by following cleverly contrived tales that we revealed the power and the presence of our Lord Jesus Christ to you, but by *becoming witnesses* (εποπται γενηθεντες) of that majesty."[1626]

[1619] Angus, *The Mystery Religions*, 54.
[1620] As at John 3:3.
[1621] 2 Corinthians 5:17, Galatians 6:15.
[1622] For example Ephesians 1:20-21, Philippians 2:9.
[1623] Galatians 1:11-12, for example.
[1624] Angus, *The Mystery Religions*, 95-96.
[1625] Galatians 6:15.
[1626] 2 Peter 1:16.

The word I have translated *witness* in this passage, *εποπτης* (epoptēs), is a technical term borrowed from the vocabulary of the mystery cults. It refers specifically to "those who have been initiated into the highest grade of the mysteries."[1627] Pagan writers described from three to five stages in the initiatory process; the final one was the *εποπτεια* (epopteia), the *ecstatic vision*. The "majesty" to which the writer refers is to the transfiguration of Jesus, of which Mark says, *και μεταμορφωθη εμπροσθεν αυτων*, "and *he was transformed before them.*"[1628] In Mark's version, Jesus' clothing becomes dazzlingly white, Moses and Elijah appear, and a voice from a cloud identifies Jesus as the beloved Son of God. Matthew's account characterizes the transformation as "the vision"[1629] and drops the verb—from which *metamorphosis* is derived—possibly because of its association with the shape shifting of the pagan gods. In fact, the true vision of the new sect was near to fruition, nearer indeed than anyone living in the 1st century could have guessed. Within the space of a few centuries the majesty of Christ would supplant the majesty of Rome itself.

1627 Angus, *The Mystery Religions*, 77.
1628 Mark 9:2.
1629 Matthew 17:9.

CHAPTER 11: SPIRIT VERSUS SPIRIT

The book of Acts records several encounters between Christian missionaries and pagan miracle workers, and it comes as no surprise that the accounts demonstrate the superiority of the power of the apostles over the powers of their pagan contemporaries—pagan accounts of Christian miracle working were equally dismissive. The stories preserve much interesting information about the role of magic in primitive Christianity, and it is to an examination of them that we turn next.

In Acts we encounter a ploy that would be used to great effect by Christians against pagan opponents and even other Christians: the accusation of magic. Klauck: "When systems competed against each other, this accusation regularly provided a handy instrument: one party would accuse the other of black magic, hurling its entire available arsenal of abuse and polemics. As for one's own group, it practiced magic of the older, unreservedly positive kind—unless one preferred a priori to avoid the risk of even the remotest connection between one's own side and the concept of magic."[1630]

The distinction was particularly essential to Christians who "either made or presupposed one central, crucial point: that magic is the work of demons, while miracles are the work of God. What this amounted to, of course, was the claim that the Christian God is true and the pagan gods are false…unlike the pagans and the Jews, Christians had no ethnic cohesion, and they asserted their group identity not only by using mysterious rituals (like the mystery religions) but also by emphasizing strongly the distinctiveness of their God and their teachings about him…for them it was first of all a truth and secondly the

---

[1630] Klauck, *Magic and Paganism in Early Christianity*, 17.

sole basis for their existence as a group."[1631] "The argument is simply: God works miracles, demons work magic...Magic may look the same but (because it is done by devils) it cannot possibly be the same. The only conclusion is that it is deceptive. The similarity is a fraud."[1632] The ploy of charging opponents with practicing magic, a tactic still in use by Christian fundamentalists, "was used to undermine the ancient and venerated cults of Greece and Rome...[and] functioned to marginalize and alienate other Christians who followed teachings or practices that certain writers rejected."[1633] In short, the charge of practicing magic appears early in the Christian arsenal of anti-Jewish and anti-pagan polemic and becomes routine in the centuries that follow as Christian sects battle each other for control. "The opponents of Jesus who witnessed his marvelous *δυναμεις* ascribed them to the influence of Satan (cf. the attitude of the Christians themselves regarding Simon Magus)."[1634]

Differentiating between miracle and magic in the New Testament is everywhere a matter of perspective. Miracles "are open to misunderstanding, and can even turn against the author; the apostolic word must then control their interpretation...What separates the magus from the gospel is neither the belief in supernatural powers, nor a charismatic performance, but the positioning of the human being before God."[1635] "Luke insults [Bar-Jesus] by describing him as a magician, because he sees his Christian preachers confronted with a situation of acute competition. There existed a wide spectrum of religious 'special offers,' often with a whiff of the exotic. The external appearance of the itinerant Christian missionaries was very similar to the 'men of God' of every shade who wandered from place to place, and

---

[1631] Kieckhefer, *Magic in the Middle Ages*, 35-36.
[1632] Hull, *Hellenistic Magic and the Synoptic Tradition*, 61.
[1633] Stratton, *Naming the Witch*, 107.
[1634] Eitrem, *Some Notes on the Demonology in the New Testament*, 4.
[1635] Marguerat, *Magic in the Biblical World*, 100, 120.

they risked being evaluated against this background and absorbed into this spectrum."[1636]

Simon Peter versus Simon Magus.

> Now those who had been scattered went through the region spreading the word. Phillip went down to the city of Samaria and preached Christ to them. Everyone in the crowd was paying close attention to the things Phillip said; while listening to him they also saw the signs he performed. Unclean spirits, screaming with a loud voice, were cast out of many of the possessed, and many who were paralyzed and crippled were being healed. There was great joy in that city.
>
> A certain man by the name of Simon, claiming to be someone great, had formerly practiced magic[1637] in the city and had amazed the people of Samaria. Everyone followed him eagerly, from the least to the greatest, saying, "This man is the Power of God, the Power called Great!" They followed him for quite some time because he had amazed them with his magical feats.[1638] But when they believed Phillip, who was preaching about the kingdom of God and the name of Jesus Christ, baptizing men and women, Simon himself believed and was baptized. He followed Phillip around constantly, astonished as he watched the signs and great miracles that occurred.

[1636] Klauck, *Magic and Paganism in Early Christianity: The World of the Acts of the Apostles*, 51-52.

[1637] *μαγευω* (mageuō), *to practice magic*, the only occurrence of this verb in the New Testament.

[1638] *μαγεια* (mageia), *magical art*, the only occurrence of this noun in the New Testament.

Samaria's connection with magic leads the Jews to accuse Jesus of being a Samaritan (John 8:48).

> When the apostles in Jerusalem heard that Samaria had embraced the word of God, they sent Peter and John to them. They went down and prayed for them so that they might receive the holy spirit because up to that point it had not fallen upon any of them. They had only been baptized in the name of the Lord Jesus.
>
> Then they laid their hands on them and they received the holy spirit. When Simon saw that the spirit was given by the application of the apostles' hands, he offered them money, saying, "Give me this power too so that anyone on whom I lay my hands may receive the holy spirit."
>
> But Peter said to him, "To hell with you and your silver! You intended to buy the gift of God with money! There is no part or share for you in this proclamation, for your heart is not upright before God. So repent of this wickedness of yours and pray to the Lord that you may be forgiven the intention of your heart, for I see in you the gall of bitterness and the shackle of unrighteousness!"
>
> Simon answered, "You must pray for me to the Lord so that nothing you have said may befall me!"[1639]

The "laying on of the hands," (*επιθεσις των χειρων*) was a technique of passing the spirit from believer to believer.[1640] This is a set phrase in the Christian vocabulary, pointing to an early ritual that probably went back to the person of Jesus. Of the application of hands in Egyptian magic, Pinch notes, "The gesture of laying a hand on the patient is sometimes linked with sealing. One spell to safeguard a child promises, 'My hand is on you, my seal is your protection.' In another spell, the goddess Hathor is described as laying her hand on a woman suffering in childbirth. Ivory rods ending in hands represented the divine hand and were part of a magician's equipment. A figure wearing an ani-

[1639] Acts 8:4-24.

[1640] 1 Timothy 4:14, 2 Timothy 1:6, Hebrews 6:2.

mal or Bes mask seems to be holding such a hand rod in a relief dating to the twenty-fourth century BC."[1641]

The story of Simon—who will be known henceforth to history as Simon Magus—is the origin of *simony*, the purchase of church offices. Although Acts does not tell us what became of Simon, the church fathers lost no time creating a substantial legend around him and his heresies, and his memory is excoriated in the *Acts of Saint Peter*, as well as by Justin Martyr, Irenaeus, Epiphanius, Hippolytus, and Pseudo-Clement.

Simon's offer of money was probably customary in his circles. If magical power is a commodity, then payment for it was quite naturally in order: "The power can be passed from one person to another. It is not a moral quality nor a learned skill but an acquisition, a property which can be conveyed either with the will of the donor, as in Luke 9.1, or without it, as in 8.46."[1642] And it was precisely the value-free nature of magical power that posed a critical problem for Christianity: "an objective consideration will note a suspicious similarity between the public appearance and working of Philip and of Simon; it is to some extent a question of interpretation, whether a successful healing is attributed to a miracle or to sorcery…most religious phenolmena were ambiguous and required interpretation. Without interpretation, the phenomena have no value; this is what makes it so difficult to distinguish the working of miracles from magical activity."[1643] There are wonder workers of every stripe in the Hellenistic world, the circumstance that motivates the temple rulers to ask, "By what power or *by what name* did you do this?" to which Peter replies, "in the name of Jesus Christ of Nazareth."[1644] There are obviously *other* effective names.

[1641] Pinch, *Magic in Ancient Egypt*, 84.
[1642] Hull, *Hellenistic Magic and the Synoptic Tradition*, 107.
[1643] Ibid, 18-19.
[1644] Acts 4:7-10.

As will be seen in the case of Paul, apostles tended to become shrill when their authority was challenged, but Peter's response to Simon's offer borders on hysteria. The apostolic diatribe contains what may be a single telling point: "There is no part or share for you in this proclamation," literally "in this word," i.e., "the word of God" the Samaritans had embraced. Simon had attached himself to Phillip, been baptized as a Christian convert, and in all likelihood had begun to preach the word himself, to spread "the word." Simon, who had formerly amazed the Samaritans with his "magical feats," now sought to perform "signs and great miracles" in the name of Jesus. That was too much for Peter. A turf war promptly ensued.

The point of the story is not as much Simon's magic as it is Peter's apostolic authority. Luke-Acts, written relatively late in the first century, long after Peter's death, reveals yet another step in the evolution of the Christian movement: the filling of an administrative vacuum. Jesus, who believed he was living on the very cusp of history, made no provision for the continuity of administrative authority. "The twelve are the bearers of personal continuity, guaranteeing and handing on to future generations everything that had happened from the baptism of Jesus until his apparitions after Easter. In this special function, they are irreplaceable..."[1645] At first this lack of continuity posed no problem; the early Christians expected the quick return of the Lord and set about preparing themselves for it. But the Lord did not return. The Jews grew weary of Christians proselytizing in their synagogues and kicked them out, while Gentiles began to join the movement in real numbers. Who now had the authority to decide what constituted true Christian practice? Who would determine the doctrinal content of the new religion? In the stories of magicians recounted in Acts we are witnessing the emergence of a new Christian pecking order, the establishment of apostolic authority as the beginning of a continuous chain of

---

[1645] Hull, *Magic and Paganism*, 7.

command that culminates in the creation of a line of bishops that starts with the apostles.

Paul versus Bar-Jesus.

> When they had gone through the whole island as far as Paphos, *they encountered a certain man, a magician, a false prophet* (ευρον ανδρα τινα μαγον ψευδοπροφητην), the Jew named Bar-Jesus, who was with the proconsul Sergius Paulus, a man of discernment, who summoned Barnabas and Saul because he wanted to hear the word of God. But Elymas[1646] *the magician* (ο μαγος)—for that is how his name is translated—resisted them, trying to turn the proconsul away from the faith.
>
> But Saul, also known as Paul, filled with the holy spirit, stared at him intensely and said, "O you who are full of every treachery and every kind of fraud, son of the Devil, enemy of all righteousness, will you not stop making crooked the straight paths of the Lord? Now look! The hand of the Lord is upon you and you will be blind, not seeing the sun for a time."
>
> Immediately *mist* (αχλυς)[1647] and darkness fell on him and he wandered around searching for someone to lead him by the hand. When the proconsul saw what had happened, he believed, having been overwhelmed by the teaching of the Lord.[1648]

The "false prophet" Bar-Jesus was only the beginning of the problem for the early church which is also plagued by false bro-

---

[1646] Probably derived from Aramaic *haloma*, an interpreter of dreams. (Labahn, *A Kind of Magic: Understanding Magic in the New Testament and its Religious Environment*, 106.)

[1647] For the magical use of αχλυς (mist), see page 335, footnote 1601.

[1648] Acts 13:6-12.

thers,[1649] false teachers,[1650] false apostles,[1651] and even false Christs.[1652] Strelan observes that "false prophets" arise from the *Christian* ranks,[1653] as do the "false brothers."[1654] "The narrator wants it understood that the charismatic power of miracle is in danger of being hijacked, as much as those who covet this force from the outside, as by the followers of Jesus."[1655] Paul addresses Bar-Jesus—which means "Son of Jesus"—as a "son of the Devil" and pronounces a classic slander spell against him, a *διαβολη* (diabolē), "a spell that ascribes unholy actions to an opponent,"[1656] causing the offended divinity to avenge itself: Bar-Jesus is struck temporarily blind even as was Paul himself for his opposition to Jesus. Paul's pronouncement, *χειρ κυριου επι σε*: "the hand of the Lord is upon you"—like the "finger of God," (Luke 11:20)—is a magical curse.

As Strelan points out, Sergius Paulus "wanted to hear the word of God," and it is over the interpretation of the "word" that Paul and Bar-Jesus are fighting. Neither Simon nor Bar-Jesus can lay claim to "the word." They are outside the prophetic circle that—as Luke is eager to show us—consists only of the apostles and their immediate associates. The conflict in sight in this passage is over true versus false representations of Christianity. Bar-Jesus, as his name strongly implies, is within or at the margins of the "Jesus community," and Paul accuses him not of denying Jesus, but of "making crooked the straight paths of the Lord," i.e., of *twisting* the gospel. As Brown remarks of Roman

---

[1649] Galatians 2:4.
[1650] 2 Peter 2:1.
[1651] 2 Corinthians 11:13.
[1652] Mark 13:22.
[1653] Matthew 7:15, 24:11, 24, 2 Peter 2:1, 1 John 4:1.
[1654] Strelan, *Biblica* 85: 65-87.
For "false brothers" see 2 Corinthians 11:26, Galatians 2:4. For Christian "false prophets," see Matthew 7:15, 24:11, 24, 2 Peter 2:1, 1 John 4:1.
[1655] Klutz, *Magic in the Biblical World*, 122-123.
[1656] Graf, *Magika Hiera*, 196.

political infighting, "resentments and anomalous power on the edge of the court could be isolated only by the more intimate allegation—sorcery."[1657] An accusation of magical practice as a tool for political advantage was already a standard rhetorical device.

That Jewish magicians like Bar-Jesus often attended Roman officials is nearly certain: "It is of some significance that the author of Acts can take it for granted that his readers will not have been puzzled by the presence of a Jewish magician and seer in the entourage of a high Roman official. That suggests that Jewish magicians and magicians who were part of the court of Roman administrators were in their eyes familiar figures."[1658] All the more reason for the Jewish missionaries of Christ to differentiate themselves.

Luke hastens to add that the *teaching* of Paul astonishes Sergius Paulus lest we assume that it is Paul's power alone that has "overwhelmed" him. However, it is "primarily as a miracle worker" that Jesus attracts attention, and his disciples' success "arose from their deeds, above all, in healing."[1659] It is noteworthy that we have again encountered the term *teaching* as a Christian code word for *magic*, and as pointed out previously, *astonishment* is the expected reaction to *magic*, not teaching. Jesus' amazing "teaching"—"they were amazed by his teaching" (εξεπλησσοντο επι τη διδαχη αυτου)—involves *exorcism*, not religious instruction previously unheard of by Jews: "and *they were all amazed* (εθαμβηθησαν απαντες)…'What is this? *A new teaching with authority* (διδαχη καινη κατ' εξουσιαν)! He commands the unclean spirits and they obey him!'"[1660] One can only conclude that specialists who interpret the account in Mark to

[1657] Brown, *Religion and Society in the Age of Saint Augustine*, 125.
[1658] Dickie, *Magic and Magicians in the Greco-Roman World*, 223.
[1659] MacMullen, *Christianizing the Roman Empire*, 22.
[1660] Mark 1:21-28.

mean that Jesus did not need to quote rabbinic authorities to support his "teaching" are simply unable to read.

The purpose of the book of Acts—the Acts of the *Apostles*—is to establish the myth of apostolic authority in the face of competing gospels. The proclamation of the true gospel belongs to the inner circle and to them alone. Henceforth the conflict between Christian sects will be characterized as a front in the universal war between the Lord and his agents of light and Satan and his army of darkness:

> Each side is represented visibly on earth by a set of human lieutenants. To the prophets correspond the false prophets, to the apostles, false apostles, to the Christ, the Antichrist. And as God empowers his "saints" to accomplish miracles that authorize their mission, Satan and his underlings enable their fiends to perform powerful works that are, or so they would seem, equivalent. These "sons of the devil" who perform such marvels are magicians.[1661]

In re: Paul and Silas.

> It so happened that as we were going to the place of prayer a certain servant girl *who had a spirit of divination* (*εχουσαν πνευμα πυθωνα*) met us. She used to turn a tremendous profit for her masters by making predictions. She kept tagging along after Paul and the rest of them,

---

[1661] My translation of: "Chaque parti est représenté visiblement sur terre par une série d'hommes-lieutenants. Aux prophètes respondent de faux prophètes, aux apôtres, de faux apôtres, au Christ l'Antéchrist. Et comme Dieu donne à ses 'saints' d'accomplir des miracles accréditant leur mission, Satan et ses satellites donnent à leurs suppôts de faire des prodiges qui sont, ou du moins paraissent, equivalents. Ces 'fils du diable' qui opèrent des merveilles sont les magiciens." *Ephemerides Theologicae Lovanienses* 15: 455.

> saying, "These men who are proclaiming a way of salvation to you are servants of the Highest God!"
>
> She went on doing this for many days. Finally at the end of his patience, Paul turned and said to the spirit, "I command you in the name of Jesus Christ to come out of her!" It came out of her that very hour. When her masters saw that their hope of profit had fled them, they seized Paul and Silas and hauled them to the marketplace to appear before the authorities.[1662]

The girl who follows Paul and Barnabas has "a spirit of divination"—*πνευμα πυθωνα*, "a spirit of the python." This curi-ous terminology derives from the myth of Apollo, the god of prophecy, who slew the dragon Python that lived in the caves of Delphi at the foot of Mount Parnassus. As a mark of his victory over the serpent, Apollo appointed a priestess, the Pythia, or "Pythoness," who spoke oracles when she was possessed by the spirit of the god, the Pythonic spirit or spirit of divination—*πυθοληπτος* (putholēptos), *seized by the python*, like the *επιληπτος* (epilēptos), *seized*, like the young prophet (2 Kings 9:11).

The Delphic oracle, which spoke continuously through its priestess for at least 2000 years, thus became synonymous with female mediums of a type known as an *εγγαστριμυθος* (engastrimuthos), or "belly talker." Such mediums, like the priestess of Apollo and the slave girl who tailed after Paul, were typically women "with little education or experience of the world,"[1663] and their presence in the ancient world is well attested. There were male "pythons" as well, but regardless of sex, possession was held to occur most readily in the "young and somewhat simple."[1664] Iamblichus described such seers as *ευηθικος* (euēthikos), *good-hearted*, or speaking bluntly, *simpletons*. Of such per-

---

[1662] Acts 16:16-19.

[1663] Dodds, *The Greeks and the Irrational*, 72.

[1664] Lane Fox, *Pagans and Christians*, 208.

sons he remarks, "In this way, through those utterly deprived of knowledge, [the god] reveals understanding that surpasses all knowledge."[1665] This description is in substantial agreement with the Christian understanding of divine revelation: to the rational mind it is folly and foolishness.[1666]

By far the most famous biblical medium is the witch of Endor. Misidentified in the *Septuagint* as an *engastrimuthos*, she is more correctly an evocator, or "soul-drawer"—a ψυχαγωγος (psuchagōgos)[1667]—as the account shows:

> When Saul saw the army of the Philistines, he was afraid and his heart trembled greatly. When Saul inquired of the Lord, the Lord did not answer him, not by dreams, or by Urim, or by prophets. Then Saul said to his servants, "Seek out for me a woman who is a medium, so that I may go to her." His servants said to him, "Behold, there is a medium at Endor."
>
> So Saul disguised himself and put on other garments and went, he and two men with him; and they came to the woman by night. And he said, "Divine for me by a spirit, and bring up for me whomever I shall name for you." The woman said to him, "Surely you know what Saul has done, how he has cut off the mediums and wizards from the land. Why then are you laying a snare for my life to bring about my death?" But Saul swore to her by the Lord, "As the Lord lives, no punishment will come upon you for this thing." Then the woman said, "Whom shall I bring up for you?" He said, "Bring up Samuel for me." When the woman saw Samuel, she cri-

[1665] *Iamblichus*: *De mysteriis*, 162-165.

[1666] 1 Corinthians 1:18-25.

[1667] "the word ψυχαγωγειν [to lead up souls, *my note*]...was first used for the magic ritual summoning of the dead...But the word came to be used for poetry, and particularly for tragedy, which possesses and beguiles the listener's soul..." (de Romilly, *Magic and Rhetoric in Ancient Greece*, 15).

> ed out with a loud voice; and the woman said to Saul, "Why have you deceived me? You are Saul!" The king said to her, "Have no fear; what do you see?" The woman said to Saul, "I see a god coming up out of the earth." He said to her, "What is his appearance?" She said, "An old man is coming up; and he is wrapped in a robe." And Saul knew that it was Samuel, and he bowed with his face to the ground, and did obeisance.
>
> Then Samuel said to Saul, "Why have you disturbed me by bringing me up?" Saul answered, "I am in great distress, for the Philistines are warring against me, and God has turned away from me and answers me no more, either by prophets or by dreams; therefore I have summoned you to tell me what I shall do."[1668]

Although we know of the evocation of ghosts by female mediums, it is not possible to tell what was thought to have possessed the girl who followed Paul. In any case Paul makes it clear that the 'proclamation of a way of salvation' will not be shared with disembodied entities, whatever their nature. The spirits of the prophets are subject to the prophets, as are also demonic spirits —not even an angel from heaven can contradict the apostolic gospel.[1669] "...humans who manifest objectionable traits and behaviour may now be *expected* to have demonic helpers..."[1670]

The account of the servant girl again raises the issue of the role of women in magical practice, a point previously touched upon in the discussion of the angelic Watchers of *1 Enoch*. There is a clear tendency to regard black magic as preeminently the work of women. "The prime model for witchcraft is the female practitioner in Exodus 22:18. In other instances the charge of witchcraft is combined with charges of prostitution and illicit sex-

---

1668 1 Samuel 28:5-15.

1669 1 Corinthians 14:32; Galatians 1:8.

1670 Flint, *Witchcraft and Magic in Europe: Ancient Greece and Rome*, 298.

uality. Prophetic texts associate harlotry and magical charms (Nah. 3:4) while historical texts denounce women as harlots who engage in sorcery (Jezebel in 2 Kings 9:22)."[1671] In addition to the Old Testament account of the ghost mistress of Endor, female necromancers are also known in Egyptian magic: "A few personal letters from the late second millennium BC preserve references to women who were called *rekhet*—'knowing one.' These wise women were consulted as seers who could get in touch with the dead."[1672] Daniel Ogden also notes the "tendency to associate a specialization in necromancy with aliens—Persians, Babylonians, and Egyptians—and with women or witches," a tendency which may reflect "cultural distancing."[1673]

Paul acknowledges that he and his fellow missionaries were treated "as deceivers"—*ως πλανοι*—a word already noted to carry the added meaning of "magician." Although Paul says little to illuminate the meaning of *πλανος* in this context, the charges brought against him by the Roman slaveholders following the exorcism of their young medium are suggestive: "These men, being Jews, are creating a disturbance in our city and *they advocate rites* (*καταγγελλουσιν εθη*) that are not lawful for us as Romans either to view with approval or to perform."[1674] As the context of the accusation makes clear, the rite peculiar to Jews in question is *exorcism*, a form of magical practice that is being distinguished from Roman rites that are legal. "The customs (*εθος*) that Paul is thus accused of promoting are economically disruptive magical practices, which as the two slave-owners correctly point out are illegal for Romans to practice in any way, shape, or form."[1675] "In practical terms magic only became magic when someone was accused of it...Why would Paul and Silas have been labeled as magicians? Their actions had resulted in harm to

---

[1671] Janowitz, *Magic in the Roman World*, 87.

[1672] Pinch, *Magic in Ancient Egypt*, 56.

[1673] Ogden, *Greek and Roman Necromancy*, 95.

[1674] Acts 16:20-21.

[1675] Reimer, *Miracle and Magic: A Study in the Acts of the Apostles and the Life of Apollonius of Tyana*, 217.

the slave-girl's owners, namely, property damage (to their slave) and the loss of their means of livelihood...the Jews were perceived to be magicians by many Romans, and exorcism was probably the main type of magic associated with Jews in this period."[1676]

Peter's magical shadow.

It is well known that magicians of antiquity sought to acquire spirit helpers. These magical assistants are given various names in ancient spell books, including "god," "angel," and "daemon," but the most common name for the assistant is *paredros* (παρεδρος), a word that moved unchanged from Greek into Latin as a technical term.[1677] The Greek magical papyri include this spell for acquiring a παρεδρος called "the shadow."

> Offering: wheat meal and ripe mulberries and [unsoftened][1678] sesame and uncooked *thrion*[1679], toss into that a beet. You will create *your own shadow* (της ιδιας σκιας) so that it will be your servant. Go at the sixth hour of

[1676] De Vos, *Journal for the Study of the New Testament* 74: 51,57,60.

[1677] See particularly Leda Jean Ciraolo's "Supernatural Assistants in the Greek Magical Papyri" in *Ancient Magic and Ritual Power* and Anna Scibilia, "Supernatural Assistance in the Greek Magical Papyri," in *The Metamorphosis of Magic from Late Antiquity to the Early Modern Period.* The role of familiar and tutelary spirits in shamanism is described by Mircea Eliade, *Shamanism: Archaic Techniques of Ecstasy,* 88-99.

[1678] Brackets indicate points at which the reading of the text is conjectural; the papyrus is defective in a number of places. All the translations from Greek are my own and will be found to differ at points from the translation offered in Betz' standard work, *The Greek Magical Papyri in Translation.*

[1679] The word is a *hapax legomenon,* a word of single occurrence in surviving Greek texts; its meaning is unknown.

the day[1680], face east *in a solitary place* (εν ερημω τοπω), girt with a new palm fiber basket, around your head a loop of scarlet cord, a falcon feather behind your right ear and behind the left that of an ibis.[1681]

Standing in the place, kneel while raising your hands and say this spell: "Make *my shadow* (την σκιαν μου) serve me now because *I know your holy names* (οιδα σου τα αγια ονοματα) and *the signs* (τα σημεια) and *the passwords* (τα παρασημα)[1682] and who you are each hour and what your name is." Having said these things, once more say the previous spell[1683] and in case [he does not listen say], "*I have uncovered your holy names* (ειρηκα σου τα αγια ονοματα) and *the signs* (τα σημεια) and *the passwords* (τα παρασημα). Therefore, Lord, make *my shadow* (την εμην σκιαν) serve me." At the seventh hour it will come to you, face to face, and you say, "Follow me everywhere." But [see to it] that it does not abandon you.[1684]

Like Jesus, driven "into the wilderness"[1685]—εις την ερημον—the magician retires to a "solitary place"—εν ερημω τοπω—to work his spell and employs a name of power like Christian magicians who use the name of Jesus—"*whatever you ask in my name* (ο τι

1680 Or *sext*, one of the minor canonical hours, which corresponds to noon. The magician performs the ritual when the sun is highest.

Not coincidentally, the hours of the magical texts tend to correspond with the hours of business and liturgy, *prime* (6 AM), *terce* (9 AM), *sext* (noon), and *none* (3 PM), bracketed by the major hours, *matins* (originally midnight) and *vespers* (sunset).

1681 As Eliade points out in his magisterial work, "*one becomes what one displays*" (179). See particularly his comments on the ornithomorphic use of feathers and cords in sorcery. *Shamanism*, 156-158, 177-179.

1682 For παρασημα, "distinguishing mark," "password," Liddell & Scott, *A Greek-English Lexicon*, 1141.

1683 The spell given previously in lines 494-536.

1684 Preisendanz, *Papyri Graecae Magicae* III, 612-632.

1685 Mark 1:12.

αν αιτησητε εν τω ονοματι μου), I will do."[1686] Or for that matter, magicians who are not followers of Jesus—"We saw someone *casting out demons in your name* (εν τω ονοματι σου εκβαλλοντα δαινομια) and we forbid him because he does not accompany us."[1687]

How is "the shadow" (σκια) to be understood? It is likely that the segment reproduced above is part of a longer ritual to establish a magical *association* (συστασις)[1688] with Helios.[1689] It is not impossible that the shadow in question is therefore the literal shadow, but other possibilities emerge in the context of Greco-Egyptian magical theory. The "Ka-shadow" was considered a real entity, an integral part of the person, "the vital power by which one lived during life and after death," and as such required "houses, shelter, and human contact."[1690]

The Egyptian magical spells of the *Leyden Papyrus* contain references to the "lucky shadow," and a spell using a boy and a lamp to summon a god concludes: "When you have finished you make [the boy] open his eyes towards the lamp; then he sees the shadow of the god about the lamp."[1691] It would appear from the magical spells that the shadow was thought to be a variety of spirit entity: "Protect me from *every demon of the air* (παντος δαιμονος αεριου) and on the earth and under the earth and *every angel* (παντος αγγελου) and *phantasm* (φαντασματος) and *shadow* (σκιασμος) and *visitation* (επιπομπης)..."[1692] "...the σκιασμος

[1686] John 14:13.

[1687] Luke 9:49.

[1688] For various meanings of *sustasis* see the comments in Hans Dieter Betz' *Greek Magical Papyri in Translation*, 2nd edition, 339.

[1689] Preisendanz, *Papyri Graecae Magicae* III, 494.

[1690] Bojana Mojsov, *Osiris: Death and Afterlife of a God*, 16.

[1691] Griffith & Thompson, *The Leyden Papyrus: An Egyptian Magical Book*, IV, 23; VI, 6.

[1692] Preisendanz, *Papyri Graecae Magicae* IV, 2700-2702.

I have translated επιπομπη as "visitation," rather than "incantation" since it appears that various manifestations of supernatural enti-

[skiasmos, *my note*] is the Semitic טלנית, *tinyth*, a shadow spirit...and the *επιπομπη* [epipompē], is an avenging daimon ..."[1693]

It appears that darkness was one of many forms the protean divine could assume: "Hidden stele: Hail, whole organism[1694] of the aerial spirit, PHŌGALŌA, Hail, spirit that extends from heaven to earth, ERDĒNOU...Hail, spirit than enters into me, and having convulsed me, leaves according to the purposes of god in abundant goodness...Hail, all spirits *of aerial appearance* (*αεριων ειδωλων*)...heavenly...ethereal, watery, earthly, fiery, like the wind, *luminous* (*φωτοειδες*), *dark-looking* (*σκοτοειδες*)...[1695] No reader of the Bible can fail at this point to recall the ominous "valley of the shadow of death,"[1696] in which the mysterious צלמות (tsalmaveth), *shadow of death*, compounded off the words for *shadow* (צל) and death (מות), seems to the reader the very personification of menace—"I will fear no evil," prays the psalmist. Keeping company with the jackal, "howling mournfully in waste places,"[1697] suggests that the shadow of death might be a creature of unhuman origin. "But you crushed us and made us a haunt for jackals; you covered us over *with the*

---

ties are in view as at *PGM* V, 169, where *επιπομπη* is linked to demons of the air and earth as well as to *μαστιξ*, *scourge* or *plague*, a form of supernatural "visitation."

For "visitations" see Faraone, *Talismans and Trojan Horses*, 82-83.

1693 Kotansky, *Greek Magical Amulets*, 385.

1694 "whole organism," my compromise for *το παν συστημα*, "the whole system." *Συστημα*, *system*, refers to "a whole compounded of several parts or members" for which the lexicographers offer the example *το ολον συστημα του σωματος*, "the whole system of the body." (Liddell, Scott & Jones, *A Greek-English Lexicon*, 1508.) The 'members' of the aerial spirit may consist of the forms it assumes.

1695 Ibid IV, 1115-1145.

1696 Psalm 23:4.

1697 Brown, Driver & Briggs, *Hebrew-English Lexicon*, 1072.
The reference is to Micah 1:8.

shadow of death" (בצלמות).[1698] That the shadow could be considered a divine entity or an extension thereof is clear: "Lord of Izida, Shadow of Borsippa, Darling of Ia, Giver of life…Good is thy shadow."[1699] "…hide me in the shadow of your wings, from the wicked who do me violence, my deadly enemies who surround me."[1700]

Although marred by racial assumptions widely current in 1921, Edward Clodd was able to accumulate an impressive list of beliefs among various cultures regarding the shadow, widely regarded as a person's living double. "The Choctaws believed that each man has an outside shadow, *shilombish*, and an inside shadow, *shilup*, both of which survive him" and malicious magic could be achieved by making a poppet of an intended victim, or by obtaining some part of his clothing, hair, or nail clippings and putting the cursed object "in some place where his shadow will fall upon it as he passes." Stabbing or stepping on a person's shadow or having it cast over food could induce illness and seeing one's own shadow might even result in death.[1701] That the shadow is an extension of the person is a widely shared notion. Describing the deference shown Hawaiian chiefs, Brenda Ralph Lewis observes "that if a commoner's shadow fell on one of them, a king or chief was polluted by it and the culprit had to die."[1702]

Given this briefly sketched background, what are we to make of this description of events from early Christianity?

> Many signs and wonders occurred among the people at the hands of the apostles and they all gathered at Solomon's Portico. None of the others dared associate with

[1698] Psalm 44:19.

[1699] King, *Babylonian Magic and Sorcery: Being "The Prayers of the Lifting of the Hand,"* 84-85.

[1700] Psalm 17:8-9 (NIV).

[1701] Clodd, *Magic in Names and in Other Things*, 28-29.

[1702] Lewis, *Ritual Sacrifice: Blood and Redemption*, 147.

> them, but the people esteemed them. A multitude of men and women began joining those who believed in the Lord with the result that the sick were carried into the streets on litters and cots so that as Peter passed by at least *his shadow might overshadow* some of them (*η σκια επισκιαση*). Crowds from the towns around Jerusalem congregated, bringing the sick and those afflicted with unclean spirits and all were healed.[1703]

Strelen points out that the shadow was not indifferently regarded as an unremarkable effect of light encountering a solid object. Peter's shadow had the same healing power as his hand or voice.[1704] A living extension of his person, Peter's shadow is Peter's double. Virtually any object associated with a successful miracle worker could transmit his power: the Christian use of amulets—or *relics of the saints* if so preferred—is obviously very ancient. Like Jesus' robe, Paul's aprons and sweat cloths are known to transmit magical power: "Such cloths were indeed amulets (*φυλακτηρια*),[1705] and though not engraved with magic words, there is little to detract from the prospect that the cloths, once used effectively, would have been deployed again and again. These magically charged reliquaries would have no doubt been reapplied with the necessary prayers or incantations: the young Christian community at Ephesus, it seems, adhered tenaciously to their magical beliefs, in some cases for up to two years after conversion (Acts 19:10)."[1706]

Regarding the "apostle's laundry," Klauck observes, "it appears that the miraculous power is thought of in material terms, so that it can be 'tapped' from the person of the wonder-worker

---

1703 Acts 5:12-16.

1704 Strelan, *Strange Acts: studies in the cultural world of the Acts of the Apostles*, 194.

1705 *φυλακτηριον* (phulaktērion), *safeguard* or *outpost*, from whence *phylactery* or *tefillin*, a small leather box containing scriptural passages worn by Jewish men during prayer, formerly used as amulets.

1706 Kotansky, *Ancient Magic and Ritual Power*, 244.

and stored for subsequent use. The cloths take on the function of amulets and talismans which were so common in the magic of antiquity."[1707] The function of such magical cloth is quite similar to the *Isis band* (τελαμων), the black strip of cloth torn from Isis' robes of mourning—*εχων τελαμωνα ολομελανα* Ισιακον, "wearing a completely black Isis strip"[1708]—that induced revelations in dreams when placed over the eyes, or to the enigmatic "Anubis cord" used to string an engraved stone amulet.[1709] Jesus' name also takes on magical power, finding its way into the magical papyri where it is particularly efficacious for exorcism: *ορκιζω σε κατα του θεου των* Εβραιων Ιησου: "I cast you out by the god of the Hebrews, Jesus..."[1710] In an important article, Šedina discusses the magical theory of "contagion," the common belief that articles of clothing or body parts such as hair serve as a "material conductor" of magical power, a belief that extended even to the names of the famous dead.[1711]

The amazing account at Acts 5:12-16 has necessitated the expenditure of strenuous effort on the part of Christian commentators to allay suspicions that anything overtly magical is being reported. Particularly strenuous in that these writers, who are professional students of religion, know that casting a shadow had clear magical implications in antiquity even if the majority of their readers are unaware of the fact. Remarking on the story of Peter's shadow, one such writer admits that the account sounds "a lot like magic."[1712]

[1707] Klauck, *Magic and Paganism*, 98.

[1708] Preisendanz, *Papyri Graecae Magicae* I, 58; IV, 176.

[1709] Ibid, I, 147.

The *Anubis cord* may have been "thread used in mummification." (O'Neil, *The Greek Magical Papyri in Translation*, 7.

See also Presedo Velo, *Religión, Superstición y Mágia en el Mundo Romano*, 89.

[1710] Ibid, IV, 3019.

[1711] Šedina, *Listy filologické* 136, 1-2: 17-23.

[1712] Kurz, *The Collegeville Bible Commentary*, 1045.

In addition to *shadow*, the word *skia* also means *shade*, or *ghost*. Certain classes of ghosts were widely considered to be sources of powerful magic in the Mediterranean world of Jesus' day and it has been suggested that Jesus himself raised the ghost of John the Baptist for magical purposes.[1713]

Although it is true that no exact equivalent of the shaman existed in the Middle East in Jesus' era, prophets and other religious figures exhibited certain traits typically associated with shamanism. As established by Eliade, a central feature of shamanism in most cultures is the incarnation of the ancestral spirits of previous shamans as a means of incorporating their powers:

> This is as much as to say that the animal spirits play the same role as the ancestral spirits...But it is clear that it is *the shaman himself who becomes the dead man*...we know that "power" is often revealed by the souls of ancestral shamans...the hereditary transmission of shamanic powers, where the decision lies, in the last analysis, with the spirits and the ancestral souls...Doubtless the *wu* was not exactly the same as a shaman; but he incarnated the spirits, and, in doing so, served as intermediary between man and the divinity; in addition, he was a healer, again with the help of spirits.[1714]

Against this we may place the prediction that John the Baptist would go before [Jesus] *in the spirit and power* (*εν πνευματι και δυναμει*) of Elijah"[1715] and the frequent claims that John the Baptist and Jesus *are* Elijah or one of the previous prophets of Israel.[1716] The passing of the mantle of prophet and miracle

---

[1713] Kraeling, *Journal of Biblical Literature* 59: 147-157.

[1714] Eliade, *Shamanism: Archaic Techniques of Ecstasy*, 95, 107, 109, 454.

[1715] Luke 1:17.

[1716] As at Matthew 11:13-15; 17:10-13; 16:13-16; Luke 4:24-30, for example.

worker, like that of the shaman in other cultures, is *ancestral* in the sense that the current prophet incarnates those who have gone before: the prophet is a figure returned from the realm of the legendary dead to the land of the living. Because he embodies the spirit and power of his predecessors, his name,[1717] word, touch, clothing,[1718] and shadow transmit magical power and after his death places and objects associated with him may retain his magic.[1719] As reworked by Paul and his school, Christianity became an ecstatic salvation cult with features of the mystery religions, and in the 2nd century fell rather easily into the preexisting matrix of a salvation religion with features enumerated by the late Arthur Evans: "the suffering of the Son of God who was born from the union of a mortal woman and the Father God," the purification of the soul, "the priority of written scripture as the defining trait of religion," increasing tendencies toward asceticism and masculine privilege.[1720]

True to form, the satirist Lucian uses shadows to comic effect: "Once we die [the shadows] denounce us and testify against us, exposing the things we've done during our lives, and some consider them exceedingly trustworthy since they're always in our company and never leave our bodies."[1721]

...seven sons of Skeva.

> God was doing uncommonly powerful works through Paul's hands, so that when handkerchiefs and aprons that had touched his skin were placed upon the sick, they were set free from their diseases and the evil spirits

---

1717 Mark 9:38-39.

1718 Jesus's robe (Mark 5:25-34), Paul's personal articles (Acts 19:11-12), for example.

1719 Elisha's bones raise a dead man that touches them (2 Kings 13:21).

1720 Evans, *The God of Ecstasy*,159-160.

1721 Lucian, *Menippus*, 11.

came out of them. *Some of the itinerant Jewish exorcists* (τινες...των περιερχομενον Ιουδαιων εξορκιστων)[1722] pronounced the name of the Lord Jesus over those having evil spirits,[1723] saying, "*I command you* (Ορκιζω υμας) by the Jesus Paul proclaims!"

There were seven sons of Skeva the Jewish high priest doing this. The evil spirit said to them by way of reply, "I know Jesus and I am well aware of Paul, but who are you?" With that, the man in whom the evil spirit was leaped upon them, overcoming them all, and so overpowered them that they fled from the house naked and wounded.

This became known among all the Jews as well as Greeks who were living in Ephesus and fear fell on all of them and the name of Jesus was exalted. Many of those who had believed came forward, confessing and publicly disclosing their practices. A good number of those who *were dabbling in such matters* (τα περιεργα πραξαντων) collected their books together and burned them before everyone and when their value was calculated, it came to fifty thousand silver coins.[1724]

"Lots of magic was practiced in the early churches: Acts 19.19 suggests the extent of it in Ephesus (the magical books of those

---

[1722] εξορκιστης (exorkistēs), *exorcist*, the only occurrence of the word in the New Testament. The related verb εξορκιζω (exorkizō), *to put under oath*, is used of the high priest putting Jesus under oath to answer his question (Matthew 26:63).

Garrett notes that *exorcist* occurs nowhere else in the New Testament "perhaps because it too had magical connotations, as did the closely related verb 'adjure.'" *The Demise of the Devil*, 92.

[1723] τους εχοντας τα πνευματα τα πονηρα: "those having evil spirits…" (Acts 19:13). In this case the context indicates that "to have" an evil spirit is to be possessed by one.

[1724] Acts 19:11-19.

Christians who could be persuaded to burn them were valued at about $320,000)."[1725]

It is widely acknowledged that there was no Jewish High Priest named Skeva, another bit of Lukan pseudo-history. The name was probably concocted from the Latin *scaevus*, *left-handed*, or from *scaeva*, an *omen*. The diminutive, *scaevola*, often referred to a phallic good luck charm. Strelan discusses other possible meanings.[1726]

The *seven* Jewish exorcists reflects the widespread belief in the magical power of the number seven. The *Sepher Ha-Razim* contains this spell: "Take water from seven springs on the seventh day of the month, in the seventh hour of the day, in seven unfired pottery vessels…Expose them beneath the stars for seven nights; and on the seventh night take a glass vial, *etc*…"[1727] An apologetic reading might assume that Luke merely meant to parody magical practice by portraying seven exorcists driven out by a demon—the demon asks the names of the exorcists before casting them out, a surprise role reversal—but that seven was thought significant is clear. The spurious ending of Mark tells of seven demons driven from Mary Magdalene[1728] and Revelation has seven churches and seven spirits,[1729] seven stars and seven lampstands,[1730] and seven torches that are identified with seven spirits,[1731] to cite but a few examples from a book riddled with magical sevens. Magical sevens are also common in the *Leyden Papyrus*: "…utter these charms seven times…take seven new bricks…seven palm sticks…seven clean loaves…seven lumps of salt…stamp on the ground with your foot seven times...call

---

[1725] Smith, *Jesus the Magician*, 94.
[1726] Strelan, *Strange Acts*, 109-110.
[1727] Morgan, *Sepher Ha-Razim*, 26.
[1728] Mark 16:9.
[1729] Revelation 1:4.
[1730] Revelation 2:1.
[1731] Revelation 4:5.

down into the middle of his head seven times..."[1732] A spell against fever specifies that the magican is to take oil in his hands and say "Sabaōth" seven times.[1733] However, as Kotansky points out in an essay on the "seven sons" episode in Acts, the Hebrew שבע (shaba) means both *seven* and *adjure, take an oath*, or *imprecate, curse.* In short, "to adjure" is "to seven."[1734] If based on an Aramaic source, the story may have originally referred to "adjuring sons" rather than "seven sons,"[1735] but that the author of Acts considered the number seven to be magical seems clear when seen in its wider religious context. In any case, Jewish conjurers "were renowned throughout the Roman world for their skill in magic arts."[1736]

The magical papyri furnish multiple examples of prolonged vocalization of the seven vowels along with other vowel strings: "IŌĒ MIMIPSŌTHIŌŌPH PHERSŌTHI *AEĒIOUŌ* [the seven Greek vowels, *α ε η ι ο υ ω*] IŌĒ EŌ CHARI PHTHA, come out from [Name]...*This is the conjuration: I conjure you by the god of the Hebrews, Jesus* (*εστιν δε ο ορκισμος ουτος ορκιζω σε κατα του θεου των* Εβραιων Ιησου)..."[1737] The seven vowels were thought to "signify the seven planets, the seven spheres and their ruler, the Αναγκη [Fate or Destiny personified, *my note*]. They signify the whole *κοσμος* [order], ultimately the creator and leader of the *κοσμος*...Magicians, pagans as well as Christians, had, however, been impressed by the mysterious powers of these letters..."[1738] "*Stoicheion* came to mean *both* letter *and* element. Thus, the cosmic elements (earth, air, fire, water) and the letters

---

[1732] Griffith & Thompson, *The Demotic Magical Papyrus of London and Leyden* II, 14-15; III, 5, 8-9; V, 1, 6; X, 16-17.
[1733] Preisendanz, *Papyri Graecae Magicae* VII, 211-212.
[1734] Brown, Driver & Briggs, *Hebrew-English Lexicon*, 989.
[1735] Kotansky, *Ancient Magic and Ritual Power*, 243.
[1736] Guignebert, *The Jewish World in the Time of Jesus*, 240.
[1737] Preisendanz, *Papyri Graecae Magicae* IV, 3010-3020.
[1738] Eitrem, *Some Notes on the Demonology in the New Testament*, 26-27.

of the alphabet could in some sense be said to mirror each other ..."[1739]

Early Christians were clearly aware of the magical power of sevens, including the seven vowels, *τα επτα φωνηεντα* (ta hepta phōnēenta). The church historian Eusebius says that "the combination of the seven vowels" is the equivalent of the "four letters" that the Hebrews "*apply to the supreme power of God*," (*επι της ανωτατω του θεου δυναμεως*),[1740] the tetragrammaton, יהוה, the secret name of Yahweh that is so holy it must not be pronounced. Christian magicians are in agreement with pagan magicians: *names of divinities transmit power*, particularly when combined with the seven letters: "I command you, all evil and unclean spirits, by *the seven letters* (*τα επτα γραμματα*) written in the heart of Helios and no one deciphers them except the Lord God..."[1741] The belief in the power of the seven letters survived for centuries in Christian circles. A Coptic spell from the 11th century includes the vowels twice (ⲁ ⲉ ⲏ ⲓ ⲟ ⲩ ⲱ) along with the typical closing, "Now! Hurry!" (ⲁⲓⲱ ⲧⲁⲭⲏ).[1742] Besides proving that even Christian magicians never acquired the gift of patience, this late spell testifies to the power of the seven vowels in Christian magic.

Acts 19:19, the *locus classicus* of Christian book burning, reveals that the Ephesian Christians were dabbling in matters "pert[aining] to undue or misdirected curiosity,"[1743] i.e., magic, the meaning of *περιεργος* (periergos) in this context. "Concerning the burning of the magical books at Ephesus, described in Acts 19.19, Deissmann points out that *ta perierga* and *prassein* are technical terms in the vocabulary of magic and that the papyrus

---

[1739] Miller, *Classical Mediterranean Spirituality*, 497.

[1740] Eusebius, *Praeparationis Evangelicae* XI, 6.36.

[1741] Delatte, *Anecdota Atheniensia*, 231.

[1742] Adcock, *The Bulletin of the American Society of Papyrologists* 19: 101.

[1743] Bauer & Danker, *Greek-English Lexicon of the New Testament*, 800.

codices may in general be similar to those burnt by the Christians."[1744] Regarding the charges brought up against Simon Magus by the church father Irenaeus, Dickie notes, "The list begins with exorcisms and incantations and moves on to amatory spells and spells that draw a person and ends with the use of familiar spirits and the sending of dreams and whatever other curious and excessive practices (*periergia*) they pursue...Now excessive or curious practices in this context mean interfering in what ought to be left undisturbed, which is to say, practicing magic."[1745]

It was essential that the apostles distinguish themselves early and clearly from the other wonder-workers of the day such as the itinerant Jewish exorcists: "The external appearance of the itinerant Christian missionaries was very similar to the 'men of God' of every shade who wandered from place to place, and they risked being evaluated against this background and absorbed into this spectrum."[1746] They are everywhere at a disadvantage compared to professional orators—"of rude speech" as the church historian Eusebius freely admits—and they "proclaimed the knowledge of the kingdom of heaven only by the display of the divine spirit working in them and by what the wonder-working power of Christ accomplished through them."[1747] In short, Eusebius attributed the success behind Christian preaching to *thaumaturgy*, not doctrine: *θαυματουργω του Χριστου δυναμει*: "by the wonder-working power of Christ." "The manhandling of demons—humiliating them, making them howl, beg for mercy, tell their secrets, and depart in a hurry—served a purpose quite essential to the Christian definition of monotheism: it made physically (or dramatically) visible the superiority of the Christian's patron's power over all others."[1748]

[1744] Hull, *Hellenistic Magic and the Synoptic Tradition*, 17.

[1745] Dickie, *Magic and Magicians in the Greco-Roman World*, 231-232.

[1746] Klauck, *Magic and Paganism*, 52.

[1747] Eusebius, *Ecclesiastical History*, III, 24, 3.

[1748] MacMullen, *Christianizing the Roman Empire*, 28.

Origen says that "except for *powerful works and marvels*" (*δυναμεων και παραδοξων*) the new doctrines and teachings of the apostles would have made no progress.[1749] Quoting Paul's boast that his preaching succeeded not due to human wisdom but due to "displays of the spirit and powerful works,"[1750] Origen conceded that "the divine word says what is spoken is not sufficient in itself no matter how true and completely believable it may be" to affect the soul "unless *some god-given power* (*δυναμις τις θεοθεν*) is granted."[1751] "Unless you see *signs and wonders* (*σημεια και τερατα*), you will not believe."[1752] In short, the gospel so lacked persuasive power that it necessarily advanced on the basis of magical performance.

Guy Williams has made a convincing proposal that Paul's claim to have fought wild animals in Ephesus[1753] is a reference to confrontation between himself and other magicians:

> Paul viewed the confrontations and physical threats that he experienced in Ephesus as instigated by the evil spirits, or 'beasts', at work in the demon-possessed, sorcerers, and idolaters of the city...in the vocabulary of magic, magicians summoned various spirits through the imagery of wild animals...The book of Acts remembers Paul's time in Ephesus as characterized by exorcisms, magical rivalries, and violent controversies regarding idolatry, while the epistle to the Ephesians also presupposes that evil spirits gravely challenged the early Christian community there.[1754]

[1749] Origen, *Contra Celsum* I, 46.
[1750] 1 Corinthians 2:4.
[1751] Origen, *Contra Celsum* VI, 2.
[1752] John 4:48.
[1753] 1 Corinthians 15:32.
[1754] Williams, *Journal of Theological Studies* 57 (2006): 45.

In the lifetime of Paul, Ephesus was the capitol of Asia Minor and the site of the temple of Artemis,[1755] the ever-virgin goddess of childbirth. In Asia, however, Artemis was patterned after the ancient Mother Goddess, Cybele, a fertility deity. It was here that Christian converts, "many of those who had believed," came forward with their books of magic and burned them. With magic, as with all life's endeavors, success is copied, and given the cultural context, one might fairly ask if the Ephesian Christians regarded themselves as having truly *discarded* magic along with their books, or instead to have simply traded up.

Evidence that the Christians from Ephesus had, in effect, basically exchanged one magical system for another even more potent comes from the epistle to the Ephesians itself which invokes an impressive string of magical 'power words':

> ...and what is the surpassing greatness *of his power* (της δυναμεως αυτου) for the use of us believers, according to *the operation of the power of his might* (κατα την ενεργιαν του κρατους) that he put into effect when he raised Christ up from the dead and seated him at his right in the heavens above, far above all rulership and authority and power and lordship and every name named, not only in this age, but that to come.[1756]

"The writer introduces the power of God in an extremely emphatic fashion. He uses the adjectival participle of υπερβαλλω combined with the adjective μεγεθος to emphasize in bold relief the incredibly mighty power of God. Both of these rare terms

[1755] One of the seven wonders of the ancient world, some 260 feet wide, 430 feet long, and 60 feet high, with 127 columns. The central cella, or sanctuary, contained the famous Διοπετης (Diopetēs), *fell-from-Zeus*, in all probability a meteorite seen as a heaven-sent cultic object. Likewise, "the primary image of Aphrodite was aniconic. It was…a black meteoric stone kept in her temple at Kouklia (Old Paphos), Cyprus." Jones & Pennick, *A History of Pagan Europe*, 21.

[1756] Ephesians 1:19-21.

may have been chosen by the author to communicate especially to those converted from magic in Asia Minor. They both appear in the magical papyri and also in a number of inscriptions from Ephesus...The author provides still another expression to emphasize the comprehensive scope of Christ's supremacy. 'Every name that is named' (*πας ονομα ονομαζομενος*) is encompassed in the mighty reign of the Lord Jesus Christ. This particular phrase is loaded with significance for exorcism and magical incantation both in Judaism and the pagan world. Every conceivable name of both known and unknown deities and supernatural 'powers' is called upon in at least one of the magical papyri. In fact, the very term *ονομα* is so important in the magical papyri that in the index to his collection, Preisendanz lists close to 400 occurrences of it."[1757]

Consistent with the necromantic focus of magical power, the writer does not fail to mention "*the operation of the power of his might* (*κατα την ενεργιαν του κρατους*) that he put into effect *when he raised Christ up from the dead* (*εν τω Χριστω εγειρας αυτον εκ νεκρων*)."[1758] The Ephesians were once enthralled "*by the Aeon of this world, the ruler of the powers of the air*" (*κατα τον αιωνα του κοσμου τουτου κατα τον αρχοντα της εξουσιας του αερος*) that even now "*works his power* (*ενεργουντος*) in the sons of disobedience." [1759] The Christians in Ephesus battle not "against blood and flesh, but against *the rulers* (*τας αρχας*), against *the authorities* (*τας εξουσιας*), against *the world powers* (*τους κοσμοκρατορας*) of this darkness," [1760] demonic powers, "angelic and also evil in character."[1761] The *κοσμοκρατωρ* (kosmokratōr), *cosmic ruler*, "may well have been a term used in the first or second century A.D. of magical or astrological traditions.

[1757] Arnold, *Ephesians: Power and Magic*, 54, 72-73. Arnold's is by far the most comprehensive discussion in English of the many references to magic in the epistle to the Ephesians.

[1758] Ephesians 1:19-20.

[1759] Ephesians 2:2.

[1760] Ephesians 6:12.

[1761] Schnackenburg, *Ephesians: A Commentary*, 77-80.

In fourth-century magical papyri it is used as one of the magical titles of Helios, Hermes, and Sarapis."[1762] A spell to invoke Helios begins, "I invoke you, greatest god, eternal lord, *world ruler* (*κοσμοκρατορα*)..."[1763]

Except for later writings that quote it, the dimentional terms "the breadth and length and height and depth (*το πλατος και μηκος και υψος και βαθος*)[1764]...never occur in succession except for their appearance in PGM IV.965, ff. This text twice uses the *four* dimensions—and appears to use the combination as an expression of supernatural power. The expression occurs in the context of a magical formula for the obtaining of a vision while awake...It is doubtful that the Ephesian passage influenced the magical texts I have cited. The two spells betray no sign of Christian influence, much less any influence by the Ephesian epistle...If the recipients of the epistle had come from a background of magical practices it is likely that the dynamic significance of the four dimensions would be readily intelligible to them."[1765]

As Arnold notes, the text of Ephesians duplicates the wording of the magical spell: "...say this spell seven [times]. Spell: I invoke you, the Living God...*Iaō Iaō*...*A E Ē O U Ō*... (**Ιαω Ιαω...α ε η ι ο υ ω**) give your strength, raise your demons and enter into this flame and *'enspirit' it with divine spirit* (*ενπνευματοσον αυτον θειου πνευματος*)...and let there be light, breadth, depth, length, height...I conjure you, holy light, holy brightness, breadth, depth, length, height, brightness, by the holy names...Iaō, Sabaōth..."[1766]

[1762] Hoehner, *Ephesians: An Exegetical Commentary*, 276-288, 826-827.
[1763] Preisendanz, *Papyri Graecae Magicae* IV, 1599.
[1764] Ephesians 3:18.
[1765] Arnold, *Ephesians: Power and Magic*, 91-92.
[1766] Preisendanz, *Papyri Graecae Magicae* IV, 960-981.

Several features of the spell merit comment. In addition to the dimensions previously mentioned, the spell invokes names of "the Living God" (*το θεον τον ζωντα*), recalling the confession, "You are the Christ, *the Son of the living God* (*ο υιος του θεου του ζωντος*).[1767] Other epithets derived from Hebrew are employed, the familiar *Iaō*, the Greek approximation of the tetragrammaton, and *Sabaōth*, a transliteration of צבאות, tsabaōt, (*God*) *of war*. The spell is to be recited the typical seven magical times, the seven vowels pronounced, and the ritual fire will be 'enspirited' (*ενπνευματοσον*) or *filled* with holy spirit. It is scarcely any wonder the Ephesian converts found in Christianity a new magical home with all the furnishings and appliances to which they were previously accustomed.

Public manifestations of repentance and book burning notwithstanding, Christian miracles and pagan magic would exist in an uneasy alliance for centuries to come, proven by the survival of this Christian magical spell:

Ablanathamala…Akrammachamari
Kaicha k aia, Lord God,
Lord of all gods, heal Thaēsas!...
Release [him] in the name of Jesus Christ!
(a row of magical characters follows)
Heal Thaēsas, now, now, quickly, quickly![1768]

As late as the mid-4th century, the church council of Laodicaea prohibited the practice of magic by the Christian clergy, a prohibition repeated in 398 at the council of Carthage, and in 667 the council of Toledo threatened to excommunicate clergy who said requiem masses for the living to induce "death by sor-

---

[1767] Matthew 16:16.

[1768] Daniel & Maltomini, *Supplementum Magicum*, I, 55-56.

The Greek text: Αβλαναθαμαλα…Ακαμμαχαμαρι καιχα κ αια κυριε θεε κυριαι θεων παντων θεραπευσαν Θαησαν…απολυσον ονοματι Ιησου Χριστου…θεραπευσον Θαησαν ηδη ηδη ταχυ ταχυ.

cery."[1769] Christians, like Jews, used passages from their scriptures as incantations.[1770] It is known, for example, that the Latin *Iesus autem transiens per medium illorum ibat*: "Jesus passed through their midst"[1771] and *Et verbum caro factum est*: "And the Word became flesh"[1772] were used as talismans.[1773] Plus ça change...

"...in practice probably a very substantial percentage of contemporary Christians wore amulets of some kind or other. If this were not so, this part of [Chrysostom's] homily would not make sense, any more than similar condemnations by other Christian authors, for Chrysostom's preaching is addressed to Christians, not to pagans...That some kind of specifically Christian magic had in fact developed is clear from rulings of the Synod of Laodicea in the middle of the century when it was found necessary to forbid Christian clerics in major or minor orders to be magicians, charmers, soothsayers, or astrologers, or to fabricate amulets; wearers of such amulets were to be banned from the Christian community. Incidentally, this same Council of Laodicea had to forbid the exaggerated cult of angels, which had apparently assumed the form of magic."[1774] Of the early Church, Brown says, "Such a group pullulated saints and sorcerers...St. Ambrose, to name only one saint, was associated with twelve deaths—more deaths than stand to the credit of any Late Roman *maleficus*."[1775] Regarding a papyrus spell (P.Lund IV 12), Daniel and Maltomini note, "The magical names and words in this text are clearly pagan, but two considerations suggest that the amulet may stem from a Christian milieu...We may have

---

[1769] Peters, *Witchcraft and Magic in Europe: The Middle Ages*, 181.

[1770] Chadwick, *Priscillian of Avila*, 2-3.

[1771] Luke 4:30.

[1772] John 1:14.

[1773] Kieckhefer, *Magic in the Middle Ages*, 77-78, 102-103.

[1774] Barb, *The Conflict Between Paganism and Christianity in the Fourth Century*, 106-107.

[1775] Brown, *Religion and Society in the Age of Saint Augustine*, 129-130.

yet another instance of Christians resorting to the use of pagan magic..."[1776]

The talismanic SATOR-AREPO magic square, believed to have originated as an anagram of the opening words of the Lord's Prayer, first came to light in a Christian house in Pompeii, and it was in Ephesus—where else?—that an ecumenical council, convened in 430 to decide the status of Mary in the Christian pantheon, declared that "the Holy Virgin is the Mother of God."[1777] Under Theodosius II (423 CE), pagan rites were finally declared to be sacrifices to demons. Morton Smith observed, "With this the reversal is complete. Christianity which previously, by Roman law, was magic, has become the official religion, and the official religion of ancient Rome has become, by Roman law, magic. The notion that magic has no history could hardly be more conspicuously refuted.[1778]

[1776] Daniel & Maltomini, *Supplementum Magicum*, I, 35.

[1777] **Θεοτοκος** (theotokos), *god-bearing*. Madonna and child icons are still called *theotokos* icons in the Greek Orthodox Church.

[1778] Morton Smith, *Studies in the Cult of Yahweh*, 215.

CHAPTER 12: THE MAGIC OF THE HERETICS

Within mere decades after the death of Jesus, Christians were in open warfare with each other. Their writings speak of little else than doctrinal perversion and matters of internal discipline, and in keeping with well-established apocalyptic style, the spats between the various sects are characterized as the final battle between Light and Darkness, between God and Satan: "...in the last times some will fall away from the faith, misled by deceptive spirits and teachings of demons...for some have already turned away to follow Satan...having a sick craving for controversies and fights about words."[1779] "The one who sins is from the Devil because the Devil has been sinning from the beginning. That is why the Son of God was made manifest, to destroy the works of the Devil."[1780] "Even as there were false prophets among the people, so also there will be false teachers among you who will introduce destructive heresies."[1781]

The beleaguered flock, hemmed in on all sides by wicked powers, is warned "not to fight about words...to the utter ruin of those listening," "nor to be misled by Jewish myths," but to "reject the heretical man."[1782] "Those who do not remain in the teaching of Christ do not have God. The one who remains in the teaching has both the Father and the Son," but of the man who deserts the fold: "This is the imposter and the Antichrist."[1783] The Antichrist arises from the *Christian* ranks: "now there have come to be many Antichrists...they went forth from

---

[1779] 1 Timothy 4:1, 5:15, 6:4.

[1780] 1 John 3:8.

[1781] 2 Peter 2:1.

[1782] 2 Timothy 2:14, Titus 1:14.

[1783] 2 John 7, 9.

us."[1784] Pseudo-Paul's "some will fall away from the faith"—*αποστησονται τινες της πιστεως*—employs the verbal form of *αποστασια*, *apostasy*, *defection* from the faith, a new category of crime that will lead untold numbers to the rack and stake under the rule of totalitarian Christianity. As the last pagan emperor of Rome prophetically remarked, "no wild beasts are as dangerous to man as the Christians are to one another."[1785] To leave the church became a capital offense. Virtually the only consistent trait that connects Christian sect to sect through the centuries is the propensity to have *a fight over the interpretation of words*, *λογομαχια* (logomachia).[1786]

Viewing church history through the optics of the eventual victors who emerged from the incessant squabbles of the first centuries, later writers, including the majority of New Testament scholars, tend to divide early Christians into orthodox and heterodox, "true" Christians and "false" Christians, heretics. It would be far more in keeping with the evidence to claim that there were as many "gospels" in primitive Christianity as there were preachers. One might point to Paul's repeated reference to "my gospel,"[1787] for example, or to clear references to the "gospels other than the one we preached."[1788] The very fact that the proto-orthodox felt constrained to write voluminous tracts against the heterodox indicates that they identified them as *Christian*, albeit false Christians—"something must be Christian, at least to some degree, to qualify as a heresy."[1789] The crowning achievement of the apologetic movement was the creation of the illusion of "a single orthodox faith"[1790] with an

---

[1784] 1 John 2:18-19.

Or in the immortal words of Pogo, "We have met the enemy and he is us."

[1785] *Julian's Against the Galileans*, 32.

[1786] 1 Timothy 6:14.

[1787] Romans 2:16; 16:25.

[1788] Galatians 1:8.

[1789] Tuzlak, *Magic and Ritual in the Ancient World*, 423.

[1790] Brakke, *The Gostics*, 5.

unbroken tradition that could be traced back though bishops to apostles and ultimately to Jesus, the "rule of faith" figment reflected in Origen's distinction between those who are making up nonsense about "ass-headed archons" and "the [people] of the Church" (*των απο της εκκλησιας*).[1791]

Before the end of the 1st century, Christianity had become rabidly anti-Semitic. As James Carroll, following Pagels, points out: "The Jews, which occurs 16 times in Matthew, Mark, and Luke combined, is found 71 times in John where *the Jews* has become synonymous with all that is in opposition to God."[1792] In Revelation, the Jews are called "the synagogue of Satan"[1793] and by the Middle Ages Christian anti-Jewish sentiment had escalated to the point that a Christian woman who had sexual relations with a Jew could be burned alive as punishment. It is no coincidence that conventicles of witches were called *sabbaths* or even *synagogues*, "a sign of anti-Semitism" by which the church conflated its murderous opposition to both Judaism and sorcery.[1794] Christianity also spread a new category of crime: "reject ...the heretical man." *Heresy*—from *αιρεσις*, *sect* or *school*—enters the Christian lexicon and seals the fate of millions. Deviation from the teaching of a particular sect had also become a capital crime. If for Jesus the apocalypse marks the rescue of the world *from* Satan, for the primitive church the failure of the apocalypse marks the abandonment of the world *to* Satan, who has become, in the words of Paul, "the god of this age."[1795] But few 'followers of Satan' would ultimately celebrate cruelty with a frenzy that matched that of the followers of Jesus. New Testament rhetoric notwithstanding, the rise of Christianity produced the paradoxical effect of empowering Satan.

[1791] Origen, *Contra Celsum* VI, 38.

[1792] Carroll, *Constantine's Sword*, 92.

[1793] Revelation 3:9.

[1794] Kieckhefer, *Magic in the Middle Ages*, 197.

[1795] 2 Corinthians 4:4.

It is largely to the church historian Eusebius that we owe the illusion that Jesus passed a coherent body of doctrine to his apostles who then bequeathed the Christian religion to a succession of bishops. The purpose of Eusebius' "history" was the creation of "a new vision of the church...The fantasy of a well-ordered, centralized, and monolithic church" based on an unbroken line of authoritative bishops.[1796] To the contrary, what the documents of the era show is that Christians were taking the leap of faith off every available cliff.

Origen's demonology.

Origen believed explicitly in the reality of demons and more than any other early Christian writer obliges the modern reader with an explanation of how magicians were thought to exercize their powers. Demons are the *handiwork of God* (*δημιουργηματα του θεου*) *only insofar as they are rational beings of some kind* (*μονον καθο λογικοι τινες*).[1797] His belief in the reality of demonic magic follows logically—the story of a magician carried by an arrow is credible if "it happened due to some kind of collusion with a demon" (*κατα τινα δαιμονιου συνεργιαν γεγονεναι*).[1798] Pagan magic is therefore real; the "Egyptian magical works" (*μαγγανειας...Αιγυπτιων*) that occur at the shrine of Antinous are accomplished "by the demon that has been established there" (*υπο του εκει ιδρυμενου δαιμονος*).[1799] Origen, like most of his contemporaries, believed that each thing implied its opposite: "magic and sorcery, *produced by evil demons*" (*ενεργουμενην υπο πονηρων δαιμονων*) imply that "*works of divine power* (*θειας δυναμεως*) must be observed among men." Of critical importance for our understanding is that demons "are spell bound, constrained by magical arts" (*κατακλησεσι περιεργοις θελγο-*

[1796] Moss, *The Myth of Persecution*, 228, 229.

[1797] Origen, *Contra Celsum* IV, 65.

[1798] Ibid, III, 31.

[1799] Ibid, III, 36.

μενων) and therefore forced to "obey magicians" (*γοησιν υπακουοντων*).[1800] As previously observed, *the magician controls the demon*: "but also by magicians and sorcerers and *by their spells that bewitch demons*" (*των επωδαις αυτων κηλουμενων δαιμονων*).[1801]

Like his pagan contemporaries, Origen believed in the magical power of names. Christians prevail by the name of Jesus: "demons and other unseen powers...*fear the name of Jesus as superior* (*φοβουμεναι το ονομα του Ιησου ως κρειττονος*)" and the demons fly away "at the recitation of his name" (*τω ονοματι αυτου απαγγελλουμενω*).[1802] Origen's belief coincides exactly with the superstitious nonsense derided by Lucian: "...the fever or the swelling *is in fear of a divine name* (*δεδιοτος η ονομα θεσπεσιον*) or barbarous invocation (*ρησιν βαρβαρικην*) and because of this flees from the inflammed gland."[1803]

The Christian confessions of faith that Celsus regards as "vulgar words" (*ιδιωτικους λογους*) are for Origen "just like spells that have been filled with power" (*ωσπερει επωδας δυναμεως πεπληρωμενους*).[1804] Origen provides us with the cultural context necessary to understand why death on the cross resulted in Jesus having "the name that is above every name" (*το ονομα το υπερ παν ονομα*) and that "in the name of Jesus" (*εν τω ονοματι Ιησου*) every knee would bend, the "heavenly" (*επουρανιων*), those "on earth" (*επιγειων*), and those "under the earth" (*καταχθονιων*).[1805] The other "names" placed in subjection to Christ are demons: "I am Osiris who Seth slew (**ⲁⲚⲞⲔ ⲠⲈ ⲞⲤⲒⲢⲈ ⲠⲈⲚⲦⲀ ⲤⲎⲦ ⲦⲀⲔⲞ**), arise infernal demon (*αναστηθι δαιμων καταχθονιε*) ..."[1806] "if you call upon *the heavenly gods*" (*τους επουρανιους*

[1800] Ibid, II, 51.
[1801] Ibid, V, 38.
[1802] Ibid, III, 36.
[1803] Lucian, *The Lover of Lies*, 9.
[1804] Origen, *Contra Celsum* III, 68.
[1805] Philippians 2:9-10.
[1806] Preisendanz, *Papyri Graecae Magicae* I, 253.

θεους)...;[1807] "I say to you, *demon of the underworld...*" (*τω καταχθονιω δαιμονι*);[1808] "I invoke you, *every demonic spirit* (*παν πνευμα δαιμονιον*)...I conjure you by the *seal* (*σφραγιδος*) that Solomon put on the tongue of Jeremiah...whatever kind you might be, heavenly (*επουρανιον*) or aerial (*αεριον*), whether earthly (*επιγειον*) or subterranean (*υπογειον*) or of the Underworld (*καταχθονιον*)..."[1809] "...according to *the ruler* [or *archon*] *of the authority of the air* (*τον αρχοντα της εξουσιας του αερος*), *the spirit* (*του πνευματος*) that even now works in the sons of disobedience..."[1810]

Of gnostics and gnosticism.

Although scores of specialists writing over a period of decades have thoroughly refuted the notion that magical practice is in any way foreign to the New Testament or "orthodox" Christianity, magical ritual as a peculiar mark of heresy survives as a scholarly and popular conceit. Following the lead of ancient proto-orthodox polemics, several generations of writers have characterized some early Christian sects accused of magical practice and heterodoxy as being 'typically gnostic.' The division between 'orthodox' and 'gnostic' that has been imposed on primitive Christian groups has recently begun to break down under a barrage of criticism and will be disregarded for the purposes of this work.[1811] "Every ancient observer of the Gnostics (including

---

[1807] Ibid, IV, 225.

[1808] Ibid, IV, 2088.

[1809] Ibid, IV, 3039-3044.

[1810] Ephesians 2:2.

[1811] See particularly Williams, *Rethinking "Gnosticism": An Argument for Dismantling a Dubious Category.*

The term "Ophite"—from *οφις* (ophis), *snake*—and "Naassene" —from נחש (nakhash), *snake*—are terms coined by "heresiologists" such as Hippolytus and applied to other Christians, doubtless to link them to the abhorred serpent of Genesis. Some Christian sects regard-

the non-Christian Porphyry) identifies them as Christians..."[1812] The sort of "dualistic, soteriological and esoteric philosophy" that are the supposed hallmarks of "Gnosticism" were "widely diffused in the Roman empire...Thanks to its esotericism and consequent lack of formal restraints, all gnosticism tended to be anarchically speculative; and Christian gnosticism was worst of all, a many-headed hydra, as the heresiologists put it, likely to devour and regurgitate, often in virtually unrecognizable form, any idea that came into view."[1813]

A movement so protean as to be undefinable should probably simply remain undefined. Nevertheless, Merkur calls attention to one feature of gnosticism that distinguished such sects from proto-orthodox Christianity: "The so-called redeemer figures of Gnosticism were teachers of gnosis. They did not save gnostics. They taught the means by which gnostics might save themselves."[1814] This valuable insight captures what Christian gnostics shared with their pagan Greco-Egyptian contemporaries: secret knowledge, *magic*, is the means by which one saves onself. That said, it is notable that "gnostic elements are relatively few in the magical papyri."[1815] Since Christian magic, not theology, orthodox or otherwise, is the subject of this book, the interested reader is referred to the standard works that treat the complex belief system of gnostics.[1816]

---

ed the serpent as a revealer of knowledge. (Genesis 3:1-6.) See Rasimus, *Paradise Reconsidered in Gnostic Mythmaking*, 20-22, 26.

[1812] Brakke, *The Gnostics: Myth, Ritual, and Diversity in Early Christianity*, 83.

[1813] Fowden, *The Egyptian Hermes: A Historical Approach to the Late Pagan Mind*, 113.

[1814] Merkur, *Gnosis: An Esoteric Tradition of Mystical Visions and Unions*, 176.

[1815] Brashear, *Aufstieg und Niedergang der Römischen Welt* II, 18.5: 3422. The only text in the Preisendanz collection considered to retain clearly "gnostic" content is XIII, 139-213, 442-563.

[1816] Rudolph, *Gnosis: The Nature and History of Gnosticism*; Jonas, *The Gnostic Religion: The Message of the Alien God and the Beginnings of*

It is worth pointing out that our information on gnosticism basically derives from only a few sources: Irenaeus, who died around the year 200 and wrote his magnum opus, *Adversus Haereses*, around 180, Origen's *Contra Celsum*, composed in the mid-3rd century, and the Nag Hammadi texts—most of the information on heterodox Christian groups used by other "heresiologists" appears to have been derived from Irenaeus. The Nag Hammadi trove came to light only in 1945 when 52 documents in Coptic, written on papyrus and leather-bound into 12 codices or books, were discovered in Upper Egypt. It is surmised that the Nag Hammadi cache was hidden by monks in the late 4th century in response to a campaign of book burning by Athanasius, bishop of Alexandria, the "Father of Orthodoxy," who in his Easter letter of 367 CE declared the 27 books of the current New Testament to be the only ones acceptable to the church. After the Nag Hammadi texts were published, scholars labeled them "gnostic," assumed their heretical status, and set about associating each document with a particular gnostic sect based on perceived internal characteristics matching the descriptions of "gnostic" belief given by Irenaeus and Origen. David Brakke has published a nuanced analysis of this complex process, to which interested readers are referred.[1817]

A relatively early mention of Christian gnostics appears in Origen's rebuttal of Celsus: "Granted that some also profess themselves to be gnostics" (*εστωσαν δε τινες και επαγγελλομενοι ειναι γνωστικοι*).[1818] Besides this bare stipulation, Origen says nothing

---

Christianity; Brakke, *The Gnostic: Myth, Ritual and Diversity in Early Christianity* contain detailed discussions of gnostic theology.

[1817] Brakke, *The Gnostics: Myth, Ritual, and Diversity in Early Christianity.*

[1818] Origen, *Contra Celsum* V, 61.

"Celsus may have been misinformed, confused, dishonest, or all three, and may have reported different characteristics of Christians in such a way as to suggest that each one defined a different group... Some of the characteristics he listed may have been shared by several

here about the specific beliefs of the Christian gnostics, but simply concedes that such a sect or sects existed as Celsus claimed.

In general, gnosticism has been presented as encompassing particular traits: a specialized vocabulary, a dualistic philosophy that considers the material world as inherently flawed,[1819] belief in multiple heavens ruled by spirit powers, a subordinate lesser god who is the Creator or Demiurge (δημιουργος),[1820] strict sexual continence, or, alternatively, sexual libertinism, a spiritual elect distinguished from ordinary believers, and, of course, devotion to magical ritual. Buckley reminds us "that not a single, self-described Libertine Gnostic document has yet come to the fore. Personally, I think the term [Gnostic, *my note*] should be discarded...ascetic forms of Gnosticism are often taken as the norm; it is as if ascetic orientations are self-evident..."[1821]

The New Testament writers sometimes use "gnostic" terminology such as the oft-cited "because in him *all the fullness* (παν το πληρωμα) was pleased to dwell,"[1822] or "for in him *the entire*

---

groups; etc. Granting such possibilities, we must also grant that Celsus' report does seem, in the main, probably true." (Smith, *The Rediscovery of Gnosticism*, 801).

1819 "Some supposedly Gnostic ideas, such as cosmological dualism, can be found in a wide variety of non-Gnostic literature, while they may be absent from many of the so-called Gnostic works...the texts show a variety of cosmological positions..." (King, *What Is Gnosticism?*, 8, 13).

1820 The notion that the supreme God is not directly involved in the act of creation is hardly limited to gnostic thought. As Brakke points out "a lower divine principle mediates between God and the creation" (*The Gnostics*, 60) which is variously identified as Christ (Colossians 1:16), the Word (John 1:1-3), or Wisdom (Proverbs 8:22-31).

1821 Buckley, *Journal of Early Christian Studies* 2:1, 15.

An informative essay, "Giving Birth to *A New New Testament* and Retiring the Idea of Gnosticism," *A New New Testament: A Bible for the Twenty-First Century*, 529-536, summarizes the history of the scholarly conflict over the term and proposes it be discarded.

1822 Colossians 1:19.

fullness of the divine (*παν το πληρωμα της θεοτητος*) lives bodily"[1823] in which *πληρωμα* (plērōma) is taken in the gnostic sense to mean the ineffable primordial divine totality from which the *aeons*, (*αιων*, aiōn), *lesser gods*, emanate in various generations. That said, nothing about 'gnosticism' is specifically Christian, and nothing about Christianity specifically 'gnostic,' but in the era in which Christianity emerged religious speculation, like magic, borrowed promiscuously from whatever philosophy or system came to hand and it is little surprise that some, many, or perhaps all Christian sects shared 'gnostic' beliefs. Since he could hardly deny their existence, a favored tactic of the apologist Origen was to compare the multitude of Christian groups to schools of philosophy and medicine.[1824] Given the welter of early Christian sects, known to us mainly through the biased testimony of their opponents and a relative handful of surviving, sometimes fragmentary, texts, I have adopted the point of view that "Gnosticism, as a unified subject of study, is a modern invention, which embraces many different and contradictory world-views."[1825] On the origins of "Gnosticism," which he defines as "a system of relations with the divine based on magic rites, mostly private, made known by revelations, efficacious rites vis-à-vis gods and demons, rites that were outside or were placed outside the covenant between Yahweh and the Jewish people,"[1826] see Mastrocinque's summary.

[1823] Colossians 2:9.

Pagel's *The Gnostic Paul: Gnostic Exegesis of the Pauline Letters* catalogues numerous examples of "gnosticizing" vocabulary in the epistles generally attributed to Paul or his school.

[1824] As in *Contra Celsum* V, 61, for example.

[1825] Alexander, *The Cambridge History of Judaism*, III, 1053.

[1826] Mastrocinque, *From Jewish Magic to Gnosticism*, 47-53.

For an informative, if perhaps dated, view of "Gnostic" ritual as it related to proto-orthodox belief, see Smith, *Ancient Christian Magic: Coptic Texts of Ritual Power*, 59-62, in which the gnostics are described as "religious bricoleurs."

Belief in a multi-tiered heaven ruled by an angelic spirit hierarchy was common, perhaps even universal, around the Mediterranean and magical texts quite naturally reflect such belief. An amulet among those discussed by Kotansky (number 52) begins, "I adjure you by *the one above heaven* (τον επανω του ουρανου), Sabaōth..." and continues, "I invoke you in the name of the One who created the All, I invoke the one seated *upon the first heaven* (επι του προτου ουρανου), Marmariōth, I invoke the one seated upon the second heaven, Ouriēl," and so on through "the seventh heaven" (επι τω εβδουμω ουρανω).[1827] In short, belief in multiple heavens, stacked one upon the other, was not diagnostic of any particular religious group and "orthodox" Christians quite obviously believed in multiple heavens: "the one who ascended *above all the heavens*" (υπερανω παντων των ουρανων).[1828] Paul's famous ascent to the 'third heaven'[1829] likewise reflects a common belief in the multiple heavens implied by the Hebrew expression השמים ושמי השמים (hashamayim ushemi hashamayim), "the heavens and the heaven of the heavens."[1830]

As noted by Morton Smith, "By our academic prerogative, without considering ancient usage [of the term γνωστικος, "gnostic," *my note*], we recognize certain schools as 'gnostic'; hence the ideas held by those schools become 'typically gnostic'; hence 'gnosticism' will be defined; and the resultant definition of 'gnosticism' will prove the 'gnostic' character of these schools. Since Plato said 'the most perfect of forms' was the most completely circular (Ti. 33b), we may describe this research program as Platonically perfect."[1831] In short, the "Gnostics" of scholarly debate were not self-described as such, and the Christian sects currently labeled "gnostic" did not consider themselves "sects,"

[1827] Kotansky, *Greek Magical Amulets*, 276-277.

[1828] Ephesians 4:10.

[1829] 2 Corinthians 12:2-4.

[1830] As at Deuteronomy 10:14; 1 Kings 8:27, etc.

[1831] Smith, *The Rediscovery of Gnosticism, Volume Two, Sethian Gnosticism*, 798.

much less "heretics." The interested reader is referred to Karen King's succinct and informative essay that concludes, in part, that "Gnosticism" is a modern construct based on "defining and maintaining a normative Christianity" in an century in which normative Christianity had yet to emerge.[1832] An essay that argues in favor of "retiring" the idea of gnosticism concludes that "it is not an accurate way to characterize anything in early Christianity" and attributes the term to "Christianity's persistent need to declare groups within its circle, but with different ideas, as heretics."[1833] It is important to stress that the "orthodox" church of the 4th century destroyed all the "heretical" writings it could lay hands on and that what "gnostics" believed can only be inferred from the reports of their enemies and that fractional part of their writings that has survived. "What we have referred to as Gnostic magic was in fact Gnostic religion."[1834]

The pagan critic Porphyry, who gathered Plotinus' writings into the form known as the *Enneads*, includes a rebuttal of Christian gnosticism, *Προς τους Γνωστικους*, "Against the Gnostics," in which he points to the end result of such teaching: its followers despise the world and everything in it.[1835] Pagans generally were alert to Christianity's apocalyptic predisposition to see the world as inherently evil and to exchange the fantasy of the failed apocalypse for the equally delusional New Jerusalem. Christians were not citizens of their native lands—Christians were citizens of heaven, of a city built by God.[1836] The Christian faithful confess "that they are strangers and temporary residents on the earth."[1837] The term *παρεπιδημος* (parepidēmos), *temporary resident*, used by Christians as a self-description, was used generally of civil servants on temporary assignment in foreign coun-

---

[1832] King, *What is Gnosticism*, 1-27.

[1833] Taussig, *A New New Testament*, 529, 531.

[1834] Mastrocinque, *From Jewish Magic to Gnosticism*, 204.

[1835] Porphyry, *Ennead* II, 9, 15.

[1836] Revelation 3:12, 21:2, Philippians 3:20, Hebrews 11:10.

[1837] Hebrews 11:13: *οτι ξενοι και παρεπιδημοι εισιν επι της γης*: "that they are strangers and temporary residents on the earth."

tries, and the term *παροικια* (paroikia), from whence *parochial*, meant *sojourn* in a foreign land. The founding documents of Christianity declared its adherents to be mere planetary tourists. Some gnostic sects took rejection of the world to a logical extreme—the creator and his world were literally evil incarnate. "The Christians, Celsus complains, inherit from the Jews the notion that the world was made solely for the benefit of mankind. When it does not conspicuously serve this purpose, they immediately call for a new order that suits them, ascribing their failures to an increase of evil ordained by their god."[1838]

Irenaeus

Irenaeus (130-202), the bishop of Lyon, considered to be the most important theologian of the 2nd century, composed *Detection and Refutation of Falsely-called Knowledge*—Ελεγχος *και ανατροπη της ψευδονομου γνωσεως*[1839]—a work in five books that survives in the form of an early Latin translation, *Adversus Haereses* (*Against Heresies*). The Greek text of the first book, thought to have been composed around CE 180, is still mostly extant in the form of quotation. Irenaeus was a contemporary of Celsus and his accusations against other Christians, which Irenaeus calls "the so-called gnostic heresy" (*της λεγομενης γνωστικης αιρεσεως*)[1840] confirms an explosion of Christian sects and

---

[1838] Hoffman, *Celsus On the True Doctrine*, 40.

[1839] Quoted from 1 Timothy 6:20, "the empty speech and contradiction of the falsely-called knowledge" (*κενοφωνιας και αντιθεσεις της ψευδωνομου γνωσεως*). It is clear that *divisions* (*σχισματα*) and *factions* (*αιρεσεις*)—schisms and heresies—already existed among Christians in the mid-1st century. Compare 1 Corinthians 11:18-19; Galatians 5:19-20; 2 Peter 2:1; 1 Timothy 4:1.

The apologist Justin "reports that Jesus had predicted" divisions and sects would appear although "this saying does not appear in any of the Gospels that we know and may be a conflation of Paul's statements." (Brakke, *The Gnostics*, 106-107.)

[1840] Irenaeus, *Adversus Haereses* I, 10, 2.

the composition of "an uncountable profusion of spurious and obscure writings" (*αμυθητον πληθος αποκρυφων και νοθων γραφων*) with which they "amaze the foolish who are not well versed in the true scriptures."[1841] The "gnostics" fabricate some new nonsense every day, something that has never occurred to anyone else.[1842] Irenaeus identified one such writing by name, a "gospel of Judas."[1843]

Irenaeus accused a number of Christian groups of practicing magic. Marcus, for example, is "very skilled in magical flimflam (*μαγικης υπαρχων κυβειας εμπειροτατος*)...*most knowledgeable* (*γνωσιτκωτατω*) and possessing *the greatest power* (*δυναμιν την μεγιστην*) from the unseen and nameless regions...an *expert in magic* (*μαγικης εμπειρος*)...he probably even *has a demon as a familiar* (*δαιμονα τινα παρεδρον εχειν*)" and he concocts "*philtres* (*φιλτρα*) and *attraction spells* (*αγωγιμα*)" by means of which he "defiles the bodies" of vulnerable women.[1844] Thee observes that these accusations appear to "go beyond conventional religious polemic" and concludes, "the charge of magic would seem to be sustained."[1845] "The success of Irenaeus' enemies in recruiting and retaining adherents particularly irked and threatened him and was specifically attributed to magic (Ad Haer 1.13.1-6)...Irenaeus' enemies have effective supernatural powers on their side who bring about their successes."[1846]

Besides the usual spellwork, Irenaeus describes early Christian speculation about letters, particularly the way in which letters generated more letters: "When at first the Father...wished that *that which cannot be expressed* (*το αρρητον*) be manifested and *that which is unseen* (*το αορατον*) be given form, He opened his mouth and *brought forth a Word* (*προηκατο λογον*) like Him-

[1841] Ibid, I, 20, 1.
[1842] Ibid, I, 21, 5.
[1843] Ibid, I, 31, 1.
[1844] Ibid, I, 13, 1-6.
[1845] Thee, *Julius Africanus and the Early Christian View of Magic*, 346.
[1846] Janowitz, *Magic in the Roman World*, 17-18.

self...He spoke the first letter of his name which is *Beginning* (αρχη)[1847] which was a combination (συλλαβη)[1848] *of* four *letters* (στοιχειων)...the letter delta contains within itself five [letters], the delta and the epsilon and the lambda and the tau and the alpha, and *those letters are written by yet other letters* (ταυτα παλιν τα γραμματα δι' αλλων γραφεται γραμματων) and these others by others yet...the *real essence* (υποστασις) of delta increases to infinity...and the word became a name and the name became what we know and speak, Christ Jesus... " Of other names the gnostics claim, "*you possess only its sound* (φωνην...εχεις), but *you do not know* [its] *power* (δυναμιν αγνοεις),[1849] *Jesus*, on the other hand, *is a remarkable name* (Ιησους...εστιν επισημον ονομα), having six letters known to all who are chosen...know therefore that these, your twenty-four letters, *represent the dominion* (απορροιας υπαρχειν...εικονικας)[1850] of the three powers, the entire number *of the letters* (στοιχειων) in the upper realm..."[1851] The *letters* or *elements*—στοιχειον (stoicheion)—the components of speech and/or matter, assume a mystical relationship since the material world was *spoken into existence* (Genesis 1:3-26). The elements of speech are therefore connected to the elements of the world because speech is creative and therefore magical.

The significance of letters is clear from the formulas of the magical papyri: "I called you—then write the 59 [letter] *IAEŌ spell* (IAEΩ λογον)—grant victory because I know the names of the good demon (ονοματα του αγαθος δαιμονος), HARPON CHNOUPHI BRITATĒNŌPHRI BRISAROUZAR BASEN..."[1852] "Great [is]

[1847] Compare John 1:1, "In the *beginning* (αρχη) was the Word (λογος)..."

[1848] A *combination* (συλλαβη) of letters, the obvious source of "syllable."

[1849] Or "you are ungnostic" (αγνοεις), i.e., αγνωστος (agnōstos), *ignorant.*

[1850] *Dominion* or *influence*, απορροια (aporrhoia) is used of planetary influences on human affairs.

[1851] Irenaeus, *Adversus Haereses* I, 14, 1-5.

[1852] Preisendanz, *Papyri Graecae Magicae* VII, 1021-1023.

the Lady Isis! Copy of a sacred book discovered in the archives of Hermes. The method is the one using *the* twenty-nine *letters* (*τα γραμματα*) by which Hermes and Isis, who went seeking her brother and husband, Osiris..."[1853] "And say the seven letters of the magicians..."[1854] "Running through all of these traditions that connect the word with the charm is an emphasis on the power or forcefulness of words. Compulsion...was built into the nature of language."[1855] So much for Christian magical alphabetology.

Carpocrates and magic.

What little is known about Carpocrates has come down to us from his sworn enemies. Aside from a brief mention in Clement, Irenaeus may be our only other primary source.[1856] Hippolytus (2nd century) and Eusebius (early 4th century) refer to Carpocrates, but they are almost certainly quoting Irenaeus. It is not known what Christian books the Carpocratians may have accepted. Irenaeus lumps them together with "gnostics," but the teachings he attributes to them, reincarnation and reminiscence of previous lives, are derived from Platonism.[1857] Although considered to be a Christian heretic, it is unknown how the Carpocratians would have defined themselves and the church saw to it that none of Carpocrates' writings survived. Clement preserves a short quotation of a philosophical tract written by Carpocrates' son Epiphanius, but aside from its radical egalitarianism there is nothing particularly scandalous about it. The conspiracy theorist Hippolytus argued that the Carpocratians with their magical spells had been sent by Satan to discredit the church.[1858]

[1853] Ibid, XXIVa, 1-5.
[1854] Ibid, LXIII, 5.
[1855] Miller, *Classical Mediterranean Spirituality*, 494.
[1856] Smith listed every extant reference to Carpocrates (Appendix B) in *Clement of Alexandria and a Secret Gospel of Mark*, 295-350.
[1857] Pearson, *Gnosticism, Judaism, and Egyptian Christianity*, 205-206.
[1858] Benko, *Pagan Rome and the Early Christians*, 115.

Like Clement, Carpocrates taught in Alexandria, his career overlapping the reigns of Hadrian (117-138 CE) and Antoninus Pius (138-161). He is awarded six paragraphs in the polemic *Adversus Haereses* (*Against Heresies*).[1859] Subtracting the venom and the libel, Irenaeus' sketch of the Carpocratians leaves us with a picture of a dualistic antinomian Christian sect that regarded the material world as fallen and escape from the cycle of reincarnation as possible only by experiencing all human conditions, which may have included all sexual behaviors. Pansexuality, whatever its value for any given individual, was justified as ritually necessary to escape the prison of the lower world and ascend into heaven. The heterogeneous mix of sects labeled "gnostics," which clearly included Christian groups, shared a belief in "a cosmos filled with semi-divine beings displaying a wide array of sexual characteristics"[1860] that conveniently reflected the human condition.

Primitive Christianity appears to have had two beliefs about the world: that the world is about to end, *apocalypticism*, or that it is a hopelessly flawed inferior creation, *dualism*, both of which assume that the world and its affairs are of scant importance. The approach that eventually prevailed in normative Christianity, *asceticism*, resulted in the rejection of the world and renunciation of its pleasures, the alternative, *libertinism*, regarded behavior as morally neutral—if the world scarely matters, how one conducts oneself in it matters little as well. "These responses to the eschaton, in turn, correspond to rival theological outlooks in the early church: the antinomian emphasis…took its cue from Paul's (and doubtless other missionaries') stance against the law…as the Christian is saved by grace and faith rather than by works, anything is permissible."[1861]

[1859] Irenaeus, *Adversus Haereses*, 1, 25, 1-6.
[1860] Kuefler, *The Manly Eunuch*, 222.
[1861] Hoffman, *Celsus on the True Doctrine*, 14.

Two reported characteristics of Carpocratian practice are relevant for our purposes: the elements of mystery and magic. On these two points at least, Irenaeus is more forthcoming: the Carpocratians taught that Jesus "spoke privately in mystery to his disciples and apostles..." (Iesum dicentes in mysterio discipulis suis et apostolis seorsum locutum...)[1862] and performed various sorts of magic. The belief in secret apostolic teaching came in very handy given the incessant theological conflict among early Christians: "The claim to have apostolic traditions was common in the ancient church and, since new apostolic traditions were discovered to settle new disputes as they arose, it must have been believed that the traditions had been secret before the times of their fortunate discovery. Therefore, this common method of doctrinal argument presupposes a general belief in a considerable body of secret apostolic tradition to which privileged members of clergy had access."[1863]

If Irenaeus was vague about what "speaking in mystery" revealed, he was much more specific about magic. His remarks are preserved not only in Latin, but also in Greek in the form of quotations by other church officials.

> They also perform *magical arts* and *enchantments* (*τεχνας ...μαγικας...επαοιδας*), *potions and erotic spells* (*φιλτροι και χαριτησια*), and use *magical assistants* and *messengers of dreams* (*παραδρους και ονειροπομπους*) and other such evil works, *alleging they* already *have authority* to be the masters *of the princes* [or *archons*] (*φασκοντες εξουσιαν εχειν...των αρχωντων*) and the creators of this world.[1864]

A *φιλτρον* (philtron), *potion* or *philtre*, is a spell for controlling the actions or emotions of others; used of horses (*φιλτρον ιπ-*

[1862] Irenaeus, *Adversus Haereses* 1, 25, 5.
[1863] Smith, *Clement of Alexandria*, 29.
[1864] Irenaeus, *Adversus Haereses* 1, 25, 3.

πειον) it means *the bit.*[1865] A φιλτροκαταδεσμος (philtrokatadesmos) is an erotic binding spell. In the Carpocratian sect, as in the magical papyri, prayers and spells were likely synonomous; "religion and magic, at least with regard to prayer, are coterminous."[1866] "A *philtron* or *amatorium* may then be the substance put into food or drink to induce sexual passion in the person who consumes or imbibes it; it may be a substance used as an ointment; it may be a substance accompanied by a spoken spell designed to elicit the same result; and it may be a spoken spell intended to provoke sexual desire."[1867]

The term χαριτησιον (charitēsion), *erotic spell*, "covered not only prayers and amulets but more directly material technologies for stimulating and managing sexual feelings, such as penis ointments and love potions...if you can throw your handkerchief over lizards copulating it will be a χαριτησιον μεγα (a great spell to produce charm); the tail worn as an amulet promotes erection..."[1868] That the Greek words had become technical terms in magic is suggested by the fact that the Latin version of *Against Heresies* simply transliterates them. The word for magical assistant, παρεδρος, is also carried over into Latin as *paredros.* "The 'assistant,' as one of the many spirits or stellar angels or daemons of the dead, may contribute anything, including dream transmissions and revelations by dreams."[1869] *Oneiropompos*, "dream sender," also a technical term, is likewise simply transposed into Latin. Winkler discusses the complex interrelation between sex magic and dreams and notes Celsus' charge that "Mary Magdalene's encounter with the risen Jesus was only the ονειρωγμος ["wet dream," *my note*] of a sexually excited woman."[1870] "Sorcerers offered spells for conjuring up prophetic dreams and considered the arts of 'dream-seeking' and 'dream-

[1865] Liddell & Scott, *A Greek-English Lexicon*, 1680.

[1866] Graf, *Magika Hiera*, 194.

[1867] Dickie, *Magic and Magicians in the Greco-Roman World*, 17.

[1868] Winkler, *Magika Hiera*, 220.

[1869] Eitrem, *Magika Hiera*, 180.

[1870] Winkler, Ibid, 230.

sending' to be a central part of their business."[1871] Dream sending, *ονειροπομπεια* (oneiropompeia), is multiply attested in the magical papyri.[1872]

The *princes* or *archons* (*αρχωντων*) over whom the Carpocratians boasted of their authority (*εξουσια*) were likely demonic entities like those referred to in Mark where the scribes accuse Jesus of expelling demons due to his authority over "the prince of demons" (*εν τω αρχοντι των δαιμονιων*).[1873]

Justin Martyr

Irenaeus thus confronts us with clear evidence for varied magical practice in the primitive church, with a sexual component being preserved among some factions. It is against this background that Justin Martyr's *Apology* must be read. Justin, a student of several schools of philosophy, was born in Samaria (present-day Palestine) around the year 100 and was executed early in the reign of Marcus Aurelius, probably about the year 165. He converted to Christianity around 130 and wrote his protest against the persecution of Christians shortly after 150 CE. Justin's work, although poorly and incompletely preserved, is nevertheless a valuable window into the practices of early Christians, particularly as perceived by their pagan contemporaries. Justin's writings are of particular relevance because he was a near contemporary of Carpocrates and his followers.

Justin's argumentation is muddled and his writing discursive in the worst sense. There are two overriding assumptions in the *Apology*: the mere antiquity of the Old Testament is its guarantee of truth and that because Jesus fulfilled the prophecies of the

[1871] Lane Fox, *Pagans and Christians*, 151.

[1872] Muñoz Delgado, *Léxico de magia y religion en los papiros mágicos griegos*, 94.

[1873] Mark 3:22.

Old Testament—which Justin quotes exhaustively—he must be the promised Messiah. Greco-Roman culture regarded religious novelty with deep suspicion while equating truth with antiquity, so the appeal to Jewish scripture, widely acknowledged to be of great age, possessed a logical inevitability. However, Christians of Justin's era went much further. Some denied that the Jewish scriptures had anything to do with the Jews, but rather pointed forward in anticipation to the Christians as the true Israel of God. I have reproduced only those portions of Justin's discourse that deal with charges that Jesus and his disciples practiced magic. In fact, it is not until the thirtieth section of his tract that Justin finally manages to come to the crux of this issue, posing the question much as pagans undoubtedly did:

> What prevents him we call Christ, a man born of men, *having performed what we call powerful works by magical art* (*μαγικη τεχνη ας λεγομεν δυναμεις πεποιηκεναι*) and by this means appear to be a son of God?

Like his Christian contemporaries, Justin is not only familiar with magicians and their practices, but apparently includes many of his coreligionists as formerly among their number: "...and we who once employed magical arts have now consecrated ourselves to the good and unbegotten God..."[1874]

> For even necromancy *and haruspexy using uncorrupted children* (*και αι αδιαφθορων παιδων εποπτευσεις*), and calling up human souls, and those who among the magicians are called senders of dreams and familiars, and all things done by those with such skills, may these persuade you that even after death souls are sentient and men seized and thrown down by souls of the dead, who everyone calls demon-possessed (*δαιμονοληπτος*) and madmen, and which is known to you as "prophesying,"

[1874] Justin, *Apology* 14.2.

> Amphilochus and Dodona and Pytho and whatever others there are...[1875]

Munier, whose Greek text of Justin I have used, translates the passage on haruspexy, "les divinations faites sur les entrailles d'enfants innocents..." or "divination using the entrails of innocent children..."[1876] Since Justin is adducing the evocation of souls of the dead as proof of a conscious afterlife, this translation, which imputes the murder of children to pagan magicians, is almost certainly correct. The verb Justin uses, εποπτευω, is used (as previously noted) in the mystery cults for revelation of ultimate truth, and if by such usage Justin implies that the ultimate revelation for pagans was to be glimpsed in the guts of dead children it comes as little surprise that he finally managed to get himself executed.

It would appear that many Christians were still practitioners of magic. Justin says as much, citing the sect of Simon the Samaritan, who "by the art of working with demons performed feats of magic" and noting that "all who belong to his sect are, *as we have said, called Christians*" (ως εφημεν Χριστιανοι καλουνται). "Justin goes on to register his frustration with the fact that 'real' Christians are persecuted by the Roman authorities while Simonians are allowed to preach their heresies unmolested."[1877] It is against this sect that the following accusations are leveled:

> Whether those legendarily evil works they perform—overturning the lamp, unrestrained intercourse, and feasting on human flesh—are true we do not know, but they are neither persecuted nor put to death by you on account of the doctrines they hold...[1878]

[1875] Ibid, 18.3-4

[1876] Munier, *Saint Justin Apologie pour les Chrétiens*, 60.

[1877] Tuzlak, *Magic and Ritual in the Ancient World*, 424.

[1878] Justin, *Apology* 26.2,6,7.

Justin returns to the subject of sexual license to reiterate, "promiscuous intercourse is not a mystery of ours."[1879] From the foregoing it is plain that Justin not only knew of accusations that Christian ritual included sexual free-for-alls—"overturning the lamp" so that the participants could engage in sexual intercourse under the cover of darkness—he joins in with the chorus of accusers by stipulating which sects he thought engaged in such practices. The charges of cannibalism and incest, whether true or not, point to general claims that Christian cults weakened the social fabric and promoted disorder.[1880] Are such charges to be taken seriously? Christians charging other Christians with gross sexual indecency was certainly not new in Justin's day: the later books of the New Testament claim that nonconforming Christians behaved like "irrational animals"[1881] and generally portray the members of competing Christian sects as prisoners of unbridled lust. To these charges later writers added cannibalism and the ritual ingestion of semen and menstrual blood.[1882]

Origen on magic.

Origen, whose name is thought to mean "son of Horus," (185-254 CE) was a controversial figure both in life and death. While still in his late teens he replaced Clement as chief catechist in Alexandria, and sometime early in his adult life, according to the historian Eusebius, he 'made himself a eunuch "for the king-

---

[1879] Ibid, 29.2.

[1880] McGowan, *Journal of Early Christian Studies* 2:3, 418.

[1881] 2 Peter 2:1-2, 12-14, Jude 10, 18.

[1882] Ehrman, *Lost Christianities*, 197-202.

Eusebius reports that Christians were repeatedly accused of cannibalism: *Ecclesiastical History* IV, 7.11, V, 1.14, 52.

On ritual murder in magic, Wolff, "La norme religieuse et les brigands à travers les sources littéraires," *La Norme religieuse dans l'Antiquité*, 53-72.

dom of heaven."[1883] Although regarded as one of the most important pre-Nicene Christian intellectual figures, his teachings included several ideas that were heretical by the standards of later theology. Origen's writings confirm that magical thinking and praxis was hardly confined to heretical Christian splinter groups.

Of Origen's extensive writings, I have reproduced several short sections from his apologetic magnum opus, *Contra Celsum*, a paragraph-by-paragraph refutation of an extensive critique of Christianity by Celsus, an early pagan opponent of Christianity. Origen composed his rebuttal around 248 CE, many years after Celsus, who wrote the Αληθης Λογος, *True Doctrine*, had already died. The curious result of Origen's delayed refutation was the substantial preservation of Celsus' polemic, a text that has been reconstructed by Joseph Hoffman.[1884]

Besides the unintended consequence of preserving Celsus' arguments nearly in their entirety, *Contra Celsum* records a number of crucial observations about the Christianity of Origen's day by one of its most highly educated insiders. By far the most interesting material for the purpose of this study concerns Origen's understanding of Christian miracles.

> After these things, through what motivation I do not know, Celsus says that Christians appear to exercise powers by using *the names of demons and by incantations* (*δαιμονων τινων ονομασι και κατακλησεσι*), hinting, I presume, at those who drive out demons by incantations. For not *by incantations* (*κατακλησεσιν*) do Christians appear to have power over demons, but by the name of Jesus, combined with *recitals of the accounts about him* (*της απαγγελιας των περι αυτον ιστοριων*), for recitation of these things has often succeeded in having

---

[1883] Matthew 19:12.

[1884] Hoffman, *Celsus On the True Doctrine.*

> driven the demon from men, and especially so when those reciting them speak with a healthy attitude and a believing frame of mind. Indeed, the name of Jesus is so powerful against the demon that now and then it is effective even when named by unworthy men, just as Jesus taught when he said, "Many will say to me in that day, *we cast out demons* (δαιμονια εξεβαλομεν) and performed powerful works in your name."[1885] Whether Celsus overlooked this from intentional malice or lack of understanding, I do not know.
>
> Next he even accuses the Savior *of having performed wonders by practicing sorcery* (ως γοητεια δυνηθεντος α εδοξε παραδοξα πεποιηκεναι) and, foreseeing that others are destined to acquire the same knowledge and brag about doing the same things by the power of God, Jesus banishes such men from his kingdom. Celsus' accusation is that if such men are justly banished, while Jesus himself does the same things, then he is morally base and subject to the same punishment, but if Jesus is not evil for performing such works, neither are they who do as he does. On the other hand, even if it is conceded to be beyond demonstration how Jesus did these things, it is clear that Christians reject the practice of using incantations. Rather they accomplish it by the name of Jesus together *with other words in which they have faith*.(μετ' αλλων λογων πεπιστευμενων) according to the divine Scripture.[1886]

Even from this brief passage it is clear that Christian exorcists used the name of Jesus together with *other words in which they had faith*, which included "recitations of accounts about him." Although Origen did not consider such performances to be

---

[1885] Origen quotes from the form of the saying recorded at Matthew 7:22. The parallel saying in Luke 13:27 has Jesus call the miracle workers "workers of wickedness."

[1886] Origen, *Contra Celsum*, I, 6.

magical, the present-day scholar certainly classify such "recitations" as examples of *historiolae*—what Origen calls *ιστορια* (historia)—"short stories recounting mythical themes"[1887] designed to magically duplicate the miracles of the story. In another passage, Origen mentions *το του Ιησου ονομα μετα της περι αυτου ιστοριας*, "the name of Jesus and stories about him" as the source of healing power.[1888] Regarding the magical use of *historiolae*, Brashear observed that, "mythical events (archetypes) 'once upon a time' (in illo tempore) retain their supernatural forces forever and can be reactivated at any given time by the simple act of recounting them…the precedent having been cited, the god is obligated to act the same way now as then."[1889]

Concerning the power to convert sinners, Origen says of Christian preaching, "we consider it just like *charms that have been filled with power*"—*επωδας δυναμεως πεπληρωμενους*.[1890] "…early Christianity rapidly developed a distinctive form of magic which cohered with its reality construction; early Christian writers unwittingly mapped the contours of Christian magic in their apologetic program developed in rebuttal to pagan and Jewish charges that Christians practiced sorcery."[1891] "According to the belief of these first Christians the efficaciousness of the exorcism pronounced in the name of Jesus had nothing to do with Jesus himself; it was from the five letters J-E-S-U-S arranged in that particular order that the curative action proceeded!"[1892] The notion that *the name alone* carries with it the power of its owner is very old. It is the basis for the use of the divine name, the

---

[1887] Kotansky, *Magika Hiera*, 112. The author elsewhere mentions "the problem that one faces when presented with prayers for salvation that seem embedded in an indisputable magical context" (123).
[1888] Origen, *Contra Celsum* III, 24.
[1889] Brashear, *Aufstieg und Niedergang der Römischen Welt* II, 18.5: 3439.
[1890] Ibid, III, 68.
[1891] Aune, *Aufstieg und Niedergang der Römischen Welt*, II, 23.2, 1520.
[1892] Oesterreich, *Possession Demoniacal and Other Among Primitive Races*, 168.

שם המפורש (shem hammefōrash), "which was indispensable," "an invincible charm," in Jewish amulets.[1893]

The point is that these "recitations," undoubtedly combined with prayers and gestures—which may have included the laying-on of hands[1894]—would have been indistinguishable from incantations, for Celsus and other pagans at any rate, regardless of how the actions were interpreted by Christians. Oesterreich is almost certainly correct when he claims that exorcism "was accompanied by the laying on of hands, the breath of the Spirit was breathed on the possessed, and signs of the cross made."[1895] Benko observes, "it is clear that when Christians accepted the existence of demons who inhabited the air and discussed their influence on human life, they were really talking in the context of contemporary pagan magic, which was based on the assumption that demons can be made to obey the will of the person who knows how to approach them properly."[1896] Origen's understanding of how power words work, particularly names invested with magical power, coincides exactly with surviving magical texts:

> Yea, to you, lord, god in heaven, *all things have been made subject* (παντα υποτετακται) and not one of the demons or spirits will oppose me because *I have invoked your great name* (το μεγα ονομα επεκαλεσαμην) for the magical rite. *Again I call on you* (παλιν επικαλουμαι σε) according to the Egyptians, PHNŌ EAI IABŌK, according to the Jews, ADŌNAIE SABAŌTH, according to the

---

1893 Spoer, *Journal of Biblical Literature* 23: 99, 104.

1894 The church historian Eusebius (3rd century) has the disciple Thaddeus tell Abgar, τιθημι την χειρα μου επι σε εν ονοματι αυτου: "I lay my hand on you in his name..." *Ecclesiastical History*, I, 13, 17. The implication is that the laying on of hands was not uncommon. Ananias cures Saul's blindness by laying his hands upon him (Acts 9:17).

1895 Oesterreich, *Possession Demoniacal and Other*, 166.

1896 Benko, *Pagan Rome and the Early Christians*, 121.

> Greeks, HO PANTŌN MONOARCHOS BASILEUS,[1897] according to the high priests, "hidden, unseen, overseer of all things," according to the Parthians, OUERTŌ[1898] PANTODUNASTA.[1899] Accomplish and empower this object for me, for all the span of my glorious life. The names engraved on the back of the stone are these: IAŌ SABAŌTH ABRASAX.[1900]

Naomi Janowitz summarizes Origen's belief about the power of names: "…divine names do not 'represent'; they manifest divine power…Language is not of human origin, and names are not arbitrary…The power of a divine name is automatic and not based on the intention of the speaker…a Christian must be careful not to speak the name of other heavenly powers, for the power would still be, as it were, turned on."[1901]

In fact, the language of this spell contains a number of terms familiar to Christians from their own scriptures: all who "*invoke the name of the Lord* (επικαλεσηται το ονομα κυριου) will be saved."[1902] Saul, *authorized* (εχει εξουσιαν) to arrest "*all who invoke* [Jesus'] *name*" (παντας τους επικαλουμενους το ονομα),[1903] subsequently pens a letter to "all *who call upon the name of the Lord*" (τοις επικαλουμενοις το ονομα του κυριου).[1904] Significantly, "not one of the demons or spirits" will oppose the will of the magician because he invokes the name of the lord to whom all

---

[1897] Ο παντων μονοαρχος βασιλευς, "the king, sole ruler of all…"

[1898] Ritner: "OUERTO corresponds to the Egyptian epithet 'the great one of earth.'" *The Greek Magical Papyri in Translation*, 163.

[1899] παντοδυναστα, "master of all…"

[1900] Preisendanz, *Papyri Graecae Magicae* XII, 261-266.

That terms had to be labeled as "Jewish" implies that the spells including them were in use by non-Jews. (Mastrocinque, *From Jewish Magic to Gnosticism*, 59-60).

[1901] Janowitz, *History of Religions* 30/4 (1991), 360-362.

[1902] Acts 2:21; Romans 10:13.

[1903] Acts 9:14.

[1904] 1 Corinthians 1:2.

are subject, just as the disciples report, "Lord, *even the demons are subject to us in your name*" (τα δαιμονια υποτασσεται ηνιν εν τω ονοματι σου).[1905] The reader will recall "the *spirits of the prophets are subject to the prophets*" (πνευματα προφητων προφηταις υποτασσεται).[1906]

The magical practice of engraving magical names on stones, well known from the discovery of magical gems, is referenced in Revelation: "I will give him a white stone and *upon the stone a new name is written* (επι την ψηφον ονομα καινον γεγραμμενον) that no one know except the one who receives it."[1907] "It seems probable that the name on the ψηφον λευκην [white stone, *my note*] refers to he secret name of God and/or Jesus."[1908] A secret, magical name to be incised on a stone is a frequent topos in the spellbooks: the name of Serapis is incised on the back of an agate;[1909] the magical names ACHA ACHACHA CHACH CHARCHARA ACHACH are written on a stone which is then worn as an amulet.[1910]

By quoting Matthew 7:22, Origen tacitly admits that the performance of exorcism was considered knowledge—μαθημα (mathēma), from which we derive *math*—and that such knowledge not only could, but would *inevitably* be acquired by others: "foreseeing that others are destined to acquire the same knowledge." The "others" in question are those "unworthy men" who Origen admits were even then using Jesus' name to perform exorcisms. "...the name of Jesus was understood to have power of its own (e.g., Mark 9:38; Acts 3:6; 16:8; in a negative context Matt. 7:22-23; Acts 19:15)."[1911]

1905 Luke 10:17.

1906 1 Corinthians 14:32.

1907 Revelation 2:17.

1908 Thomas, *Magical Motifs in the Book of Revelation*, 170.

1909 Preisendanz, *Papyri Graecae Magicae* V, 449.

1910 Ibid, I, 143-146.

1911 Achtemeier, *Aspects of Religious Propaganda in Judaism and Early Christianity*, 151.

One might fairly ask why, *if even unworthy men could learn to perform successful exorcisms using Jesus' name*, exorcisms performed by *anyone* in Jesus' name should not be considered magical since their performance did not depend on religious merit, but worked *ex opere operato* as previously noted. Origen's description of the performances by Christian exorcists has in common the basic assumption of the Jewish magicians of whom the Christians were the direct religious descendents: magic is "an *acquired body of technical knowledge.*"[1912]

> Moreover, seeing that [Celsus] often *speaks of the secret doctrine* (ονομαζει κρυφιον δογμα) in this also he stands accused—nearly everyone in the world knows the preaching of the Christians better than those things that tickle the fancy of the philosophers. For who does not know that Jesus was born of a virgin, and was crucified, and that his resurrection has been believed by many, and that the judgment of God has been proclaimed in which the wicked will be punished in keeping with their sins, but the righteous correspondingly rewarded? Yet not having discerned the mystery of the resurrection, it is chattered around derisively among unbelievers.
>
> So on this basis, to speak of the hidden doctrine is entirely out of place. But that certain doctrines not revealed to the majority are attained *after the public ones* (μετα τα εξωτερικα) is not unique to the teaching of Christians only, but also to that of the philosophers for whom some things were public teachings, *but others private* (ετεροι δε εσωτερικοι). Even some of Pythagoras' listeners accepted his statements without proof, whereas others were taught about those things not to be spoken

[1912] Bohak, *Ancient Jewish Magic: A History*, 27.

"Magic is something which can be taught (τεχνη, *ars*); the teachers are Egyptian priests in Memphis, and it takes a certain amount of time to learn their art." Graf, *Envisioning Magic: A Princeton Seminar and Symposium*, 94.

> (εν απορρητω διδασκομενοι) to profane and insufficiently worthy ears. All the mysteries everywhere, the Greek and the non-Greek, although being secret have not been slandered, therefore it is in vain that Celsus misrepresents what is secret in Christianity.[1913]

Origen nowhere denies that the Christianity of his day—in common with the Greek mystery cults to which he alludes—had *inner teachings*, esoteric doctrines not for public consumption, and though he condemns Celsus for misrepresenting what was secret about Christianity, he leaves unrevealed just what those secrets were. It is probable that one of the Christian mysteriers "from which the uninitiated should be excluded" was the Eucharist.[1914] In another reversal of fortune, Origen—who like Clement was a stalwart defender of the faith—was himself subsequently declared to be heretical due to his belief in the subordination of the Son and the preexistence of human souls.

In short, our earliest extracanonical writers on Christian doctrine use the language of the mystery cults to describe their faith, and concede that secret doctrines were taught privately to an inner circle, much like the lore of the Egyptian magicians "stored up in *secret writings*" (scriptis arcanis).[1915] A probable reference to such private revelations survives in the text of Colossians where the ambiguous phrase α εορακεν εμβατευων, which from the evidence of ancient inscriptions should be translated "entering an oracle for interpretation of what he has seen,"[1916] is more often rendered "taking his stand on visions,"[1917] thus saving early Christianity from an overt association with mystery cults. Lane Fox: "Among the Colossians, by contrast, there were

---

[1913] Origen, Contra Celsum I.7.

[1914] Benko, *Pagan Rome and the Early Christians*, 112.

[1915] *Ammianus Marcellinus*, II, XXII, 16.

[1916] Danker, *Greek-English Lexicon*, 321. The verb εμβατευω, used only once in the New Testament, was apparently a term peculiar to the mystery cults.

[1917] Colossians 2:18, *Revised Standard Version*.

people who trusted other visions, worshipping angels and 'vaunting the things which they have crossed the threshold and seen'...Paul's word for 'crossing the threshold' is the word for visitors who 'entered' a temple like Claros and penetrated its tunnels."[1918]

As pointed out repeatedly in this work, Christian rite and wonder working shared the presumptions, processes and procedures of Jewish and pagan magic. It was, in fact, inevitable that pagan authorities would see Christianity in terms of magical practice as described by Stratton: "The Christians met in secret and at night. They took oaths to each other, worshipped an executed criminal, and shared a sacred repast consisting of their hero's flesh and blood. Furthermore, the invocation of someone who had died violently (*aōros*) figures prominently in ancient curse tablets (*katadesmoi*); Christian invocation of Jesus' name, therefore, would have resembled magic to most people living in the ancient world. Additionally, the Bacchanal and other nocturnal rites were associated with women in Roman tradition and were, on this account, especially suspect. No doubt, the fact that female slaves held leadership positions in this new religion, combined with its nighttime assemblies, triggered long-held fears of hysterical women, unrestrained promiscuity, and the violation of traditional patriarchal codes. Christianity thus smacked of magic, superstition, and possible treason from the viewpoint of an ancient Roman."[1919]

To these observations may be added the refusal of Christians to participate in the state cult, to acknowledge the *numen* of the emperor, and their accusation that the gods of the pagan religions were evil spirits. To the Roman mind, their attitudes openly invited the wrath of the gods that protected the continuity of the Roman state. In the apocryphal acts, "magic

---

[1918] Lane Fox, *Pagans and Christians*, 380. Claros was an oracular shrine of Apollo.
[1919] Stratton, *Naming the Witch*, 118.

discourse functions to attack Roman values and institutions."[1920] The Roman populace despised the Christians in their midst for a reason. Christians were traitorous and subversive.

Origen believed that divine names were invested with miraculous power, a claim that formed the very basis for Greco-Egyptian magic. "Origen believed in magic: not just as fraud or sleight of hand, or as a system of demonic responses, but as something that really existed, based on the nature of things."[1921] His defense of Christian exorcism explains the rationale for such belief:

> If, in reference to what has been mentioned, we are able to call attention to the nature of *effective names* (ονοματων ενεργων), some of which are used by the wise men of the Egyptians, or by *the Persian magi* (Περσαις μαγων), or the Indian philosophers called Brahmins, or by the Samaneans, and others from different nations, we will establish that *magic so-called* (η καλουμενη μαγεια) is not, as Epicurians and Aristotelians suppose, a totally incoherent affair, but as those of great skill prove, organized, having words known but to exceedingly few. Now we say that *the name Sabaoth and Adonai* (το μεν Σαβαωθ ονομα και το Αδωναι), and others handed down and uttered with great reverence by the Hebrews, treat not of ordinary engendered things, but belong rather to *a secret theology* (θεολογιας απορρητου) which refers to *the Maker of everything* (τον των ολων δημιουργον).[1922] Accordingly, these names, pronounced in a way appropriate to their nature, are effective, but others, *spoken in the Egyptian language* (κατα αιγυπτιαν εκφερομενα

[1920] Ibid, 135.

[1921] Thee, *Julius Africanus and the Early Christian View of Magic*, 367.

[1922] The δημιουργος, the Demiurge, *craftsman*, the Maker of the lower material world identified with Yahweh by some early Christian sects generally understood as "gnostic." The term is used here in the usual sense of *Creator*.

> φωνην), work against certain demons capable of only certain things, others in the Persian dialect, and so on for each of the nations as appropriate. And so it will be found that to the demons rooted in various places, there correspond appropriate names according to region and national dialect.[1923]

Origen's explanation for the use of particular power words to expel demons explains Mark's concern to preserve Jesus' words of power verbatim:[1924] demons, like people, are native to various regions and accordingly respond to different languages. Ancient tongues constitute a sort of *lingua franca* recognized by demons. The exorcist must use the regional dialect in order to make himself understood, because "these names…pronounced in the right set of circumstances, naming the right demon for a particular task, in the proper language of his area, have great power …incantations are vitiated by translation."[1925] In fact, Origen's explanation agrees in every detail with the magician's understanding of magical praxis, accounting for the insertion of Coptic words—"the Egyptian language"—as well as "Sabaoth" and "Adonai," words belonging to a Hebrew "secret theology"—into magical spellbooks.[1926] Arignotus, describing the procedure for laying a ghost, says, "Taking my books—for I have a large number of Egyptian works on the subject...I resorted to my most

---

[1923] Origen, *Contra Celsum* I, 24.

[1924] Mark 5:41; 7:34.

[1925] Thee, *Julius Africanus and the Early Christian View of Magic*, 371.

[1926] Bohak's observation on the magic use of Hebrew names is particularly relevant: "the non-Jewish practitioners who invoked these divine names often had no sense of their original meanings, and even little sense that they all were the names of a single god." (*Prayer, Magic, and the Stars in the Ancient and Late Antique World*, 71).

Morton Smith remarked that many, probably most, of the magical names derived from Judaism that are found in the magical papyri were, in fact, interpolations added willy-nilly to magical spells, becoming "elements of a transcultural magical lingo." *Studies in the Cult of Yahweh*, 2, 245.

terrifying invocation, *speaking in the Egyptian tongue* (αιγυπτιαζων τη φωνην), pinned him in a dark corner, *and laid him to rest with an incantation*" (καταδων αυτον...οικηματος).[1927]

"The name of God, in all its manifest forms, is the highest goal of the mystic...the one who knows it can claim to be, not only master over the Torah, but also over the universe and, in the end, over God. God himself, together with the angels, has submitted to the power of magic."[1928] Correspondingly, Greek and Coptic spells take care preserve the Hebrew names of patriarchs and divine epithets as in this example:

> Excellent ritual for driving out demons. *Spell to be recited over his head* (λογος λεγομενος επι της κεφαλης αυτου): Hail, *God of Abraham* (**ⲫⲛⲟⲩⲑⲓ ⲛ̄ⲁⲃⲣⲁⲁⲙ**), hail, *God of Isaac* (**ⲡⲛⲟⲩⲧⲉ ⲛ̄ⲓⲥⲁⲕ**), hail, *God of Jacob* (**ⲡⲛⲟⲩⲧⲉ ⲛ̄ⲓⲁⲕⲱⲃ**), Jesus Chrēstos...Bring *Iao Sabaoth* (**ⲓⲁⲱ ⲥⲁⲃⲁⲱⲑ**)...drive away this unclean demon..."[1929]

"...Christianity was not the initial motivation for the introducetion of the Coptic script...the consistent use of the Greek alphabet to write (perhaps we should really say 'spell') Egyptian seems to have been motivated by the need to record and retrieve precise vocalized pronunciations, specifically in texts of ritual power!"[1930] The role of divine names was central to both theurgy and magic. For the theurgist Iamblichus "certain names not only call to mind the gods to which they refer, but actually provide a chain of emanation to the transcendent...[the Egyptians and Assyrians] were the first to whom the gods revealed the

---

[1927] Lucian, *Lover of Lies*, 31.

[1928] Schäfer, *Envisioning Magic: A Princeton Seminar and Symposium*, 42.

[1929] Preisendanz, *Papyri Graecae Magicae* IV, 1227-1239.

[1930] Meyer & Smith, *Ancient Christian Magic: Coptic Texts of Ritual Power*, 20.

secret language, which again, is no mere human invention but exists in the very sinews of the structure of the cosmos."[1931]

Bohak remarks on "the well-known tendency of magical rituals, names, and figures to migrate from one culture to another and from one generation to the next," and cites the "invocation of the קטיריא"—a transliteration of the Greek χαρακτηρες, *charaktēres*, magical "characters," or "signs," basic geometric shapes of which the asterisk is typical—in an Aramaic magical recipe. "This process," the author notes, "was aided by the fact that קטיריא bears a close resemblance to the Aramaic word for 'knots.'"[1932] That Jewish Christians also borrowed from Egyptian theology is suggested by the inclusion of terms such as "lake of fire" and "second death,"[1933] terminology found in Egyptian funerary texts.[1934]

Origen knew that the names of God that were used by Christian exorcists also appeared in magical books:

> Combined with the name of God, so great are the names [of the Jewish patriarchs] that not only do the people of the nations employ them *in their prayers to God* (εν ταις προς θεον ευχαις), even *to subdue demons by charms* (κατεπαδειν δαιμονας), "The God of Abraham, and the God of Isaac, and the God of Jacob" is used by nearly *all those engaged in casting spells and doing magic* (παντας τους τα των επωδων και μαγειων πραγματευομενους). Such an invocation to God will be found *in many places in the magical books* (εν τοις μαγικοις συγ-

---

[1931] Struck, *Magic and Ritual in the Ancient World*, 394-395.

[1932] Bohak, *Bulletin of the American Society of Papyrologists* 36: 33.

[1933] Revelation 19:20; 20:10, 14, 15; 21:8.
See also Thomas, *Magical Motifs in the Book of Revelation*, 3.

[1934] Morenz, *Egyptian Religion*, 207.

> γραμασι πολλαχου), using the name of God as appropriate by these men who expel demons.[1935]

Casting out demons by prayer, using the epithets of "the God of Abraham, and the God of Isaac, and the God of Jacob," provides the authentic cultural setting for Jesus' words to his disciples, "This kind cannot be expelled in any way except *by prayer*," (τουτο το γενος εν ουδενι δυναται εξελθειν ει μη εν προσευχη).[1936] Incantations to drive out demons are prayers to be delivered from evil. "It is remarkable that no names of historical persons from Greek, Egyptian, or Persian traditions are used in the papyri as names of deities in spells, although many such persons are named as authors of spells or magical books."[1937]

Regarding the use of Jesus' name, Origen says:

> A similar philosophy of names also applies to our Jesus, in whose name, in fact, innumerable demons are seen already driven out of souls and bodies, *so effective it was* (ενεργησαν) on those from whom [the demons] were driven. And on the topic of names, we have mentioned that those who are experts in the use of incantations relate that *the spell pronounced in the appropriate dialect achieves the very thing commanded* (την αυτην επωδην ειποντα μεν τη οικεια διαλεκτω ενεργησαι οπερ επαγγελεται η επωδη), but said in another tongue becomes weak and capable of nothing. Therefore it is not the things signified, but the qualities and peculiar properties of the words that have a certain power for this or that.[1938]

Origen's understanding of the power of magical names pronounced in their mother tongues sounds suspiciously like that

---

[1935] Origen, *Contra Celsum* IV, 33.
[1936] Mark 9:29.
[1937] Smith, *Jesus the Magician*, 114.
[1938] Origen, *Contra Celsum* I, 25.

of the magical papyri: *εξορκιζω σε κατα της εβραικης φωνης και κατα της αναγκης των αναγκαιων...*,[1939] "I conjure you by the Hebrew sound and by the Necessity of the Fates" appears to take "the Hebrew sound" as a personified power like Necessity with which it is paired; the Hebrew sound "appears itself to be a name of power."[1940] The Hebrew sound or "language" is almost certainly a reference to other power names of Yahweh mentioned in the section that begins, "Come to me, *O Greatest in heaven* (*ο μεγιστος εν ουρανω*), for whom heaven became a *κωμαστηριον* (kōmastērion),"[1941] references the *Sun* (*Ηλιος*) that shines over the entire inhabited earth, and continues, "*I am Adam, the forefather* (*εγω ειμι Αδαμ προγενης*). My name is Adam. Accomplish for me the [Named] deed, because *I pray to you* (*ενευχομαι σοι*) by the god Iaō (*κατα θεου Ιαω*), the god Abaōth, the god Adōnai (*θεου Αδωναι*), the god Michael (*θεου Μιχαηλ*), the god Souriel, the god Gabriel, the god Raphael, the god Abrasax (*θεου Αβρασαξ*)..." However, the spell is catholic in the pagan sense for in addition to Hebrew names, it invokes a Coptic word of unknown meaning (ΟΙϪΟΥ), Seth-Typhon (*Σηθ Τυφων*), like Yahweh a god of storms and the desert, and Mithra (*Μιθρα*) among others.[1942] "...names point to the deepest meaning of objects, signifying their nature...This is a function of Hebrew being the language of creation and the language of God's revelation."[1943] Origen clearly believed that names retained some magical essence in original languages—"Each effort to make these powerful names generally comprehensive using translation

[1939] Preisendanz, *Papyri Graecae Magicae* III, 119.

[1940] LiDonnici, *Heavenly Tablets: Interpretation, Identity and Tradition in Ancient Judaism*, 92.

[1941] The reference is unclear. Dillon translates it "a dancing place" (Betz, *The Greek Magical Papyri in Translation*, 21), based no doubt on the meaning of *κωμος*, a *festival procession* of song, dance, and revelry, but Liddell & Scott offers the definition, "an assembly of priests" in Egypt (Liddell & Scott, *A Greek-English Lexicon*, 866), related perhaps to *κωμασια*, a ritual procession of images of the gods.

[1942] Preisendanz, *Papyri Graecae Magicae* III, 86-151.

[1943] Martin, *The Politics of Orality*, 264.

or a definition of their meaning will, on the contrary, result in a disruption of the magical contact."[1944] The magical power of names represents "a profound and inexpresable question about the nature of names" (*βαθυς και απορρητος λογος περι φυσεως ονοματων*),[1945] "a certain mysterious principle" (*τινα απορρητον λογον*) that Origen accepts as self evident, although unable to explain it.[1946]

Belief in the inherent power of names in their original languages explains the reaction of the crowd—"women, old men and boys"—who pray and fall to their knees in awe as the religious fraud Alexander "blurted out *some meaningless words* (*φωνας τινας ασημους*), something like Hebrew or Phoenician, he struck senseless those who did not even know what he was saying..."[1947] After a careful analysis of the use of "Hebrew" names by magicians of the period, Bohak concludes "Lucian, who knew Alexander quite well, was certain that the 'words' uttered by him were not real Hebrew or Phoenician words but his own playful inventions."[1948]

Origen provides the modern reader with a sketch of 'magic in theory and practice,' which completely undermines his apologetic intentions. Instead, he demonstrates that Christian miracle workers shared exactly the same worldview as pagan magicians, worked from identical presuppositions, and obtained similar results. His words confirm the suspicion that the difference between *miracle* and *magic* was, and is, merely semantic and that the spirit of Jesus worked no differently than the ghost of any powerful prematurely dead man. Christians in later centuries extended the names of power to include saints and Old Testament figures, as illustrated from a Coptic spell dated from around the

---

1944 Šedina, *Listy filologické* 136, 1-2: 18.
Compare *Contra Celsum* I, 25.

1945 Ibid, I, 24.

1946 Ibid, I, 25.

1947 Lucian, *Alexander the False Prophet*, 13.

1948 Bohak, *Prayer, Magic, and the Stars*, 79.

11th century that invokes ⲍⲉⲧⲣⲁⲕ (Zetrak), ⲙⲉⲍⲁⲕ (Mezak), and ⲁϥⲧⲉⲛⲁⲕⲱ (Aftenakō), better known as Shadrach, Meshach and Abednego, the Babylonian names of Hananiah (ⲁⲛⲁⲛⲓⲁⲥ), Misahael (ⲙⲁⲍⲁⲏϩ) and Azariah (ⲁⲍⲁⲣⲓⲁⲥ), the three faithful youths of Daniel,[1949] whose name (ⲧⲁⲛⲓⲏⲗ) is also included.[1950] The writer is careful to include *all* the known names —the number of names functions as a coefficient of power. In this particular case the invocation of the survivors of the fiery furnace seems particularly apropos since the incantation drives away fever.

Origen's arguments set the stage for all future Christian apologetics that seek to distinguish religion from magic. True Christian magic is "religion" (*θεοσεβεια*), false Christian magic is "magic and sorcery" (*μαγεια..και γοητεια*); true Christian incantations are "the prayers that have been prescribed" (*ταις προσταχθεισαις…ευχαις*), false Christian incantations are just "magical stuff" (*περι των κατα την μαγειαν*)[1951] and so on. Surviving Christian magical texts and amulets, of which there are many, remove any need to take Origen's distinctions seriously. To the contrary, *Contra Celsum* has saved the archaeology of magic a mountain of spadework by confirming that primitive Christians sang "expiatory psalms" (*λυτηριους ωδας*), intoned *counter-spells* (*αποπομπιμους φωνας*), used amulets (*λιθων*)[1952] as *counter-charms* (*αλεξιφαρμακα*) and that some Christian "elders" (*τισι πρεσβυτεροις*) were discovered to have books "full of the barbarous names of demons" (*βαρβαρα δαιμονων ονοματα εχοντα*).[1953] Confronted with beliefs and practices that made

---

1949 Daniel 1-3.

1950 Adcock, *The Bulletin of the American Society of Papyrologists* 19: 99-100.

See Brashear on the names of the three Magi in Coptic spells (*Aufstieg und Niedergang der Römischen Welt* II, 18.5: 3438).

1951 Origen, *Contra Celsum* VI, 39, 41.

1952 "stones with inscriptions graven on them.." Thee, *Julius Africanus and the Early Christian View of Magic*, 369, 385.

1953 Origen, *Contra Celsum* VI, 39-41.

him uncomfortable and finding himself unable to simply deny their existence, Origen simply attributed them to "false" Christians, making the "no true Scotsman" fallacy the oldest trick in Christianity's apologetic repertoire.

The Sethians and magic.

The Christians whom the proto-orthodox "heresiologists" labeled "Sethians" appear to have emerged from a pre-Christian Jewish wisdom tradition that appropriated and reworked elements of Christian theology. Turner states that "Sethianism" is "the earliest form of Gnosticism for which we possess a great deal of textual evidence" but concedes that "we have no record of any group, Gnostic or otherwise, who called themselves 'Sethians,' even though this convenient description was used by the Church Fathers."[1954]

The Biblical Seth, son of Adam or the Egyptian god, Seth-Typhon? With which figure did the Christian Sethians identify? In the documents generally accepted as Sethian, these early Christians self-identify as the "seed of Seth," or "children of Seth," "another race." The gospel of Luke pretends to trace the geneology of Jesus back to Adam through Seth: "the [son] of Enoch, [son] of Seth, [son] of Adam, [son] of God" (*του Ενως του Σηθ του Αδαμ του θεου*).[1955] The Sethian Christians, working from the Greek translation of the Old Testament as did most 1st century Jews of the Dispersion, could cite the text of Genesis, "she bore a son and called his name Seth, and said, 'God *has raised up* (*εξανεστησεν*) for me *another seed* (*σπερμα ετερον*) to replace Abel…'"[1956] The verb *εξανιστημι*, *raise up*, could apply to both a rising generation of children[1957] as well as rising from the

---

[1954] Turner, *Sethian Gnosticism and the Platonic Tradition*, 57-58.
[1955] Luke 3:38.
[1956] Genesis 4:25, *Septuagint*.
[1957] Mark 12:19, for example.

dead.[1958] The Genesis account of the birth of Seth therefore provided ample room for mystical speculation about the "seed of Seth" reborn in the risen Jesus.

Enoch is a well known figure of Jewish religious speculation, including that of some proto-orthodox Christians,[1959] as is Adam. Seth, who might be thought of as a "second Adam," is not an object of conjecture in the canonical New Testament, but was clearly a figure of interest to some early Christian sects. That figures such as Adam could form the basis for extended allegory is clear from Paul's writing in which "the first man, Adam, became a living soul, *the last Adam, a spirit that gives life* (*ο εσχατος Αδαμ εις πνευμα ζωοποιουν*)."[1960] To an emanationist theology that tends to regard each divine entity as the source from which the next issues, the figure of Seth would appear an obvious target of mystical exegesis and that such identification occurred seems secure: "The first is Seth (**ⲥⲏⲑ**), who is called Christ ..."[1961] in which the Seth of reference appears to be the biblical Seth, since other aeonic figures, ultimately derived from Judaism, called Adamas (**ⲁⲇⲁⲙⲁⲥ**)[1962] and Adonaios (**ⲁⲇⲱⲛⲁⲓⲟⲥ**) are also mentioned.[1963] One might point to other Coptic sources

---

[1958] As at Philippians 3:11 or 1 Clement 26:2 where resurrection of the faithful is compared with the rising of the mythical phoenix.

[1959] Jude 1:14, in which Enoch is demoted to seventh in line from Adam. The pseudonymous letters of Peter contain material derived from the Enoch tradition (1 Peter 3:19-20; 2 Peter 2:4-5).

[1960] 1 Corinthians 15:45.

[1961] Ehrman & Pleše, *The Apocryphal Gospels: Texts and Translations*, 405. The text quoted is the *Gospel of Judas*, 52.

The Egyptian Seth was also persistently connected with homosexual rape, hardly an association Christians would want to make with Christ, the Second Seth, assuming, naturally, that they were aware of such a linkage to begin with. (te Velde, *Seth, God of Confusion*, 31, 33-46, 50-52).

[1962] See Van Den Broek, *Studies in Gnosticism and Alexandrian Christianity*, 48-55.

[1963] *Gospel of Judas*, 48, 52.

in which Seth and Christ are assimilated: "...your only-begotten son, whose true name is Seth, Seth the living Christ."[1964] Were the Christians inclined to merge Christ with an Egyptian god, Osiris would seem to have seemed a more attractive choice than Seth: "Osiris is death from which life arises, Seth is life that produces death."[1965]

Ancient writers were given to etymologies that are fanciful by modern standards. It is possible that the Greek ΙΑΩ (IAŌ), the transliteration of the Tetragrammaton, the ineffable name of Yahweh that was much used in magic, became associated with the Coptic ⲉⲓⲱ (ĪŌ), *ass* or *onager*,[1966] an animal associated with the Egyptian god Seth-Typhon, simply through a naïve penchant for homophony. A clear association between IAŌ, *Yahweh*, and ĪŌ, *ass*, occurs at least once in the magical papyri: "... with a bronze stylus draw *an ass* (*ονον*), and on its face, *ÏAŌÏŌ* (*ιαωιω*)...and on its chest, *Sabaōth* (*Σαβαωθ*), under its feet, Abraxas, smear it *with the blood of Typhon* (*αιματι* Τυφω-*νος*)..."[1967] The archons, the ruling powers of the seven heavens in some apocryphal Christian texts, assume therianthropic forms which include the ass: "And these are the bodies belonging with the names: the first is Athoth, he has a sheep's face; the second is

---

1964 Meyer & Smith, *Ancient Christian Magic: Coptic Texts of Ritual Power*, 195.

1965 te Velde, *Seth, God of Confusion*, 95.

Regarding a Coptic amulet for snakebite—"He rebuked all the poisonous snakes"—Frankfurter notes "the ritual repulsion of the desert god Seth and his manifestation in snakes and scorpions...allows a formal link between the image of Horus defeating Seth's reptiles and powers attributed to Jesus..." (*Ancient Christian Magic: Coptic Texts of Ritual Power*, 102, 108).

1966 Crum, *A Coptic Dictionary*, 75-76.

Egyptologists have variously identified the enigmatic "Seth-animal" with the wild ass, the oryx, greyhound, fennec fox, jerboa, okapi, camel, long-snouted mouse, wild hog and the giraffe, confirming that Seth as the god of chaos. (te Velde, *Seth, God of Confusion*, 13).

1967 Preisendanz, *Papyri Graecae Magicae* IV, 3255-3260.

Eloaiou, he has a donkey's face..."[1968] In a spell likely riddled with interpolated material, the magician begins to address the sun god Helios, "I invoke you, the greatest god, eternal lord, ruler of the world, over the world and under the world...I invoke your holy and great and hidden names which it pleases you to hear...Abaōth, Sabaōth, Adonai, the great god...the shining Helios...*you are the great Snake* (*συ ει ο μεγας* Οφις), ruler of all the gods, *who controls the beginning of Egypt* (*ο την αρχην της* Αιγυπτου *εχων*)...in the first hour *you assume the form of a cat* (*μορφην εχεις αιλουρου*)...in the second *you have the form of a dog* (*μορφην εχεις κυνος*)...in the third hour *you have the form of a serpent* (*μορφην εχεις οφεως*)...in the fifth hour *you have the form of a donkey* (*μορφην εχεις ονου*)..."[1969]

"Neither Seth, son of Adam, nor Christ is ever welded with the Egyptian god Seth-Typhon."[1970] Yet Seth, "a chaotic storm and desert god associated with the borderlands and eventually with foreign people" became associated not only with the Greek Typhon, but with Yahweh, a god of storms and deserts: "Seth and the Israelite God frequently co-occur, and both of them are linked to the donkey."[1971] The ancient association of ass wor-

---

[1968] *The Apocryphon of John*, 11.

Compare Ezekiel 4:10 (NIV): "Each of the four had the face of a human being, and on the right side each had the face of a lion, and on the left the face of an ox; each also had the face of an eagle."

[1969] Preisendanz, *Papyri Graecae Magicae* IV, 1601-1665.

Another spell addressed to Helios includes "in the sixth hour you have the form of a donkey" (*ωρα εκτη μορφην εχεις ονου*), III, 515. Evidently the magicians could not keep straight which animal went with which hour.

[1970] Fossum & Glazer, *Zeitschrift für Papyrologie und Epigraphik* 100: 92.

[1971] LiDonnici, *Heavenly Tablets: Interpretation, Identity and Tradition in Ancient Judaism*, 93.

Kotansky considers *οι* Σηθθ on an amulet (document number 36) to represent *ειω* Σηθ: "The vowels *οι* that appear before the name Σηθ

ship, *onolatry* (*ονολατρεια*), with Yahweh is discussed in some detail by Schäfer who notes the lack of "unequivocal evidence" (56) for identifying Seth-Typhon with Yahweh for reasons other than "belittling the Jewish religion," (62)[1972] but that the connection between Yahweh and Typhonian Seth made its way into the magical texts and was not thought to diminish Yahweh's magical power appears clear—the magicians were not concerned with theological purity, after all, but with the acquisition of power through names. Disregard for religious pedigree, so characteristic of magic, is also obvious in many early Christian texts. The works generally considered to represent 'Sethian gnosticism' often betray a Christian framework that is "very thin ...The same discrepancy between framework and contents ap-

---

[Seth, *my note*] may be a variant on the usual *ειω*, Coptic for 'ass,' the usual designation of Seth." (*Greek Magical Amulets*, 188).

[1972] Schäfer, *Judeophobia: Attitudes toward the Jews in the Ancient World*, 55-62, 168.

"The close connection of Seth with foreign countries and the god Baal was not only fatal to the cult of Seth, but also to the symbolism of the reconciliation of Horus and Seth. Egyptian nationalism and its dark reverse, the anti-Semitism that Egypt bequeathed to the ancient and modern world, supplanted the myth of the reconciliation of Horus and Seth, now odious as the god of the Semites..." (te Veldt, *Seth, God of Confusion*, 66, 109-110, 120-125).

The early Christians were seen as just another sect of Judaism and Jesus, conflated with Yahweh, becomes a donkey, leading to Tertullian's famous *somniastis caput asininum esse deum nostrum*, "you have dreamed the head of an ass is our God." (*Apology* XVI). That the Jews worshipped an ass was widely believed; it appears in Plutarch (*Quæstiones Conviviales* 4.5.2), Tacitus (*Historiae* 5.5), Minucius Felix (*Octavius*, IX, XXVIII) and Epiphanius (*Panarion* XXVI, 12. 1-4) among others. Tertullian (*Apology* XVI) even records a pagan placard, DEUS CHRISTIANORUM ΟΝΟΚΟΙΤΗΣ, "GOD OF THE CHRISTIANS ΟΝΟΚΟΙΤΗΣ" in which *ονοκοιτης* has been read "lying in the asses' stall" or as "ass-worhip" (Liddell & Scott, *A Greek-English Lexicon*, 1056), but given that *κοιτη* (koitē), *bed*, can also refer to *coitus*, the message might have carried the even more derogatory connotation, "donkey-screwed" or "son of an ass."

pears even more clearly in the most 'Christian' of all Sethian writings, the *Apocryphon of John*" which exhibits "a New Testament coloring" that fades as the work progresses until the conversation between Jesus and John has "no specifically Christian traits."[1973] But the essential point is not what was or was not "really" Christian—from its very beginning Christianity was many things to many people, freely mixing apocalyptic fervor with mystery cult terminology, personal revelation with spirit possession, borrowing magical techniques and inserting Christian elements into pagan spells and vice versa.

Of Yahweh the psalmists sing, "He parted the heavens and came down; dark clouds were under his feet. He mounted the cherubim and flew; he soared on the wings of the wind. He made darkness his covering, his canopy around him—the dark rain clouds of the sky. Out of the brightness of his presence clouds advanced, with hailstones and bolts of lightning."[1974] "When you, God, went out before your people, when you marched through the wilderness, the earth shook, the heavens poured down rain, sing to God, you kingdoms of the earth, sing praise to the Lord, to him who rides across the highest heavens, the ancient heavens, who thunders with mighty voice."[1975] Yahweh is exactly the kind of power source with which any magician worthy of the name would think to make connection, but on the basis of surviving evidence it would appear that the Seth of Sethian Christianity is the Seth of Genesis,[1976] not the Seth-Typhon of Egypt who is weakly assimilated to Yahweh due to shared elements such as storms,[1977] the desert, the wild ass, and

---

[1973] Schenke, *The Rediscovery of Gnosticism, II, Sethian Gnosticism*, 611.

[1974] Psalms 18:9-12 (NIV).

[1975] Psalm 68: 7-8, 32-33 (NIV).

[1976] The gnostic Seth is Adam's son, "considered by many Gnostics as their founder." (Mastrocinque, *From Jewish Magic to Gnosticism*, 54).

[1977] te Velde, *Seth, God of Confusion*, 25-26, 28-29, 85. Seth is associated with "atmospheric disturbances," i.e., storms and thunder, as well as being "an animal of fatality, a beast of ill omen, an angel of

homonymous titles. Some early Christian sects appropriated Sethianism, but scholars such as Schenke now regard Sethianism as essentially "non-Christian and even pre-Christian" and point out that "most writings of our [Sethian] text group contain no Christian elements at all."[1978]

Regarding Christian dissatisfaction with the lower world, the pagan theurgist Plotinus observed,

> But they themselves most of all impair the inviolate purity of the higher powers in another way too. For when *they write magic chants* (επαοιδας γραφωσιν), intending to address them to those powers, not only to the soul but to those above it as well, what are they doing except making the powers obey the word and *follow the lead* (αγεσθαι) of people *who say spells and charms and conjurations* (γοητειας και θελξεις και πεισεις λεγουσι), any one of us who is well skilled in the art of saying precisely the right things in the right way, songs and cries and aspirated and hissing sounds and everything else which *their writings say has magic power* (μαγευειν γεγραπται). in the higher world? But even if they do not want to say this, how are the incorporeal beings affected by sounds? So by the sort of statements with which they give an appearance of majesty to their own words, they, without realizing it, take away the majesty of the higher powers. But when they say they free themselves from diseases, if they meant that they did so by temperance and orderly living, they would speak well, just as the philosophers do; but in fact they assume that *the diseases are evil spirits* (τας νοσους δαιμονια ειναι), and claim to be able to drive them out *by* their *spell* (λογω); by this claim they might make themselves more impressive in the eyes of the

---

death" linked to the crocodile and hippopotamus, both renowned to this day as killers of men, and he causes spontaneous abortion as well.

[1978] Schenke, *The Rediscovery of Gnosticism, II,* 607.

> masses, *who wonder at the powers of magicians* (οι τας παρα τοις μαγοις δυναμεις θαυμαζουσι), but would not persuade sensible people...[1979]

According to pagan critics, "these Christians used incantatory formulas (επαοιδαι), witchcraft (γοητεια), spells (θελξεις), persuasive words (πεισεις), songs (μελη), cries (ηχοι), blowing (προσπνευσεις), and hissing (σιγμους της φωνης) to attract the attention of the higher entities and draw them to themselves."[1980] That forms of specifically Christian magic had in fact developed early and persisted is clear from rulings of the Synod of Laodicea (363-364 CE) when it was found necessary to forbid Christian clerics in major or minor orders to be magicians, charmers, soothsayers, or astrologers, or to fabricate amulets; wearers of such amulets were to be banned from the Christian community. This same Council had to forbid the exaggerated cult of angels, which had apparently assumed the forms of magic.[1981]

Signs, symbols and magical passwords.

Celsus possessed a diagram in use among certain Christian sects, "a map of celestial and supracelestial regions in the form of circles"[1982] that listed the angelic theriocephalic archons that controlled the journey of the soul through each region. To pass these gatekeepers required a password and Origen conceded the existence of such a map (or one of very similar content) and to prove the superiority of Christian understanding not only disclosed the names and forms of the gatekeepers, but also the

---

[1979] Porphyry, "Against the Gnostics," *Ennead* II, 9.14. I have mostly followed Armstrong's translation with a few minor changes.

[1980] Mastrocinque, *From Jewish Magic to Gnosticism*, 44.

[1981] Barb, *The Conflict Between Paganism and Christianity in the Fourth Century*, 107.

[1982] Rasimus, *Paradise Reconsidered in Gnostic Mythmaking*, 16.
Origen's information on the "Ophite" rituals is suspect (Rasimus, 246).

passwords. Nevertheless, Origen took pains to distance the "real" Christians from the group identified by Celsus: "Next he takes up the subject of the seven ruling demons, by no means acknowledged among the Christians, but, I suppose, an accepted teaching among the Ophites...we discovered that he who is honored in holy scripture as the angel of the Creator (*αγγελον του δημιουργου*)[1983]...is called '*Michael the lion-formed*' (Μιχαηλ *τον λεοντοειδη*)." Origen then lists the theriomorphic gatekeepers in order, among them *Souriel, in the shape of a bull* (Σου*ριηλ...ταυροειδη*), *Raphael, serpent-shaped* (Ραφαηλ...*δρακοντοειδη*)—according to some Coptic texts, the Seraphim are *serpent-shaped* (ⲙ̄ⲙⲟⲣⲫⲏ ⲛ̄ⲇⲣⲁⲕⲱⲛ) angels[1984]—*dog-faced Erathaōth,*[1985] (*κυνος προσωπον*...Επαθαωθ), and *Onoel, "found to be somewhat donkey-shaped*" (Ονοηλ...*ονοειδης τις τυγχανων*). The angelic name is obviously formed off the Greek word for *donkey* (*ονος*) plus the standard Hebrew suffix *-el* (אל) to form *Onoel*, "donkey angel."

Origen also reveals the magical passwords needed to move sucessfully through the "gates of the ruling Æons" (*πυλας αρχοντων αιωνι*), each ending with "Grace be with me, yea, Father, be with me" (*η χαρις συνεστω μοι ναι πατερ συνεστω*).[1986] Origen, eager to contrast "the doctrines of true Christians" (*αληθως* Χ*ριστιανων λογοις*) with those of his real opponents—"*the sorcerers* (*οι γοητες*) deceive those carried away by the imaginary names [of magic]"—accuses Celsus of propagating "things magical and foolish" (*ουσα περιεργια και φλυαρια*), and then lists several of the magical names in use by both pagan and Christian magicians: Ialdabaōth (Ι*αλδαβαωθ*), Iaō (Ι*αω*), Sabaōth (Σ*αβαωθ*), and Adōnaios (Α*δωναιος*) among others well-known from the magical papyri and amulets.[1987] Celsus knew many details

---

[1983] Or, "angel of the Demiurge" if so desired.

[1984] Rasimus, *Paradise Reconsidered in Gnostic Mythmaking*, 69.

[1985] Apparently derived from *Thoth*.

[1986] Origen, *Contra Celsum* VI, 31.

[1987] Ibid, VI, 32.

about gnostic theology, including heavenly "gates that open spontaneouly" (*αυτοματως ανοιγομενας πυλας*) by magic.[1988]

An early form of Jewish religious practice known as היכלות (heykalōt), *palaces* (a reference to the lower heavens), or מרכבה (merkabah), *chariot* mysticism (in reference to the chariot throne of the first chapter of Ezekiel[1989]) promised ascent to the highest heaven and a vision of the throne of God. The "palaces" or seven heavenly spheres of Jewish mysticism are generally believed to have influenced the "gnostic" belief in seven heavens above which lay an eighth realm, the Ogdoad, the highest spiritual plane.[1990] Both systems taught that magical passwords and angelic names were necessary in order to ascend through each of the seven heavens—"frauds and sorcerers and that bunch who learn *the names of the doorkeepers* (*τα ονοματα των θυρωρων*) through wretched memorization."[1991]

"The magical names designated either angels or aspects of the godhead and were described as seals that were to be shown as passports to the angelic gatekeepers of the seven palaces."[1992] A spell for *a vision* (*αυτοπτος*) requires the magican to declare the "mystic symbols" (*συμβολα μυστικα*) of the god, who is addressed, "Hail, Serpent" (*χαιρε δρακων*), "EŌ AI OY AMERR OOUŌTH IYIŌE," etc.[1993] In this case the symbols are *sounds* produced by vowel chanting. "...invoking God shatters human words, breaking them up into their elemental parts. Indeed, language is

[1988] Ibid, VI, 34.

[1989] Ezekiel 1:4-26.

[1990] The *Ogdoad* (*ογδοας*), "Eight-fold," so called after the eight deities or æons in four male-female pairs in Egyptian/Gnostic theology. The seven heavens were the regions of the seven known planets, the eighth, above them, the *empyreum* (from *εμπυρος*, "on fire"), the realm of light, plane of the fixed stars and constellations.

[1991] Origen, *Contra Celsum* VII, 40.

[1992] Merkur, *Gnosis: An Esoteric Tradition of Mystical Visions and Unions*, 176-177.

[1993] Preisendanz, *Papyri Graecae Magicae* IV, 930, 945.

sometimes so shattered that only its most basic elements, the vowels, remain."[1994] Lucian, of the Babylonian mage: "At the same time he mixed in some foreign-sounding *meaningless names of many syllables*" (ασημα ονοματα και πολυσυλλαβα).[1995]

In other spells the magician declares, "I know your *signs* (τα σημεια) and *the passwords* (τα παρασημα) and forms...I have discovered your *signs* (τα σημεια) and *passwords* (τα παρασημα)...I know your *sacred names* (τα αγια ονοματα) and your *signs* (τα σηνεια) and your *passwords* (τα παρασημα)..."[1996] "*Prayer* (ευχη): I call on you, *every-formed* (πανμορφον) and *many-named* (πολυωνυμον), double-horned goddess Mene...and the first component (ο...συντροφος)[1997] of the name is silence, the second *popping* (ποππυσμος), the third *groaning* (στεναγμος), the fourth hissing, the fifth a joyful shout, the sixth moaning, the seventh, barking...the twelfth, *a wind-creating sound* (ο... ηχος ανεμοποιος)...I have found the signs and symbols of your name so that you might hear me..."[1998] Given that the Æons are theriomorphic, it would seem perfectly natural that they would be summoned and addressed in animal "languages" such as barking and hissing, hence Porphyry's mention of the "Gnostic" invocation by *cries* (ηχοι),[1999] hissing, and blowing. Luke's description of the coming of the spirit at Pentecost can be placed in this cultural context: "Suddenly *a sound* (ηχος) like a

---

1994 Martin, *Classical Mediterranean Spirituality*, 495.

1995 Lucian, *Menippus*, 10.

1996 Preisendanz, *Papyri Graecae Magicae* III, 500, 537, 624.

1997 "Component," rather than "companion" (Grese, *The Greek Magical Papyri in Translation*, 139), taking συντροφος in the sense of "natural, congenital," a natural property or constituent element of the magical "name" (Liddell & Scott, *A Greek-English Lexicon*, 1502).

1998 Ibid, VII, 756-788.

1999 Compare, "I adjure you by the three cries, which the son sent forth from the cross, Eloi Eloi Elema Sabaktani..." (Meyer & Smith, *Ancient Christian Magic: Coptic Texts of Ritual Power*, 229). The "cries" are considered magical due to their relation to death by execution.

violent wind (πνοης βιαιας) came from heaven and filled the whole house..."[2000] The word πνοη (pnoē), *wind*, *breath*, usually translates the Hebrew נשמה (neshamah), the *wind* or *breath* of Yahweh, by turns destructive or life-giving.[2001]

Gate imagery is not uncommon in the New Testament: "The one who enters *through the gate* (δια της θυρας) is the shepherd of the sheep. *The gatekeeper* (ο θυρωρος) opens for him and the sheep hear his voice and he calls his sheep by name and leads them out...*I am the gate* (εγω ειμι η θυρα) of the sheep."[2002] "After that I looked and beheld *a door opened in heaven* (θυρα ηνεωγμενη εν τω ουρανω) and the first voice I heard spoke to me like a trumpet and said, 'Come up here and I will show you what must happen after this.' And suddenly I was in [the] spirit and beheld a throne..."[2003] The gods of magic are gatekeepers: "Hekate and Pluto, Kore and chthonic Hermes...*gatekeeper* (πυλωρε) of the everlasting bars..."[2004] "Then open [your] eyes and you will see *the doors* (τας θυρας) open and the world of the gods that is behind the doors...your spirit runs forward and ascends...Having said this you will see *doors flung open* (θυρας ανοιγομενας) and seven virgins...with the faces of vipers."[2005]

2000 Acts 2:2.
2001 As in "the breath of life" of Genesis 2:7.
2002 John 10:2, 7.
2003 Revelation 4:1-2.
2004 Preisendanz, *Papyri Graecae Magicae* IV, 1465-1466.
2005 Ibid, IV, 625-626, 661-662.

CHAPTER 16: A DIALOGUE WITH THE DEAD

Drawing attention to the multiple correspondences between Judeo-Christian and pagan magic, instances of cross-cultural plagiarizing, similarities in magical vocabulary, in theory and practice, is often interesting, sometimes tedious, and occasionally even amusing work. To see themes develop, supporting evidence amass, and a book take shape partially repays weeks spent in reference libraries, lingering dissatisfaction with the best translation one seems able to achieve, and the certain knowledge that important data has been slighted or overlooked altogether due to the author's many limitations. At the end of this fascinating and frustrating process, one must ask, *why this book*?

A facile answer would invoke pure scholarship, supposing such a creature exists, knowledge for its own sake, the past illuminating the present—given the size of the public likely to read a book such as this, a feeble ray of illumination indeed. One might mention the venerable tradition of the *religionsgeschichte Schule*, the "history of religions" movement that sought to draw enlightening comparisons between the cults of the ancient world. But to write an honest history of the formation of Christianity is in fact more akin to documenting the emergence of an incredible *lügenhaft geschichte*, a tall story, a lie. Of all the tall stories widely discussed in this, Anno Domini 2014, the story of Jesus is certainly one of the tallest although it must be conceded that it has some equally impressive brethren.

The New Testament is more than theologized history. The New Testament is a book of magic, magic in the worst sense, fraudulent and ultimately even murderous. The only difference between ancient Christian gobbledygook and ancient pagan gobbledygook is that Christian gobbledygook seems less ridiculous for being more familiar. The raving Christians in Paul's house churches were "speaking into the air," their minds "fruitless" (*ακαρπος*), a "blank,"[2006] mere noise, with no more comprehensible content than the nonsense letter strings that litter the magical papyri: "SAPHPHAIOR BAELKOTA KIKATOUTARA EKENNK LIX…IPSENTANCHOUCHEŌCH DŌOU SHAMAI ARABENNAK ANTRAPHEU BALE SITENGI ARTEN, etc."[2007]

The elevated titles and doxologies of the New Testament are no different in kind than the titles and doxologies of the magical spells. The "hymns" of the magical papyri, once assumed to have been plagiarized from "religious" sources turn out to be compositions of magicians: "No direct literary connections between the magical hymns and religious hymns can be detected…No one has been able to demonstrate any direct borrowing."[2008] The elevated theological language of the books of the New Testament is a mirror image of the language of the spell books:

> Who is the image *of the invisible god* (*του θεου του αορατου*), *firstborn of all creation* (*πρωτοτοκος πασης κτισεως*), because *everything in heaven on on earth was created* by him (*εκτισθη τα παντα εν τοις ουρανοις και επι της γης*), *the seen and the unseen* (*τα ορατε και τα αορατα*), *whether thrones* (*ειτε θρονοι*) or lordships or rulers or authorities. Everything has been created through him and for him. He is before all things and *everything is joined together in/by him* (*τα παντα εν αυτω συνεστηκεν*) and he is *the head of the body* (*η κεφαλη του σωματος*), the church. *Who is the beginning* (*ος εστιν αρχη*), the firstborn of the dead, that he might have the first place in everything so that in him *all the fullness was pleased to live* (*ευδοκησεν παν το πληρωμα κατοικησαι*) and

[2006] 1 Corinthians 14:9, 14.

[2007] Preisendanz, *Papyri Graecae Magicae* IV, 1-8.

[2008] Segal, *Studies in Gnosticism and Hellenistic Religions*, 352.

> through him to reconcile all things to him, whether on earth or in heaven through the blood of his cross.[2009]
>
> "I invoke you, greater than all, *creator of all* (*τον παντα κτισαντα*), self-begotton, who sees all but is not seen... when you appeared, the cosmos came to be and light appeared. *All have been subjected to you* (*σοι παντα υποτετακται*),[2010] whose true form none of the gods are able to see, who assumes every form, *you are invisible* (*αορατος ει*), Æeon of Æeons."[2011]

To be the *firstborn*, *πρωτοτοκος* (prōtotokos), was clearly of magical significance. The magician is to rub the wick of a magical lamp with the fat "of a male firstborn and first-reared" (*αρενος πρωτοτοκου και πρωτοτροφου*) black ram,[2012] and another spell calls for pouring a libation of milk from a black cow, "firstborn and first-raised" (*πρωτοτοκου και πρωτοτροφου*).[2013] A spell to open a door calls for "the umbilical cord of a firstborn ram" (*πρωτοτοκου κριου ομφαλιου*).[2014] A series of spells includes the formula, "and he handed over the scepter of the first-created god" (*και επεδωκεν τω θεω τω πρωτοκτιστω το σκηπτρον*)[2015] and another spell is addressed to "the first-begotten and firstborn god" (*του πρωτοφυους θεου και πρωτογενους*).[2016] Or this Christian spell: "I adjure you today by the blood of the firstborn which was poured out violently..."[2017] Likewise, the gods of

---

[2009] Colossians 1:15-20.

[2010] Compare Ephesians 1:22, "and subjected all under his feet" (*παντα υπεταξεν υπο τους ποδας αυτου*) and similar language at 1 Corinthians 15:27, Hebrews 2:5,8, etc.

[2011] Preisendanz, *Papyri Graecae Magicae* XIII, 70-71.

[2012] Ibid, IV, 1093, 1102.

[2013] Ibid, IV, 3150.

[2014] Ibid, XXXVI, 312.

[2015] Ibid, XIII, 118, 187.

[2016] Ibid, I, 195.

[2017] Meyer & Smith, *Ancient Christian Magic: Coptic Texts of Ritual Power*, 329.

magic are, like Jesus, gods of creation. An incantation begins, "The great living god…who created every soul and race…"[2018] or "eternal lord *who created everything* (ο παντα κτισας), the only god…"[2019]

Jesus is *the head of the body* (η κεφαλη του σωματος), the church; Cerberus is adjured by the head of the chthonic gods: "I adjure you, Cerberus, *by the holy head of the underworld gods…*" (κατα της ιερας κεφαλης των καταχθονιων θεων).[2020] Christ joins everything together in himself (τα παντα εν αυτω συνεστηκεν) just as the gods and angels invoked by the magicians. The "angel of the air" is "joined with a powerful [magical] assistant" (συσταθεν κραταιω παρεδρω),[2021] "*I am joined to you* (συνισταμαι σοι) by the great chief commander, Michael, lord, the great archangel …"[2022] As this brief set of examples demonstrates, the language of the New Testament is the language of magic and has no greater claim to truth.

New Testament Christianity is the perseveration of an ancient religious quackery: the generation Jesus promised would by no means disappear before the glorious return of the Son of Man died awaiting his return and so has every generation since. Failing that return, Christianity's credentials as a non-prophet organization were firmly secured, but the fledgling religion did not wither on the vine or even appear to suffer any longterm reversal. Although this confounds rational expectations, a quick survey of apocalyptic Christian sects in America and elsewhere will prove that discredited predictions—of which there have been many—almost never lead to the disappearance of the groups that make them. Despite the fact that *every apocalyptic*

[2018] Preisendanz, *Papyri Graecae Magicae* IV, 1040.

[2019] Ibid, XIII, 987.

More examples could be cited: PGM XIII, 145; III, 395, 554; IV, 1710.

[2020] Ibid, IV, 1917.

[2021] Ibid, I, 180.

[2022] Ibid, XIII, 927.

prediction made to date by Jesus and his followers has proven false, end-of-the-world preachers continue to flourish in the Cloud-cuckooland of fundamentalist Christianity whose financial beneficiaries merely rewrite their prophecies of a Christian *tausandjahriger Reich*. As Lucian remarked about the Christians of his time, "However, if some fraud (*τις...γοης*) or crafty individual who is able to work matters to his advantage hangs around among them for a while, he can sneer at the ill-informed people while becoming very rich in a short time."[2023] There is no shortage of irony in the fundamentalist position, which proclaims a fake end of the world while hastening the real end of the world through opposition to population control and measures to protect the environment.

In fact, Christian intolerance and rejection of the world has already produced a real apocalypse. "The invasion of the barbarians who conquered the Roman Empire has destroyed infinitely less than did the Christian hatred and persecution of the heathen. Never in the world's history has so vast a literature been so radically given over to destruction. Nor is its historical value the only thing involved: the influence of antiquity on the present would have been still greater had more of the literature of its later times been preserved."[2024] The abysmal moral failure that contemplates the destruction of the world as a thing most devoutly to be wished—'I am dead to the world and the world is dead to me'[2025]—represents a terminal failure of imagination, a spiritual second death. It is a failure that has produced, in the words of Thomas Berry, "an extinction spasm…a kind of ultimate manifestation of that deep inner rage of Western society against its earthly condition."[2026]

[2023] Lucian, "On the Death of Peregrinus," *Lucian: A Selection*, 154.
[2024] Oesterreich, *Possession Demoniacal and Other*, 160.
[2025] Galatians 6:14.
[2026] Laszlo, *The Chaos Point: The World at the Crossroads*, 124-125.

If this book makes one overarching claim, it is that public understanding of what the New Testament says about primitive Christianity has receded, not advanced, and that this failure of comprehension is partly due to what passes for New Testament scholarship. It is inevitable that the majority of students of the New Testament come to the subject armed with a previously established belief in the truth of Christianity and its founding texts, and that their course of study in religious schools is largely designed to reinforce that belief, prepare them to proselytize and to serve as pastors. It nearly goes without saying that the professoriate in such schools—which in the case of "Bible colleges" are nothing more than Christian madrassas—teach and interact within a shallow pool, an intellectually incestuous tendency that actively discourages investigation while promoting fundamentalist orthodoxy. Despite the superficially impressive strings of degrees such teachers award each other, critical study of the New Testament within their ranks is in most cases an interminable Sunday school for overachievers.

At the beginning of the 21st century the primary purpose of such seminaries is the defense of the steadily eroding subcontinent of literalist belief from the surrounding ocean of contrary fact and opinion. Theologically motivated apologetic is dressed up in the clothing of the prevailing *secular* paradigm. Special creation must now be defended as 'creation science' in much the same way that Christian 'miracle' once borrowed from the same frame of reference as magic. Homosexuality is 'healed' by Christian 'therapists' spouting religious psychobabble in place of exorcistic formulas. In each case, the vaunted transcendence of modern Christian discourse is belied by its persistent plagiarism from secular science, psychology and politics, just as the original Christians borrowed from the cultural framework of their own era. One could hope that every two millennia or so the wheel of the collective consciousness will turn sufficiently to permit a renewed relationship between humanity and the cosmos, but if we now know anything with certainty it is that the cosmos will endure long after humanity's time has run out.

REFERENCES

Abusch, Tzvi. *Mesopotamian Witchcraft: Toward a History and Understanding of Babylonian Witchcraft Beliefs and Literature*, 2002, Brill.

Achtemeier, Paul. J. "Jesus and the Disciples as Miracle Workers in the Apocryphal New Testa-ment," *Aspects of Religious Propaganda in Judaism and Early Christianity*, E.S. Fiorenza, ed, 1976, University of Notre Dame Press.

Adams, Christina. "Shades of Meaning: The Significance of Manifestations of the Dead as Evidenced in Texts from the Old Kingdom to the Coptic Period," *Current Research in Egypto-logy 2006: Proceedings of the Seventh Annual Symposium*, 2007, Oxbow Books.

Aland, Barbara & Kurt. *Novum Testamentum Graecae*, 27th edition, 1993, Deutsche Bibel-gesellschaft.

Alcock, Anthony. "A Coptic Magical Text," *The Bulletin of the American Society of Papyrolo-gists* 19/3-4: 97-103.

Alexander, Philip S. "The Demonology of the Dead Sea Scrolls," *The Dead Sea Scrolls After Fifty Years*, II, P.W. Flint & J.C. Vanderkam, eds, 1999, Brill.

—. "Jewish elements in gnosticism and magic c. CE 70—c. CE 270," *The Cambridge History of Judaism*, III, W. Horbury, W.D. Davies & J. Sturdy, eds, 1999, Cambridge University Press.

Alfayé Villa, Silvia. "Nails for the Dead: A Polysemic Account of an Ancient Funerary Practice," *Magical Practice in the Latin West: Papers from the International Conference held at the University of Zaragosa 30 Sept.-1 Oct. 2005*, 2010, Brill.

Anderson, Janice Capel & Stephen D. Moore. "Matthew and Masculinities," *New Testament Masculinities*, S.D. Moore & J.C. Anderson, eds, 2003, Society of Biblical Literature.

Angus, Samuel. *The Mystery Religions: A Study in the Religious Background of Early Christianity*, 1975 (reprint of 1928 edition), Dover Publications.

Archambault, Georges. Justin: *Dialogue Avec Tryphon*, 1909, Librairie Alphonse Picard et Fils.

Arnold, Clifton E. *Ephesians: Power and Magic*, 1989, Cambridge University Press.

Audollent, Augustus. *Defixionum Tabellae quotquot innotuerunt tam in Graecis Orientis quam totius Occidentis partibus praeter attias*, 1904, Alberti Fontemoing.

Aune, David E. "Magic in Early Christianity," *Aufstieg und Niedergang der Römischen Welt*, II, 23.2, 1507-1557, H. Temporini & W. Haase, eds, Walter de Gruyer.

—. "The Apocalypse of John and Graeco-Roman Revelatory Magic," *Apocalypticism, Prophecy, and Magic in Early Christianity*, 2006, Baker Academic.

—. "Magic in Early Christianity," *Apocalypticism, Prophecy, and Magic in Early Christianity*, 2006, Baker Academic.

Avalos, Hector. *The End of Biblical Studies*, 2007, Prometheus Books.

Bailliot, Magali. *Magie et sortilèges dans l'Antiquité romaine: Archéologie des rituels et des images*, 2010, Hermann Éditeurs.

Ball, David Mark. *'I am' in John's Gospel: Literary Function, Background and Theological Implications*, 1996, JSNT Supplement Series 124.

Barb, A.A. "The Survival of Magical Arts," *The Conflict Between Paganism and Christianity in the Fourth Century*, A. Momigliano, ed, 1963, Clarendon Press.

Barton, Stephen C. *Discipleship and Family Ties in Mark and Matthew*, 1994, Cambridge University Press.

Becker, Jürgen. *Jesus of Nazareth*, 1998, Walter de Gruyer.

Becker, Michael. "Μαγοι—Astrologers, Ecstatics, Deceitful Prophets: New Testament Understanding in Jewish and Pagan Context," *A Kind of Magic: Understanding Magic in the New Testament and its Religious Environment*, M. Labahm & B.J. Lietaert Peerbolte, eds, 2007, T&T Clark.

Bell, Richard H. *Deliver Us from Evil: Interpreting the Redemption from the Power of Satan in New Testament Theology*, 2007, Mohr Siebeck.

Benko, Stephen. *Pagan Rome and the Early Christians*, 1984, Indiana University Press.

Bentley, James. *Restless Bones: The Story of Relics*, 1985, Constable.

Bergman, J. "ידע," *Theological Dictionary of the Old Testament*, G.J. Botterweck & H. Ringgren, eds, 1986, William B. Eerdmans.

Bernhard, Andrew E. *Other Early Christian Gospels: A Critical Edition of the Surviving Greek Manuscripts*, 2006, T&T Clark.

Bertram, Georg. "ενεργεω," *Theological Dictionary of the New Testament*, G. Kittel, ed, 1964, William B. Eerdmans.

Betz, Hans Dieter. *Galatians: A Commentary on Paul's Letter to the Churches in Galatia*, 1979, Fortress Press.

—. "Magic and Mystery in the Greek Magical Papyri," *Magika Hiera: Ancient Greek Magic and Religion*, C.A. Faraone & D. Obbink, eds, 1991, Oxford University Press.

—. *The Greek Magical Papyri in Translation: Including the Demotic Spells*, 2nd ed, 1992, University of Chicago Press.

—. "Secrecy in the Greek Magical Papyri," *Secrecy and Concealment: Studies in the History of Mediterranean and Near Eastern Religions*, H.G. Kippenberg & G.G. Stroumsa, eds, 1995, E.J. Brill.

Blondel, Carol. *Μακαριου Μαγνετος Αποκριτικος Η Μονογενης*, 1876, Klincksieck.

Blumell, Lincoln H. *Lettered Christians: Christians, Letters, and Late Antique Oxyrhynchus*, 2012, Brill.

Bohak, Gideon. "Greek, Coptic, and Jewish Magic in the Cairo Genizah," *Bulletin of the American Society of Papyrologists* 36 (1999): 27-44.

—. "Hebrew, Hebrew Everywhere? Notes on the Interpretation of *Voces Magicae*," *Prayer, Magic, and the Stars in the Ancient and Late Antique World*, S. Noegel, J. Walker & B. Wheeler (eds), 2003, Pennsylvania State University Press.

—. *Ancient Jewish Magic*, 2008, Cambridge University Press.

Bompaire, Jacques. *Lucien Œuvres*, I, 2003, Les Belles Lettres.

Bonner, Campbell. "Traces of Thaumaturgic Technique in the Miracles," *Harvard Theological Review* 20 (1927): 171-181.

Borg, Marcus J. & John Dominic Crossan. *The Last Week: The Day-by-Day Account of Jesus' Final Week in Jerusalem*, 2006, Harper San Francisco.

Boswell, John. *Same-Sex Unions in Premodern Europe*, 1994, Vintage Books.

Botha, Pieter J.J. "Health and Healing in New Testament Times: Historical understanding and the healthcare debate," *Health Sa Gesondheid* 1, No. 2 (1996): 3-11.

Bouillet, Marie-Nicolas. *Les Ennéades de Plotin: Chef de l'École Néoplatonicienne*, Tome Troisieme, 1864, Librairie de L. Hachette.

Bowe, Barbara E. "Dancing into the Divine: The Hymn of the Dance in the Acts of John," *Journal of Early Christian Studies* 7 (1999): 83-104.

Brakke, David. *The Gnostics: Myth, Ritual, and Diversity in Early Christianity*, 2010, Harvard University Press.

Brashear, William M. "The Greek Magical Papyri: An Introduction and Survey, Annotated Bibliography (1928-199)," *Aufstieg und Niedergang der römischen Welt* II, 18.5: 3380-3730, H. Temporini & W. Haase, eds, Walter de Gruyer.

Bremmer, Jan N. "Magic, martyrdom and women's liberation in the Acts of Paul and Thecla," *The Apocryphal Acts of Paul*, J.N. Bremmer, (ed), 1996, Kok-Pharos.

Brenk, Frederick E. "In the Light of the Moon," *Aufstieg und Niedergang der Römischen Welt*, II, 16.3, 2068-2143, H. Temporini & W. Haase, eds, Walter De Gruyter.

Brenton, Lancelot C.L. *The Septuagint with Apocrypha: Greek and English*, 2003, Hendrickson Publishers.

Breyfogle, Todd. "Magic, Women, and Heresy in the Late Empire: The Case of the Priscillianists," *Ancient Magic and Ritual Power*, M. Meyer & P. Mirecki, eds, 2001, Brill Academic Publishers.

Brier, Bob. *Ancient Egyptian Magic*, 1981, Quill.

Brown, Francis, S.R. Driver & Charles A. Briggs. *Hebrew and English Lexicon: With an appendix containing the Biblical Aramaic*, 1906, Hendrickson Publishers, Inc.

Brown, Jeannine K. "Just a Busybody? A Look at the Greco-Roman Topos of Meddling for Defining αλλοτριεπισκοπος in 1 Peter 4:15," *Journal of Biblical Literature* 125 (2006): 549-568.

Brown, Peter. *Religion and Society in the Age of Saint Augustine*, 1972, Faber & Faber.

—. *The Cult of the Saints: Its Rise and Function in Latin Christianity*, 1981, University of Chicago Press.

—. *The Body and Society: Men, Women and Sexual Renunciation in Early Christianity*, 1988, Columbia University Press.

Brown, Raymond. "Diverse Views of the Spirit In the New Testament," *Worship* 57 (May, 1983), 225-236.

Buckley, Jorunn Jacobsen. "Libertines or Not: Fruit, Bread, Semen and Other Body Fluids in Gnosticism," *Journal of Early Christian Studies*, 2/1 (1994), 15-31.

Büchsel, Friedrich. "δεω," *Theological Dictionary of the New Testament*, G. Kittel, ed, 1964, William B. Eerdmans.

Burkert, Walter. *Greek Religion: Archaic and Classic*, 1985, Harvard University Press.

—. *Ancient Mystery Cults*, 1987, Harvard University Press.

Butterworth, G. W. *Clement of Alexandria: The Exhortation to the Greeks*, 1982 (reprint), Harvard University Press.

Cameron, Ron. *The Other Gospels: Non-Canonical Gospel Texts*, 1982, The Westminster Press.
Carmichael, Joel. *The Unriddling of Christian Origins: A Secular Account*, 1995, Prometheus Books.
Carrier, Richard C. "The Plausibility of Theft," *The Empty Tomb: Jesus Beyond the Grave*, R.M. Price & J.J. Lowder, eds, 2005, Prometheus Books.
Cary, Earnest. *Dio's Roman History*, 1960, Harvard University Press.
Cavigneaux, Antoine. "Introduction à la magie mésopotamienne," *La magic en Égype: à la recherche d'un definition*, 2002, La documentation Française.
Chadwick, Henry. *Origen: Contra Celsum*, 1965, Cambridge University Press.
—. *Priscillian of Avila: The Occult nd Charismatic in the Early Church*, 1976, Oxford University Press.
Chancey, Mark A. *The Myth of a Gentile Galilee*, 2002, Cambridge University Press.
—. "How Jewish was Jesus' Galilee?" *Biblical Archaeology Review* 33 (2007): 42-50.
Chester, Stephen J. "Divine Madness? Speaking in Tongues in 1 Corinthians 14:23," *Journal for the Study of the New Testament* 27 (2005): 417-446.
Ciraolo, Leda Jean. "Supernatural Assistants in the Greek Magical Papyri," *Ancient Magic and Ritual Power*, M. Meyer & P. Mirecki, eds, 1991, Brill Academic Publishers.
Clarke, Emma C., John M. Dillon & Jackson P. Hershbell. *Iamblichus: De mysteriis*, 2003, Society of Biblical Literature.
Clay, Diskin. "Lucian of Samosata: Four Philosophical Lives (Nigrinus, Demonax, Peregrinus, Alexander Pseudomantis)," *Aufstieg und Niedergang der römischen Welt* II.36.5, 3406-3450.
Cohn, Haim. *The Trial and Death of Jesus*, 1967, Harper & Row.
Collins, Adela Yarbro. "The Function of 'Excommunication' in Paul," *Harvard Theological Review* 73 (1980): 251-262.
—. "Rulers, Divine Men, and Walking on the Water (Mark 6:45-52)," *Religious Propaganda and Missionary Competition in the New Testament World*, L. Bormann, K. Del Tredici & A. Standhartinger (eds), 1994, Brill.
Collins, Derek. *Magic in the Ancient Greek World*, 2008, Blackwell.

Comfort, Philip W. & David P. Barrett, eds. *The Text of the Earliest New Testament Greek Manuscripts,* corrected and enlarged edition, 2001, Tyndale House Publishers.

Conner, Miguel. *Voices of Gnosticism*, 2011, Bardic Press.

Conner, Randy P. *Blossom of Bone: Reclaiming the Connections between Homoeroticism and the Sacred*, 1993, Harper San Francisco.

Conner, Robert P. *Jesus the Sorcerer*, 2006, Mandrake of Oxford.

—. *Magic in the New Testament: A Survey and Appraisal of the Evidence*, 2010, Mandrake of Oxford.

Connolly, A. L. "κυναριον," *New Documents Illustrating Early Christianity: A Review of the Greek Inscriptions and Papyri published in 1979*, 1987, The Ancient History Documentary Research Centre.

Cosaert, Carl. *The Text of the Gospels in Clement of Alexandria*, 2008, Brill.

Cotter, Wendy. *Miracles in Greco-Roman Antiquity*, 1999, Routledge.

Crossan, John Dominic. *The Historical Jesus: The Life of a Mediterranean Jewish Peasant*, 1991, Harper San Francisco.

—. *Four Other Gospels: Shadows on the Contours of Canon*, 1992, Polebridge Press.

—. *Who Killed Jesus? Exposing the Roots of Anti-Semitism in the Gospel Story of the Death of Jesus*, 1995, Harper San Francisco.

Crum, Walter Ewing. *Catalogue of the Coptic Manuscripts in the British Museum*, 1905, Longsmans & Company.

—. *A Coptic Dictionary*, 1939, Clarendon Press.

Cryer, Frederick H. "Magic in Ancient Syria-Palestine and in the Old Testament," *Witchcraft and Magic in Europe: Biblical and Pagan Societies*, B. Ankarloo & S. Clark, eds, 2001, University of Pennsylvania Press.

Daniel, Robert W. & Franco Maltomini, eds. *Supplementum Magicum*, Volume I (1990) & Volume II (1992), Westdeutscher Verlag.

Danker, Frederick William. *A Greek-English Lexicon of the New Testament and Early Christian Literature*, 3rd edition, 2000, University of Chicago Press.

David, Rosalie. *Religion and Magic in Ancient Egypt*, 2002, Penguin Books.

Davies, Owen. *Grimoires: A History of Magic Books*, 2009, Oxford University Press.

Davies, Stevan L. *Jesus the Healer: Possession, Trance, and the Origins of Christianity*, 1995, Continuum.

Davies, T. Witton. *Magic, Divination, and Demonology Among the Hebrews and Their Neighbors: Including an Examination of Biblical References and of the Biblical Terms*, 1898, J. Clarke & Company, (reprinted, Ktav Publishing House, 1969).

DeConick, April D. "From the Bowels of Hell to Draco: The Mysteries of the Peratics," *Mystery and Secrecy in the Nag Hammadi Collection and Other Ancient Literature: Ideas and Practices*, C.H. Bull, L.I. Lied & J.D. Turner, eds, 2012, Brill.

Deissmann, Adolf. *Light from the Ancient East: The New Testament Illustrated by Recently Discovered Texts of the Græco-Roman World*, 4th ed, 1922, Harper & Brothers.

Delatte, Armand. *Anecdota Atheniensia*, 1927, Édouard Champion.

de Mause, Lloyd. *The History of Childhood*, 1974, Harper & Row.

Denzey, Nicola. "A New Star on the Horizon: Astral Christologies and Stellar Debates in Early Christian Discourse," *Prayer, Magic, and the Stars in the Ancient and Late Antique World*, S. Noegel, J. Walker & B. Wheeler eds, 2003, Pennsylvania State University Press.

De Romilly, Jacqueline. *Magic and Rhetoric in Ancient Greece*, 1975, Harvard University Press.

de Vos, Craig S. "Finding a Charge That Fits: The Accusation Against Paul and Silas at Philippi (Acts 16:19-21)," *Journal for the Study of the New Testament* 74 (1999): 51-63.

Deutsch, Celia. "Visions, Mysteries and the Interpretive Task: Text Work and Religious Experience in Philo and Clement," *Experientia, Volume I, Inquiry into Religious Experience in Early Judaism and Christianity*, F. Flannery, C. Shantz & R.A. Werline, eds, 2008, Brill.

Dickie, Matthew W. "The Fathers of the Church and the Evil Eye," *Byzantine Magic*, H. Maguire, ed, 1995, Harvard University Press.

—. *Magic and Magicians in the Greco-Roman World*, 2001, Routledge.

Dio Cassius. *Roman History: Books LXI-LXX*, tr. Earnest Cary, 1925, Harvard Univeristy Press.

Dodds, Eric. R. *The Greeks and the Irrational*, 1951, University of California Press.

Duff, Jeremy. *The Elements of New Testament Greek*, 3rd ed., 2005, Cambridge University Press.

Duling, Dennis C. "Solomon, Exorcism, and the Son of David," *Harvard Theological Review* 68 (1975): 235-252.

Dunn, James D.G. *Jesus and the Spirit: A Study of the Religious and Charismatic Experience of Jesus and the First Christians as Reflected in the New Testament*, 1975, The Westminster Press.

Ehrenreich, Barbara. *Blood Religion: Origins and History of the Passions of War*, 1997, Henry Holt & Company.

Ehrman, Bart D. *The Orthodox Corruption of Scripture: The Effect of Early Christological Controversies on the Text of the New Testament*, 1993, Oxford University Press.

—. "The Neglect of the Firstborn in New Testament Studies," *Presidential Lecture*, Society of Biblical Literature, 1997.

—. *Jesus: Apocalyptic Prophet of the New Millennium*, 1999, Oxford University Press.

—. *Lost Christianities: The Battles for Scripture and the Faiths We Never Knew*, 2003, Oxford University Press.

—. *The New Testament: A Historical Introduction to the Early Christian Writings*, 3rd ed, 2004, Oxford University Press.

—. & Zlatko Pleše. *The Apocryphal Gospels: Texts and Translations*, 2011, Oxford University Press.

—. *Forged: Writing in the Name of God—Why the Bible's Authors Are Not Who We Think They Are*, 2011, Harper One.

Edwards, Mark. *Christians, Gnostics and Philosophers in Late Antiquity*, 2012, Ashgate Variorum.

Eitrem, Samson. *Some Notes on the Demonology in the New Testament*, 2nd edition revised and enlarged, 1966, Symbolae Osloenses, Supplement XX.

—. "Dreams and Divination in Magical Ritual," *Magika Hiera: Ancient Greek Magic and Religion*, C. Faraone & D. Obbink, eds, 1991, Oxford University Press.

Eliade, Mircea. *Images and Symbols: Studies in Religious Symbolism*, 1969, Sheed & Ward.

—. *Shamanism: Archaic Techniques of Ecstacy*, 1972, Princeton University Press.

Elkin, Adolphus P. *Aboriginal Men of High Degree: Initiation and Sorcery in the World's Oldest Tradition*, 1977, Inner Traditions International.

Epp, Eldon Jay. "The Multivalence of the Term 'Original Text' in New Testament Textual Criticism," *Harvard Theological Review* 92 (1999): 245-281.

Epstein, Louis M. *Sex Laws and Customs in Judaism*, 1967, Ktav Publishing House.

Ericksen, Robert P. *Theologians Under Hitler: Gerhard Kittel, Paul Althaus and Emanuel Hirsh*, 1985, Yale University Press.

Esler, Philip F. *The First Christians in their Social Worlds: Social-scientific approaches to New Testament Interpretation*, 1994, Routledge.
Faraone, Christopher A. "The Agonistic Context of Early Greek Binding Spells," *Magika Hiera: Ancient Greek Magic and Religion*, C.A. Faraone & D. Obbink, eds, 1991, Oxford University Press.
—. *Talismans and Trojan Horses: Guardian Statues in Ancient Greek Myth and Ritual*, 1992, Oxford University Press.
—. *Ancient Greek Love Magic*, 1999, Harvard University Press.
—. "The construction of gender in ancient Greek love magic," *The world of ancient magic*, D.R. Jordan, H. Montgomery & E. Thomassen, eds, 1999, Bergen.
—. "Necromancy Goes Underground," *Mantikê: Studies in Ancient Divination*, S.I. Johnston & P.T. Struck, eds, 2005, Brill.
Farley, David. *An Irreverent Curiosity: In Search of the Church's Strangest Relic in Italy's Oddest Town*, 2009, Gotham Books.
Farnell, Lewis Richard. *The Cults of the Greek States*, 1977, Caratzas Brothers Publishers.
Felton, Debbie. *Haunted Greece and Rome: Ghost Stories from Classical Antiquity*, 1999, University of Texas Press.
Finucane, Ronald C. *Ghosts: Appearances of the Dead and Cultural Transformation*, 1996, Prometheus Books.
Flint, Valerie. "The Demonization of Magic and Sorcery in Late Antiquity: Christian Redefinitions of Pagan Religions," *Witchcraft and Magic in Europe: Ancient Greece and Rome*, B. Ankarloo & S. Clark, eds, 1999, University of Pennsylvania Press.
Forbes, Christopher. *Prophecy and Inspired Speech in Early Christianity and its Hellenistic Environment*, 1997, Hendrickson Publishers.
Fossum, Jarl & Brian Glazer. "Seth in the Magical Texts," *Zeitschrift für Papyrologie und Epigraphik* 100: 86-92.
Fowden, Garth. *The Egyptian Hermes: A Historical Approach to the Late Pagan Mind*, 1986, Cambridge University Press.
Fowler, Miles. "Identification of the Bethany Youth in the Secret Gospel of Mark with Other Figures Found in Mark and John," *The Journal of Higher Criticism* 5/1 (1998): 3-22.
Frankfurter, David. "Fetus Magic and Sorcery Fears in Roman Egypt," *Greek, Roman, and Byzantine Studies* 46 (2006): 37-62.
—. "Narrating Power: The Theory and Practice of the Magical *Historiola* in Ritual Spells," *Ancient Magic and Ritual Power*, M. Meyer & P. Mirecki, eds, 2001, Brill.

Freeman, Charles. *The Closing of the Western Mind: The Rise of Faith and the Fall of Reason*, 2002, Vintage.
Freyne, Sean. *Galilee, Jesus and the Gospels*, 1988, Fortress Press.
Fuhrmann, Christopher J. *Policing the Roman Empire: Soldiers, Administration, and Public Order*, 2012, Oxford University Press.
Gager, John G. *Curse Tablets and Binding Spells from the Ancient World*, 1992, Oxford University Press.
García Martínez, Florentino. "Magic in the Dead Sea Scrolls," *The Metamorphosis of Magic from Late Antiquity to the Early Modern Period*, J.N. Bremmer & J.R. Veenstra, eds, 2002, Peeters.
Garrett, Susan R. *The Demise of the Devil: Magic and the Demonic in Luke's Writings*, 1989, Fortress Press.
—. "Light on a Dark Subject and Vice Versa: Magic and Magicians in the New Testament," *Religion, Science, and Magic: In Concert and in Conflict*, J. Neusner, E.S. Frerichs & P.V. McCracken Flesher, eds, 1989, Oxford University Press.
Geary, Patrick J. *Furta Sacra: Thefts of Relics in the Central Middle Ages*, 1978, Princeton University Press.
Geller, Markham J. "Jesus' Theurgic Powers: Parallels in the Talmud and Incantation Bowls," *Journal of Jewish Studies* 28 (1977): 141-155.
Giannobile, Sergio & D.R. Jordan. "A Lead Phylactery from Colle san Basilio (Sicily)," *Greek, Roman, and Byzantine Studies* 46 (2006): 73-86.
Gifford, Edwin Hamilton (tr). *Eusebius' Preparation for the Gospel*, II, 1981, Baker Book House.
Goldin, Judah. "The Magic of Magic and Superstition," *Aspects of Religious Propaganda in Judaism and Early Christianity*, 1976, E. Schüssler Fiorenza, ed, University of Notre Dame Press.
Gordon, Richard. "Reporting the Marvellous: Private Divination in the Greek Magical Papyri," *Envisioning Magic: A Princeton Seminar and Symposium*, P. Schäfer & H.G. Kippenberg, eds, 1997, Brill.
—. "Imagining Greek and Roman Magic," *Witchcraft and Magic in Europe: Ancient Greece and Rome*, B. Ankarloo & S. Clark, eds, 1999, University of Pennsylvania Press.
Grabbe, Lester L. "The Roman Period," *Judaism from Cyrus to Hadrian*, II, 1992, Fortress Press.
—. *Priests, Prophets, Diviners, Sages: A Socio-Historical Study of Religious Specialists in Ancient Israel*, 1995, Trinity Press International.
Graf, Fritz. *Magic in the Ancient World*, 1997, Harvard University Press.

—. "How to Cope with a Difficult Life: A View of Ancient Magic," *Envisioning Magic: A Princeton Seminar and Symposium*, P. Schäfer & H.G. Kippenberg, eds, 1997, Brill.

—. "Excluding the Charming: The Devolopment of the Greek Concept of Magic," *Ancient Magic and Ritual Power*, M. Meyer & P. Mirecki, eds, 2001, Brill.

Grant, Michael. *The Jews in the Roman World*, 1973, Charles Scribner's Sons.

—. *Jesus*, 1977, Rigel Publications.

Grayston, Kenneth. "The Meaning of Paraklētos," *Journal for the Study of the New Testament*, 13 (1991): 67-82.

Greenfield, Richard P. H. "A Contribution to the Study of Palaeologan Magic," *Byzantine Magic*, H. Maguire, ed, 1995, Harvard University Press.

Griffith, F. Ll. & Herbert Thompson, eds, *The Leyden Papyrus: An Egyptian Magical Book*, 1974, Dover Publications.

Grig, Lucy. *Making Martyrs in Late Antiquity*, 2004, Duckworth.

Grundman, Walter. "ισχυω," *Theological Dictionary of the New Testament*, 1964, G. Kittel, ed, William B. Eerdmans.

Guignebert, Charles. *The Jewish World in the Time of Jesus*, tr. S.H. Hooke, 1939, Routledge & Kegan Paul.

Haardt, Robert. *Gnosis: Character and Testimony*, 1971, E.J. Brill.

Hale, John R., et al. "Questioning the Delphic Oracle, *Scientific American* 289/2 (2003): 66-73.

Hanse, Hermann. "εχω," *Theological Dictionary of the New Testament*, 1964, G. Kittel, ed, William B. Eerdmans.

Hansen, William. *Phlegon of Tralles' Book of Marvels*, 1996, University of Exeter Press.

Hanson, K.C. & Douglas E. Oakman. *Palestine in Time of Jesus: Social Structures and Social Conflicts*, 1998, Fortress Press.

Haren, Michael J. "The Naked Young Man: A Historian's Hypothesis on Mark 14,51-52," *Biblica* 79 (1998): 525-531.

Harmon, A.M. *Lucian*, III, 1921, Harvard University Press.

—. *Lucian*, IV, 1925, Harvard University Press.

Harvey, W. Wigan. *Five Books Against Heresies*, Volume I, 2013 (reprint of 1857 edition), St. Irenaeus Press.

Harris, William V. *Ancient Literacy*, 1989, Harvard University Press.

Hegedus, Tim. "The Magi and the Star in the Gospel of Matthew and Early Christian Tradition," *Laval théologique et philosophique* 59/1 (février, 2003): 81-95.

Heinichen, Frederick A. *Eusebii Pamphili: Praeperationis Evangelicae*, II, 1842, Lipsius.

Heintz, Florent. "Simon "Le Magicien": Actes 8, 5-25 et l'accusation de magie contre les prophètes thaumaturges dan l'antiquité," *Cahiers de la Revue Biblique*, 1997, J. Gabalda.

Hennecke, Edgar. *New Testament Apocrypha*, II, 1964, Westminster Press.

Hester, J. David. "Eunuchs and the Postgender Jesus: Matthew 19.12 and Transgressive Sexualities," *Journal for the Study of the New Testament* 28 (2005):13-40.

Hoehner, Harold W. *Ephesians: An Exegetical Commentary*, 2002, Baker Academic.

Hoffman, R. Joseph. *Jesus Outside the Gospels*, 1984, Prometheus Books.

—. *Celsus On the True Doctrine, A Discourse Against the Christians*, 1987, Oxford University Press.

—. *Julian's Against the Galileans*, 2004, Prometheus Books.

Hoffner, Harry A. "אוב," *Theological Dictionary of the Old Testament*, 1974, J.J. Botterweck & H. Ringgren, eds, William B. Eerdmans.

Holmén, Tom. "Jesus and Magic: Theodicean Perspectives to the Issue," *A Kind of Magic: Understanding Magic in the New Testament and its Religious Environment*, M. Labahn & B.J.L. Peerbolt, 2007, T&T Clark.

Horsley, Greg H.R. *New Documents Illustrating Early Christianity*, 1981-1987, Macquarie University Press.

Horsley, Richard A. & John S. Hanson. *Bandits, Prophets and Messiahs: Popular Movements in the Time of Jesus*, 1999, Trinity Press International.

Hull, John M. *Hellenistic Magic and the Synoptic Tradition*, 1974, SCM Press Ltd.

Hunt, Arthur S. *The Oxyrhynchus Papyri*, VIII, 1911, Egypt Exploration Society.

Isbell, Charles D. *Corpus of the Aramaic Incantation Bowls*, 1975, Scholars Press.

Jacobs, Andrew S. "A Family Affair: Marriage, Class, and Ethics in the Apocryphal Acts of the Apostles," *Journal of Early Christian Studies* 7/1 (1999): 105-138.

Janowitz, Naomi. "Theories of Divine Names in Origen and Pseudo-Dionysius," *History of Religions* 30/4 (1991), 359-372.

—. *Magic in the Roman World: Pagans, Jews and Christians,* 2001, Routledge.

—. *Icons of Power: Ritual Practices in Late Antiquity,* 2002, Pennsylvania State University Press.

Jeffers, Ann. *Magic and Divination in Ancient Palestine and Syria,* 1996, E.J. Brill.

Jennings, Theodore W. Jr. *The Man Jesus Loved: Homoerotic Narratives from the New Testament,* 2003, Pilgrim Press.

— & Tat-Siong Benny Liew. "Mistaken Identities But Model Faith: Rereading the Centurian, the Chap, and the Christ in Matthew 8:5-13," *Journal of Biblical Literature* 123 (2004): 467-494.

Johnston, Sarah Iles. *Restless Dead: Encounters Between the Living and the Dead in Ancient Greece,* 1999, University of California Press.

—. "Songs for the ghosts: Magical solutions to deadly problems," *The world of ancient magic,* D.R. Jordan, H. Montgomery & E. Thomassen, eds, 1999, Bergen.

—. *Religions of the Ancient World: A Guide,* 2004, Harvard University Press.

Jonas, Hans. *The Gnostic Religin: The message of the alien God and the beginnings of Christianity,* 2nd ed, revised, 1958, Beacon Press.

Jones, Christopher P. *Culture and Society in Lucian,* 1986, Harvard University Press.

Jones, Prudence & Nigel Pennick. *A History of Pagan Europe,* 1995, Routledge.

Junod, Eric & Jean-Daniel Kaestli. *Acta Iohannis,* 1983, Brepols-Turnhout.

Kashdan, Alexander. "Holy and Unholy Miracle Workers," *Byzantine Magic,* H. Maguire, ed, 1995, Harvard University Press.

Keck, Leander E. "Matthew and the Spirit," *The Social World of the First Christians: Essays in Honor of Wayne A. Meeks,* L.M. White & O.L. Yarbrough, eds, 1995, Fortress Press.

Kee, Howard Clark. "The Terminology of Mark's Exorcism Stories," *New Testament Studies* 14 (1967): 232-246.

—. *Medicine, Miracle and Magic in New Testament Times,* 1986, Cambridge University Press.

—. "Magic and Messiah," *Religion, Science, and Magic: In Concert and in Conflict,* J. Neusner, E.S. Frerichs & P.V. McCracken Flesher, eds, 1989, Oxford University Press.

Kieckhefer, Richard. *Magic in the Middle Ages,* 1989, Cambridge University Press.

King, Leonard W. *Babylonian Magic and Sorcery: Being "The Prayers of the Lifting of the Hand,"* 1896, Luzac and Company.

Kittel, Gerhard. "αγγελος," *Theological Dictionary of the New Testament*, 1964, G. Kittel, ed, William B. Eerdmans.

Kirby, Peter. "The Case Against the Empty Tomb," *The Empty Tomb: Jesus Beyond the Grave*, R.M. Price & J.J. Lowder, eds, 2005, Prometheus Books.

Klauck, Hans-Josef. *Magic and Paganism in Early Christianity: The World of the Acts of the Apostles*, 2003, Fortress Press.

—. *The Apocryphal Acts of the Apostles*, 2008, Baylor University Press.

Klijn, A.F.J. "Jewish Christianity in Egypt," *The Roots of Egyptian Christianity*, B.A. Pearson & J.E. Goehring, eds, 1986, Fortress Press.

Koester, Helmut. *Ancient Christian Gospels: Their History and Development*, 1990, Trinity Press International.

—. "The Text of the Synoptic Gospels in the Second Century," *Gospel Traditions in the Second Century: Origins, Recensions, Text, and Transmission*, W.L. Petersen, ed, 1990, University of Notre Dame Press.

Kolenkow, Anitra B. "Relationship Between Miracle and Prophecy in the Greco-Roman World and Early Christianity," *Aufstieg und Niedergang der Römischen Welt*, II, 23.2, 1470-1506, H. Temporini & W. Haase, eds, Walter de Gruyer.

Koskenniemi, Erkki. "Apolo

Kotansky, Roy. "Incantations and Prayers for Salvation on Inscribed Greek Amulets," *Magika Hiera: Ancient Greek Magic and Religion*, C. Faraone & D. Obbink, eds, 1991, Oxford University Press.

—. *Greek Magical Amulets: The Inscribed Gold, Silver, Copper, and Bronze Lamellae, Part I, Published Texts of Known Provenance*, 1994, Westdeutscher Verlag.

—. "Greek Exorcistic Amulets," *Ancient Magic and Ritual Power*, M. Meyer & P. Mirecki, eds, 2001, Brill Academic Publishers.

Kraeling, Carl H. "Was Jesus Accused of Necromancy?" *Journal of Biblical Literature* 59: 147-157.

Kraemer, Ross S. "Implicating Herodias and Her Daughter in the Death of John the Baptizer: A (Christian) Theological Strategy?" *Journal of Biblical Literature* 125 (2006): 321-349.

Kueffler, Matthew. *The Manly Eunuch: Masculinities, Gender Ambiguity, and Christian Ideology in Late Antiquity*, 2001, University of Chicago Press.

Kurz, William S. "The Acts of the Apostles," *The Collegeville Bible Commentary: New Testament*, R.J. Karris, ed, 1992, The Liturgical Press.

Lake, Kirsopp. *Eusebius: The Ecclesiastical History*, Books I-V, 1926, Harvard University Press.

—. *The Apostolic Fathers*, II, 1948, Harvard University Press.

Lalleman, P.J. "Polymorphy of Christ," *The Apocryphal Acts of John*, J.N. Bremmer, ed, 1995, Pharos.

Lambert, Royston. *Beloved and God: The Story of Hadrian and Antinous*, 1984, Wiedenfeld and Nicolson.

Lane Fox, Robin. *Pagans and Christians*, 1989, Alfred A. Knopf.

Lange, Armin. "The Essene Position on Magic and Divination," *Legal Texts and Legal Issues: Proceedings of the Second Meeting of the International Organization of Qumran Studies*, M. Bernstein, F. García Martínez & J. Kampen, eds, 1997, Brill Academic Publishers.

Lapin, Hayim. "Introduction: Locating Ethnicity and Religious Community in Later Roman Palestine," *Religious and Ethnic Communities in Later Roman Palestine*, H. Lapin, ed, 1998, University Press of Maryland.

Larsson, Edvin. "εχω," *Exegetical Dictionary of the New Testament*, H. Balz & G. Schneider, eds, 1991, William B. Eerdmans.

Lenormant, François. *Chaldean Magic: Its Origin and Development*, 1875, Samuel Bagster & Sons.

Lesses, Rebecca. "Speaking with Angels: Jewish and Greco-Egyptian Revelatory Adjurations," *Harvard Theological Review* 89 (1996): 41-60.

Levison, John R. *The Spirit in First Century Judaism*, 1997, Brill.

Lewis, Ioan M. *Ecstatic Religion: An Anthropological Study of Spirit Possession and Shamanism*, 1971, Penguin Books.

Lewis, Theodore J. *Cults of the Dead in Ancient Israel and Ugarit*, 1989, Scholars Press.

Licht, Hans. *Sexual Life in Ancient Greece*, 1932, George Routledge & Sons.

Liddell, Henry George, Scott, Robert & Jones, Stuart. *A Greek-English Lexicon*, 9th ed, Clarendon Press.

LiDonnici, Lynn. "According to the Jews:" Identified (and Identifying) 'Jewish' Elements in the Greek Magical Papyri," *Heavenly Tablets: Interpretation, Identity and Tradition in Ancient Judaism*, L. LiDonnici & A. Lieber, eds, 2007, Brill.

Lietaert Peerbolte, Bert Jan. "Paul the Miracle Worker: Development and Background of Pauline Miracle Stories," *Wonders Never Cease: The Purpose of Narrating Miracle Stories in the New Testament and its Religious Environment*, M. Labahn & B.J. Lietaert Peerbolte, eds, 2006, T&T Clark.

—. "Paul's Rapture: 2 Corinthians 12:2-4 and the Language of the Mystics," *Experientia, I, Inquiry into Religions Experience in Early Judaism and Christianity*, F. Flannery, C. Shantz & R.A. Werline, eds, 2008, Brill.

Liew, Tat-siong Benny. "Re-Markable Masculinities: Jesus, the Son of Man, and (Sad) Sum of Manhood?" *New Testament Masculinities*, S.D. Moore & J.C. Anderson, eds, 2003, Society of Biblical Literature.

Lipsius, Richard Adelbert & Maximillian Bonnet. *Acta Apostolorum Apocrypha*, 1959, Wissenschaftliche Buchgesellschaft Darmstadt.

Loader, William. *Sexuality and the Jesus Tradition*, 2005, William B. Eerdmans Publishing Company.

Luck, Georg. *Arcana Mundi: Magic and the Occult in the Greek and Roman Worlds*, 1985, Johns Hopkins University Press.

—. "Theurgy and Forms of Worship in Neoplatonism," *Religion, Science, and Magic: In Concert and in Conflict*, J. Neusner, E.S. Frerichs & P.V. McCracken Flesher, eds, 1989, Oxford University Press.

—. "Witches and Sorcerers in Classical Literature," *Witchcraft and Magic in Europe: Ancient Greece and Rome*, B. Ankarloo & S. Clark, eds, 1999, University of Pennsylvania Press.

—. "The 'Way Out': Philological Notes on the Transfiguration of Jesus," *Ancient Pathways and Hidden Pursuits: Religion, Morals, and Magic in the Ancient World*, 2000, University of Michigan Press.

—. "Recent Work on Ancient Magic," *Ancient Pathways and Hidden Pursuits: Religion, Morals, and Magic in the Ancient World*, 2000, University of Michigan Press.

MacDonald, Margaret Y. "Slavery, Sexuality and House Churches: A Reassessment of Colossians 3.18-4.1 in Light of New Research on the Roman Family," *New Testament Studies* 53 (2007): 94-113.

Mack, Burton L. *The Lost Gospel: The Book of Q and Christian Origins*, 1993, Harper San Francisco.

Macleod, M.D. *Lucian: A Selection*, 1991, Aris & Philips.

MacMullen, Ramsay. *Enemies of the Roman Order: Treason, Unrest, and Alienation in the Empire*, 1966, Harvard University Press.

—. *Christianizing the Roman Empire: A.D. 100-400*, 1984, Yale University Press.

Marcovich, Miroslav. *Iustini Martyris Dialogus cum Tryphone*, 1997, de Gruyer.

—. *Origenes: Contra Celsum Libri VIII*, 2001, Brill Academic Publishers.

Marguerat, Daniel. "Magic and Miracle in the Acts of the Apostles," *Magic in the Biblical World: From the Rod of Aaron to the Ring of Solomon*, T.E. Klutz, ed, 2003, T&T Clark.

Martin, Dale. *Sex and the Single Savior: Gender and Sexuality in Biblical Interpretation*, 2006, Westminster John Knox Press.

Martin, Matthew J. "Writing Divine Speech: Greek Transliterations of Near Eastern languages in the Hellenistic East," *The Politics of Orality: Orality and Literacy in Ancient Greece*, C.R. Cooper ed, 2006, Brill.

Martin, Michaël. *Magie et magicians dans le monde gréco-romain*, 2005, Editions Errance.

Martinez, David. "'May She Neither Eat Nor Drink,': Love Magic and Vows of Abstinence," *Ancient Magic and Ritual Power*, M. Meyer & P. Mirecki, eds, 2001, Brill Academic Publishers.

Mastrocinque, Attilio. *From Jewish Magic to Gnosticism*, 2005, Mohr Siebeck.

McCown, Chester Charlton. *The Testament of Solomon*, 1922, G.E. Stechert & Co.

McCullough, W.S. *Jewish and Mandaean Incantation Bowls in the Royal Ontario Museum*, 1967, University of Toronto Press.

McGowan, Andrew. "Eating People: Accusations of Cannibalism Against Christians in the Second Century," *Journal of Early Christian Studies* 2/3 (1994): 413-442.

McKay, Heather A. "Ancient Synogogues: The Continuing Dialect Between Two Major Views," *Currents in Research: Biblical Studies* 6:103-142.

Meier, John P. *A Marginal Jew: Rethinking the Historical Jesus*, I, 1991, Doubleday.

Merkur, Dan. *Gnosis: An Esoteric Tradition of Mystical Visions and Unions*, 1993, State University of New York Press.

Merrifield, Ralph. *The Archaeology of Ritual and Magic*, 1987, New Amsterdam.

Metzger, Bruce M. *The New Testament: Its Background, Growth, and Content*, 2nd ed, enlarged, 1987, Abingdon Press.

Meyer, Marvin & Richard Smith. *Ancient Christian Magic: Coptic Texts of Ritual Power*, 1994, HarperSanFrancisco.

—. "The Prayer of Mary in the Magical Book of Mary and the Angels," *Prayer, Magic, and the Stars in the Ancient and Late Antique World*, S. Noegel, J. Walker & B. Wheeler eds, 2003, Pennsylvania State University Press.

Miller, Patricia Cox. "In Praise of Nonsense," *Classical Mediterranean Spirituality: Egyptian, Greek, Roman*, A.H. Armstrong (ed), 1986, Crossroad.

Miller, Robert J., ed. *The Complete Gospels: Annotated Scholars Version, Revised and Expanded Edition*, 1994, Polebridge Press.

Miner, Edwin L., F.H. Sandbach & W.C. Helmbold. *Plutarch's Moralia*, 1961, William Heinemann, Ltd.

Morenz, Siegfried. *Egyptian Religion*, 1973, Cornell University Press.

Morgan, Michael A. *Sepher Ha-Razim: The Book of the Mysteries*, H.W. Attridge, ed, 1983, Scholars Press.

Morony, Michael G. "Magic and Society in Late Sasanian Iraq," *Prayer, Magic, and the Stars in the Ancient and Late Antique World*, S. Noegel, J. Walker & B. Wheeler, eds, 2003, Pennsylvania State University Press.

Moss, Candida. *The Myth of Persecution: How Early Christians Invented a Story of Martyrdom*, 2013, Harper One.

Mount, Christopher. "1 Corinthians 11:3-16: Spirit Possession and Authority in a Non-Pauline Interpolation," *Journal of Biblical Literature* 124 (2005): 313-340.

Munier, Charles. *Saint Justin: Apologie pour les Chrétiens*, 1995, Éditions Universitaires Fribourg Suisse.

Muñoz Delgado, Luis. *Léxico de magia y religión en los papiros mágicos griegos*, 2001, Consejo Superior de Investigaciones Científicas.

Myers, Ched. *Binding the Strong Man: A Political Reading of Mark's Story of Jesus*, 1988, Orbis Books.

Myllykoski, Matti. "Being There: The Function of the Supernatural in Acts 1-12," *Wonders Never Cease: The Purpose of Narrating Miracle Stories in the New Testament and its Religious Environment*, M. Labahn & B.J.L. Peerbolte, eds, 2006, T&T Clark.

Naveh, Joseph & Shaul Shaked. *Magic Spells and Formulae: Aramaic Incantations of Late Antiquity*, 1993, Magnes Press.

Neusner, Jacob. "Science and Magic, Miracle and Magic in Formative Judaism: The System and the Difference," *Religion, Science, and*

Magic: In Concert and in Conflict, J. Neusner, E.S. Frerichs & P.V. McCracken Flesher, eds, 1989, Oxford University Press.

Neyrey, Jerome H. *The Resurrection Stories*, 1988, Michael Glazier.

—. "Bewitched in Galatia: Paul and Cultural Anthropology," *Catholic Biblical Quarterly* 50:72-100.

Nissinen, Martti. *Homoeroticism in the Biblical World*, 1998, Fortress Press.

Nordh, Katarina. *Aspects of Ancient Egyptian Curses and Blessings: Conceptual Background and Transmission*, 1996, Uppsala Studies in Ancient Mediterranean & Near Eastern Civilizations.

Oesterreich, Traugott K. *Possession Demoniacal and Other Among Primitive Races, in Antiquity, the Middle Ages, and Modern Times*, 1930, University Books (reprint, 1966).

Ogden, Daniel. "Binding Spells: Curse Tablets and Voodoo Dolls in the Greek and Roman Worlds," *Witchcraft and Magic in Europe: Ancient Greece and Rome*, B. Ankarloo & S. Clark, eds, 1999, University of Pennsylvania Press.

—. *Greek and Roman Necromancy*, 2001, Princeton University Press.

—. *Magic, Witchcraft and Ghosts in the Greek and Roman Worlds*, 2002, Oxford University Press.

—. *In Search of the Sorcerer's Apprentice: The traditional tales of Lucian's Lover of Lies*, 2007, The Classical Press of Wales.

—. *Night's Black Agents: Witches, Wizards and the Dead in the Ancient World*, 2008, Hambledon Continuum Books.

Otto, Walter F. *Dionysus: Myth and Cult*, 1965, Indiana University Press.

Oulton, J.E.I. *Eusebius: The Ecclesiastical History*, VI-X, 1932, Harvard University Press.

Pagels, Elaine. *The Gnostic Paul: Gnostic Exegesis of the Pauline Letters*, 1975, Trinity Press International.

—. *The Origin of Satan*, 1995, Random House.

Paige, Terence. "Who Believes in 'Spirit'? Pneuma in Pagan Usage and Implications for the Gentile Christian Mission," *Harvard Theological Review* 95 (2002):417-436.

Paton, Lewis Bayles. *Spiritism and the Cult of the Dead in Antiquity*, 1921, The Macmillan Company.

Penny, Douglas I. & Michael O. Wise. "By the Power of Beelzebub: An Aramaic Incantation Formula from Qumran (4 Q 560), *Journal of Biblical Literature*113 (1994): 627-650.

Petermann, J.H.S. *Ignatii Patris Apostolici quae Feruntur Epistolae Una cum Ejusdem Martyrio*, 1849, Lipsiae.

Peters, Edward. "Superstition and Magic from Augustine to Isidore of Seville," *Witchcraft and Magic in Europe: The Middle Ages*, B. Ankarloo & S. Clark, eds, 2002, University of Pennsylvania Press.

Philostratus, Flavius. *The Life of Apollonius of Tyana*, I & II, F.C. Conybeare (tr), 1912, Harvard University Press.

Pietersen, Lloyd K. "Magic/Thaumaturgy and the Pastorals," *Magic in the Biblical World: From the Rod of Aaron to the Ring of Solomon*, T.E. Klutz, ed, 2003, T&T Clark.

Pinch, Geraldine. *Magic in Ancient Egypt*, 1994, University of Texas Press.

Piñero, Antonio & Gonzalo del Cerro. *Hechos Apócrifos de los Apóstoles*, 2004, Biblioteca de Autores Cristianos.

Pitre, Brant James. "Blessing the Barren and Warning the Fecund: Jesus' Message for Women Concerning Pregnancy and Childbirth," *Journal for the Study of the New Testament* 81 (2001): 59-80.

Plumer, Eric. "The Absence of Exorcisms in the Fourth Gospel," *Biblica* 78 (1997): 350-368.

Porter, Stanley E. "The Functional Distribution of Koine Greek in First-Century Palestine," *Diglossia and Other Topics in New Testament Linguistics*, S.E. Porter, ed, 2000, Sheffield Academic Publishers.

Porterfield, Amanda. *Healing in the History of Christianity*, 2005, Oxford University Press.

Powell, Mark Allen. "The Magi as Wise Men: Re-examining a Basic Supposition," *New Testament Studies* 46 (2000): 1-20.

Preisendanz, Karl. *Papyri Graecae Magicae: Die Grieschischen Zauberpapyri*, I & II, 2001 (reprint), K.G. Saur.

Presedo Velo, Francisco. J. "Religion y Magia en el Egipto Grecorromano" in *Religion, Supersticion y Magia en el Mundo Romano: Encuentros en la Antigüedead*, 1985, Universidad de Cadiz.

Price, Robert M. "Introduction: The Second Life of Jesus" & "Apocryphal Apparitions: 1 Corinthians 15:3-11 as a Post-Pauline Interpolation," *The Empty Tomb: Jesus Beyond the Grave*, R.M. Price & J.J. Lowder, eds, 2005, Prometheus Books.

Prieur, Jean-Marc. *Acta Andreae*, 1989, Brepols-Turnhout.

Prince, Deborah Thompson. "The 'Ghost' of Jesus: Luke 24 in Light of Ancient Narratives of Post-Mortem Apparitions," *Journal for the Study of the New Testament* 29 (1987): 287-301.

Rabinowitz, Jacob. *The Rotting Goddess: The Origin of the Witch in Classical Antiquity's Demonization of Fertility Religion*, 1998, Automedia.

Rainbow, Jesse. "The Song of Songs and the Testament of Solomon: Solomon's Love Poetry and Christian Magic," *Harvard Theological Review* 100 (2007): 249-274.

Rasimus, Tuomas. *Paradise Reconsidered in Gnostic Mythmaking: Rethinking Sethianism in Light of the Ophite Evidence*, 2009, Brill.

Reed, Annette Yoshiko. *Fallen Angels and the History of Judaism and Christianity*, 2005, Cambridge University Press.

Reimer, Andy M. *Miracle and Magic: A Study in the Acts of the Apostles and the Life of Apollonius of Tyana*, 2002, JSNT Supplement Series 235.

Remus, Harold. "Does Terminology Distinguish Early Christian from Pagan Miracles?" *Journal of Biblical Literature* 101(1982): 531-551.

Ricks, Steven D. "The Magician as Outsider in the Hebrew Bible and the New Testament," *Ancient Magic and Ritual Power*, M. Meyer & P. Mirecki, eds, 2001, Brill Academic Publishers.

Riley, Gregory J. *Resurrection Reconsidered: Thomas and John in Controversy*, 1995, Augsberg Fortress.

Ritner, Robert Kriech. "Curses," *Ancient Christian Magic: Coptic Texts of Ritual Power*, 1994, Harper San Francisco.

—. "Necromancy in Ancient Egypt," *Magic and Divination in the Ancient World*, L. Ciraolo & J. Seidel, eds, 2002, Brill.

—. *The Mechanics of Ancient Egyptian Magical Practice*, 2008, The Oriental Institute.

Rives, James B. "Magic in Roman Law," *The Religious History of the Roman Empire: Pagans, Jews, and Christians*, J.A. North & S.R.F. Price, eds, 2011, Oxford University Press.

Robinson, James M., Paul Hoffmann & John S. Kloppenborg. *The Sayings Gospel Q in Greek and English*, 2002, Fortress Press.

Rochefort, Gabriel. *L'Empereur Julien: Oeuvres Complètes*, 1963, Société D'Édition "Les Belles-Lettres."

Rolfe, John C. (tr). *Ammianus Marcellinus*, II, 1936, Harvard University Press.

Römer, Thomas. "Les Interdits des Pratiques Magiques et Divinatoires dans le Livre du Deutéronomie (Dt 18,9-13)," *Cahiers de L'Institut du Proche-Orient Ancien du Collège de France*, 2012, Editions Jean Maisonneuve.

Rudolph, Kurt. *Gnosis: The Nature and History of Gnosticism*, 1987, Harper San Francisco.

Samain, P. "L'accusation de magie contre le Christ dans les évangiles," *Ephemerides Theologicae Lovanienses* 15 (1932): 449-490.

Sanders, Ed Parish. *The Historical Figure of Jesus*, 1993, The Penguin Press.

Schäfer, Peter. "Jewish Magic Literature in Late Antiquity and Early Middle Ages," *Journal of Jewish Studies* 41 (1990): 75-81.

—. "Magic and Religion in Ancient Judaism," in *Envisioning Magic: A Princeton Seminar and Symposium*, P. Schäfer & H.G. Kippenberg, eds, 1997, Brill.

—. *Judeophobia: Attitudes toward the Jews in the Ancient World*, 1997, Harvard University Press.

—. *Jesus in the Talmud*, 2007, Princeton University Press.

Schenke, Hans-Martin. "The Phenomenon and Significance of Gnostic Sethianism," *The Rediscovery of Gnosticism, Volume II, Sethian Gnosticism*, B. Layton (ed), 1981, Brill.

Schlier, Heinrich. "δακτυλος," *Theological Dictionary of the New Testament*, 1964, Gerhard Kittel, ed, William B. Eerdmans.

Schmidt, Brian B. *Israel's Beneficent Dead: Ancestor Cult and Necromancy in Ancient Israelite Religion and Tradition*, 1996, Eisenbrauns.

—. "The 'Witch' of Endor, 1 Samuel 28, and Ancient Near Eastern Necromancy," *Ancient Magic and Ritual Power*, M. Meyer & P. Mirecki, eds, 2001, Brill.

—. "Canaanite Magic vs. Israelite Religion: Deuteronomy 18 and the Taxonomy of Taboo," *Magic and Ritual in the Ancient World*, 2002, Brill.

Schnackenburg, Rudolf. *Ephesians: A Commentary*, Helen Heron, tr, 1991, T&T Clark.

Schneemelcher, Wilhelm & Rudolphe Kasser, "Acts of Paul," *New Testament Apocrypha*, II, W. Schneemelcher, ed, 1964, The Westminster Press.

Scholem, Gershom G. *Major Trends in Jewish Mysticism*, 1941, Schocken Publishing House.

Schürer, Emil. *A History of the Jewish People in the Time of Jesus Christ*, 1923, Charles Scribner's and Sons.

Schweitzer, Albert. *The Quest of the Historical Jesus: From Reimarus to Wrede*, W. Montgomery, tr, 1910, Adam & Charles Black, Ltd.

Scibilia, Anna. "Supernatural Assistance in the Greek Magical Papyri," *The Metamorphosis of Magic from Late Antiquity to the Early Modern Period*, J.N. Bremmer & J.R. Veenstra, eds, 2002, Peeters.

Šedina, Miroslav. "Magical Power of Names in Origen's Polemic Against Celsus," *Listy filologické* 136 (2013): 7-25.

Segal, A. F. "Hellenistic Magic: Some Questions of Definition," *Studies in Gnosticism and Hellenistic Religions: Presented to Gilles Quispel on the Occasion of His 65th Birthday*, R. van den Broek & M.J. Vermaseren, eds, 1981, E.J. Brill.

Seland, Torrey. "Philo, Magic and Balaam: Neglected Aspects of Philo's Exposition of the Balaam Story," *The New Testament and Early Christian Literature in Greco-Roman Context: Studies in Honor of David E. Aune*, J. Fotolpoulos, ed, 2006, Brill.

Selwyn, Edward Gordon. *The First Epistle of St. Peter: The Greek Text with Introduction, Notes and Essays*, 1952, Macmillan & Company.

Selwyn, William. *Contra Celsum*, 1876, Cambridge University Press.

Shandruck, Walter M. "The Interchange of *ι* and *η* in Spelling *χριστ-* in Documentary Papyri," *Bulletin of the American Society of Papyrologists* 47 (2010): 205-219.

Shantz, Colleen. "The Confluence of Trauma and Transcendence in the Pauline Corpus," *Experientia, I, Inquiry into Religious Experience in Early Judaism and Christianity*, F. Flannery, C. Shantz & R. Werline, eds, 2008, Brill.

Smith, Gregory A. "The Myth of the Vaginal Soul," *Greek, Roman, and Byzantine Studies* 44 (2004): 199-225.

Smith, Jay E. "The Roots of a Libertine Slogan in 1 Corinthians 6:18," *Journal of Theological Studies* 59 (2008): 61-79.

Smith, Lacey Balwin. *Fools, Martyrs, Traitors: The Story of Martyrdom in the Western World*, 1997, Alfred A. Knopf.

Smith, Mark S. *The Early History of God: Yahweh and the Other Deities in Ancient Israel*, 1990, Harper & Row.

Smith, Morton. *Clement of Alexandria and a Secret Gospel of Mark*, 1973, Harvard Univerity Press.

—. *Jesus the Magician: Charlatan or Son of God?* 1978, Harper & Row.

—. "Pauline Worship As Seen by Pagans," *Harvard Theological Review* 73 (1980): 241-249.

—. "The History of the Term Gnostikos," *The Rediscovery of Gnosticism, Volume II, Sethian Gnosticism*, B. Layton (ed), 1981, Brill.

—. *Studies in the Cult of Yahweh*, I & II, S.J.D. Cohen, ed, 1996, E.J. Brill.

Sophocles, Evangelinus A. *Greek Lexicon of the Roman and Byzantine periods (from B.C. 146 to A.D. 1100)*, 1900, Charles Scribner's Sons.

Sorensen, Eric. *Possession and Exorcism in the New Testament and Early Christianity*, 2002, Mohr Siebeck.

Sørensen, Jørgen P. "The argument in ancient Egyptian magical formulae," *Acta Orientalia* 45: 5-19.

Spoer, Hans H. "Notes on Jewish Amulets," *Journal of Biblical Literature* 23 (1904): 97-105.

Stanton, Graham N. "Jesus of Nazareth: A Magician and a False Prophet Who Deceived God's People?" *Jesus of Nazareth Lord and Christ: Essays on the Historical Jesus and New Testament Christology*, J.B. Green & M. Turner (eds), 1994, Wm. B. Eerdmans.

—. *Gospel Truth? New Light on Jesus and the Gospels*, 1995, Zondervan.

Starr, Joshua. "The Meaning of Authority in Mark 1.22," *Harvard Theological Review* 23 (1930): 302-305.

Stone, Michael E. *Scriptures, Sects and Visions: A Profile of Judaism from Ezra to the Jewish Revolts*, 1980, Fortress Press.

Stratton, Kimberly B. *Naming the Witch: Magic, Ideology, and Stereotype in the Ancient World*, 2007, Columbia University Press.

Strelan, Rick. "Who Was Bar-Jesus (Acts 13,6-12)?" *Biblica* 85 (2004): 65-87.

—. "Outside Are the Dogs and the Sorcerers…" (Revelation 22:15), *Biblical Theology Bulletin* 33 (2003): 148-157.

—. *Strange Acts: Studies in the Cultural World of the Acts of the Apostles*, 2004, Walter de Gruyter.

Stroumsa, Guy G. *Barbarian Philosophy: The Religious Revolution of Early Christianity*, 1999, Mohr Siebeck.

Struck, Peter T. "Speech Acts and the Stakes of Hellenism in Late Antiquity," *Magic and Ritual in the Ancient World*, P. Mirecki & M. Meyer (eds), 2002, Brill.

Taylor, Gary. *Castration: An Abbreviated History of Western Manhood*, 2000, Routledge.

Tayor, Greg. "Her Sweet Murmur: Exploring the Aural Phenomenology of Border Experiences," *Dark Lore*, G. Taylor, ed, 2007, Daily Grail Publishing.

Taussig, Hal (ed.). *A New New Testament: A Bible for the Twenty-First Century*, 2013, Houghton Mifflin Harcourt.

te Velde, Herman. Seth, *God of Confusion: A Study of His Role in Egyptian Mythology and Religion*, 1967, E.J. Brill.

Thee, Francis C.R. *Julius Africanus and the Early Christian View of Magic*, 1984, Mohr Siebeck.

Thiselton, Anthony C. "The Holy Spirit in 1 Corinthians: Exegesis and Reception History in the Patristic Era," *The Holy Spirit and Christian Origins: Essays in Honor of James D. G. Dunn*, G.N. Stanton, B.W. Longenecker & S.C. Barton, eds, 2004, William B. Eerdmans Publishing Company.

Thomas, Rodney Lawrence. *Magical Motifs in the Book of Revelation*, 2010, T&T Clark.

Thompson, R. Campbell. *Semitic Magic: Its Origins and Development*, 1908, Luzac & Company.

Thomsen, Marie-Louise. "Witchcraft and Magic in Ancient Mesopotamia," *Witchcraft and Magic in Europe: Biblical and Pagan Societies*, B. Ankarloo & S. Clark, eds, 2001, University of Pennsylvania Press.

Tipei, John Fleter. *The Laying On of Hands in the New Testament: Its Significance, Techniques, and Effects*, 2009, University Press of America.

Trachtenberg, Joshua. *Jewish Magic and Superstition: A Study in Folk Religion*, 1970, Atheneum.

Tropper, Joseph. "Spirit of the Dead אוב," *Dictionary of Deities and Demons in the Bible*, K. van der Toorn, B. Becking & P.W. van der Horst, eds, 1995, E.J. Brill.

Trzcionka, Silke. *Magic and the Supernatural in Fourth-Century Syria*, 2007, Routledge.

Turner, John Douglas. *Sethian Gnosticism and the Platonic Tradition*, 2001, Éditions Peeters.

Tuzlak, Ayse. "The Magician and the Heretic: The Case of Simon Magus," *Magic and Ritual in he Ancient World*, P. Mirecki & M. Meyer (eds), 2002, Brill.

Twelftree, Graham H. "Jesus the Exorcist and Ancient Magic," *A Kind of Magic: Understanding Magic in the New Testament and its Religious Environment*, M. Labahm & B. J. Lietaert Peerbolte, eds, 2007, T&T Clark.

—. *In the Name of Jesus: Exorcism among Early Christians*, 2007, Baker Academic.

Van Den Broek. *Studies in Gnosticism and Alexandrian Christianity*, 1996, Brill.

VanderKam, James C. "1 Enoch, Enochic Motifs, and Enoch in Early Christian Literature," *The Jewish Apocalyptic Heritage in Early Christianity*, J.C. VanderKam & W. Adler, eds, 1996, Fortress Press.

Van Groningen, M. David & B.A. Van Groningen. *Papyrological Primer*, 4th ed, 1965, E.J. Brill.

Van Hoye, Albert. "La fuite du jeune homme nu (Mc 14,51-52)," *Biblica* 52 (1971):401-406.

Van Voorst, Robert E. *Jesus Outside the New Testament: An Introduction to the Ancient Evidence*, 2000, William B. Eerdmans.

Vermes, Geza. *Jesus the Jew*, 1973, Collins.

Vermeule, Emily. *Aspects of Death in Early Greek Art and Poetry*, 1979, University of California Press.

Versnel, Hendrik S. "Κολασαι τουη ημαη τοιουτουη ηδεωη βλεποντεη 'Punish those who rejoice in our misery': On curse texts and Schadenfreude," *The World of Ancient Magic: Papers from the first International Samson Eitrem Seminar*, 1997, D. R. Jordan, H. Montgomery & E. Thomassen, eds, 1999, Bergen.

Victor, Ulrich. *Lukian Von Samosata: Alexandros oder der Lügenprophet*, 1997, Brill.

Vitelli, G. *Papiri Greci e Latini*, 2004, Edizioni di Storia e Letteratura.

Voutiras, Emmanuel. "Euphemistic names for the powers of the nether world," *The world of ancient magic*, D.R. Jordan, H. Montgomery & E. Thomassen, eds, 1999, Bergen.

Wahlen, Clinton. *Jesus and the Impurity of Spirits in the Synoptic Gospels*, 2004, Mohr Siebeck.

Wasyliw, Patricia Healy. *Martyrdom, Murder, and Magic*, 2009, Peter Lang.

Watt, Jonathan M. "Of Gutterals and Galileans: The Two Slurs of Matthew 26.73," *Diglossia and Other Topics in New Testament Linguistics*, S.E. Porter, ed, 2000, Sheffield Academic Publisher.

Werline, Rodney A. "The Experience of Prayer and Resistance to Demonic Powers in the Gospel of Mark," *Experientia, I, Inquiry into Religious Experience in Early Judaism and Christianity*, F. Flannery, C. Shantz & R.A. Werline, eds, 2008, Brill.

Wiens, Devon H. "Mystery Concepts in Primitive Christianity and its Environment," *Aufstieg und Niedergang der Römischen Welt*, II, 23.2, 1248-1284, H. Temporini & W. Haase, eds, Walter de Gruyer.

Wikgen, Allen, Ernest Cadman Colwell & Ralph Marcus. "The Acts of Paul," *Hellenistic Greek Texts*, 1947, University of Chicago Press.

Wilcox, Max. "Jesus in the Light of His Jewish Environment," *Aufstieg und Niedergang der Römischen Welt*, II, 25.1: 131-187, H. Temporini & W. Haase, eds, Walter de Gruyer.

Wilken, Robert L. *The Christians as the Romans Saw Them*, 1984, Yale University Press.

Williams, Frank. *The* Panarion *of Epiphanius of Salamis*, 2nd Edition, Revised and Expanded, 2009, Brill.

Williams, Guy. "An Apocalyptic and Magical Interpretation of Paul's 'Beast Fight' in Ephesus (1 Corinthians 15:32)," *Journal of Theological Studies* 57 (2006): 42-56.

Williams, Michael A. *Rethinking "Gnosticism": An Argument for Dismantling a Dubious Category*, 1996, Princeton University Press.

Wilson, Stephen. *Saints and Their Cults: Studies in Religious Sociology, Folklore and History*, 1983, Cambridge University Press.

Winkler, John J. "The Constraints of Eros," *Magika Hiera: Ancient Greek Magic and Religion*, C. Faraone & D. Obbink, eds, 1991, Oxford University Press.

Wisse, Frederik. "The Apocryphon of John (II, 1, III, 1, IV, 1, and BG 8502,2), *The Nag Hammadi Library in English*, 1977, Harper & Row.

Wolff, Catherine. "La norme religieuse et les brigands à travers les sources littéraires" in *La Norme religieuse dans l'Antiquité*, B. Cabouret & M. Charles-LaForge, eds 2010, Diffusion Librairie De Boccard.

Worrell, W.H. "A Coptic Wizard's Hoard," *The American Journal of Semitic Languages and Literature* 46 (1930): 239-262.

SUBJECT INDEX

T

W

Printed in February 2023
by Rotomail Italia S.p.A., Vignate (MI) - Italy